MARKED MEN

MARKED MEN

White Masculinity in Crisis

Sally Robinson

 COLUMBIA UNIVERSITY PRESS   NEW YORK

Columbia University Press
Publishers Since 1893
New York   Chichester, West Sussex
Copyright © 2000 by Columbia University Press

Library of Congress Cataloging-in-Publication Data
Robinson, Sally, 1959–
Marked men : white masculinity in crisis / Sally Robinson.
p. cm.
Includes bibliographical references and index.
ISBN 0–231–11292–0 (cloth : alk. paper) — ISBN 0–231–11293–9 (paper : alk. paper)
1. White men—United States. 2. Masculinity—United States. 3. Men in popular
culture—United States. 4. Men in literature. I. Title.

HQ1090.3.R634 2000
305.31′0973—dc21   00–025916

Casebound editions of Columbia University Press books
are printed on permanent and durable acid-free paper.
Printed in the United States of America
c 10 9 8 7 6 5 4 3 2 1
p 10 9 8 7 6 5 4 3 2 1

To William Robinson

CONTENTS

ACKNOWLEDGMENTS

I owe a special debt of gratitude to the undergraduate students at the University of Michigan, who took my courses on American masculinity and became willing collaborators in this project. The excitement that these students brought to the enterprise of interrogating dominant masculinity fueled my own engagement with the project, and this is a better book than it would have been without these students' willingness to challenge their assumptions and my own. For their intellectual generosity and their feminist acumen, I thank Anne Herrmann, Patsy Yaeger, and Valerie Traub—all of whom helped me to see how work on masculinity fits into feminist scholarship. For much-needed encouragement in the later stages, I thank Tobin Siebers and the writing group he organized in Ann Arbor. Rei Terada read key parts of the manuscript at a critical point, and her astute comments helped my argument crystallize into its final form. Sandra Gunning read and reread much of the manuscript, often on short notice and always carefully, and brought me tales of what was happening at the movies when I couldn't go myself. I thank Marlon Ross not only for his reading, his ideas, and his conversation, but for telling me that he found himself laughing out loud at certain points in the manuscript—a comment that buoyed me at a moment when I was having a bit of a crisis over what audiences this book might be appealing to, and what audiences it risked alienating. For their help and support during a difficult time, I thank Suzanne Raitt, Sid Smith, and Rafia Zafar. To certain members of the Michigan English Department, thank you for convincing me I was really onto something and reinforcing my desire to see these ideas in print.

Ann Miller, my editor at Columbia University Press, has been a delight to work with on every level. Peter Lehman, who twice read the manuscript for Columbia, was enthusiastic, encouraging, and incredibly generous. Other, anonymous, readers also helped me to tighten up the argument. Thanks, also, to my copyeditor, Roy Thomas, for his work on the manuscript. Chapter 1 appeared in different form in *Modern Fiction Studies* 44.2 (Summer 1998), and I thank the editors for permission to reprint it here.

To all the friends who brought me their own stories about wounded white men and examples of the dynamics *Marked Men* analyzes, thanks for your humor. I thank my new colleagues at Texas A&M University for embracing me and my work with such enthusiasm; their welcome truly gave me the energy I needed to finally finish the book. Stan Raleigh listened to my tirades and theories with good grace and superior intelligence, and his thinking is inextricably woven into the book. He deserves my gratitude, as well, for taking such great care of our daughter, Emma Raleigh, and enabling me to work as much as I needed to. As always, my parents and siblings have supported me in countless ways; thanks, especially, to my father, William Robinson, whose skeptical, intelligent, and practical voice I often heard in my head as I tried to predict how white men of a particular age might respond to what I had to say. It is to him that this book is dedicated.

MARKED MEN

INTRODUCTION

Visibility, Crisis, and the
Wounded White Male Body[1]

Much of the recent work on specifying, theorizing, or analyzing masculinity and whiteness in society and in culture takes as its starting point the notion that *invisibility* is a necessary condition for the perpetuation of white and male dominance, both in representation and in the realm of the social.[2] Masculinity and whiteness retain their power as signifiers and as social practices because they are opaque to analysis, the argument goes; one cannot question, let alone dismantle, what remains hidden from view. This line of argument makes a good deal of sense, for it is clear that white male power has benefited enormously from keeping whiteness and masculinity in the dark. What is invisible escapes surveillance and regulation, and, perhaps less obviously, also evades the cultural marking that distances the subject from universalizing constructions of identity and narratives of experience. It is in this sense that Donna Haraway speaks of the privilege of inhabiting an unmarked body that has been the patrimony of white Western man, his inheritance through the ages that have witnessed an ever more precise marking of the bodies of others: "From the eighteenth to the mid-twentieth centuries, the great historical constructions of gender, race, and class were embedded in the organically marked bodies of woman, the colonized or enslaved, and the worker. Those inhabiting these marked bodies have been symbolically other to the fictive rational self of universal, *and so unmarked,* species man, a coherent subject" (210, emphasis added). Implicit in Haraway's claim is the connection between the unmarked and the disembodied, the marked and the embodied. To be unmarked means to be invisible—not in the sense of "hidden from history"[3] but, rather, as the self-evident standard against which all differences are measured: hidden *by* history.[4]

Making the normative visible as a category embodied in gendered and racialized terms can call into question the privileges of unmarkedness; but visibility can also mean a different kind of empowerment, as the history of move-

ments for social equality in the United States has taught us. Identity politics—
what Peggy Phelan refers to as "visibility politics"—is largely based on the assumption that invisibility is both cause and effect of political and social exclusion. "Invisibility blues," to borrow from Michele Wallace, has been the
historical malady of underrepresented populations, and one of the main impe-
tuses for women's studies and ethnic studies programs.[5] White men, conflated
with normativity in the American social lexicon, have not been understood as
practicing identity politics because they are visible in political terms, even as
they benefit from the invisibility of their own racial and gender specificity. Political power and the rights of citizenship, in this formulation, fall to those who
are not "encumbered" by racial and gender difference, and thus are not bound
by "special interests." Post-sixties gender and racial struggles are most often
conceptualized as a battle between "multiculturalists" and the white, male
spokesmen for unmarked normativity. This is the master narrative of identity
politics in post-sixties American culture, a narrative that is wittingly or unwittingly reproduced by both its critics and its champions. But, is it historically accurate, or theoretically useful, to frame whiteness and masculinity in this way?
Do white men, in fact, belong *outside* of struggles over gender and race? Have
whiteness and masculinity remained untouched by skirmishes elsewhere? The
answer, quite simply, is no.

A dominant or master narrative of white male decline in post-sixties America has developed to account for the historical, social, and political decentering
of what was once considered the normative in American culture. Versions of
that narrative can be read in books by historians, film scholars, and sociolo-
gists, some of which forward causal arguments, some of which settle for thick
description of literary or filmic genres, and some of which place the current
state of white masculinity within a larger history of American manhood.[6] That
narrative goes something like this: In the late 1960s, in the wake of the civil
rights movement, and with the rise of women's liberation, gay liberation, and
the increasing visibility of ethnic and racial diversity on the American scene,
white men begin to be decentered. Some accounts of this general shift take economic changes into account, noting that postindustrial (or post-Fordist or late
capitalist or Sonyist)[7] economies have thrown not only the working class into
crisis, but the professional managerial class, as well. While such economic shifts
clearly affect women as well as men—and people of color as much as or more
than whites—an enduring image of the disenfranchised white man has become
a symbol for the decline of the American way. Since the middle classes are arguably the source of normative representations of Americanness, those who
speak loudest and most forcibly for the decline of America in post-sixties culture speak of the middle class "falling from grace."[8] That this class is assumed
to be normatively white perhaps goes without saying; but the degree to which

the crisis afflicting the white middle class is also, and most forcefully, a crisis in masculinity, has become clear in recent years, with the vociferous cries of men who are contesting the claim that *they* are the villains in American culture. White men have, thus, been marked, *not* as individuals but as a *class,* a category that, like other marked categories, complicates the separation between the individual and the collective, the personal and the political. While the responses to, and effects of, this crisis are multiple and sometimes self-contradictory, they add up to what I will call an identity politics of the dominant, a concept that I want to use to challenge some of the key assumptions behind much recent work on making whiteness and masculinity visible.

The assumption that identity politics is practiced only by marginalized groups positioning themselves against what passes for the norm in American culture—and that those who embody that norm actively resist a politicized articulation of identity because it would endanger the very concept of the unmarked individual—is functionally parallel to the assumption that *marking* whiteness and masculinity, making them visible, will necessarily erode their power. This way of thinking makes it nearly impossible to see how whiteness and masculinity have, in fact, quite often been marked and made visible in both progressive and reactionary ways; and how those who defend the existence of an unmarked, universally available individualism or citizenship have practiced identity politics in both subtle and overt ways. While most accounts of the relationship between power and (in)visibility suggest that only the disenfranchised have a positive interest in promoting the visibility of social difference—and that the dominant can only have an interest in remaining unmarked and invisible—I will argue here that what calls itself the normative in American culture has vested interests in *both* invisibility and visibility. Invisibility is a privilege enjoyed by social groups who do not, thus, attract modes of surveillance and discipline; but it can also be felt as a burden in a culture that appears to organize itself around the visibility of differences and the symbolic currency of identity politics.

In general, when we speak of "identity politics," we mean the politics practiced by marginalized groups who understand subjectivity as inevitably grounded in the relations of power that structure a given society. Further, those relations of power are embodied in persons whose differential relationships to normativity are registered, in large part, by the evidence of visible, bodily difference. Identity politics rests on the premise that the minoritized subject is marked by the dominant culture and its representational regimes as lesser, made to embody the difference and particularity against which the norm defines itself. But a central tenet of identity politics is that the minoritized subject proudly claims her own difference from the norm, and so marks *herself* as the bearer of an embodied particularity. What makes this concept of identity a politics is the belief that being subject *to* such markings determines how one becomes subject *of* speaking, writing, and representation. In other words, identity politics links the marked body to the more abstract workings of the mind, or perspective, or creativity. Forging a firm link between the body and the mind, the material and the abstract, identity politics places into question the separations on which the notion of the abstract individual depends.

Because white masculinity has historically been understood as coterminous with the abstract individualism which an identity politics attempts to erode,[9] white men have most often been understood as the victims of, but not participants in, identity politics. When whiteness or masculinity becomes the topic of political discussion, we tend to see white men orchestrating a *backlash* against, but not fully participating in, struggles over gender and racial definition and priority. Yet the notion of backlash is an oversimplified concept that obscures the much more complicated struggle over normativity in American culture. Rather than seeing that struggle as a singular, pitched battle between the white man and his various others, it is much more accurate—and more fruitful, as well—to think about how normativity, constantly under revision, shifts in response to the changing social, political, and cultural terrain. My project in *Marked Men* is to place white men, and white masculinity, within a field of struggle over cultural priority—rather than outside of those struggles, looking on, being affected by them but not affecting them. What is at stake in this struggle is the power to define the terms of the normative. Placing white men as both subject and object of post-sixties liberationist discourses, I will show how white men both resist and welcome the *marking* of their minds and bodies. On the one hand, the forced embodiment of whiteness and masculinity is often represented as a violence; on the other, there is evidence of an undeniable attraction toward a more fully embodied, particularized identity on the part of white men. The doubleness of this response is my subject here, and while I do not want to discount the power of whiteness or masculinity to define the cultural terrain, I do want to insist that this power is neither absolute nor secure. The power to represent the normative must be constantly rewon, and to recognize this is also to appreciate the power of liberationist discourses to change the dominant discourse.

Not surprisingly, the sixties occupy a pivotal position in narratives about the decentering of white masculinity and the parallel rise of identity politics. John Updike, who resists mythologizing that decade, puts his finger on the sense of white male surprise and disbelief in the face of seemingly concerted attacks on normativity. The sixties, according to Updike, changed white masculinity from a guarantee of inalienable rights to something of a dirty secret: "My earliest sociological thought about myself had been that I was fortunate to be a boy and an American. Now the world was being told that American males—especially white, Protestant males who had done well under 'the system'—were the root of evil. Law-abiding conformity had become the opposite of a refuge. The Vietnam era was no sunny picnic for me" (*Self-Consciousness* 146). Updike points here to the making visible of white Protestant masculinity as a specific identity category; but he goes further to suggest that what had once been an unquestioned privilege has turned into a liability. No longer able to "take refuge" in the invisibility Updike names "law-abiding conformity," white men are subject to interpretations of their motives, their powers, and their identities forced upon them by others. In this brief passage, we can see the logic that will concern me throughout this study: articulations of white men as victimizers slide almost imperceptibly into constructions of white men as victims. The sixties were "no sunny picnic" for Updike, and the implication is that the sixties *were* a sunny picnic for others. Since, according to Updike, those others are now on the ascendant, concern about their victimization recedes, while the "silent majority" moves to occupy the territory of victimization. Further, Updike's use of the cliché of the "picnic" works to divert attention away from the wide-ranging social and institutional changes of the post-liberationist era, and toward the individual white man's personal experience of them. The white male victim—personally, individually targeted—is the emblem of the current crisis in white masculinity.

The idea that dominant masculinity is "in crisis" is evidenced in widely divergent discursive registers, from scholarly histories of American masculinity to popular newsmagazine coverage of the Lorena and John Bobbitt incident. From the late sixties to the present, dominant masculinity appears to have suffered one crisis after another, from the urgent complaints of the "silent majority" following the 1968 presidential election, to the men's liberationists call for rethinking masculinity in the wake of the women's movement in the 1970s, to the battles over the cultural authority of "dead white males" in academia, to the rise of a new men's movement in the late 1980s. Each of these moments comes clothed in the language of crisis, and the texts produced out of that crisis use a vocabulary of pain and urgency to dwell on, manage, and/or heal the threats to a normativity continuously under siege. In post-sixties American culture, white men have become *marked men,* not only pushed away from the symbolic centers of American iconography but recentered as malicious and jealous protectors of the status quo. From innumerable feminist critiques of white and male privilege to *Time* magazine's Valentine's Day (!) cover story, "Are Men Really That Bad?" (February 14, 1994), white men have been marked as "simply, unambiguously, essentially evil . . . : shot through with violence, megalomania, instrumental rationality, and the obsessive desire for recognition and definition through conquest" (Pfeil vii). *Time*'s answer to its own question posed images of mutilated and wounded white men (most notably John Bobbitt) against feminist claims of women's victimization, demonstrating that white men can most persuasively claim victimization by appealing to representations of bodily trauma. That the article studiously avoided uttering the word *power* suggests that the figure of the wounded white man enables an erasure of the institutional supports of white and male dominance, as we will see in many instances throughout this book. The *Time* story occupies the same emotional, political, and imaginative terrain as Warren Farrell's incendiary and almost surreal *The Myth of Male Power,* in which the scandalous lack of male power is evidenced by a numbing litany of psychological, social, and physical wounds suffered by the so-called "disposable sex." Such ideas are woven into the fictional texts I will focus on here, as well, in which concern over the place of white men in post-sixties American culture produces images of a physically wounded and emotionally traumatized white masculinity. White masculinity most fully represents itself as victimized by inhabiting a wounded body, and such a move draws not only on the persuasive force of corporeal pain but also on an identity politics of the dominant. The logic through which the bodily substitutes for the political, and the individual for the social and institutional, reveals that the "marking" of whiteness and masculinity has already been functioning as a strategy through which white men negotiate the widespread critique of their power and privilege.

Images of wounded white men, manufactured traumas, and metaphorical pains abound in post-sixties American culture, and I have chosen for analysis groups of texts which bring out the bodily crisis of white masculinity in particularly complicated and interesting ways. I stress the "manufactured" and "metaphorical" nature of these bodily traumas in order to insist that such representations function in the service of certain social, political, and artistic ends, and to insist, as well, that there is something irresistible about the logic whereby white male angst gets represented in bodily terms.[10] By calling these wounds, and the crises they herald, metaphorical or fantasized or manufactured, I do not mean to suggest that they are unreal; on the contrary, the persistent representation of white male wounds and of a white masculinity under siege offers ample evidence of what is felt to be the *real* condition of white masculinity in post-liberationist culture.[11] Further, the question of what constitutes "real" or "authentic" trauma and pain is very much at issue, and a good deal of confusion over where the "political" meets the "personal" is a hallmark of these fictions of crisis.

I am using the term *post-liberationist* in order to emphasize the centrality of resistance and rebellion to the zeitgeist I am excavating, not to suggest that the liberationist moment is *over,* but to suggest that after 1968 "liberation" becomes the dominant trope for expressing a wide array of struggles over sociocultural priority and value. While it is true that white masculinity has attempted to reconsolidate its centrality and power in the wake of the liberationist movements of the late sixties and early seventies, it is also the case that the "ordinary" Americans who might seem most invested in such a reconsolidation have also been irresistibly drawn to rhetorics of "liberation." White male rebels of various sorts populate the post-liberationist cultural terrain, and the narratives through which such rebellions are articulated and embellished are remarkably similar, and clearly owe a debt, to the narratives that have villainized white men. In other words, stories of white men rebelling against the forces that would mark them and deprive them of power are organized around the same narrative of resistance or rebellion that characterizes the liberationist movements that these men are, allegedly, lashing back against. In each of the five chapters that follow, we will see white men taking up the position of rebel or resistance fighter, fighting the power and the status quo. The irony, of course, is that the status quo is embodied, these somewhat paranoid narratives suggest, in the minority. Thus, the very idea of the normative, the majority, is itself under attack and in need of "liberation."

The dominance of liberationist rhetoric explains the irresistible appeal of identity politics and the ambivalent attraction to group identity on the part of those individuals who, simultaneously, have vested interests in the fictions of unmarked individualism. Crucially, identity politics is only mobilized after the perception of victimization or injury; just as crucially, the appeal of collectivity appears to depend on a felt experience of disempowerment. This is evident in the language in which calls for groups rights are couched; that language draws heavily on the moral and symbolic power of pain, victimization, and crisis, whether articulated from economic and social centers or their margins. Throughout this era, identity politics pits the individual against the collective and, thus, enacts, again and again, a struggle central to American self-definition. For white men, conflated with the normative individual in American culture, the appeals of collectivism have always appeared thin: white men do not willingly fold their individual identities into a group identity except around perceived losses of power, articulated as impingements of rights.[12] Anxiety over loss of privilege competes with a desire to forge a collective white male identity around claims of victimization.

It is tempting to read the white male victim as just another ruse of white patriarchy, a last-ditch strategy to hang onto a privilege that is perceived to be slipping away. This view has been articulated by numerous critics, most often analyzed through the logic of the commodity, as in this formulation of the motives behind claims of white victimization: "Because they lack multicultural cachet, whites allegedly endure social disempowerment. By painting themselves as the victims of multiculturalism, whites can go multicultural identity one better. As the victims of victims, whites can believe that they have the richest and most marginalized identities around" (Newitz and Wray 62).[13] But, as we will see, the construction of the white male victim is not merely a cynical exploitation of the power of victimization; nor is it simply an opportunistic or appropriative gesture on the part of the privileged. The logic of victimization—based on shifting distinctions between insiders and outsiders, inclusion and exclusion—exercises a pull that even the most privileged seem unable, or unwilling, to resist. Its seductiveness stems in large part from the fact that "grouping" in the United States is almost always linked to perceived experiences of victimization. In American culture, group or collective identity is claimed primarily to argue for rights or restitution; individuals enter into a collective only as "victims" of some wide-ranging legal or otherwise institutionalized neglect or discrimination.[14] Individuals give up their claims to individuality, pledging allegiance to a collectivity, only, it would seem, when (1) they have never been recognized as unmarked "individuals" in the first place; or (2) they experience a felt victimization at the hands of some other collectivity, or indeed, of collectivism itself; or (3) they imagine themselves victimized by an alien or alienating state—a fantasy that, for white men, requires the erasure of systemic and institutionalized white and male privilege. Claiming a collective or group identity is particularly fraught for those individuals who have enjoyed the privileges which come from invisibility; to identify with a collective entails the sacrifice of uniqueness, individuality, and unmarked normativity.

The conflict between individualism and collectivism often gets coded as a conflict between the personal and the political, the "authentic" and the sham. Representations of wounded white men most often work to *personalize* the crisis of white masculinity and, thus, to erase its social and political causes and effects. The opposition between the personal and the political, the authentic and the sham, is itself a tenuous one and must constantly be reinvented. It also produces a good deal of confusion and contradiction, as what once was imaged as "personal" now becomes "political" (sexuality, for example), and what was once imagined as "political" now becomes "personal" (the feminist critique of male privilege, for instance). Representations of wounded, victimized white men do not resolve these contradictions; on the contrary, such representations and the emotions they generate more often have the effect of contributing to the confusion. On the one hand, the substitution of an individually suffering white male body for a social class or gender and racial identity under attack betrays a desire to materialize, literalize the wounds to white and male privilege that come from puncturing the aura of "universality" and "umarkedness" historically claimed by whiteness and masculinity. On the other hand, individualizing a more properly social wound is a way to evade, forget, deny the very marking that has produced those wounds in the first place. In other words, narratives about wounded white men spring from, but obscure, the marking of white masculinity as a *category*. What this means is that representations of wounded white male bodies signal a crisis elsewhere, and one that is simultaneously caused and managed by narratives of crisis and the wounded bodies displayed within those narratives. Displaying wounded bodies materializes the crisis of white masculinity, makes it more real, like other bloody battles over race and gender in American history; but such a materialization, in turn, threatens to expose the lie of disembodied normativity so often attached to white masculinity. Paradoxically, in representing a materialized, wounded white male body as the new norm of white masculinity in the post-liberationist period, the texts I will examine themselves evidence the impossibility of recuperating the fiction of abstract individualism and unmarkedness. White masculinity, then, becomes fully embodied *through* its wounding.

In arguing that white masculinity is "in crisis," I do not mean to suggest that the hegemony of a particular construction of masculinity, or the hegemony of masculinity per se, is in danger. Feminist and pro-feminist critics writing from a variety of different disciplines have cautioned against putting too much stock in the possibilities for social change offered up by the much-announced "crisis" in white masculinity. Tania Modleski, for example, warns that "however much male subjectivity may currently be 'in crisis,' as certain optimistic feminists are now declaring, we need to consider the extent to which male power is actually consolidated through cycles of crisis and resolution, whereby men ultimately deal with the threat of female power by incorporating it" (7). Modleski rightly worries that deconstructive insights about the ways in which patriarchy is divided against itself—and about the contradictions which splinter any notion of a dominant masculinity—can function to reauthorize patriarchal power relations and masculine hegemony under new and ever more complicated guises.[15] But "optimistic feminists" who see a crisis in masculinity as cause for joy are missing the same point that Modleski misses when she implies that a crisis would be a good thing if, in fact, it were real. While it is true that "crisis" might signify a trembling of the edifice of white and male power, it is also true that there is much symbolic power to be reaped from occupying the social and discursive position of subject-in-crisis.[16]

While some historians have cautioned against using the notion of "crisis" to characterize shifts in configurations of gender, I remain convinced that crisis is, in fact, the best way to understand the contemporary condition of white masculinity. Further, objections to the crisis model are based on several faulty assumptions about how crisis works and what kind of cultural work it does. First, some worry that by chopping up history into discrete chunks of crisis and calm, the crisis model constructs history as a linear narrative containing turning points leading to a determined end. However, a *cyclical*, as opposed to linear, understanding of crisis is perfectly suited to a history that appears to move through waves of crisis and resolution. Crises are managed in multiple and sometimes contradictory ways and, while most scholars of masculinity have assumed that crisis leads to a resurgence of old models of masculinity, the idea of crisis in no way requires a singular outcome or, indeed, any outcome at all. Similarly, some historians have complained that the crisis model constructs masculinity as a necessarily defensive, reactive identity formation, always looking to recoup its power, and men to *re*masculinize themselves in traditional ways.[17] But crises produce both retrenchments and recodings, and while new models of masculinity might share some features with old, assuming that history is comprised of a struggle between "traditional" and "alternative" constructions of masculinity misses the dynamism of shifts in gender meanings. When Gail Bederman rejects the claim that, at the turn of the twentieth century, dominant masculinity found itself in crisis, she does so because she sees "no evidence that most turn-of-the-century men ever lost confidence in the belief that people with male bodies naturally possessed both a man's identity and a man's right to wield power" (11). But crisis need not signify a loss of belief in male power or privilege; nor need it be resolved through a *re*masculinization in a narrow or stereotypical sense. As Bederman's own work on the discourse of manliness and civilization suggests, the rhetoric of crisis *gets used* by white men to negotiate shifts in understandings of white masculinity, and so rejecting the idea of crisis seems counterproductive at best. The question is how that rhetoric enables both backward and forward movement.

Marked Men is not about a decades-long, progressive crisis in white masculinity that gets resolved once and for all. While it might be tempting to impose a master narrative on the period—bracketed on one end by the 1968 election and on the other by the culture wars of the late 1980s—it is important to stress that a linear and escalating sense of crisis is not evident in the period. As opposed to more contained historical crises, like the Iranian hostage crisis, for instance, the crisis I am analyzing here has murkier boundaries, no clear beginning, middle, or end. Yet even the rhetoric of "the Iranian hostage crisis," so named by those interested in representing it and thus framing its significance to the American national body and national narrative, participates in the logic of crisis I will attend to here. Announcements of crisis, both direct and indirect, are *performative,* in the sense that naming a situation a crisis puts into play a set of discursive conventions and tropes that condition the meanings that event will have. A crisis is "real" when its rhetorical strategies can be discerned and its effects charted; the reality of a particular crisis depends less on hard evidence of actual social trauma or do-or-die decision-making than on the power of language, of metaphors and images, to convincingly represent that sense of trauma and turning point. While the Iranian hostage crisis was certainly "real," the discursive maneuverings performed by the language of crisis determined, at least to some extent, the course this situation would take and how it would resolve itself. The language of crisis imposes a certain narrative logic on an event or, more nebulously, a social trend or cultural formation. And while we might assume that logic to be governed by a teleological drive toward resolution and closure, the rhetoric of crisis actually functions to defer that closure. The rhetorical power of "crisis" depends on a sense of prolonged tension; the announcements of crisis are inseparable from the crisis itself, as the rhetoric of crisis performs the cultural work of centering attention on dominant masculinity. The question of whether dominant masculinity is "really" in crisis is, in my view, moot: even if we could determine what an actual, real, historically verifiable crisis would look like, the undeniable fact remains that in the post-liberationist era, dominant masculinity consistently represents itself as in crisis.

The rhetoric of crisis is flexible enough to accommodate a range of narratives driven by competing investments and intentions. In general terms, the fictions of crisis I will read here are characterized by competing interests: to heal a wounded white masculinity, and thus to remasculinize America, but also to dwell in the space of crisis and thus to reimagine the dominant meanings of white masculinity. The very idea of "remasculinization," the ground of so much work on masculinity, needs to be placed into question; for although there is undoubtedly compelling evidence to support a claim that post-sixties American culture is engaged in an ongoing process of remasculinization, there are other narratives evident that require a different interpretation. Those narratives include an undeniable attraction to masochism on the part of white men attempting to come to terms with the feminist critique of male power and privilege, most often evident in the remarkable frequency of images of wounded white men in the texts I will analyze here. Masochistic narratives, structured so as to defer closure or resolution, often feature white men displaying their wounds as evidence of disempowerment, and finding a pleasure in explorations of pain.

Masochism is, apparently, an irresistible psychic grid not only for novelists, filmmakers, therapists, and others invested in working out ways of being white and masculine in post-sixties America, but also for feminists and men's studies scholars intent on analyzing the cultural constructions of masculinity in the past as well as the present. When the prestigious feminist journal *differences* published a special issue on "Male Subjectivity" in 1989, dominant masculinity became visible primarily as *wounded*. Of the six essays published in this issue, three take male suffering, male masochism, and/or male hysteria as their subject, and a fourth has at least one reference to Freud's essay on masochism, "A Child Is Being Beaten."[18] Quite a number of other essays, and even a couple of books, contributing to the new masculinity studies circa 1989 also focus on masochism. That year also saw the release of Steven Soderbergh's surprisingly successful *sex, lies, and videotape,* a film whose "hero" is a man suffering from impotence and other wounds and whose villain is a man who stereotypically embodies most of the signifiers of phallic, virile masculinity.[19] Male masochism and male pain continue to compel feminists and masculinists alike, as scholarly books with titles like Carol Siegel's *Male Masochism* (1995) sit cheek by jowl in the library stacks with popular books like Warren Farrell's *The Myth of Male Power: Why Men Are the Disposable Sex* (1993). Why is it that when dominant masculinity becomes visible, it becomes visible as *wounded*?

The answer, one that I will elaborate throughout this book, has to do with the logics of victimization I sketched out above, and the dominance of a particular mode of identity politics in U.S. culture. Announcements of a crisis in white masculinity, and a widely evidenced interest in wounded white men, themselves perform the cultural work of *re*centering white masculinity by *de*-centering it. In other words, in order for white masculinity to negotiate its position within the field of identity politics, white men must claim a symbolic disenfranchisement, must compete with various others for cultural authority bestowed upon the authentically disempowered, the visibly wounded.[20] The strategies through which this is accomplished are neither entirely deliberative nor entirely innocent. And while we might sneer at the white male victim as the latest ruse of a white supremacist patriarchy under attack, the effects of this crisis are far more complicated than this. If post-sixties American culture is characterized by an escalating remasculinization, as some have argued, it is also the case that the masculinity such an agenda promotes is increasingly distant from the putatively "healthy" or "stable" masculinity that preexisted the crisis.

The rhetoric of crisis I analyze here makes ample use of certain tropes that highlight the cyclical nature of crises in white masculinity, as well as the centrality of masochism and male wounds to the narratives detailing those crises. These tropes often have to do with representing a conflict between a dominant masculinity defined by an unrestricted freedom of verbal, emotional, and sexual expression and a dominant masculinity defined by a pain-inducing repression of male language, emotions, and sexuality. The language of crisis carries with it a vocabulary of blockage and release, sometimes explicitly, sometimes only implicitly: like the dominant model of (male) sexual pleasure as based on building tension and the relief of discharge, so too do representations of crisis draw on the image of a pent-up force seeking relief through release. As this analogy suggests, the language of blockage and release (and the language of crisis and resolution) invokes a bodily economy and helps to explain, at least in part, the centrality of the white male body to explorations of crisis. But the release that men seek, and the resolution that might be found at the end of a crisis, are always deferred, and this is why we might say, following Gaylyn Studlar, that an aesthetic of masochism rules representations of dominant masculinity in crisis in the post-sixties era.

The psychic economy of masochistic desire, theorized by psychoanalysis, is remarkably similar to the narrative economy of "crisis" evident in individual texts and in the larger cultural landscape as I understand it. "The pleasure of masochism," Studlar writes, "is inseparable from the pain of suspense. Masochism's dynamic of pleasure does not depend on resolution or the recreation of the original plenitude" (60).[21] The original plenitude corresponds, in the fictions of crisis I will read here, to the illusory "true" masculinity whose apparent decline motivates and fuels the crisis. Kaja Silverman echoes this formulation when she notes that masochistic desire and fantasy are characterized by "the endless postponement of the moment at which suffering yields to reward, and victory to defeat" (*Male Subjectivity*, 199). Masochism, more about fantasy than it is about actual experiences of pain (Studlar 16), is governed by a narrative economy that privileges infinitely deferred release, theatricality, and display. Masochism depends on an audience, as both Studlar and Silverman argue: the masochist's suffering must be made *visible* in order for him to experience the pleasure in pain. The visibility of white male suffering, understood within a masochistic frame, challenges the critical assumptions about visibility, pleasure, pain, and power with which I began this introduction, and raises a number of key questions: Why is it that a crisis in white masculinity gets represented in corporeal terms? In what ways are pleasure and power made available through representations of white male bodies in crisis? What kind of power springs from narrative explorations of powerlessness? How and why do rhetorics of disempowerment rely on bodily figures?

The display of wounds and of male suffering is central to elaborations of a crisis in white masculinity, but masochism always competes with the more clearly phallic pleasures of release. The fact that Freud saw masochism as a perversion of the pleasure principle with its focus on male heterosexual release, and that feminists turn to masochism in search of a subversively nonphallic masculinity, suggests that gender and power are implicated in the relationship between pleasure and pain. The biologistic language of blockage and release that characterizes discussions of male sexual pleasure is central to the narratives I will attend to here. Blockage—of male speech, male sexuality, male privilege—becomes synonymous with not only repression but oppression, while release gets equated with "liberation." Oppression and liberation are figured primarily in individualist rather than social terms, and what could be more individual than the body? Yet because white masculinity has retained so much of its power through what Michael Warner calls "rhetorics of disincorporation," an emphasis on the body always risks plunging white masculinity into the morass of materialist politics—body politics, identity politics—that provoked the crisis in the first place. Because of the impossibility of resolving the crisis, what most clearly characterizes white masculinity in this era, I will argue, is a perpetual state of crisis that confuses causes with effect, symptom with cure, disempowerment with empowerment. As Wendy Brown argues, the perpetuation of a crisis state is the price to be paid for identity politics: "Politicized identity thus enunciates itself, makes claims for itself, only by entrenching, restating, dramatizing, and inscribing its pain in politics; it can hold out no future—for itself or others—that triumphs over this pain" (74). If we hope to find our way out of this impasse, Brown warns that we must guard "against abetting the steady slide of political into therapeutic discourse, even as we acknowledge the elements of suffering and healing we might be negotiating" (75). And although she is addressing the uses and problems of identity politics for marginalized groups, her point is equally applicable to what I am calling an identity politics of the dominant. Perhaps more so, since, as we will see, the slide into the therapeutic, the depoliticized personal, definitively characterizes representations of a wounded white masculinity. After all, the alleged emphasis on the "political"—responsible for the marking of white masculinity in the first place—is most often identified as the disease that must be cured.

Despite sometimes overwhelming evidence of a backlash against, or at least a backsliding away from, the gains of the liberation movements of the sixties and seventies, I want to insist that the liberationist movements and discourses that arose in the late sixties—particularly feminism and black power—have radically changed the American cultural landscape, and not just those areas which are most often understood as having been influenced by the sixties. Similarly, while it is clear that much of the radical language and representational practices of that time have been appropriated by the mainstream, commodified and, thus, to some degree, deprived of their revolutionary power; it is also clear that, in absorbing such languages and representations, the "mainstream" has been undeniably altered. The "mainstream" is, in fact, a far more volatile space than is usually acknowledged in literary or cultural criticism, as most critics assume that the action is found on either end of a high-low cultural, and class, divide. The middle, as I see it, is an essentially *defensive* cultural and political formation, one characterized by suspicion, even paranoia, about the passing of a now delegitimized cultural order.

The "mainstream"—also called the "Middle American," the "vast middle," the "middlebrow," the location of "ordinary" Americanness—is a site of struggle over the meaning of normativity, in political and cultural terms. In political terms, the "Middle American" or ordinary American is the hero of a vast array of American narratives, pursued by the right and the left, apprehended paradoxically as both uniquely individual and representatively American. The Middle American is the great unmarked, the phantom figure against whom differences become visible—but, as we will see, himself deeply invested in coming to visibility. The Middle American is *the* American individual, and his fortunes parallel the fortunes of dominant conceptualizations of American identity. While it is obvious that both the left and the far right practice identity politics—witness the rise of the Christian identity movement alongside the rise of multiculturalism in American universities—it is not immediately evident how and to what effect the broad "middle" participates in a renegotiation of gender and racial differences in post-liberationist American culture. In cultural terms, the "middlebrow" is territory that has always been up for grabs, the subject of a good deal of cultural angst and subject to often vicious battles over the cultural hierarchies that are also always social hierarchies. On the run not from the attacks on its value from the high, as was the case in the earlier decades of this century,[22] but from a mass culture relentless in its efforts to "feminize" and commodify identities and aesthetics, the middlebrow is nevertheless anxious about the place of the "literary" or the "artistic" in contemporary American culture. John Updike and John Irving, novelists of the middlebrow, belong next to the "culture warriors" of the late 1980s who mourn the death of a particular configuration of cultural hierarchy and, indeed, the death of cultural hierarchy itself. The middlebrow is associated with the establishment, the delegitimized center; while the avant-garde fits into, or can be made to fit into, revolutionary projects, and mass culture can be read as a potential source of individual and collective empowerment,[23] middlebrow appears impotent from either direction, out of touch with the masses and out of touch with the elites. I seek to elaborate the effects of a marking of white masculinity in the middlebrow or, more simply, the "mainstream," because that's where the normative lives. While one could certainly make the argument that it is in mass culture—Hollywood blockbusters, to use the limit case—that the normative finds its expressions, I want to excavate a different cultural territory, and one that has received little attention.

By focusing on reconstructions of white masculinity within the middlebrow in this era, I aim to zero in on a number of discursive and social sites where the normative gets reconfigured in response to, and in contestation with, liberationist ideology. Because the middlebrow is so defensive, so full of contradictions and paradoxes, it is an incredibly fertile ground for examining cultural hierarchies and values, for uncovering anxieties and desires. And while it would be inaccurate to say that the middlebrow is an exclusively white and male category, it *is* the case that the cultural anxieties defining and shaping the middlebrow are very similar to social anxieties afflicting white men. The defensiveness of the middlebrow as a cultural sphere is parallel with the defensiveness of white men on the social and political fronts. As we all learned during the 1994 midterm congressional elections, the angst of "ordinary Americans" became most fully visible via the image of the "angry white man," a defensive figure if there ever was one. Those anxieties have to do with the power to represent the norm. Whereas white male novelists, for example, might have until recently been read simply as "novelists," many might now find themselves categorically defined *as* white male novelists: they might find themselves *marked,* not read for their expression of a personal, individualized vision but, like women writers or African American writers, habitually read as the exemplars of a particularized—gendered and racialized—perspective. Like the marginalized or minoritized subject who is first marked by the dominant culture, and then appropriates that marking for her own purposes, the so-called average American—straight, white, male, middle-class—also experiences a mark imposed on him by others and then learns to restage his identity as marked. Paradoxically, it is through the acceptance of this marking that the crisis in white masculinity gets managed—but by no means resolved.

Marked Men is organized around five sites or moments of crisis that, roughly speaking, chart a movement from the political to the personal that also characterizes, in broad terms, the period from the late sixties to the late eighties. Those sites are the political (in the literal sense of social and governmental policy), the academic, the cultural, the emotional, and the sexual. While these sites of crisis are never fully separable from one another—the political is grounded in the cultural, the emotional in the sexual, for instance—I have organized the chapters in this way in order to highlight the connections and disjunctions between a variety of different discursive and social registers. Chapter 1 ("Marking Men, Embodying America") locates the birth of the current crisis in white masculinity in the "discovery" of Middle America following the 1968 election of Richard Nixon. In a backlash against liberation movements and discourses that had become so vocal, and the bodies of women and people of color that had become so visible, the "silent majority" emerges from its invisibility to compete for attention on the national scene. But "backlash" is not, ultimately, the most accurate way to describe how this crisis in white masculinity gets managed. The accounts of Middle American angst are riven by a paradox that can neither be acknowledged nor openly disavowed: to claim disenfranchisement based on gender and racial discrimination, these wounded white men must own up to their own gender and racial locations, thus giving the lie to their claim to represent America per se. The paradoxes of white male visibility circa 1969 are linked to a desired and feared embodiment in an influential and widely read set of novels, John Updike's "Rabbit" series. I argue that Updike's novels chart the transformation of white masculinity from an unmarked normativity to a specific, embodied category. The story the Rabbit novels tell is not a simply linear narrative of progressive decline or disempowerment. While Updike does spend some narrative energy bemoaning the "disenfranchisement" of his representative Middle American, the overall political effect of the novels is far more ambiguous.

Chapter 2 ("Pale Males, Dead Poets, and the Crisis in White Masculinity: Scenes from the Culture Wars") focuses on what I take to be another moment of crisis in an identity politics of the dominant, this time unfolding within the relatively rarified world of academia. I read between the lines of the "culture wars" to argue that recent conservative critiques of the academy (and its identity-based politics) speak of and for a white masculinity suffering the pains of its fall from a disembodied universality into an embodied specificity. These critiques offer sensationalist stories of a white and male professorate under attack, producing spectacles of embodiment and displays of vulnerable white male bodies at the mercy of "gender and race warriors." The crisis evident in texts as diverse as Allan Bloom's *The Closing of the American Mind* (1987) and Dinesh D'Souza's *Illiberal Education* (1991) is instigated by a marking of white masculinity as a specific and embodied (racial and gendered) identity. Yet underneath philosophical arguments against the corruption of higher education, a discourse on the mind, these texts betray an almost obsessive interest in the body. As we will see, that bodily discourse functions to muddy the oppositions that these cultural critics are invested in upholding, including the opposition between the abstract and the material, the individualist and the collectivist, the universal and the particular, the disinterested and the political. D'Souza and Bloom each stage a crisis in which the social trauma inflicted on the cultural authority of white masculinity gets displaced onto a more personal and even bodily plane. These critics move in to occupy the position of true rebel, true victim, in a culture war that works to reshape, rather than rise above, identity politics. In order to connect ivory-tower debates more fully with the middlebrow, I frame my analysis with readings of two widely popular texts, one a novel of ideas (Michael Crichton's explosive 1993 bestseller *Disclosure*), the other a highbrow film (Peter Weir's 1989 Academy Award–nominated *Dead Poet's Society*).

In chapter 3 ("Traumas of Embodiment: White Male Authorship in Crisis"), I examine middlebrow texts that more fully literalize these anxieties around, and pleasures derived from, the cultural decentering of white masculinity: Philip Roth's *My Life as a Man* (1974), John Irving's *The World According to Garp* (1978), and Stephen King's *Misery* (1987).[24] In these narratives, as in the documents of "culture war" which provide their context, bodies and texts exist in a synecdochic relation, making the link between white male bodies and "culture" absolutely explicit. Together these texts construct a picture of a white masculinity in crisis, and the effects of that crisis are somatic. The individual authorial body stands in for the cultural body of aesthetic standards, both bodies threatened by women who are engaged in victimizing white male authors and mutilating the cultural sphere. These fictions go much further, however, in their representations of a white male authorship in crisis; they positively revel in the spectacle of white male bodies in pain, and in the spectacle of a weak masculinity at the mercy of the feminine. While representing wounded masculinity in order, then, to recuperate it at the end of a narrative—making it stronger and more resilient in the process—is not new to American popular culture, I argue here that recuperation is not the only effect of these representations. If the goal of the aesthetic separation of the masculine high and feminine low culture is the separation of the creative imagination from the material body, that body will always return with a vengeance. Although it is primarily women, the feminine, or feminism that initiates the return of the body, these fictions are not simply misogynist, antifeminist, or gynophobic—even if they are occasionally all of these things. These texts insist that there is something *pleasurable* in the wounding of the white male body, a pleasure not unlike that produced by the spectacular staging of wounds within masochistic narratives. This surplus of pleasure keeps the representations from being geared entirely toward the revenge of masculinity on the feminine; and the fact that none of the three novels ends with an entirely triumphant and newly empowered male body suggests that this is not possible even if it were desirable.

While the first three chapters touch upon evidence of the psychological wounds of a crisis in the meanings of white masculinity, chapter 4 ("Masculinity as Emotional Constipation: Men's Liberation and the Wounds of Patriarchal Power") enters fully into the terrain of the psychological and analyzes a set of texts concerned with the emotional, verbal, and sexual "blockage" suffered by middle-class white men. In the 1970s, feminist-inspired critiques of masculinity, patriarchy, and the "male role" produced a large body of writing about a crisis in masculinity. Men's liberation discourse participates in the move to substitute the personal and bodily for the public and social, as a feminist analysis of systematic gender oppression gives way to a description of the personal emotional and physical ills traceable to the burdens of patriarchy. Central to this substitution is a conceptualization of emotion as a psychophysical essence, rather than as a socially conditioned and situated process, one that makes it possible to argue for the positivities of male "release" while ignoring the contemporaneous women's liberationist critique of various forms of male expressivity. Arguing that the release of blocked male "energies" is an a priori good, these male libbers construct "liberation" as a personal, highly therapeutic enterprise. Yet the men's liberationists should not be seen as orchestrating a backlash against the women's liberationists; they are best understood as attempting to change the terms of the discourse on gender to make room for narratives at odds with those forwarded by the "marking" of white men as the carriers of power and privilege. Men must survive, not the erosion of their power begun by a feminist critique, but rather the "myth of male privilege" that qualifies the feminist critique by making men, too, subject to the traumas of gendered experience. Like other rebel males we will see in this study, these brave fighters against patriarchy are represented as suffering bodily wounds that cause this discourse to veer into the melodramatic and to obscure certain pressing questions: What are the *costs* of male release? Will an ethos of emotional and sexual release necessarily be in the interests of women? Will expressing emotion liberate men or, instead, "feminize" them? I then turn to two contemporaneous novels that take on these questions in complicated and fascinating ways, and suggest that the very model of blockage and release on which the men's liberationists depend is itself deeply complicit with the "expression" of patriarchal power. John Irving's *The Water-Method Man* (1972) and Leonard Michaels's *The Men's Club* (1978) expose the problems in men's liberationist discourse, but also contribute to a growing sense that white masculinity is, in fact, in crisis.

Chapter 5 ("Expression, Repression, and Male Hysteria: Marked Men and the Wounds of a Dammed Masculinity") picks up from this argument and looks at the complicities between a liberationist focus on male "release" and a patriarchal and racialized construction of a "savage" masculinity lurking in men's natures. Here I look at popular sexology and argue that prescriptions for the "liberation" of a white male sexuality often mask a desire to liberate the emotional energies that issue in violence against the self and against others. I then turn to James Dickey's 1970 novel *Deliverance* and argue that it enshrines an age-old narrative about the damage inflicted on white men from a "civilizing" culture that tamps down, or represses, men's "nature." But John Boorman's film of Dickey's novel actively contests this mythology, and instead constructs a much more contemporary, historicized narrative about a white masculinity in perpetual and unresolvable crisis. Central to Boorman's rescripting of Dickey's narrative is the recognition that competing constructions of masculinity in post-liberationist culture paralyze men, and produce a hysterical male body as evidence of that paralysis. I use Pat Conroy's 1986 novel, *The Prince of Tides*, to trace that hysterical male body into the next decade. Both Boorman's film and Conroy's novel frame the male body as the site of simmering emotional and physiological energies that must remain dammed up if civilization is to be saved from a dangerously violent masculinity. But Barbra Streisand's 1991 film of Conroy's novel returns us to the apolitical and ahistoricist stance that was evident in Dickey's novel, as this film erases the social and political valences of the crisis Conroy details, instead cashing in on the new visibility of white male victim. Streisand's film confirms that the sympathetic representation of wounded white masculinity, and a belief in the efficacy of a therapeutic cure for those wounds, command more cultural and economic capital than Conroy's more politicized, overtly feminist meditation on the crisis in dominant masculinity.

My central argument, then, is that white masculinity can most fully and convincingly represent itself as victimized by inhabiting a wounded body, and that such a move draws not only on the persuasive force of corporeal pain but also on an identity politics of the dominant. Making a virtue of necessity, the wounded white male stakes a claim to an entire set of cultural conventions originally designed to identify those bodies and subjectivities made to suffer so that white men could retain privileged access to a disembodied norm. Yet such representational strategies can produce unexpected effects—as can *analyses* of those strategies. I am, of course, fully aware that my analysis of the marking of white masculinity in the post-liberationist era contributes to, and exacerbates the effects of, that marking. *Marked Men*, thus, might help to perpetuate the crisis, and with possibly contradictory effects. On the one hand, I might be read as joining up with Modleski's "optimistic feminists," who believe that a masculinity in crisis is necessarily a masculinity disempowered. On the other hand, in further marking white masculinity, *Marked Men* inevitably adds fuel to the fire, further entrenching an image of a damaged white masculinity and thus providing another alibi for the performance of its wounds. Even if I were able to be perfectly clear about my own intentions and investments, I would not necessarily be able to keep at bay the assumption that analyzing dominant masculinity means "you're either gonna whomp 'em or join 'em," as Fred Pfeil puts it (viii). My position is more than slightly different from Pfeil's, who to some degree cannot help but identify with his "white guys" in much more complicated ways than I can ever know; but my position in relation to this material is, by no means, disinterested.

Marked Men is motivated by both a political aim and a scholarly fascination. I construct a feminist argument that means to make a difference in how we read representations of wounded white men in contemporary culture, even as I admire the ingenuity of, and find great cultural interest in, those representations. I have also developed a good deal of respect for the difficulty of seeing with fresh eyes a category, white men, that much of my feminist training has prepared me to see as singular, monolithic, and singularly, monolithically powerful. But, as a feminist who was educated to believe that only women "have" gender and as a white woman who was indoctrinated to believe that "race" belongs only to people of color, I'm not going to spend a lot of time worrying that I am unfairly generalizing about an obviously heterogeneous category. In fact, I take a certain delight in imagining one possible response to my arguments here: How can we lump *all* white men, regardless of their differences, into one, seemingly monolithic, category? The delight comes both from the irony of this question—what feminist woman wouldn't laugh at this? what victim of racial profiling wouldn't snicker at this payback?—and from the fact that anyone who articulates it will be further confirming the arguments I am making. White men in post-liberationist American culture *have,* in fact, been lumped into one category; and the sometimes violent and sometimes whiny responses to that lumping is the subject of this book. Marked with the homogenizing brush of gender and racial categorization, white men are experiencing what women and people of color have long experienced: being made to signify the particular and the material. But, unlike the marking of "other" bodies that Haraway and others have identified as a technology of control practiced on behalf of the putatively universal and abstract, *this* marking does not depend on the existence of an unmarked norm existing elsewhere. In other words, while the identity politics of the dominant shares many assumptions and rhetorics with an identity politics of the marginalized, the two politics are not, and never can be, fully commensurate. Like arguments for "reverse racism" or "reverse sexism," the strategies through which white men represent themselves as disempowered depend on a systematic erasure of ways in which white and male power are socially and institutionally embedded. What makes that power so deeply embedded is, precisely, a historically verifiable, if sometimes tenuous, equation between white masculinity and a disembodied, unmarked, abstract personhood. In analyzing the cultural work performed by the current crisis in white masculinity, I am to make that equation more tenuous. It is just possible that doing so might push us closer to liberating men as well as women.

CHAPTER 1

MARKING MEN, EMBODYING AMERICA

John Updike and the Reconstruction
of Middle American Masculinity

In a 1974 self-help book entitled *The Male Dilemma: How to Survive the Sexual Revolution*, Anne Steinmann and David J. Fox describe the "pain of transition" suffered by ordinary Middle American men attempting to come to terms with the radical changes wrought by the civil rights and sexual liberation movements. Steinmann and Fox draw attention to the forced invisibility of these normative Americans who have been decentered in an era marked by the coming to visibility of others:

> Whenever there is a major revolution or change in the power structure of some aspect of society, the outs, the insurgents, the underdogs always become the center of attention and receive the major share of publicity. Thus, in the United States, the activities of racial minorities and youthful rebels are given center stage, while their adversaries, the white, middle-class, middle-age establishment, sink into the shadows. In the sexual revolution, the male has been cast as the adversary, the "enemy." (9)

The felt social, cultural, and political marginalization of Middle American white men that Steinmann and Fox allude to here gets most famously articulated through the metaphor of the "silent majority." Like Richard Lemon's *The Troubled American,* in which he laments the American "common man's" lack of a spokesperson or voice, Steinmann and Fox's contribution to the portrait of white Middle American male angst represents ordinary American men as the victims of a profound silencing. Whereas for Lemon "Middle American" is mostly defined as white, victimized by civil rights legislation and racially conceived entitlement programs, for Steinmann and Fox the villain is feminism and women: "The publicity surrounding the 'women's lib' movement has been formidable, but rarely, if ever, in the avalanche of words by or about women, has man been mentioned at all. He is told he must move over, but no one has bothered to tell him where or how. Like the establishment, he has become a symbol, a shadow" (9). This avalanche of women's words literally threatens to suffocate men, who are thus not only silenced but also at risk of injury. Whether traced to the rising voices of women, or the upsurge in black visibility, these texts announce a crisis in white masculinity and, in drawing on a rhetoric of personal and sociocultural injury, make that crisis more real.

Throughout their book, Steinmann and Fox make liberal use of the figure of the "shadow" to describe the paradoxical condition in which white men find themselves vis-à-vis the revolutionary movements of the era: at once invisible behind the "underdogs" who have taken center stage, and newly visible as the "enemies" of change and of liberation, middle-class white men become a shadowy presence-absence on the American scene. White men are but a shadow of their former selves, enjoying but a shadow of their former power and entitlements; but they also cast a dark shadow on the sunny fields of free love, heady protests, and optimistic political claims. The sixties, to recall John Updike's lament discussed in the introduction, were "no sunny picnic for" Protestant white males who had now become "the root of evil" in a major ideological, symbolic, and cultural shift (*Self-Consciousness* 146). Such paradoxical utterances—simultaneously claiming power and disempowerment, recognizing might and vulnerability—are a hallmark of texts that attempt to negotiate this moment of crisis. Updike's Rabbit novels provide the most sustained literary treatment of the paradoxes of (in)visibility as experienced by "average" white men as the twentieth century progresses, and will be my primary focus here. Harry "Rabbit" Angstrom is not representative of America per se, as some of Updike's critics have suggested; nor does he exactly stand in for a general American Everyman, as others argue;[1] he is, instead, a figure for middle-class white heterosexual masculinity, and the story of his decline (along with his triumphs) charts the ideological fortunes of that most normative of Americans: the Middle American.

"Middle American" is a term that came into wide public use on the American political and social scene around 1969, the year in which Updike set the second novel in the Rabbit series, *Rabbit Redux* (1971). In the first section of this chapter, I analyze the emergence of the "Middle American" as white and male, arguing that, paradoxically, this figure is created as the spokesperson for a normative American identity unmarked by gender and race *and* as a specific gendered and racialized identity. In the second and third sections, I analyze the complex enactments of an identity politics of the dominant found in the middle two Rabbit novels (*Rabbit Redux* and *Rabbit Is Rich* [1981]). As I argued in my introduction, while most accounts of the rise (and fall) of identity politics in post-liberationist American culture position white men *outside* the struggles over gender, race, and identity, my reading of the "silent majority," and Updike's exploration of it, suggests that such a view misses the vital fact that the meanings of whiteness and of masculinity are just as much at stake in such struggles as are the meanings of blackness or of femininity. While, on the one hand, it is accurate to read in the silent majority a "backlash" against liberation movements, the minority discourses that had become so vocal, and the bodies of women and people of color that had become so visible, it is also the case that the white men who so loudly proclaim their own "silencing" and decentering in post-liberationist American culture are fully participating in the struggles they are supposed to be lashing back against. In other words, in claiming to be deprived of the right both to represent "America" and to enjoy the fruits of a formerly secure entitlement, the spokesmen for Middle America paradoxically draw on the identity politics that were just beginning to emerge as the model of critique within radical thinking and activism. From the pages of *Newsweek* to the halls of academe, cultural commentators were busily making the Middle American visible—and visible as a victim. This move carries risks as well as payoffs, for in arguing that white men are victimized *because* they are white men, the spokespersons for the "silent majority" unwittingly corroborate claims that the rewards and punishments of social life in the United States are apportioned based on racial and gender identity, rather than merit or hard work or, simply, citizenship. While this new visibility enables a symbolic reempowerment of white men, now positioned as the "underdogs" of American culture, it also threatens to disempower white men by forcing the recognition that masculinity and whiteness are specific gender and racial categories modifying identity—rather than simply the invisible standard of American identity per se.

The Rabbit novels—spanning the decades from 1969 to 1980—chart the decentering of white masculinity, from its secure position as synecdoche for American identity *tout court* to its tenuous position as a specific (limited, historically circumscribed, dependent) category of American identity. Rabbit's story is the story of a shift in the status of white heterosexual masculinity away from its position as the self-evident (and invisible) standard against which all other identities are measured and found to be "different." It is under cover of this self-evidence that white masculinity has hidden both its claims to universality and its anxieties about its place in a culture that increasingly understands identity as specific, embodied, and marked by gender and race. The unmarked becomes the marked in Updike's novels, and Rabbit's engagement with the major historical and political forces of the late twentieth century demonstrates a wide range of reactions to and against this marking.[2] While the fall of white masculinity into specificity does, indeed, entail a degree of disempowerment, it is also the case that a growing group consciousness of middle American white men makes possible a different type of empowerment, one modeled on the various liberation movements which challenge the self-evident dominance of white masculinity on the American political, social, and sexual scene. That empowerment, paradoxically, is to be found in claims of victimization, and the Rabbit novels exhibit a pull in two contradictory directions: simultaneously dwelling on what might be called a feminizing disempowerment of the masculine *and* moving toward a recuperation of a fully phallic masculinity, the novels articulate dominant masculinity as structured by the competing attractions of power and vulnerability. It is primarily through changing representations of Rabbit's body that Updike expresses the condition of white masculinity in contemporary culture, and the crisis the novels narrativize is, thus, a crisis of embodiment. Rabbit is made to bear the marks of his own gendered and racialized identity—his body gets marked by others—but Updike turns this social and political crisis into a much more personal, bodily crisis, as Rabbit's body comes to signify the wounds to white and male privilege in post-liberationist American culture. Given the weird combination of pleasure and pain that characterizes Updike's representation of the powerfully vulnerable, vulnerably powerful white man, it comes as no surprise that in the last novel of the series, *Rabbit at Rest* (1990), Harry owns up to the "masochistic Christian" in himself, the "soldier," the man who takes pain over the "soft," "uncritical love" offered by women (64).

While it might appear that Updike makes white masculinity visible in order to disempower it, and could thus be seen as instigating a critique of the privileges that attend invisibility, my reading of the Rabbit novels suggests a far more ambivalent intention and a less clearly recognizable effect. Updike's novels are symptomatic of a cultural shift in which the visibility of white masculinity is both resisted and welcomed. These fictional texts both reflect and feed the growing crisis in white masculinity announced in the discourses around the discovery of Middle America, and do so by foregrounding the dilemmas of visibility and invisibility studiously suppressed in the nonfictional accounts. But the tension that animates these novels is not the tension between the fictional exposition of a cultural disease and its authoritative diagnosis, or between Rabbit as spokesman of the "silent majority" and Updike as its critic.[3] Rather, the tension emerges from the textual enactment of a crisis in white masculinity that is productive of both pleasure and pain, power and vulnerability. The novels, together, represent the state of white masculinity as perpetually in crisis; each of the (eventually) four Rabbit novels is structured around a moment of crisis in Harry's narrative and in the national narrative, but while isolated, historically discrete crises might get resolved within Updike's series, the overwhelming narrative impulse is to keep the crisis in suspension—much as masochistic narratives keep warding off the end result of a desire for pleasure in pain.[4] In fact, each of the novels almost hysterically evades closure. Most spectacularly, *Rabbit at Rest* leaves Rabbit on the verge of death with no hope for recovery; that Updike doesn't actually kill him suggests that, despite evidence to the contrary, white masculinity might just survive even the most severe attacks on its authority and centrality. In fact, it might just be the case that male masochism, and the rhetoric of crisis so consonant with it, will lead the way to that survival.

THE "DISCOVERY" OF MIDDLE AMERICA AND THE MARKING OF WHITE MASCULINITY

The discovery of Middle America by the media and political parties in the late 1960s causes a shift in representations of "Americans," away from the spectacular images of campus and urban unrest, youthful demonstrations against the war and against racist laws and practices; and toward far less sensational images of "workers," "hardhats," housewives, and ordinary folk, all white and all middle-aged. The construction of Middle America permeated mainstream culture through what Godfrey Hodgson calls a "complex process of feedback": popular opinion polls, media representations, and public policy all conspired to elevate Middle Americans into the spotlight and to make civil rights, radical thought and action, and the Vietnam War taboo topics (370). While we might be tempted to argue that these representations simply sought to diagnose an already existing sociocultural disease—and prescribe a cure—it is in fact more accurate to say that, in announcing the dilemma of the silent majority, these discourses actually *produced* and *enacted* that crisis in dramatic narrative terms. Because of this, it becomes increasingly clear that, far from resolving that crisis, analyses of the silent majority instead worked to recenter white men as subjects-in-crisis, in a culture that was proving itself to be ever more interested in such subjects. The announcements of crisis thus actually function to ward off a "cure" since it is through dwelling on crisis that the threats to the normativity of white masculinity get managed.

While women are included within the category "Middle American," the hero/villain who dominates books like Lemon's *The Troubled American*, Steinmann and Fox's *The Male Dilemma*, Donald Warren's *The Radical Center* (1976), and Richard Scammon and Ben Wattenberg's *The Real Majority* (1970) is white, male, heterosexual, and of a vast but hazily defined middle class. The technical inclusion of women does nothing to obstruct the construction of the Middle American as normatively male, and the masculinity at the center of this construction becomes clear in those moments when a commentator poses Middle Americans (ungendered) against Middle American women, or notes that the prevalence of women in the workplace "contributes to the sense of disorientation and alienation" (Lemon 58) that characterizes the Middle American (again ungendered). Women's liberation, of even the tamest variety, is lumped under the category of "the new moral permissiveness" (Lemon 58) along with pornography, student protests, and loosened sexual mores. At the same time as Middle America is speaking against (or constructed as speaking against) civil rights and social justice, the "average Joe" is represented as speaking *for* "traditional" (patriarchal) values. "Traditional values" are linked with a white masculinity that escapes the "softness" pervading American culture in the wake of the "permissive" sixties.[5] An unimpeachably masculine working class, attached to these traditional, virile values, thus, is used to heal over middle-class anxieties about the "feminization" that many saw corrupting American manhood in the sixties. The dominant image of a resurgent machismo in a hard hat is fueled by Spiro Agnew's widely quoted rhetoric against the national mood of masochism promulgated by that "effete corps of impudent snobs who characterize themselves as intellectuals" (quoted in Carroll 6). Symbolic constructs of femininity are used in contradistinction to the values of Middle America, and thus Middle America is firmly masculinized.

The normativity of white masculinity is confirmed by the data and testimony offered by Lemon, Scammon and Wattenberg, and Warren.[6] The factoring out of all but white Americans from the category "Middle American" suggests that nonwhite Americans are the "problem" and white Americans the "victims" of that problem. But the category "white Americans," and its cognate "Middle Americans," is not nearly as unified as this conclusion would imply. Scammon and Wattenberg's *The Real Majority* and Lemon's *The Troubled American* reveal that the "middle" is a slippery and inexact term, meant to signal a homogeneous group defined by negatives: "unyoung, unpoor, unblack." The homogeneity of the category "Middle American" is dependent upon the erasure of class and gender differences and thus Middle America comes to mean a unified and dissatisfied white America. But it is also dependent on the erasure of *individual* differences, for the category of "Middle American," like the category of "white masculinity," implies a collective, a unified grouping. What unifies this "politically and philosophically varied place, and the one thread that ties all its groups together is resentment" against the gains of the various liberation movements that were loudly claiming rights and restitution (Lemon 26). Ironically, however, it is by *joining* that chorus of voices that these normative Americans aim to differentiate themselves from the "young, the poor, and the black."

Middle America comes into wide public view via a discourse that subtly collapses class, gender, and sexual tensions and differences among whites into a polarized debate about race, and thus threatens to erase the individualist values on which the Middle American stakes his normativity.[7] The blurring of class boundaries in this discourse serves an important purpose in polarizing white against black Americans, but it also, paradoxically, places white men in a marked category that is known *not* for the differences of its individual members, but for its coherence, its sameness. At the same time, the Middle American comes to occupy the space of "difference," as he replaces other rebels and takes his place as the hero of what looks an awful lot like a liberationist narrative. It is here that we begin to see that an identity politics of the dominant arises to compete with an identity politics of the marginalized, as voiceless and decentered Middle Americans are irresistibly drawn toward a collectivism that threatens to invalidate the very terms of normativity on which the category "Middle American" would seem to depend. Middle America becomes visible as wounded, weakened, and vulnerable, and while this might compromise the power and position of white masculinity, such a representation also enables white men to lay claim to a newly emerging center: white men, too, can claim civil rights and restitution against their injuries. What defines Middle American white men in this period is a sense that they have lost what was rightfully theirs; they experience a "deep alienation from a social system which, *by rights,* they ought to dominate" (Lemon 21, emphasis added). Part of that lost entitlement is the power to represent America per se, and to determine the terms of American normativity. It is in this sense that these Middle Americans, so angry at others' use of the logic of victimization, position themselves as victims.

The degree to which this new discourse on "Middle America" assumes a victimized beleaguered whiteness as its prime identity category is striking, as "Middle America" is defined against civil rights and the fledgling social programs of the 1960s.[8] A heavily coded discourse on whiteness pervades these studies of "troubled Americans," in which whiteness hides behind what Updike refers to as "law-abiding conformity" (*Self-Consciousness* 146) and blackness is coded by "welfare," "law and order," "urban decay," and "crime." Whiteness takes cover behind the term "Middle American," and it is a powerful enough, if often silent, signifier that all other differences become meaningless in the face of the racial binary. Scammon and Wattenberg, despite some awareness about "racial coding," unwittingly paint a picture of a growing obsession with race which defines whiteness in the period. Importantly, though, the racial binary is skewed by the fact that "white" is a normative category and "black" a racial one. By 1974, when Wattenberg publishes *The Real America*, whiteness has so fully disappeared again into the normative that he can write with sturdy pragmatism and absolutely no self-consciousness: "It has become apparent that 'law and order' is [for Middle America] no mere code phrase for racism—it is shorthand for civilization itself" (118). In this ambiguously racialized discourse, overt discussion of gender recedes behind an elaborate set of metaphors meant to "feminize" poverty and the "permissiveness" of the youth culture, and to construct masculinity as normatively white, whiteness as normatively masculine.

"Middle Americans," as a discursive construct, thus enters political discourse as antiblack, anti-civil rights, and, despite this aggressive posture, as the objects of institutional neglect if not blatant racial discrimination. This is not to say that the majority of Americans of middle income were racist; it *is* to say that the discourse around their "discovery" as a group constructed them as first and last concerned with race. In an intriguing 1976 study of a group he dubs the "Middle American Radicals" (MARs), Donald Warren makes a distinction between Middle Americans, primarily identified as such through income level, and MARs, whose unifying feature is ideology. Although this ideology is characterized by a general disillusionment with the way institutions are working, particularly the federal government, its most marked characteristic is racial: resentment of African Americans, all of whom receive "special" treatment and, importantly, a sense of solidarity with other white Americans. Warren's study makes explicit and clear what was kept hidden in earlier treatments of Middle Americans: the most vocally alienated spokespersons for the "silent majority" are united by racial, rather than class, concerns. What emerges from Warren's portrait of the MARs is a construction of whiteness as an identity marker, and the making of white men into a distinct social group united by race and, secondarily, by gender. Drawing his conclusions from interviews with MARs, Warren speculates: "The emphasis which MARs place on ethnic and racial ties has implications for the way in which more traditional and 'visible' ethnic and racial minorities may compare. Therefore, one perspective on the MAR phenomenon is to view it as *yet another new group consciousness,* albeit one formed out of other ethno-religious groupings" (98, emphasis added). In terms of racial (and nationalist) feeling, Warren concludes that MARs are more like the "visible" racial minorities than they are like other (presumably "invisible") whites. Further, the MARs feel that they are disempowered as a group, that is to say, disempowered *because they are white.* Warren identifies the MARs as being in the "early stages of militancy" as a racial group, and one that feels it "is beginning to have some power" (103).[9] This claim is echoed by a majority of Lemon's "troubled Americans" who complain that no one speaks for Middle America's interests, for instance: "The middle class has the numbers, but they feel too cut off from the entire society to change things. Someone has got to show them how to get a voice in this country" (Lemon 20).

For the Middle American Radicals, group interests must necessarily conflict with the individualism that, according to Warren, defines them. Anxious not to join the chorus of middle-class writers bashing Middle Americans even while making them the heroes of a new American narrative, Warren suggests a deeper understanding of the group in the context of "traditional" American values:

"rugged individualism, self-reliance and autonomy" (48). While not exactly ex-
onerating the MARs of the charges against them—and, in fact, much of his research confirms the central place of racism in MAR ideology—Warren stresses
that a very American emphasis on individualism, autonomy, and self-reliance
makes it difficult for MARs to accept what they see as "special treatment" of
minorities and women. At the same time, of course, this individualism makes it
difficult for the MARs to claim that they, as a group identified by race, are the
objects of discrimination. As George Lipsitz persuasively argues, an ideology
and a language of liberal individualism has secured white dominance while
hiding the fact that white Americans benefit in untold ways from their membership in a *group*. Noting the "overdetermined inadequacy of the language of
liberal individualism to describe collective experience," Lipsitz goes on to argue
that this language "serves as a cover for coordinated collective group interests"
(383). Although concerned with the rise of a reactionary white supremacist
fringe in the early 1990s, Lipsitz makes a number of points which are also applicable to the reaction against civil rights gains in the late 1960s. For instance,
Warren's work makes it clear that in 1969 there was already a "broadly shared
narrative about the victimization of innocent whites by irrational and ungrate-
ful minorities" which hides "the disciplined, systemic, and collective *group* activity that has structured white identities in American history" (Lipsitz 382–83).
    The MARs participate in a collective mobilization for "white rights," but do
so by positioning themselves as socially situated individuals (white individuals)
fighting against a corrupt collectivity—usually figured as "an unholy alliance
growing between the liberal and minority establishment at [their] expense"
(Warren 3). What Lipsitz calls the "possessive investment in whiteness" includes, for the MARs, an investment in the language of liberal individualism
which, paradoxically, makes collective mobilization in the name of whiteness
taboo. Similarly, "rugged individualism" encodes a particular construction of
(white) American masculinity, and the ideal of masculinity prized most by the
Middle American Radicals makes it difficult, again, for them to mobilize into a
group united against individuality and for racial solidarity. As Warren explains,
Middle American men avoid political action groups because "the lower middle
class male defines all organizations which demand verbal skills and organized
political activity as incompatible with his self-image. His 'ideal self' is a physically strong, hardworking, dependable person. Social aggressiveness and verbal
ability are seen exclusively as feminine attributes" (6). Warren's interviewees
define their individualism and autonomy—guarantees of masculinity—in
opposition to group behaviors which might, within this frame, be coded as
feminine.
    There is a paradox here that marks every effort on the part of white mas-
culinity to situate itself as a specific identity category based on gender and race

and a social group mobilizing around perceived discrimination; and, *simultaneously*, as the spokesmen for, and figures of, an individualism that brooks no talk of discrimination based on race and gender. Warren's work on the Middle American Radicals suggests that this paradox finds added fuel in the late sixties. This suggestion is confirmed by a number of other books which imply, mostly obliquely, that the white man as figure for an American individualism meets the white man as object of discrimination in the late sixties.[10] This confluence marshals in an era in which white masculinity begins to make claims based on group rights and wrongs while trying, at the same time, to hold onto the privilege of representing the American individual. The tension between representativeness and individual uniqueness is at the heart of the late sixties crisis in white masculinity. It is also at the heart of Updike's Rabbit series, where, as many critics have argued, Harry is constructed both as a representative of "America" and as a unique individual. The primary impulse of *Rabbit Redux* is to resituate white masculinity, conceived of as "middle Americanness," in a landscape radically altered during the course of a turbulent decade. Harry feels as if he has been made "invisible" and, as we shall see, this anxiety over invisibility produces bodily, as well as political, insecurities. At the same time, he has been made visible as a gendered and racialized body and this, too, causes problems.

RABBIT REDUX: BLACK POWER, THE COUNTERCULTURE, AND THE DECENTERING OF WHITE MASCULINITY

On the surface, *Rabbit Redux* is a novel all about the ways in which racial and sexual "otherness" can impinge on "Middle America." Set in the summer of 1969, the novel is an explosive representation of the effects of the sixties youth movements on that portion of the population which perceives itself and its interests as ill served, if not endangered, by those movements. As such, the novel is situated at the very beginning of an era marked by a crisis in the symbolic (if not social) position of white masculinity. As Susan Jeffords points out, by the late 1980s scores of texts are responding "to the chief challenges offered to white male authority in the preceding decades—the loss of the Vietnam War, the civil rights movement, and feminism" (*Hard Bodies* 118). Updike's novel all but ushers in this era, but does not end with the recuperation of white male authority: while taking some steps toward remasculinization, particularly in response to anxieties over the waning of male sexual power, Updike's narrative resists the temptation to pump Rabbit back up. Instead, Updike represents his American "Everyman" as a subject split between a desire to recharge the power of white masculinity and a desire to entertain disempowerment as a positive element in the construction of a new white male identity.

In *Rabbit Redux*, Updike submits his protagonist to a number of forces which, together, work to diminish the power "naturally" afforded to white masculinity in American culture. Harry is plunged into a morass of politics—racial, sexual, and national—that threatens his construction of "America" and his privileged place within it. The novel takes great pains to place Rabbit in a disempowered position and, as many critics of the novel have argued, Updike represents him primarily as passive. This is a Rabbit who can't walk, never mind run, and he appears to have lost the impulse to quest which defined him in *Rabbit, Run* (1960). The beginning of the later novel finds Rabbit with a wife newly energized (and sexualized) by the women's liberation movement; a job endangered by proto–affirmative action programs and, in any case, soon to be made obsolete by new print technology; a family on the verge of dissolution and death; an unfashionable "hawkish" view of the war (and deep regret about being too old to serve); and a town with "too many Negroes." The novel almost revels in Rabbit's impotence in the face of a world which seems to have stripped him of his privilege, and thus sets the stage for a recuperation of white masculinity. But things get worse, rather than better, for our representative Middle American: his wife leaves without their son, tying Rabbit to domesticity; he endangers his position in the community by taking in a white woman who represents the counterculture he despises, then Skeeter, a Vietnam vet who claims to be the black Jesus; he gets laid off because linotyping is rendered obsolete by offset printing; he finds himself impotent with women several times during the course of the novel; he allows himself to be passively dragged along on Skeeter's "trip," never understanding what it means. He can't protect his home (it burns down), his woman (Jill perishes in the fire), or his son (who blames him for both). Like the Middle Americans who define themselves against the "black, the poor, and the young," Rabbit imagines enemies of American normativity everywhere. The difference is that Rabbit *welcomes* these enemies, and with them entertains the possibility that the normalizing power of white masculinity is no longer secure in a culture that has made "white men" visible, and visibly lacking.[11]

The novel offers its readers an almost illicit look into the disempowerment of white masculinity, and the pleasures of readerly voyeurism match Rabbit's own pleasure in his vulnerability. Updike ties that vulnerability to a general condition of lack, but a lack that is most clearly fed by Rabbit's hungry interest in, and desire for, black masculinity. Updike's construction of whiteness requires proximity to, not distance from, blackness; and, as Jan Clausen suggests, "the world of the Rabbit novels is overwhelmingly white—which is to say furtively, almost pruriently obsessed with race" (47). Rabbit is literally held in thrall to Skeeter, a representation based on Eldridge Cleaver's performance of black masculinity in *Soul on Ice*. The novel expresses this obsession with race (and gender) through a focus on bodily manifestations of gender and racial difference, and through an investigation into the embodiment of white masculinity. As white masculinity moves further away from its status as a (disembodied) norm, as it does in post-sixties culture, white men's consciousness of corporeality becomes more pressing. In *Rabbit Redux*, Harry Angstrom both invites and resists the embodiment into the particularity of his white and masculine identity—invites it as a way into the "action" taking place on various revolutionary fronts in the United States; and resists it because of the vulnerability it entails. Being embodied, thus, means power to participate in (and control) sexual, gender, and racial upheavals, all of which put the body on the line; but it also means an experience of disempowerment produced by the consciousness of inhabiting a material body, an experience exacerbated by the nagging suspicion that white male bodies simply fail to measure up—to black bodies, to female bodies, or to the universalist claims of an unmarked body.

From the very first sentence, the novel works its representation of white male bodies as bland, bleached out, and enervated:

> Men emerge pale from the little printing plant at four sharp, ghosts for an instant, blinking, until the outdoor light overcomes the look of constant indoor light clinging to them. . . . The sky is cloudless yet colorless, hovering blanched humidity, in the way of these Pennsylvania summers, good for nothing but to make green things grow. Men don't even tan; filmed by sweat, they turn yellow.
> (13–14)

White male bodies are dead, distanced from nature and fecundity, trapped in the artificial light of technology. As Charlie Stavros, Rabbit's rival, later says, "I don't find technology that sexy" (45). Charlie, himself dark and ethnically "other" to the "big Swede" Rabbit (who refers to him as a "spic"), makes the lighter man feel "pasty and nervous" (165) as does Rabbit's black coworker Buchanan. The description of these unhealthy, "yellowing" white men predicts Skeeter's discourse, "borrowed" from both Cleaver's *Soul on Ice* and Mailer's "The White Negro," in which white masculinity is linked to a disembodied existence, and to the rise of mechanization: "You are white but you are wrong," Skeeter tells Rabbit; "we fascinate you, white man. We are in your dreams. We are technology's nightmare. We are all the good satisfied nature you put down in yourselves when you took that mucky greedy turn" (208).[12] As Richard Dyer remarks, the "idea that nonwhites are more natural than whites also comes to suggest that they have more 'life', a logically meaningless but commonsensically powerful notion." And, " 'life,' " Dyer continues "tends to mean the body, the emotions, sensuality and spirituality" (55).

This commonsensical notion is fully activated in Updike's novel, where "life" is linked with blackness and death with whiteness. White bodies can't hold up to black, the difference between color and colorlessness written on the skin, as in this vibrant description of Skeeter's body:

> Physically, Skeeter fascinates Rabbit. The lustrous pallor of the tongue and palms and the soles of the feet, left out of the sun. Or a different kind of skin? White palms never tan either. The peculiar glinting lustre of his skin. The something so very finely turned and finished in the face, reflecting light at a dozen polished points: in comparison white faces are blobs: putty still drying. The curious greased grace of his gestures, rapid and watchful as a lizard's motions, free of mammalian fat. Skeeter in his house feels like a finely made electric toy; Harry wants to touch him but is afraid he will get a shock.
>
> (221)

What is even more striking here than Rabbit's (barely even repressed) sexual desire for Skeeter is what appears to be a loving fascination with the material black body, and a fascination that would appear to depart significantly from the standard American iconography of racial differentiation. That fascination springs from Rabbit's envy of an elemental, animalistic, lizard-like masculinity; but, in addition to the projection of a "primitive," natural masculinity onto Skeeter, Updike also articulates a *cultural* appreciation of the black body as aesthetically more appealing than the white body. Skeeter's body is likened, *not* to a force of nature, but to a work of art: "so finely turned and finished in the face, reflecting light at a dozen polished points." Although this description does not entirely avoid fetishizing blackness, the kind of overt projections that Toni Morrison analyzes in white American literature are missing in it. What this passage does accomplish is to make whiteness visible in relation to blackness, and in its momentary visibility, whiteness shows itself to be bland, *un*finished, *un*formed—like "putty still drying." Rabbit's estranged wife expresses this best, with her distaste for "his white body, his spreading slack gut, his uncircumcised member hanging boneless as a rooster comb from its blond roots. . . . She sees a large white man a knife would slice like lard" (39). Rabbit's body is in decline, and that decline is linked up with the fledgling women's movement—it is the newly "liberated" Janice who criticizes it so devastatingly; and the new visibility of black masculinity embodied in a vibrant and "electric" form.

It is the increased visibility of women and people of color in Rabbit's world that forces him to think about his own embodiment, his own gendered and racial body, and the fact that his body can signify "otherness." Culturally, too, whiteness pales in contrast to blackness, as we see in Rabbit's response to the music and ambiance of Jimbo's, a predominantly black bar: "everything is warm, wet, still coming to birth but himself and his home, which remains a strange dry place, dry and cold and emptily spinning in the void of Penn Villas like a cast-off space capsule" (121). Updike's language, linking blackness with lithe lively bodies and whiteness with dead, dry, or cold bodies, points to what I will call the novel's anxiety of blandness. And although black masculinity represents a vital force, Rabbit's own sense of male privilege and empowerment is severely compromised—not least by Janice coming into a fiercely desired bodily life with Charlie. That this anxiety about blandness seems so focused around bodily matters suggests that what has been a privilege of white masculinity—its closeness to a disembodied norm—has now become a liability. The reference to the space capsule reminds the reader that, in the summer of 1969, a vessel of white men was streaming across space, and that the most marked characteristic of those white male bodies was to become their *weightlessness*. Liberated from bodily mass (although vulnerable to bodily cataclysms), these images of floating white male bodies, encased in protective suits, fail to ignite Rabbit's imagination, despite his patriotic pride. The novel's representation of the moonwalk emphasizes a weightlessness and abstraction; in fact, Updike has Rabbit failing to hear the famous words spoken by Neil Armstrong: "A man in clumsy silhouette has interposed himself among these abstract shadows and glare. He says something about 'steps' that a crackle keeps Rabbit from understanding" (92). Addressing both this monumental historic event and the more personal event of Janice's leaving him for Charlie Stavros, Rabbit remarks to his mother, " 'I know it's happened but I don't feel anything" (93).[13]

White male anxiety about blandness flows beneath the more overtly political discourse around the "discovery" of Middle America, in which, as Richard Lemon's *The Troubled American* most clearly demonstrates, white men are reacting against their perception that their central position in American culture has been usurped. Although Lemon does not say so explicitly, he hints that Middle American anger at the increasingly vocal and visible "troublemakers" has something to do with the fact that Middle America in the late 1960s lacks a "poet" to sing its experiences. Lamenting that "common men" are "no longer seen in the most respectable novels or movies. They rarely appear on television, and their values are not to be found in most popular songs," Lemon concludes that "in American culture today, the common man is like the buffalo of the Great Plains—not quite but almost extinct" (105). David Roediger identifies a similar anxiety as stemming from a history in which "white culture" becomes increasingly less vital and vibrant than other American cultures. Following up on Toni Morrison's work in *Playing in the Dark*, Roediger argues that whiteness "is the empty and therefore terrifying attempt to build an identity based on what one isn't and on whom one can hold back" (*Towards the Abolition of Whiteness*, 13). This is true, in part, because, according to Roediger, there is no such thing as "white culture"—or, if there is, it is a pale imitation of various ethnically specific American cultural traditions: "Whiteness describes, from Little Big Horn to Simi Valley, not a culture but precisely the absence of culture" (13).[14]

Making a useful distinction between the appeals *of* whiteness and appeals *to* whiteness, Roediger describes a historical situation in which whiteness appears to avenge itself against nonwhiteness, precisely because of a kind of anxiety of blandness.

> Whiteness exercises such political force despite its thorough discrediting as a "cultural color," despite its having become the fair game of standup comics who reflect on the vacuity of "white culture" in a nation in which so much that is new, stirring, excellent and genuinely popular—in music, fashion, oratory, dance, vernacular speech, sport and increasingly in literature, film, and nonfiction writing—comes from African American, Asian American and Latino communities. We face, in short, a mad and maddening situation in which the *appeals of* whiteness are at their most pitifully meager and the effectiveness of *appeals to* whiteness—from Howard Beach to Simi Valley to the ballot boxes—are at a terrible height.
>
> (*Towards the Abolition of Whiteness*, 6, emphasis added)

While Roediger's formulation shies away from a causal argument, I will risk one here: whiteness—or, rather, white masculinity—must recuperate the symbolic power lost through its "discrediting as a 'cultural color.'"

In *Rabbit Redux*, that recuperation never gets off the ground, although Updike intimates that whiteness can get recharged by siphoning off and drinking in draughts of blackness. Rabbit gets a charge out of his entertainment of blackness, and by his voyeuristic appreciation of Skeeter's body and sexuality. But, rather than increasing his power, his attraction to Skeeter only works to diminish it. Constantly watching Skeeter, Rabbit feeds off of the vibrancy he sees in that body, but this voyeurism reflects back on Rabbit in dangerous ways, implicating him both in a homoeroticism that threatens because it is *not* demasculinizing and in the self-canceling denigration of whiteness. Spying on Skeeter masturbating, for instance, Rabbit flees "into the white realm where an overhead frosted fixture burns on the landing. His heart skips. He has escaped. Narrowly" (248).[15] Rabbit narrowly escapes from homoeroticism, but also from a desire to embrace the blackness that threatens to overwhelm him. But what does he escape with? Into? The novel offers no sanctuary for Rabbit or for a white masculinity that suffers such an intense crisis of cultural, sexual, and political authority. As the story of Rabbit and Skeeter plays itself out, we expect whiteness to recuperate the power it has lost. Whiteness needs to become bigger and better for having absorbed blackness; whiteness must be remasculinized. But while Updike offers Skeeter as a kind of reservoir of hypermasculinity, Rabbit never quite recoups his power, and white masculinity remains a pale imitation of black.

Throughout the novel, Updike dwells on the fascinations and fears of and for white masculinity as it encounters both black masculinity and a reconceptualized white femininity. What is at stake here is a conception of white masculinity as coextensive with "America"—endangered not only by the youth movements of the sixties but also by the battles of the Cold War. Updike explicitly sexualizes (and genders) the Vietnam War, first through Skeeter's theories about American imperialism as masculinity: "How can money and jizz make their way if we don't keep a few cunts like that open? Nam is an act of love, right?" (232); and then through Rabbit's echo: "A woman is blank until you fuck her. Everything is blank until you fuck it. Us and Vietnam, fucking and being fucked" (270). Fucking is what fills in the blank, what masculinizes, what makes whiteness powerful, what makes whiteness more like blackness. Skeeter tells Rabbit what he already knows, that he feels "de-balled" (224) by not fighting in Vietnam and Skeeter enables Rabbit to get "re-balled," vicariously as it were.[16] But the fact that he *needs* Skeeter to heal his own masculinity indicates that white masculinity can only know its power through the mediation of blackness. The fact that this strategy doesn't work, and Rabbit remains de-balled, suggests that the price to be paid for the mediation of black masculinity is the knowledge that white masculinity is dependent and fragile. Black masculinity, thus, becomes the *norm* of masculinity, and white masculinity its differentiated other.

What I'm suggesting here is that, alongside the racist fantasies that *Rabbit Redux* clearly expresses, we can glimpse a different fantasy, a fantasy of white male *dis*empowerment. For, while a history of constructions of the black male body as virile and, thus, dangerous to white masculinity's sense of its own potency might lead us to expect Updike's novel to destroy that body, at least symbolically, the opposite occurs. Skeeter escapes relatively intact and leaves in his wake a white male body conscious of its own impotence and even figurative deadness. The white girl is dead, literally.[17] But this novel isn't about the destruction and death of the lost but privileged white woman; she is simply a catalyst or an occasion for the battle between black and white masculinity, and once that battle is over, she can be disposed of, as Skeeter says: "The thing about a cunt, man, it's just like a Kleenex, you use it and throw it away" (246). As ugly as the sexual politics of the novel are, women are not the point, although *gender* clearly is. Gender is articulated less to biological sex than it is to race, and what is at stake in the novel's racial politics is the question of an American masculinity. Is there a masculinity that can accommodate Rabbit's attraction to, and fascinated fear of, the black man? Or, to put it the other way round, can white masculinity survive the new national context of race relations, structured as they are around fear and attraction? *Rabbit Redux* does not answer these questions, and they take a very different form in the next novel, where Harry's new membership in the professional managerial class insulates him against the black presence that so fascinated and worried him in the earlier novel.

Making whiteness visible in *Rabbit Redux* coincides with Harry's fall from both literal and metaphorical heights: Harry appears to lose both social and symbolic power. Socially, his privilege as a Middle American white man has been endangered by black men (Buchanan keeps his job while Harry loses his); and by white women (Jill challenges his beliefs, and Janice will demand equal power as the price for her return). Symbolically, the new "heroes" of American culture are not ordinary white individuals like Harry, but the various groups who organize collectively around rights, and against injustices. In order to recuperate some of that symbolic power—the social power will return in the next novel, where Janice's wealth enables an economic recuperation—Updike represents Rabbit as a new underdog, victimized *because* he is white and male. But this gesture can never fully heal white masculinity because, first, it is a gesture originating with those others who have helped to mark white masculinity; and, second, the figure of the white male victim contains a recognition that white masculinity can never recapture the invisibility upon which its normative power has rested.

RABBIT IS RICH: FEMINISM, THE THIRD WORLD, AND THE SCREWING OF WHITE MASCULINITY

Unlike the uneasiness with which critics greeted *Rabbit Redux, Rabbit Is Rich* met with nothing but accolades. It won the Pulitzer Prize for Literature, the American Book Award, and the National Book Critics Circle Award. It was on the *New York Times* bestseller list for six months. And, while some critics simply claim that it's a "better book" than its predecessor, I don't think it is too far-fetched to suggest that the critical reception of *Rabbit Is Rich* is, in part, fueled by relief that the trauma for Middle America represented in *Rabbit Redux* by *the* chronicler of the American middle class has given way to bliss. One of the standard lines on *Rabbit Redux* (and on the decade it represents) is best articulated by Donald Greiner: "*Rabbit Redux* is filled with disease and death as if Harry's personal predicament were a metaphor for the social collapse of traditional American values in the 1960s" (65).[18] Those values, as we have seen, include white and male supremacy, often articulated as "rugged individualism" and self-reliance. In this narrative, social contradictions are displaced onto personal ills, with the consequence that larger social and historical forces are rendered irrelevant.[19] Indeed, as Greiner implies, *Rabbit Is Rich* reinstates the separation between the public and the private that was temporarily breached by the "sick" sixties.[20] What ailed Harry in the sixties was a white masculinity made weak by challenges to its sovereignty as "self" or individual or "American"; that self seems to have recuperated in the seventies, at least to some degree, as the political gives way to the personal in the overwhelmingly consumerist, therapeutically oriented "Me Decade."

Perhaps because *Rabbit Is Rich* has no major black characters and little sustained discussion of race, critics of the novel have unequivocally designated it as the "economic" novel of the series, where *Rabbit Redux* might be called the "race" novel. White masculinity *appears* to be untroubled in *Rabbit Is Rich,* in which Harry rests secure in the paradise of his new middle-class position. In this novel, whiteness is freed of the burden of representing racial difference; that is to say, Harry is freed of the necessity to assume, or own up to, the racial identity forced upon him in *Rabbit Redux.* This freedom is bought, quite literally, by Harry's new wealth, his stable position in the middle class of the late seventies, and his consequent separation from the working class, African Americans, and the other "dark" shadows who people the margins of Brewer, and of Harry's consciousness. The brief moment in *Rabbit Redux* when Skeeter makes Harry realize that black and white men can unite, bonded by class interests, against a wealthy white elite, is long gone. As Donald Warren suggests, the "silent majority" starts to splinter into two distinct groups in the mid-seventies. "In one camp is the more content and secure portion of America's broad, middle income strata of blue-color workers and white-color functionaries," a group credited with casting the "happiness vote" for Nixon in 1972. The second group, "more militant, more aggressively dissatisfied," responded most fully to Agnew's attack on the liberal elite during the 1972 campaign and is embodied in the construction worker protests in Manhattan and the truckers' protest against the "energy crisis" in 1974 (Warren xv–xvi). Harry belongs in the first group, throwing his support behind oil interests and even government policy: " 'I don't blame the oil companies,' Harry says tranquilly. 'It's too big for them, too. Mother Earth is drying up, is all' " (*Rich* 5). Having entered fully into what has now become the professional managerial class, Harry has little contact with the class he has left behind; for instance, he no longer rides the city buses, the site of his everyday contact with the black population of Brewer. Racial and class differences are subsumed into a vast and only vaguely represented "underclass" in this novel, and Rabbit's new membership in the professional managerial class insulates him against the black presence that so fascinated and worried him in *Rabbit Redux*.

Whiteness does not become conscious of itself except in those moments when Harry becomes aware of the "wrong elements" (80) on the fringes of his city and consciousness. A Hispanic population has become visible in the years between the end of the second novel and beginning of the third, thus making the nonwhite population more diverse and less a singular mirror held up to whiteness. But despite the narrative ghettoization of people of color, blackness cannot so easily be exorcised. A mere twenty-five pages into the book returns Updike and Rabbit to questions of race—predictably through the medium of Skeeter whose death Rabbit has just learned of. As if materialized by the ghost of the black man, Harry notes "dark youths thinking in languages of their own," staring at him as he drives by (29), and nostalgically yearns for the paradise lost of a monocultural Brewer and its "vanished white giants" of buildings (30). The threat of blackness has been defused, primarily because it has so fully been appropriated by whiteness, a move that Updike contextualizes in relation to an explosion of consumerism. Harry approves the Bee Gees whom he hears on the radio, thinking of them as "white men who have done this wonderful thing of making themselves sound like black women" (30). But actual black women, in the person of Donna Summer, are only wonderful if they stay within the gender and race parameters set up by the white male imagination. No gender or race bending for Donna, whom Harry "liked best in the days when she was doing those records of a woman breathing and panting and sighing like she was coming" (33). The rhetoric and images of black power, of women's liberation, and indeed, the entire repertoire of countercultural imagery and language has been commodified into "lifestyle" choices that can be purchased by what Ben Wattenberg describes in *The Real America* as a "Massive Majority Middle Class." For Wattenberg, as for Updike, the "tens of millions of middle classians are in fact middle class because they fit the criteria they themselves have established for such status" (Wattenberg 57). Circular reasoning aside, Wattenberg's formulation expresses a prevailing sense that class is determined by the goods one purchases and the lifestyle one chooses to pursue.

This is the milieu of *Rabbit Is Rich*, in which any revolutionary insights Harry might have taken from Skeeter, Jill, and television coverage of antiwar protests and urban uprisings have given way under a consumerist ethos that substitutes "style" for politics. The only lasting impression of his experience in and with the sixties seems to be that the decade legitimized longer hair styles for men. Commodified and domesticated, the signifiers of "liberation" and "revolution" become just another set of "cultural resources available for consumption," and the new middle classes an avid market for that consumption

(Clarke 106–107). Harry's illicit fascination with blackness endangered his normativity in the late sixties of *Rabbit Redux;* in the late seventies, Middle Americans can purchase the spiciness of black cultural forms, even while continuing to project the same old racist sexual fantasies onto African American figures. In *Rabbit Is Rich,* white masculinity gets a needed injection of "blackness" from several quarters, including South African gold coins, and a trip to a Caribbean island. But while consumer culture makes possible the co-optation of American rhetorics of liberation and cultural difference, a darker and less known challenge hovers on the international horizon in *Rabbit Is Rich.* White masculinity, having recuperated a good deal of its power on the domestic scene, finds itself challenged on the international stage, not only by individual "enemies" but also by the ways in which increasing globalization has decentered America. As we will see, the threat to the American body politic gets figured in *Rabbit Is Rich* by a fearful fascination with violation of bodily boundaries, most fully registered through Harry's near obsession with anal penetration.

The first words of *Rabbit Is Rich,* "running out of gas," signal that this novel will deal with an age of diminished resources and of diminished expectations, but Harry is swimming against this particular tide. He is doing just fine, selling gas-saving Toyotas at the car dealership he runs, thanks to his father-in-law's providential death *and* thanks to the energy crisis. Rabbit is rich by the standards of Middle America, and the novel is, in part, a meditation on the pleasures and dangers of materialism. Harry "likes having money to float in, a big bland good guy is how he sees himself" (4), blandness once again having become a badge, a sign of normality. As the embodiment of normative Americanness, Harry measures his personal situation against the national one, and finds that, sexually, blandness can produce an energy crisis of his very own: "Somewhere early in the Carter administration his interest, that had been pretty faithful, began to wobble and by now there is a real crisis of confidence" (45). Harry is quoting his president, who warned the nation in July 1979 that America was suffering a "crisis of confidence" stemming from the decline, in the sixties and seventies, of traditional American values: "hard work, strong families, close-knit communities and our faith in God."[21] No prude, Harry blames his crisis on having too much money, being too satisfied for sexual desire to flourish, but there is more than a little hint that the waning of his desire for Janice owes to her increased independence. Janice, a beneficiary of the women's and sexual revolutions (villains of Carter's America), requires more out of Harry, leading him to experience performance anxiety (84). The diminishment of Harry's sexual energy, in fact, seems more linked to the increase in Janice's than to his new wealth. Lacking desire and initiative, he can only get it up when Janice is unconscious, silent and undemanding: While she is asleep and snoring, "he decides to fuck her. . . . The climax freezes his scalp and stops his heart, all stealthy; he hasn't come with such a thump in months. So who says he's running out of gas?" (50). Harry's claim that being rich has sapped him of sexual desire is especially ludicrous in light of the scene in which he and Janice make love covered by the gold Krugerrand he has just purchased. This scene, in which Harry lies on the bed "tumescent amid scattered gold" (201) with "his prick up like a jutting piece of pink wreckage" (202) establishes clearly enough that money and wealth turn him on—just as the language here suggests that Harry's sexuality is, indeed, in desperate need of some kind of healing, the kind that can only be found among this currency marked by blackness.

The image of a prick as a "jutting piece of wreckage" installs an unmistakable gap between the penis and the phallus and, thus, undermines the "naturalness" of male dominance. As a number of feminist theorists and analysts of masculinity have pointed out, the assumption that the penis is (or even represents) the phallus is shattered by the recognition of the penis as a corporeal, and thus vulnerable, organ.[22] What this means is that consciousness of corporeality threatens phallic power. As Susan Bordo puts it, "actual men are not timeless symbolic constructs, they are biologically, historically, and experientially embodied beings; the singular, constant, transcendent rule of the phallus is continually challenged by this embodiment" ("Reading the Male Body," 696). Male power is dependent on stalling the recognition of male embodiment, and particularly, white male embodiment, for, as Bordo also points out, nonwhite men have been forced to carry the symbolic burden of *over*embodiment. Updike's novels do nothing to challenge this representation of corporeal black masculinity, where the image of the virile black man is everywhere evident; but they do exhibit a good deal of interest in the corporeality of white men, and in how an awareness of corporeality can endanger phallic power even as it engenders new avenues of experience. Whereas in *Rabbit Redux,* proximity to black masculinity made Rabbit aware of his own relative sexual impotence—not to mention his own illicit desires for Skeeter—in *Rabbit Is Rich* it is the proximity of a sexually liberated femininity that threatens his sexual potency. But it also produces in Rabbit a desire to experience a "feminizing" sexual experience. In both cases, a politicized discourse—black power and women's liberation—has made Rabbit aware of the potential pleasures to be found in occupying a minoritized, less than fully entitled, positionality.

If the rise of the silent majority after 1968 is, in part, evidence of what some commentators call "blacklash" against civil rights gains, the visibility of racial minorities, and the turned-up volume of racial discourse in the United States, the rise of a vocal conservative minority in the 1970s evidences a backlash against a feminism that threatens a specifically white, middle-class masculinity. But "backlash" doesn't tell the whole story, for while a growing group consciousness of middle-class white men is produced, in part, by the sexual liberation movements that Steinmann and Fox see marking white men as the "ene-my," it is also the case that the representation of white men wounded by that marking opens up new possibilities for dominant masculinity. The women's movement has forced Rabbit to think of men *as men*, that is, as a group which denies the rights of another group, women. But Harry manages to evade that marking, in part by himself taking up a position of vulnerability, as we will see, and in part by projecting male guilt onto Nelson, the son who activates a kind of reverse Oedipal complex in Rabbit. Making Nelson over into a representa-tive of a dominant and violent masculinity, the formerly feminized son (he used to be called "Nellie") becomes for Harry almost a caricature of the domi-nating man vilified by feminist rhetoric—for it is Nelson's existence in a male body that makes him guilty, "one more pushy man in the world, hairy wrists, big prick" (209). This appropriation of feminist language is an example of what Dilvo Ristoff suggests is a general "absorption" of the counterculture by the conservative forces Rabbit represents in the seventies: "Rabbit, like middle America, absorbs the forces of change but discards them just as easily once they have outlasted their exchange value or threaten the very existence of the sys-tem" (138). While I think Ristoff's cynicism is warranted, it is also important to recognize that, just as Rabbit wanted to identify with Skeeter's ascendant pow-er in the earlier novel—a power made all the more attractive for its survival in the face of social injuries—here he wants to identify with women, the most vis-ible of newly empowered "underdogs" in this women's liberation era.

The irony of Rabbit offering a critique of phallic power would not be lost on many readers, especially in a novel that talks so incessantly about "pricks." In fact, *Rabbit Is Rich* seems downright obsessed with penises, asses, and anal eroticism and, more specifically, with the threatening and titillating idea that male bodies can be penetrated. Along with Janice's money, the other thing that excites Harry are images of male bodies both penetrating and penetrated. Lamenting that "he's running out of pictures" to turn him on, he fantasizes a woman penetrated by men "at both ends," and puts himself in *her* position: "the woman's sensations seem nearer to him than the man's, the prick in his mouth like a small wet zucchini, plus the other elsewhere, in and out, in and out, a kind of penance at your root" (130). Rabbit's fantasies about homosexual penetration is one way to literalize, materialize what Updike takes to be the wounds suffered by dominant masculinity. A penetrable body is a vulnerable body, and Rabbit expresses a desire to experience a kind of erotic disempower-ment through the breakdown in his bodily boundaries. Becoming more and more "sodden" (208), he no longer experiences his body as a solid shell, but more as a fluid and, increasingly, penetrable entity. It should come as no sur-prise, then, that Harry is "fascinated by fags" (178).

Updike suggests that anal eroticism (or, as he puts it, "buggery") is simply one stop on Harry's "somatic pilgrimage," "his lifelong journey into the bodies of women" (*Odd Jobs* 870), but it seems to me that the novels' escalating interest in anal eroticism and homosexuality signals a perhaps unconscious desire on Updike's part to figure the disempowerment of white masculinity through a sexual metaphor. For it is the bodies of *men* which inflame Rabbit's interest throughout the series—from Skeeter's "electric" body to the bodies of the male porn stars Rabbit fantasizes about in *Rabbit at Rest* (372).[23] It could be, as Judie Newman argues in a stunning reading of *Rabbit Is Rich,* that anal fantasies are simply part of the novel's overall concern with "dirty" materialism (61–67); but, coupled with the interest in representing the penis, it seems safe to say that one of the main concerns of the novel is the question of penetration, who's doing and who's being done to. Recall Skeeter's discourse on Vietnam, in which American "money and jizz" invade "cunts" like Vietnam (*Redux* 232). In Rabbit's terms, American foreign policy is all about "fucking and being fucked" (270), and in Updike's 1960s, there's no question of who's doing what to whom. In the seventies, however, American imperial might is diminished, its energy in crisis, and America itself is "held hostage" to foreign powers. America is getting fucked in the seventies, and this state of affairs is articulated in the novel through Rabbit's obsession with anal penetration—for there is no doubt that "America" as Updike envisions it is a masculine construct.

That construct is endangered in the seventies by a series of crises in American involvement abroad, as well as through representations of Jimmy Carter as a "feminine" president. As Susan Jeffords argues, America under Carter suffers a crisis of manhood, according to popular representations and, in no small part, thanks to Richard Nixon, whose 1980 book, *The Real War,* attacks Carter directly for his "failure of will" (Jeffords, *Hard Bodies,* 7–8). Updike's Nelson articulates the American lack of (phallic) resolve in relation to Afghanistan, another Third World country challenging America's might: "'At least the Russians, Dad, *do* it when they're going to do it. We *try* to do it and then everything gets all bogged down in politics. We can't do *any*thing anymore'" (354). "Doing it," of course, is sexual as well as military, and Nelson's description represents the United States as impotent if not penetrated. Carter, then as now perceived as politically "incompetent," "communicated images of hesitancy, obfuscation, ultimately of impotence" (Carroll 212). Metaphors of "softness" and "limpness" mark criticisms of Carter, whose inability to resolve the hostage crisis was seen as a sign of his diminished masculinity. Once again, white American manhood finds itself at the mercy of the Third World, as it was in Vietnam. Even as early as 1969, this was articulated by one of Richard Lemon's "troubled Americans": "Americans have been so conditioned to believe we're all powerful. Suddenly they have to confront a situation in which a bunch of half-naked brown guys, little bitty ones running around in sneakers, are beating the shit out of those good American boys with crew cuts and heavy, hobnailed boots and the latest technology" (Lemon 113).

Rabbit Is Rich attempts to mitigate this emasculation by also envisioning the Third World as a place where white American masculinity can get regenerated, as seen in the "spouse-swapping" incident in the Caribbean. Classic seventies fare, this episode recharges Rabbit's battery—or fills his gas tank—by reassuring him that his penis still works, and even with a wide-awake woman. The trip to the unidentified island is Harry and Janice's real entrance into middle-class culture and, at the same time, potentially offers the very antithesis of that culture. Winter vacations in the tropics signal, for white middle-class America, the ultimate in "escape" from the very life they prize so highly. That the island is inhabited by others, and that it might have a history, is irrelevant except to the extent that its being a former English colony explains why the "natives" drive on "the wrong side of the road" (372). The fact that Updike does not name the vacationers' island getaway is, in itself, significant. The island is important only as it supplies a reinvigoration of the tourists and, particularly, a little dose of exoticism to spice up a white masculinity "running out of gas." Not only does Rabbit get reinvigorated sexually, he also gets to fulfill his fantasy of anal penetration, as white America has fun in the "uninhibited" Third World: "since fucking Thelma up the ass he's felt freer, more in love with the world again" (403), he says later. Civilization has been left behind (golf notwithstanding), and the Americans have license to break their own laws. Meanwhile, "those to whom this island is no vacation" (375)—Harry *does* at least notice them—bring drinks to the tourists, clean their hotel rooms, and provide a soupçon of danger to enhance the experience: "Everything down here is guarded, theft is rampant, thieves and even murderers pour outward from the island's dark heart to feed on its rim of rich visitors" (374).[24]

Harry, as the embodiment of America, has temporarily overcome an impending loss of manhood by reerecting his bodily boundaries. Still penetrating, but not penetrated, Harry and his country can bask for another moment in the knowledge of safety and sovereignty. It is important to note that in the discourse around the feminization of America, American manhood is made weak primarily by experience in and with the Third World. The wounds of Vietnam are exacerbated by the situation in Teheran, where not just Americans but the nation finds itself at the mercy of another Third World country. ABC television's *Nightline* was inaugurated in the crisis, naming that crisis and bringing it into America's living rooms nightly. "America Held Hostage" proclaimed a national crisis, a few short years after the devastating end of the Vietnam War. It would be years before America would fully recover by "penetrat[ing] the Iraqi airspace, while their airplanes ejaculated their missiles over the unresisting land. By proving its mastery of air, sea, and land in Iraq,

America imagines itself cured of its trauma of (destructive) impotence whose origin lay in another Third World country—Vietnam" (Shohat 148).

But it is Nelson who articulates a national, masculinist dream of healing the wounds inflicted upon American manhood by experience in the Third World. Mass-mediated fantasies of violent masculine regeneration afflict Nelson, whose attendance at the now quiet and blessedly apolitical Kent State signals both his envy of Vietnam-era activism and his relief at having missed it. Like his father's friend Buddy Inglefinger who remarks, "Jesus, those Arabs . . . Wouldn't it be bliss just to nuke 'em all?" (159), Nelson's belief in American supremacy is a belief in white supremacy and patriarchy.

> He thinks of those hostages in Teheran and it's like a pill caught in his throat. . . . Take a single big black helicopter in there on a moonless night, commandos with blackened faces, a little piano wire around the throats of those freaky radical Arabs, *uuglh, arg,* you'd have to whisper, women and children first, and lift them all away. Drop a little tactical A-bomb on a minaret as a calling card. Or else a tunnel or some sort of boring machine like James Bond would have.   (*Rich,* 298)

That Updike puts these thoughts in Nelson's head rather than Rabbit's means, first, that Rabbit comes off as more tolerant than the much ballyhooed pacifist and socially humane younger generation; and, second, that the United States can look forward to more traditional macho militarism (rather than *less*) in the post-Vietnam generation.

CODA: THE DEATH OF WHITE MASCULINITY?

By the end of *Rabbit Is Rich,* representations of race have become more complicated in a country that is increasingly dependent on an international economy. Arab peoples and the Japanese are new enemies to American interests— there conceived of as the interests of middle-class white men; but, at the same time, these complications make it possible for those very white men to profit. The novel ends, appropriately enough, with the Superbowl. As Harry watches the game, Updike makes clear his character's faith in the recuperation of "America" and with it, his own privileged relation to it.

> At half-time, a lot of girls in colored dresses and guys that look like fags in striped jerseys dance. . . "Energy is people," they sing. "People are en-er-gy!" Who needs Khomeini and his oil? Who needs Afghanistan? Fuck the Russkis. Fuck the Japs, for that matter. We'll go it alone, from sea to shining sea. (436)

Harry, cheerleader for America, manages, at least for the moment, to rescue his country from its foreign enemies; and to recoup its culture from the "kids" who "try to jitterbug but don't have the swing" (435).

In *Rabbit at Rest*, the "kids" (that is, Nelson) threaten to destroy the Angstrom family, while the American national family is palpably threatened by Japan and the Arab nations. Toyota takes the franchise away from Springer Motors, *literally* "disenfranchising" our Middle American white man;[25] and Harry obsesses over the terrorist bombing of the jet over Lockerbie. In this, the last novel of the tetralogy, Rabbit is (not so slowly) killing himself through the consumption he worshipped in *Rabbit Is Rich*. America in the 1980s is sunk into practices of inappropriate consumption: drug use, overeating, and unsafe sex are just three of the "addictions" with which this novel of the Reagan-Bush era is obsessed. The "war on drugs" and AIDS figure as the battleground for a Middle America besieged by the consequences of its own consumption—as well as by the racial and sexual "others" who have invaded the urban and even suburban territory. At the end of the Cold War, the enemies of America are once again located within the borders of the United States, although one of the main anxieties is that those borders are permeable. As Jan Clausen points out, "People of color (along with gay men and Jews) are everywhere in [*Rabbit at*] *Rest* waiting to take over" (47). But Rabbit, as before, has an ambivalent attitude toward the "others" inhabiting the periphery of his life. White masculinity, tired as it is in this novel, still seeks that injection of blackness to pump itself up, and Rabbit journeys to the "dark" sections of town where he can manage to "steal a little life for himself" (154) and his dying body. This novel takes straight white masculinity about as close to death as possible without killing it outright. As the final chapter in Updike's chronicle of white Middle American masculinity, this novel leaves little hope for the recuperation of that most normative of American identities.

Rabbit at Rest makes literal what the previous two novels in the series left figurative: the decline of American culture is embodied in an ailing white male body. *Rabbit at Rest* registers the growing obsession with white male embodiment as the twentieth century progresses; the novel is, in fact, so obsessed with bodies and experiences of embodiment that it almost disproves my thesis that white men, "free" from gender and racial specificity, do not primarily experience themselves as corporeal or embodied beings. Almost, but not quite; for, in order to represent Rabbit's descent into a claustrophobic embodiment, Updike must rely on metaphors of femininity. Rabbit's growing consciousness of his own embodiment, and the limitations that imposes, is represented as a feminization. Further, and continuing on with the series' representation of whiteness as blandness, Rabbit's body is whiter than ever, and here that whiteness is represented as sickly. Harry is a marked man in this novel, not only because of his impending death but also because he can no longer represent a generalized, normative "America." Updike is absolutely explicit about that here, having Harry, in one scene, parade down the streets of town as Uncle Sam. If Rabbit embodies America, then America is embodied in a pale and lifeless form. Harry's middle-aged body carries the evidence of decay and decline; the once healthy athlete's body has gradually deteriorated, and Harry imagines his body as "enormous . . . menacingly white and pink and sodden with sodium-retained water" (57). He "remorsefully feels the bulk, two hundred thirty pounds the kindest scales say, that has enwrapped him at the age of fifty-five like a set of blankets the decades have brought one by one" (4). Later, when he has a heart attack on a sailboat, his body becomes entirely alien (111). The American body politic is, likewise, in decline, evidence of decay found in the wild and irresistible proliferation of consumer culture that produces addictions of all kinds.

Consumer culture is out of control in *Rabbit at Rest,* producing a nation of bloated bodies and weak hearts.[26] Updike uses Harry's compulsive eating as a metaphor that, paradoxically, works to materialize the consumerism of consumer culture. Like Harry's lover Thelma's lupus, the disease of consumerism eating up American culture and American power is a kind of autoimmune disease "in which the body attacks itself, antibodies attack your own tissue, self-hatred of a sort" (272). This representation of lupus, however, merely prepares the way for an exploration of AIDS and drug addiction, two diseases of contemporary American culture that, according to Updike, are destroying the body politic—and, somewhat surprisingly, white masculinity.[27] Harry's awareness of his own fragile embodiment produces an unrecuperable wound to his sense that he represents a disembodied norm of "divine" individualism.

Rabbit at Rest thus connects the death of Harry Angstrom to the death of a particular conceptualization of the social body that depends on an equivalency between white masculinity and an unmarked individualism. As we saw, throughout *Rabbit Redux* and *Rabbit Is Rich,* Harry Angstrom both wallows in the wounds to his white and male privilege, and luxuriates in recuperations of that privilege. In *Rabbit at Rest,* no such recuperations are possible. While undoubtedly sprinkled with some of the baldest unreconstructed racism and sexism to shadow the pages of contemporary American literature, Rabbit's self-representation is marked by what I take to be a genuine interest in offering up his entitlements, in experimenting with what it might mean to live life as "other." Rabbit's envy of the racial and sexual others who have changed the shape of his world suggests that, for Updike, the invisibility of white masculinity is, at best, a mixed blessing—in the same spirit as laments over the "silent majority," but in another spirit as well. For, while Updike's protagonist might qualify as one of Richard Lemon's "troubled Americans," his fascination with and undeniable attraction to his own symbolic disempowerment complicates that connection. What troubles Rabbit is consciousness of a bland white body, regret at missing out on the action of the sixties, and an ambivalent fascination with the breakdown of bodily and social boundaries. The crisis of white masculinity in the background of the Rabbit novels is not a singular episode or condition that can get resolved; rather, the novels show that white masculinity in the 1960s and 1970s is rocked by a series of crises, and that pleasure, as well as pain, is to be found in the exploration of crisis.

The prevailing image of the Middle American is of a wounded white man who aggressively speaks up for his "natural" rights and entitlements, even as he trumpets his own "silence" and invisibility. In the discourse around the "discovery" of Middle America, and in the political and economic retrenchments of the decade that follows, we can see how anxieties about the endangered dominance of white men produced a collectivity that was disavowed, hidden under the language of liberal individualism and the catchall term "Middle America." In the late sixties, this amorphous group signifies nothing so much as whiteness, and its aggressive posture and sense of "natural" entitlement identify Middle Americans as the figures for a national masculinity trying to recuperate its power in the wake of a "permissive" and "open" decade. By the seventies, such openness has become a boon of the middle class and of consumer culture, and Middle Americans just another market for the signifiers of class uplift.

What Updike's novels teach us, and this is a lesson confirmed by late sixties and seventies treatments of wounded and disenfranchised white middle-class men, is that while a fantasized disempowerment can lead to recuperation, it can also lead to subtle but still meaningful changes in the social relations of American culture. While laments about the silent majority certainly helped fuel the rise of the New Right, the discourse on the emergence of the Middle American also helped to make whiteness and masculinity visible in such a way as to threaten their normativity. In this sense, the laments of a "silent majority" or the militancy of "angry white men" can work in the interests of interrupting the stubborn equation of white masculinity with Americanness itself. In the next chapter, we will turn to an episode in the cultural history of the United States in which the laments over the decentering of the "silent majority" appear to have materialized into the worst nightmare imagined by those who claimed that the white man has been silenced, deprived of a voice. But in the discourses of culture war in the late 1980s, to which I now turn, the wounded white man has come up in the world: no longer the working-class stiff whose woes were hymned by the liberal elite knowledge industries, the beleaguered white man is now garbed in tweeds and leather, and the liberal elite has taken over the universities. Here, too, we will see the double meanings of the crisis in white masculinity. While the wounds to white and male privilege might enable the repetition of narratives of recuperation and healing, the representational system which produces a normative masculinity as the model of the human subject works most often "by being *disabled,*" as Steven Cohan and Ina Rae Hark point out. "What," they ask, "are we to make of a masculinity that can preserve its hegemony only by confessing its anxieties at every turn?" (2). The desire to confess anxiety is fraught with the ambivalence which necessarily attends any move that requires even a temporary or provisional (or even rhetorical) surrender of power. Will the payoff be worth the risk, or will some unexpected social or discursive maneuver render white male dominance as truly obsolete as some would claim it already is? Can the representational system misfire?

CHAPTER 2
PALE MALES, DEAD POETS, AND THE CRISIS
IN WHITE MASCULINITY

Scenes from the Culture Wars

It is in Michael Crichton's 1993 bestseller *Disclosure* that the figure of the white male victim fully emerges from the political into the personal, and becomes visible as a marked man whose endangerment signals the triumph of a liberationist zeitgeist that tramples all innocents in its path. This novel, a Byzantine tale of white male victimization in the workplace and in the streets, offers evidence of the crisis in dominant masculinity and contributes to the perpetuation of that crisis. Sexually harassed by his predatory female boss, Crichton's hero Tom Sanders barely has time to register the effects of this assault on his masculinity when that boss, Meredith Johnson, turns around and accuses *him* of sexual harassment. Passing on the opportunity to truly explore what Crichton claims to "know" about sexual harassment—that it's not about gender, it's about power[1]—the novel instead opts for a far more paranoid narrative, making its hero a poster-boy for marked men everywhere. Not only is he victimized by Meredith's humiliating and disconcertingly arousing advances, Tom is further victimized by *her* false claims of victimization.[2] Cashing in on a "contemporary climate where men were assumed to be guilty of anything they were accused of" (269), a climate where men are marked as the always already guilty bearers of a malignant power and unearned privilege, Meredith is aided by an identity politics and a feminism that equates masculinity with violence and femininity with victimized innocence. But Crichton, delighting in one of the "role-reversals" that he claims help us excavate the truth of fraught politico-sexual conflicts from beneath "traditional responses and conventional rhetoric" ("Afterword"), reveals that strong and ambitious women are the truly violent ones; as *Disclosure*'s most vocal feminist puts it with vengeful zeal, "[Sanders is] resentful, and he's violent. He's a typical man. And let me tell you, before I'm through with him, he'll wish he had never been born" (353). The harassment narrative is reinforced in countless ways, as various characters be-

moan the silly rules that require companies to remove pinups from men's lock-
er rooms, to hire unskilled and inadequate female and minority workers, and
to promote vicious women instead of sincere men. That climate is further
characterized by references to the havoc wrought on innocent fathers and other men who fall victim to the manipulations of mothers and psychiatrists indiscriminately and deliberately utilizing "recovered memory" to mark men—
always unfairly—as sexual predators of children. Exhibiting an extraordinary
indifference to the suffering of victims in his zeal to detail the effects of false
accusations, Crichton nevertheless uses a language of victimization, bodily
violation, and "rape" to characterize the suffering of the men who run afoul
of what can only be called a crazy conspiracy against the powerful and their
entitlements.

These simmering resentments come to a boil in a discursive aside, in which
Tom ponders the wounds of white and male privilege. Using a bodily metaphor
to explore a more properly social wound, Crichton signals his participation in
the reconstruction of white masculinity that is the subject of this book. As Tom
watches his colleague Mary Anne on their morning commute, he speculates on
what it's like to be a woman and, thus, subject to the bodily and psychic violation of rape. But this meditation soon mutates into a fantasy of white male disempowerment that depends on the substitution of vulnerable male subjectivities for vulnerable female bodies:

> He watched her walk away, a slender, compact figure in exercise clothes, car-
> rying a leather briefcase. She was barely five feet tall. The men on the ferry
> were so much larger. He remembered that she had once told [his wife] Susan
> that she took up running because of her fear of rape. "I'll just outrun them,"
> she had said. Men didn't know anything about that. They didn't understand
> that fear.
>
> But there was another kind of fear that only men felt. He looked at the
> newspaper column with deep and growing unease. Key words and phrases
> jumped out at him:
>
> *Vindictive . . . bitter . . . can't tolerate a woman . . . blatant hostility . . .*
> *rape . . . crimes of males*   (266, emphasis and ellipses in the original)

Those words and phrases, articulated by none other than the rabid feminist
journalist quoted above, jump out, attack, and *mark* Tom. While Crichton's use
of a rape metaphor to describe victims of verbal assault might be understand-
able within a cultural context where speech is increasingly subject to legal controls via harassment laws, campus speech codes, and the like, *Disclosure* is not a
novel that approves of such laws and codes. On the contrary, the novel explicitly argues against *any* regulation of speech, and by implication, sexuality. Speech

and sexuality have, indeed, become intricately entangled in recent years, as harassment claims and speech codes have caused us to rethink the distinctions between thought, speech, and action. But it is primarily *male* sexuality and *male* speech which have come under censure and control, and Crichton's novel is most invested in detailing how laws that function to block male expression of any kind lead us down a slippery slope into an Orwellian nightmare. The use of a rape metaphor to describe "dangerous" language betrays Crichton's desire to flesh out "the fear that only men felt," to impress upon his readers the visceral, corporeal force of these fighting words, their power to wound: raped bodies recede behind the horror of a raping language. But it also works to undermine his more central claim, that the regulation of speech and of male sexuality is as dangerous to civil and sexual freedoms as fighting words and sexual assaults are to individuals. Because the novel cannot recognize this contradiction, it is somewhat incoherent, except insofar as Crichton remains convinced that speech codes, harassment law, affirmative action, and other sins of the "liberal" state target, mark, and wound white men. In a novel so devoted to celebrating the victimization of "pale males" (81), Crichton's troping of masculine hurts through the metaphor of rape is part of his effort to explore the pains—and the pleasures—of wounded white male bodies and subjectivities. While the novel unsurprisingly punishes Meredith and exonerates Tom, the time that Crichton spends dwelling on the injuries suffered by seemingly powerful white men evinces the novel's true focus on the victimization of "pale males" as a newly disenfranchised social group marked for extinction. Unwittingly, then, the novel falls prey to the very logic it attacks.

I begin with this hot-button novel because the contradictions and illogics of Crichton's attack on affirmative action, political correctness, and the regulation of speech and sexuality is symptomatic of the crisis in white masculinity fueling what Carol Stabile calls the "PC monologues," and others have referred to as the "culture wars" of late 1980s.[3] These culture wars erupted with the publication of a number of now infamous books that announced loudly and confidently that post-liberationist American culture was in a state of crisis and, in doing so, worked to reshape the cultural terrain they were purportedly just describing. Beginning with the publication of William Bennett's 1984 national report on the state of higher education, these announcements of crisis take off from the apparently irresistible claim that something has been *lost* in American culture, something has been displaced, decentered, and generally pushed to the margins by a host of competing forces and trends in social, cultural, and political life. By now, of course, this is *the* dominant narrative in American political life and one that is often used to delegitimize attempts to revivify liberationist rhetoric or action. The title of Bennett's report, *To Reclaim a Legacy,* invokes this narrative, as do the titles of countless other books, essays, and editorials that, together, make up the culture wars.

Like the laments over the forced invisibility of the "silent majority" (see chapter 1), the jeremiads announcing the decline of American culture per se mask a much more specific crisis: the forced *visibility* of the white and male norm, as white men experience the "marking" that endangers their position as unmarked, and universalizing, norm. An overwhelming sense of loss pervades these discourses of culture war, as the angry denunciations of the contemporary climate that Crichton excoriates mutate into something else: a portrait of the powerful turned powerless, of white masculinity subject to the definitions and machinations of others. Such a portrait, paradoxically, works to reconceptualize a newly centered white masculinity in a radically changed cultural, educational, and professional terrain. I have chosen to focus on the most widely read (and reviewed) and the most sensationalist of these books on the losses suffered in post-liberationist American culture: Allan Bloom's *The Closing of the American Mind* (1987) and Dinesh D'Souza's *Illiberal Education* (1991), respectively. While these texts are quite distinct in their aims, their audiences, and their discursive strategies, they both offer a good deal of evidence to support my claim that the current crisis, as it is played out in the halls of academe, is instigated by a marking of white masculinity as a specific and embodied (racial and gendered) identity—*and* that the mere enunciation of crisis does the cultural work of recentering white masculinity in a remapped academic context. *Illiberal Education* and *The Closing of the American Mind* perpetuate that sense of crisis, keeping its resolution in suspension. These announcements of crisis do not, thus, function to alleviate that crisis, and to recuperate and "unmark" white masculinity once more; on the contrary, in *enacting* and, in fact, *producing* that crisis, these texts work toward a recentering of white masculinity (and the various symbolic extensions of it) precisely as endangered, victimized, wounded.

Although I am most interested in the discourse of the culture wars as a *performance* of crisis, a dramatic rendering of the current crisis in white masculinity that simultaneously creates, manages, and perpetuates that crisis, the specific contours of the narratives these discourses construct and the rhetoric they utilize are also significant to the current crisis as I understand it. Perhaps more than any other instance under analysis in this book, the culture wars evidence the effects of shifting hierarchies in post-liberationist American culture. The term *post-liberationist,* as I have said, best reflects what I take to be the major social upheavals of the post-sixties era and their cultural and literary consequences: the gradual shift from a politicized notion of liberation to a personal one; the critique of normativity and the proliferation of marked identities produced by that critique; the rise of popular culture and the diffusion of cultural authority among multiple audiences and forms. Both *The Closing of the American Mind* and *Illiberal Education* emerge from this context, and they offer the usual suspects as the villains in a narrative about the decline of American culture. But they also fully enter into the terrain they claim to rise above, and thus carve out an identity politics of the dominant that functions covertly within narratives about the rise of "victimism" in American culture and about the coincident decline of standards of academic disinterestedness.[4] Both of these books attempt to reinstall white masculinity at the center of cultural study (and American identity) by erasing the marks scripted onto white and male bodies by several decades of politically motivated and egalitarian-minded theory and pedagogy.[5] But rather than reading this relatively obvious goal as evidence of a simple backlash against the remapping of the cultural, educational, and social fields by various "others"—what Bloom refers to as the "barbarians at the gate"—I want to insist that D'Souza, Bloom, and their brethren must instead be understood as participating equally in struggles over gender and racial identity and priority in American culture. By "participating equally," I do not mean to say that all players in the field of identity politics command the same amount of cultural, economic, or political capital; what I do mean to suggest is that white masculinity, too, is at stake in identity politics, and the usual understanding of white men as the *victims* of identity politics and political correctness works to reinforce the absurd notion that white men are not gendered and racialized actors struggling to retain and reshape their places in American culture. What is so interesting about the culture wars as they are played out in Bloom and D'Souza is that just when such actors seem most invested in freeing themselves from a politicized, marked identity, they end up indulging in the very logics that place them smack dab in the center of the skirmishes against which they explicitly position themselves.

My strategy in this chapter, then, is not to rebut the arguments Bloom and D'Souza offer, nor to defend the educational and activist projects they criticize. Instead, I want to trace the unexpected effects of the rhetorical moves these writers make in their efforts to rise above the contested field of identity politics and "victimism." Underneath the overt narratives of these critiques can be discerned more subterranean agendas having to do with all manner of anxieties about the fall of white masculinity from the heights of disembodied "universality" into the depths of embodied particularity. The critique of universalism has produced a cultural field in which whiteness and masculinity have joined nonwhiteness and femininity as social constructions; and in which white men enter into a complicated relationship with an identity politics heretofore practiced *against* them. The disparate responses to the crisis in the hegemony of a white male norm clearly suggest that those who speak for the dominant in American culture have a vast armory of discursive strategies at their disposal, including the very rhetoric of crisis. It is by analyzing how this rhetoric works, pointing out its investments and its contradictions, that we can fully understand how the conservative critique remaps identity politics, rather than retreating from them.

SPECTACLES OF (DIS)EMBODIMENT

Like Crichton's *Disclosure*, Dinesh D'Souza's *Illiberal Education* is a dramatization of what happens when putative "victims" rise up demanding restitution and find sanction for those demands within gullible and nervous institutions. Crichton and D'Souza both take on the mask of objective cultural observers, anthropologists seeking out the truth in a climate in which truth has become a dirty word. Likewise, both writers craft melodramatic narratives featuring villains and victims. When I say that *Illiberal Education* is melodramatic, I do not mean that as an indictment; in fact, it is precisely the novelistic, melodramatic form of D'Souza's narrative that interests me here, for it is so clearly an *interested* narrative invested in convincing his readers that we are living in a moment of crisis.[6] The cultural work performed by *Illiberal Education* is to reconstruct a common American narrative about victimization and the underdog so that the unmarked, seemingly disembodied liberal individual becomes the disenfranchised victim, pursued by those (feminists and multiculturalists) whose fantasized power makes ridiculous their own claims to victimization. At times a paranoid fantasy of white male disenfranchisement, *Illiberal Education* does manage to stumble onto what I take to be some pretty convincing truths about how higher education conducts itself in the midst of an ambivalent struggle over democratization.[7] Such truths are incidental, I think, to the larger purpose of the book, which is to stage a crisis in higher education as a crisis afflicting the beleaguered spokesmen for what D'Souza takes to be a genuinely "liberal" university and the "special interests" that threaten that liberalism. This narrative, of course, will be familiar to anyone who has followed the rhetorical strategies of the neoconservative movement in the United States. But what is intriguing about D'Souza's book is that, in the middle of this relatively standard critique, his desire to construct a scandalous narrative meant to provoke reader indignation pushes him to indulge in the very logics and rhetorical ploys that neoconservatives are generally wont to criticize as the mark of the "special interest."

In *Illiberal Education*, Dinesh D'Souza explores the pains and pleasures of white male embodiment, as he presents white male "victims" suffering so enjoyably their visibility as gendered and racial beings. These newly anointed victims replace those named in one of D'Souza's chapter titles, "The Victim's Rev-

olution on Campus." Feminists and "minority activists," trendy Duke humanists, and those who insist on locating truth in standpoints determined by race
and gender turn academia away from the search for truth and toward the celebration of victims. In contrast to an ideal of disinterested and disembodied
thought, D'Souza gives us Women's Studies and African American Studies programs that encourage "org[ies] of consciousness-raising" (135). Like other conservative attacks on the academy, D'Souza's relies on a construction of gender
and race as matters of the body and, like migraines or the appetite for unhealthy foods, something to be overcome, transcended. This move implies that
certain sectors of the university are free from bodily matters, although this
freedom is continuously under attack. The evacuation of race and gender from
"the Tradition" carries with it a longed-for disembodiment, a freeing of the
universal from the "contingencies" of gender and race, as Roger Kimball puts it
(xv). The body, in this view, impedes but does not ground intellectual activity;
and gender and race, likewise, just get in the way.

Throughout the book, D'Souza seeks to rescue the speech of the great white
male minds he imagines have been silenced in the contemporary academy; endangered by the crusade against "Dead White Males," these figures compel our
sympathy because they suffer a violence that can only be called gendered and
racially motivated. In a reversal of the arguments he attributes to his "minority
activists," D'Souza represents dead white male authors as subject to the will of
a tyrannous minority, a minority that university administrations legitimize for
fear of being called racist or sexist. Like the "fear that only men knew" (Crichton), anxiety over accusations of racism or sexism cow the powers-that-be on
campuses nationwide, as putatively powerful white men find themselves held
hostage to the hysterical demands of a small but vocal minority. As in *Disclosure*, little credit is given to the idea that such accusations might be true;
D'Souza always places phrases like "institutional racism" in scare quotes, dele-
gitimizing the idea as it reaches the reader's eyes. While there is some potentially interesting material here—one might, for example, question how being
cowed by "minority activists" might affect those who allocate rewards and punishments in the university—D'Souza leaves such questions behind in his desire
to construct a Manichaean and melodramatic narrative in which there are clear
villains and clear victims. The master narrative unifying D'Souza's "eyewitness"
accounts of specific outrages on college campuses goes like this: a true liberal
education, in which students learned to appreciate the great minds of Western
culture and the universal truths they discovered, has been displaced through a
"victim's revolution" fueled by the liberation movements of the sixties and seventies, and transformed by new forms of politicized scholarship. Because the
focus is on victims, racial and gender sensitivity, and diversity as a priori values, D'Souza argues, standards of intellectual rigor and objectivity have disap-

peared. If this language sounds gendered, it is, as the university D'Souza gives us is a weakened, feminized institution dominated by the "others" who focus on "soft," rather than "hard," intellectual endeavor. Indeed, as the story of a Princeton Dante scholar who unsuccessfully but heroically fought against the formation of a Women's Studies program in the early 1980s makes explicit, the feminization of the academy is nearly complete. When the measure passed, this scholar testifies, the scene "confirmed what [he] had feared about the program": "'Women were embracing and kissing on the floor. This struck me as odd. Was this an academic discussion or a political rally? Were we discussing ideas or feelings?'" (6). The palpable distaste, if not nausea, expressed by this scholar is produced by this display of bodily enthusiasm in an environment in which the body must be transcended. D'Souza uses this episode to prove a larger point: Women's Studies and Ethnic Studies programs are conceptualized as bodily enclaves, where all attention is devoted to analyzing, celebrating, and in general getting all worked up about corporeal attributes. In contrast, traditional liberal arts programs emerge as the space of nobly disembodied and disinterested thought—exemplified in Stanford's now defunct Western Civilization course, fallen victim to the "victim's revolution" on campus.[8]

Like the Dante scholar disgusted by displays of bodily and emotional expression, D'Souza implies that Dante himself (along with Shakespeare and other great white male minds) is turning over in his grave. The rhetoric of crisis that characterizes D'Souza's accounts of curricular and cultural change in the academy suggests that "dead white males," in the shorthand of the moment, are in danger of suffering another, more permanent, death by being displaced from their positions at the center of the canon. Victimized and moving toward obscurity, these great minds are in need of rescue, and D'Souza finds the perfect candidates in a small band of intrepid defenders of the liberal tradition who, themselves, must be saved from the fighting words and wounding accusations of "gender and race warriors." He presents the National Association of Scholars, for example, "as a small group of faculty crusaders," "outside the mainstream of the academy," that is bravely "launching a bold but somewhat quixotic effort to arrest the pace of the revolution" (18). In positioning a small group of elite white men as hero-victims, *Illiberal Education* draws on the very rhetoric of victimization D'Souza claims has destroyed academic standards and academic freedom, individualizing it, and thus stripping collective claims of victimization of their legitimacy: we must worry about the fate of Homer, the singular, individual artistic genius and his defenders, but claims of collective hurts based on institutionalized racism or sexism deserve only skepticism. Behind the rhetoric of victimization, however, we can discern a desire to get in on the (bodily) action, to put white male bodies on the line. Because a "norm" or a universal cannot pose as a compelling victim, cannot offer the sensational spectacle of a suffering body, bodies are needed to flesh out the narrative of innocents under attack.

In the best example of this strategy, D'Souza gives us the spectacle of a white male victim suffering at the hands of an all-powerful "elite" of race and gender warriors who practice the "tyranny of the minority." The case concerns Harvard history professor Stephan Thernstrom, who was charged with "racial insensitivity" by three black students, a complaint then arbitrated by Harvard's Committee on Race Relations. D'Souza quotes Thernstrom's wounded and surprised response to what comes off as a racially motivated witch hunt that ends with a "rape":

> I felt like a rape victim, and yet the silence of the administration seemed to give the benefit of the doubt to the students who attacked me. Maybe I was naive, but I expected the university to come to my defense. I mean, that's what academic freedom is about, isn't it? Instead I was left out there by myself, guilty without being proven guilty. I could not even defend myself, because the charge of racism or racial insensitivity is ultimately unanswerable.
> (quoted in D'Souza, without cited source, 196)

This strategic use of rape as metaphor for a primarily discursive conflict brings a wounded body into public view. Thernstrom's opening gambit—"I felt like a rape victim, and *yet* the silence of the administration seemed to give the benefit of the doubt to [my attackers]"—suggests his belief, now troubled, that social and legal institutions always come to aid victims of physical assault. Either naive or disingenuous, this belief gives way, *not* from evidence of the rape of female bodies, but of male minds and academic freedom.[9] Thernstrom not only compares physical assault to verbal assault; the wounded objects of racist remarks disappear behind the shocked face of the wounded subject of that utterance. Thernstrom's invocation of rape points to a canny participation in the politics of identity as understood by D'Souza and other conservative critics. Lamenting the fact that others reduce his psyche and his speech to a bodily gender and racial essence, Thernstrom nonetheless *uses* this conflation of body and speech to pose as a victim of a gender and racial system which discriminates against white men. D'Souza makes Thernstrom speak for an identity politics that locates racial difference in the body and claims restitution for personal injuries done to that body, even while denying the significance of gender and race.[10]

In a narrative woven throughout *Illiberal Education*, white men, speaking for disinterested thought, are incalculably damaged by an identity politics which demonizes them by *essentializing* them. While the logic here might sound vaguely familiar to those who have, historically, been marked as the visibly different other to the white male self, D'Souza does not stop to pursue this irony. He is too invested in showing white men to be the innocent victims of a malicious marking, even as he attempts to resuscitate the illusion that the norm is valuable precisely because unmarked. He notes that minority students "aspire to victim status," and describes perfectly the posturing of Thernstrom: "They do not yearn to be oppressed, of course; rather, they seek the moral capital of victimhood . . . they tend to see their lives collectively as a historical melodrama involving the forces of good and evil, in which they are cast as secular saints and martyrs. These roles allow them to recover the sense of meaning, and of place, which otherwise seems elusive" (242). For Thernstrom and other white male victims, this melodrama of good and evil is played out against the background of a loss of a "sense of meaning, and of place"—a loss, that is, of the power to signify the universal, the general, the normative, and the true. Claiming that the minority victim "becomes a victimizer while continuing to enjoy superior moral credentials" (243), D'Souza, hungry to validate the moral superiority of the "minoritized" white man, ignores the ironies of his own utterance.[11] But something more serious is going on underneath all this posturing, and that something else has to do with D'Souza's implicit argument for de-racing and de-gendering academic work, an argument that is based on the premise that gender and race are mere bodily attributes which just get in the way of intellectual endeavor and academic freedom. White men only experience embodiment when forced into it—as when Thernstrom feels "raped" or when University of Virginia law professor Thomas Bergin appears "visibly shaken" by an anonymous note accusing him of racism, and articulates his pain through a bodily metaphor: "I have never been so lacerated" (6).

D'Souza's melodramatic presentation of Bergin's story is typical of Illiberal Education and makes this book more akin to the scandal sheets of popular culture than to Bloom's The Closing of the American Mind. The sensationalism of such stories favors certain interpretations and forecloses on others: these stories of scandalously misunderstood white male professors draw attention to the individual hurts experienced by these men and obscure the larger social and political struggles that provide the context for these stories. The most striking effect of this surprisingly effective strategy is to make these accused men appear, by definition, the innocent victims of apparently powerful minority and women students. This logic is exactly the same as the logic Michael Crichton decries when he complains of a "contemporary climate where men were assumed to be guilty of anything they were accused of" (269); the effect is to make accusers necessarily guilty, and the accused necessarily innocent. More striking even than the ironies of this reversal is the depth of the entitlement that enables these wounded white male professors to be so appalled that anyone would question their motives and innocence, their disinterestedness and objectivity. This is the response of the unmarked: secure in their own freedom from the marks of gender and racial specificity, these innocents seem truly incapable of understanding that women or African American students might bring to the classroom experiences of being "lacerated," as Bergin puts it. And it is this sense of entitlement, coupled with and sanctioned by a faith in the principles of disinterestedness and objectivity, that, paradoxically, evidences the need for what D'Souza so pejoratively calls "minority activism." Rather than quietly ponder the validity or absurdity of the accusation—what teacher hasn't been wounded by the anonymous comments on student evaluations?—Professor Bergin instead paraded his wounds in front of his class, along with his antiracist credentials, and as his "eyes filled with tears," confessed, "'I can't go on,'" and "rushed out of the classroom, unable to control himself" (6).

This melodramatic performance—both by Bergin and by D'Souza—is typical of *Illiberal Education*'s staging of the victimization of white men. It doesn't matter if this story is true, it does the narrative work that D'Souza means it to.[12] And it works again when D'Souza relates a conversation with two "liberal" white male students at Michigan who are "wounded and outraged at being on the racism suspect list" and have now withdrawn their sympathy with "black suffering"; D'Souza concludes that these young white men "have transferred their sympathies to themselves, in a belief that an old victim class has turned upon its former oppressors and their children with a vengeance—whites are the real victims now" (131–32). D'Souza calls this new view a "sort of liberation," a freedom from guilt that makes one student "crack a smile" (131). What better evidence of the weird mix of pleasure and pain that comes from a "liberation" into victimization? It is important to note here that anxieties about political correctness have mutated into a legitimization of racist ideas and speech; part of what these students are "liberated" into, as D'Souza wants to claim, is a newly authorized racism. That he blames institutions and "minority activists" for this new racism does not blunt the fact that the logic he details here is, in fact, evident throughout American culture. It is unclear, however, how a return to so-called merit-based admissions and a traditional curriculum will do anything to ameliorate what D'Souza calls the "new racism." That D'Souza ends his book with "Three Modest Proposals"—surely an unwitting reference to genocide?—does little to reassure us that the "new" university will look any different than the university as it was organized and inhabited in the pre-liberationist era.

Because this book is so invested in the idea of disinterested scholarship, D'Souza's attack on the academy relies on a construction of gender and race as mere corporeal attributes. The effort to *unmark* the white and male minds that are under attack, and to rescue the cause of disinterestedness and universality, competes in this book with a desire to fully embody these wounded white men as endangered victims who suffer bravely to uphold the truth. It seems unlikely that even D'Souza is convinced by his lame arguments for the total irrelevance of gender and race. The case, instead, rests on his ability to present the suffering of white men and the risks to the tradition they uphold as dramatically and convincingly as possible. It is in this effort that the book's "logic" begins to unravel, as Thernstrom, Bergin, and others come off as pleasurably wounded by their new position as men whom the "system" has done wrong. While D'Souza attempts to make gender and race irrelevant to the scholarly and educational life by insisting that they are matters of the body that, quite simply, don't matter in the classroom or the library, *Illiberal Education* stumbles on the body again and again as D'Souza winds his melodramatic way through the campus scandals that compel his imagination. These scandals have everything to do with a conflict between the abstract and the material, the intellectual and the bodily, and it is this conflict that D'Souza enacts for his readers throughout the book.

The "minority activists" D'Souza tracks down speak for the materiality of gender and racial difference, while the beleaguered spokesmen for what D'Souza deems a truly "liberal" education press the claim that gender and racial difference has no material bearing on education, the distribution of resources, or access to the abstract principles of democracy and humanism. While D'Souza's main interest is in showing how silly the former are and how noble the latter are, the truth is that *Illiberal Education* inevitably and repeatedly demonstrates that the crisis created by these conflicts is irresolvable because everyone—including the traditionalists—is obsessed with gender, race, and the relationship between the body and the mind. In other words, it's not only the "minority activists" who are responsible for keeping gender, race, and the body center stage. Whiteness and maleness, as D'Souza tells us repeatedly, are the insignia of infamy on campus, and white men of a more traditionally "liberal" bent are constantly marked and in danger because they try to fight the power. Just as the visibility of black skin and the outward signifiers of femaleness have marked those "minority activists," the visibility of white skin and the outward signifiers of maleness are marking the hapless individuals who just want to be appreciated for their contributions to their respective fields, regardless of race and gender.

To be white and male means to be forced to embody values or ideas or politics that might have nothing to do with one's own, as the hapless Lee Atwater found out at Howard University when students protested his appointment to the board of trustees: "Atwater's main problem," D'Souza states, "was simply that he was a white man who came along just when black students were ready for an ambush" (107). Of course, the fact that Atwater was responsible for the Bush campaign's Willie Horton ads had nothing to do with it. D'Souza refuses to see that, for the students, the issue here is speech, not identity—and not the speech that Atwater was scheduled to make at Howard, but that which he had already broadcast to the entire nation. Just exactly who is playing identity politics here? And just where is D'Souza *himself* located in these struggles?

I ask the last question because, although he speaks for the importance of placing white masculinity back in the cultural center where he thinks it belongs, D'Souza himself is not white, although he is male. In fact, D'Souza gets his identity cards on the table at the outset in what is either a clever rebuttal of the identity politics he excoriates or a canny and covert participation in them. As is somewhat typical of the self-effacing, objective persona he tries to project in the book, he "outs" himself as a man of color only under the prompting of the "curious" students who often asked him where he was " 'coming from' " (21). What follows is a somewhat cryptic argument for how his "outsider" position (he moved to the United States from India in 1978) places him in a privileged position to analyze the gender and racial struggles on American campuses. Two things are cryptic here: First, it's unclear how being a man of color in the United States offers him "critical distance" on American struggles over race, gender, and ethnicity. Is he suggesting that his experience in another country, also fractured by race and class difference, gives him grounds for an "objective" comparison that might be illuminating? Second, is he implicitly challenging American students' claims of racism by asking that if people of color habitually experienced racism on campus, then why has he not had such an experience? Just as we're pondering exactly what he means, he offers a "personal anecdote [that] may clarify" his point but which, in my view, further muddies the waters.

He tells a story about asking a "beautiful young woman" to a high school dance under the urging of his American host family. The woman he asks must ask her parents for permission, and so Dinesh approaches her the next day only to find that she has no idea what he's talking about. "At first I was simply astounded," he says, "but then I realized, with a sinking feeling"—the reader shares this feeling, it's clear where this story is going—"that I had approached *the wrong girl.* It was only later that I realized what my problem was: I thought all white women looked alike" (22). Wasting no time at all, D'Souza goes on to make fun of a black woman at Dartmouth who claimed that being mistaken for another black woman was " 'grossly racist,' " and ends with this moral: while he is sympathetic with this woman, he can't be "totally outraged" because his own experience has taught him that "no matter what our skin color or background, it is not easy to transcend our cultural particularity. Provincialism is a universal problem which all groups must confront; it is not a moral deformity confined to whites" (22).

Now, I must admit that this anecdote doesn't exactly clarify things for me.

First off, the woman at Dartmouth is *not* in D'Souza's position; on the contrary, she is on the receiving end of a white student's "provincialism," and it is thus unclear how *his* experience illuminates *hers*. Surely the point of the "minority activists" D'Souza represents as overly sensitive is that such positions are not, in fact, interchangeable. Second, D'Souza seems not to notice that his anecdote also says something about *gender* that's not reducible to provincialism. When Dinesh "reluctantly" agrees to ask out "someone," the idea seems to be that any woman would do—the family just wants to be sure that Dinesh is fully experiencing American high school culture. Now, if the white woman had mistaken him for some other Indian man, the story might work; but, instead, what we get is a portrait of a man of color who feels no sting of racism, but who, himself, is limited by his "provincialism." Or we get a picture of a man who thinks all "beautiful young women" look alike and are, in fact, interchangeable as objects and as representatives of "difference." Either way, the story, oddly, goes against the central pressure of the book which is, precisely, to argue that it is necessary to "transcend" what he claims here to be unable to transcend—racial and gendered specificity. Perhaps the message here is that only the white woman is free of "provincialism"—even if she is a cipher—and, thus, it is only incumbent upon people of color to "transcend" their particularity. In any event, substituting the more innocent "provincialism" for the inflammatory "racism," D'Souza ends by saying, "I feel a special kinship with minority students, and believe that the university is the right location for them to undertake their project of self-discovery" (23). It is hard to reconcile this feeling with the rest of the book, but one thing is clear: D'Souza's "outing" of his own minority "credentials" and his own "provincialism" works to undermine the claims of the "minority activists" and their faculty sponsors he asserts kinship with. This is playing identity politics by pretending you're not playing identity politics, and leads me to credit Jon Weiner's cynical view that "after ten years of searching for and cultivating young neocon ideologues, the Olin Foundation and the American Enterprise Institute finally got everything they could have hoped for in Dinesh D'Souza and his book: a Best-seller attacking multiculturalism and the campus left and, best of all, a right-wing book written by a young person of color" (195).

D'Souza is certainly canny enough to know that "political correctness" might impede just the kind of critique I'm offering here, not to mention Weiner's more direct attack. Fearing to appear racist, I might, as a white woman, refrain from attacking a person of color; further, as a *feminist,* and one who believes in the saliency of gender and racial difference in the formation of intellectual and scholarly perspective, I might back away from *Illiberal Education* because it appears to challenge the link between identity and politics that I am pursuing in this book about white masculinity in crisis. But this would be to misunderstand my project, much as D'Souza misunderstands how the claims of identity function within a larger educational and political project. One need not be white to speak for whiteness. To the extent that he speaks for the unmarked, he speaks for white masculinity, a point that he makes better than I could in the following justification of the universality of the "classics":

> It seems unlikely that being white and male are the reasons for anyone's greatness of thought; rather, those are the features, historically accidental, that happened to coincide with great minds who were working at particular times in particular environments. If whiteness and maleness are the cause of great civilization, then nonwhites and females are truly deprived in an incurable sense. . . . Fortunately, the great thinkers of the white male perspective did not think of themselves in this way.   (85–86)

While, on the one hand, we might be happy to applaud the democratic impulse behind D'Souza's hope that being white and male confers no special privileges on the individuals whose bodies can be characterized in those terms, on the other hand it is precisely the understanding of gender and race as *bodily* attributes that makes this defense both naive and all too canny. In his attempt to un-mark white male minds—to allow Homer and other now unfairly marked white men to reclaim their right to universality—D'Souza argues for a transcendence of the body and of bodily specificity. Yet if the body and its legible gender and racial attributes are, in fact, reducible to an "accident of history," history itself becomes an accident and the only thing that remains is a body of *texts* by people who just happen to be white and male. Surely the point is that white male thinkers have never *had* to think of themselves as white and male— not because these things are accidental or incidental but because white men have enjoyed, historically and not accidentally, a privileged proximity to the "universal" and the normative. While D'Souza wants to argue that it's not Homer's fault that he was born a white man, and to whip up our indignation that he's being punished for this transgression, what he actually does in this passage is argue *not* for the irrelevance of gender and race but for the un-markedness of masculinity and whiteness. Nonwhites and females are marked and, if not "deprived in an incurable sense," at least subject to the laws of the body that such a diagnosis invokes. As we will see in *The Closing of the American Mind,* white men are immune to the contingencies and specificities that af-flict women and people of color. D'Souza's defense of white masculinity be-comes not less, but more, convincing since it requires him to "transcend" his particularity. It's not too much of a stretch, either, to see how D'Souza's self-identification is, in fact, a savvy attempt to forestall critique of his own project by playing the "race card."[13]

My goal, in any event, is *not* to argue that political correctness does not exist, nor to defend a naive identity politics of the sort that D'Souza caricatures and that his "confession" attempts to delegitimate. Rather, my goal is to suggest that *Illiberal Education* participates in the skirmishes D'Souza claims to be outside of; in other words, and as that weird little anecdote suggests, the melodramatically and simplistically rendered battle between villains and victims is, in actuality, a much more entangled struggle compelling not only minority activists but the guardians of the old, traditional view of liberalism, as well. In more direct ways,too, D'Souza's critique of multiculturalism makes ample political use of the logic of identity. The charge of racism leveled against Thernstrom is "unanswerable," for instance, because being white, he is read as speaking for a white perspective; he is guilty, as Crichton puts it, simply by being accused. But this identitarian logic that forces Thernstrom into a pigeonhole also gets him off the hook. Thernstrom's story marks a political moment in which white men claim to become the victims, not just of "rape culture" but of metaphorical rapes. Rape culture marks all men as potential rapists, natural victimizers; but Thernstrom's story and Crichton's novel take this logic a step further to claim that this marking of white men constitutes a victimization of them, a violation akin to rape. White men, as a *class*, are positioned as always already "rapable" because they are vulnerable as a group, and ironically, vulnerable *because* they are perceived to be powerful. The success of identity politics produces the logic of white male "dispossession" identified by Todd Gitlin: "Here [white men] can compete for victim status. In a world of racial and gender definitions, are they not a race and a gender too?" (*Twilight* 119). This "victim envy," though, is only part of the story, for in other ways, majoritarian politics in American culture have always been identity politics. Rather than focus on white male appropriation of disenfranchisement (made possible, even necessary, by the identity politics of women and people of color) it is possible to tell the story of identity politics differently.

Such an alternative story might suggest, as I did in chapter 1, that identity politics really gets off the ground in the late 1960s, when Richard Nixon and his pundits were busily constructing "the silent majority," described by Richard Scammon and Ben Wattenberg as the "unyoung, unpoor, unblack" (45). The identity politics of the dominant pioneered by the chroniclers of the "silent majority" gets reborn, in the 1980s, and announces a new cycle of the crisis in white masculinity. Where the spokesmen for, and analysts of, the silent majority were relatively honest about their appropriation of the victim position from the "others" who had only recently claimed it, the cultural, social, and political terrain of the 1980s has forced that crisis to go underground. Like the laments over the forced invisibility of the silent majority, the voices that most loudly proclaim the more recent crisis in the normativity of white masculinity clash against a number of contradictions. Claiming at once that they are rendered invisible by the coming to visibility of others and that they've been made newly visible as the much-maligned embodiment of the status quo, those who speak up against the current state of an American culture run aground on identity politics in the 1980s position themselves both inside and outside of the struggle over identity and politics.

As I suggested in the introduction, identity politics is best understood as a strategy for combating perceived losses of power, a strategy for healing the wounds that mark the individual as the carrier of racial and gender "particularity." The focus on "victims" makes it possible for white men to claim injury without claiming to be oppressed systemically by white supremacist patriarchy. To speak of victims, as opposed to oppressions, and of identities, as opposed to institutions, lifts "difference" out of the realm of the institutional and places it in the realm of the individual. The focus on injured bodies facilitates this slide from a discourse of oppression to one of victimization, and this is true of the right as well as the left. Joan Scott notes that, during the Reagan-Bush years, personal injury, aided by an individualistic and entrepreneurial turn of the law,

> became the sign of an oppressed identity and identity was then articulated as the experience of injury. The language of experience and personal suffering (intersecting with the therapeutic discourse of victimization) replaced the language of rights and history as victims demanded their due. . . . Deciding among competing claims of injury meant abandoning structural, historical, and ideological analyses—all of which attended to power—and substituting instead questions about who had suffered the greater hurt or who had the more "authentic" experience   (297).

Talk of personal injury simultaneously invokes and obscures the body; injury and hurt are lifted out of the bodily arena and refigured as emotional pain or verbal restraint. But the bodily metaphor is too powerful and too tempting, even for those whose histories do not evidence systemic violence. The turn toward the personal and away from the institutional has enabled privileged Americans a share in the symbolic value of the victim, even while diverting attention from systemic racism and sexism. D'Souza, for one, refuses to ratify the claim that American culture is racist; instead he positions himself carefully on the side of the "authentic" victims of intolerance, showing sympathy for the ongoing quest for civil rights in a society still suffering from isolated racist incidents. He even manages to find (or invent) a black female student willing to testify that "the only overt racism she has encountered at Columbia involves hostility directed against whites" (10). The "authentic" is a property of individuality and individualism gets cast as a symptom of authenticity. The logic of this closed circuit excludes collective injury and collective guilt or responsibili-ty. Further, because his attack on identity politics is based on the faulty as-sumption, common on both the left and the right, that women and minorities have marked *themselves,* D'Souza can make a distinction between guilty and innocent victims.[14] That is, because the key spokespersons of the "victim's rev-olution" have themselves stressed their gender and racial specificity, they "de-serve" to be caught in their own logical traps, and *Illiberal Education* is full of scenes detailing these guilty victims doing exactly that. But because white men have been marked by others, they are the innocent victims.

The question of who constitutes a class of "authentic" victims is absolutely central to the conservative critique of political cultures, as when Charles Sykes laments the "politicization" of rape by feminists who care little for the "authen-tic," individual victims of assault. Wanting to make a distinction between au-thentic and inauthentic victims, Sykes makes explicit what D'Souza's account of Thernstrom's trauma left implicit. There are genuine traumas and then there are manufactured traumas; the former are personal, and the latter are "political." After acknowledging that rape and sexual harassment are not just "politicized fantasies" (showing that he's not an unfeeling brute), Sykes goes on:

> But just as the genuine and unquestionable martyrdom of the early victims
> of racist violence in the civil rights movement was appropriated and trivial-
> ized for political ends, the genuine suffering of victims of sexual assault and
> harassment has proven eminently exploitable by those for whom rape is a
> convenient symbol of society's oppression of women. Typically, the result is
> confusion, as genuine concern is overlaid with shrill victimist indignation,
> and distinctions between truth and fiction are obscured.   (184)

The political is opposed to the personal, the collective to the individualist, and individual, personal hurts are thus more compelling than any institutional or group oppressions. It is here that these conservative commentators, who else-where tend to excoriate postmodernism as the destruction of Western civiliza-tion as we know it, become most postmodern. Not only do they cannibalize discourses whose political and social agendas are at odds with their own; but Sykes, D'Souza, and others who speak for the ungrounded and decontextual-ized personal participate in what Susan Bordo terms the paradigmatic post-modern conversation. Interestingly, in entering this conversation, D'Souza un-wittingly aligns himself with two of the "enemies" of the traditional humanties: deconstruction and popular culture. What Bordo points out as the link be-tween a "celebratory, academic postmodernism" and the talk show seems equally applicable to some of D'Souza's arguments: "it has become highly unfashionable—and 'totalizing'—to talk about the grip of culture on the body" ("Material Girl" 117). "What the body does," Bordo concludes, "is immaterial, so long as the imagination is free. This abstract, unsituated, disembodied freedom . . . celebrates itself only through the effacement of the material praxis of people's lives, the normalizing power of cultural images, and the sadly continuing social realities of dominance and subordination" (129). Such realities, indeed, are denied within the universe of *Illiberal Education,* making of D'Souza's purportedly anti-postmodernist polemic itself a symptom of postmodernism.

AMERICAN MINDS AND AMERICAN BODIES: REPRODUCING ELITISM

Although never uttering the word *postmodern,* Allan Bloom rails against what he takes to be the sins committed under the banner of the contemporary. Unapologetically elitist, *The Closing of the American Mind* argues that the values on which a university is founded—exclusivity, difference from the mainstream, the pursuit of absolute truth, and a communion with the great minds of the Western tradition—have been destroyed by a liberationist ideology that preaches "value relativism" as opposed to truth, and equal, as opposed to "natural," rights. The university should transmit knowledge of "the good," a knowledge that can only come from sustained and "open" study of the great minds of the Western tradition; instead, our universities have become vocational institutions devoted to egalitarian principles of diversity and difference, dependent on the political will of weak administrators and contemporary-minded faculty and students. Although its critics have placed *The Closing of the American Mind* in a category with other, more pointed attacks on affirmative action, political correctness, and the rise of "tenured radicals," Bloom is in fact only peripherally concerned with such matters. Bloom does attack the university for supporting antiracist, antisexist, antielitist modes of scholarship and texts, and touches on black "separatism" and feminist dogma as symptoms of the triumph of relativism and egalitarianism over truth and universalism; but his arguments about the dominance of race, ethnicity, and gender in the curriculum are in service to a different kind of argument, a much more abstract argument for the value of an exclusive, traditional liberal arts education. In what follows, I want to use "elitist" and "exclusive" in the way Bloom uses them—not as a political indictment but as a simple description of the kind of institution *The Closing of the American Mind* longs for. Because Bloom feels no need to counter arguments for affirmative action and cultural studies, for instance, his case rests on what he takes to be the self-evident value of elitism and exclusivity fostered by a classical education of the "Great Books" variety.[15] There's no question what kind of university Bloom remembers. As his critics have not tired of pointing out, as if Bloom did not already know this himself, this is a university that feeds off of, rather than feeds, civil society, and it is a university that is rather stunningly cut off from the social and political contexts in which it exists. For Bloom, the loss of *this* university has produced an irreparable cultural wound, and he means *The Closing of the American Mind* to evoke in his readers a deep but *unrealizable* longing for its healing. For, where *Illiberal Education* is a call to arms that exacerbates the crisis it purports to describe objectively, *The Closing of the American Mind* narrativizes a crisis that is unresolvable. The book, in other words, is about a desire that can never be fulfilled and thus is permeated with a painfully pleasurable melancholy that can be discerned beneath the more overt anger and bitterness of its tone. Bloom's contribution to American education and cultural life in the post-liberationist era is, thus, an elaborate elegy for a dead institution, and it is meant to provoke the appropriate emotions in his readership.

The crisis anatomized in *The Closing of the American Mind* begins at Cornell in 1969 when, as one canny reviewer noted, Western philosophy died "with Bloom in attendance. Intellectual history and Bloom's autobiography [thus] coincide" (Pattison 9).[16] The social crisis and the personal crisis are collapsed together in a narrative performance that mourns the death of the Western tradition as it mourns the cultural delegitimation of the great white male minds (including Bloom's). Like *Illiberal Education*, Bloom's book attempts to invoke sympathy for the white men who have embodied the "tradition," but have otherwise spoken for the value of a universalist, unmarked, disembodied truth. Enthusiastically occupying the position of one of D'Souza's "quixotic" minoritized and put-upon white male professors, Bloom tilts at everything from rock music to the "lame" eroticism of his students, to the misreading of Nietzsche that has produced a "Nihilism, American Style."[17] Because Bloom also presents himself as bravely but hopelessly at odds with the debased culture he claims to describe, this book is a lengthy lament *and* celebration of his own marginality vis-à-vis the current zeitgeist. Eschewing solutions to the crisis he details, he instead aims to provoke sympathy and anger for the wounds that tradition (and himself as its spokesman) has suffered. The pathos of that loss, Bloom implies, can only be fully understood and appreciated by a small group of fellow thinkers, and it is this small group that is both subject and projected audience of this book. As one particularly hostile reviewer put it, Bloom argues that "this nation's higher education ought to be organized around the edification of the *few* who embody philosophy rather than the *many* who embody America" (Barber 82).[18] While this comment is meant to warn Bloom's readers to be on the lookout for elitism, it also unwittingly happens upon what I take to be a central concern of the book: the importance of *(dis)embodiment* to Bloom's philosophical project. While this book announces itself as concerned with the "souls" of today's students, it is at least as concerned with student bodies and sexuality. In the process of mourning the Western tradition of Great Minds and Great Books, Bloom constructs an argument for an education based on the sexual exchange of ideas between an elite group of men devoted to the study of a few great minds. For Bloom, sexuality is vital to the study of the classics and to a true education, but it is only a nondomesticated, explicitly male, and highly sublimated sexuality that he seeks. In order to make this argument, Bloom must banish women and other marked bodies from his educational paradise.

Like D'Souza, Bloom locates gender and race in the bodies of women and people of color, and positions the "great minds" of Western culture above these "contingencies" of bodily existence, above the "particularities" which impede communion with timeless universals. Black students and feminists twist American egalitarianism by confusing a respect for universal natural rights with a belief in the sanctity of personal identity and the equality of all differences. Here, the "particular" is posed against the "universal," and "particularity" becomes a code word for racially marked (that is, nonwhite) bodies and for female bodies. Following Plato, Bloom aligns the body with the particular, the soul with the universal, and argues that a universal respect for "natural rights" comes into conflict with the particularities on which arguments for respecting ethnically specific cultures are based. Given Bloom's passion for Plato, it is perhaps not all that surprising that *The Closing of the American Mind* mounts an argument for the importance of the soul over the body. As Elizabeth V. Spelman has pointed out, Plato defines a philosopher by his desire to "free the soul from the lazy, vulgar, beguiling body" (113). The soul is what transcends material life, what unites disparate men and cultures, and what links individual men with universal Man. Bloom blithely claims that "everyone knows that the particular as particular escapes the grasp of reason, the form of which is the general or the universal" (173), and mounts an argument against those who focus on particularity (feminists and multiculturalists) instead of universality. Bloom wants to save the humanities (and the social sciences) from these barbarians who would ignore "that part or aspect of man that is not the body" (356). The classical philosophers Bloom reads so passionately evidently either had no bodies or found their bodies somehow separate from the *"je ne sais quoi* pertaining to man" which eludes the natural sciences (357). Indeed, as Spelman argues, the division of the body from the soul is *the* project of Western philosophy, and it is a project informed by the desire to create hierarchies of human beings. " 'Flesh-loathing' is loathing of flesh by some particular group under some particular circumstances. . . . Somatophobia historically has been symptomatic not only of sexism, but also of racism" (Spelman 128).[19] Bloom's discussions of race and ethnicity do suggest a kind of somatophobia, most evident when he bemoans what he sees as a tribal and primitive obsession with the visceral, corporeal battles over class, race, and gender now corrupting higher education. He argues, for example, that "the 'ethnic' differences we see in the United States are but decaying reminiscences of old differences that caused our ancestors to kill one another" (192–93). This quasi-biologistic strain of Bloom's discourse keeps returning in what borders on an obsessive interest in reproduction, couched in language drawn from social Darwinism, eugenics, and sociobiology. Those who argue for multiculturalism, Bloom implies, are unable to understand that it is only by forgetting the bodily specificities of gender and race that "outsiders" can "make themselves into that universal, abstract being who participates in natural rights"—"or else be doomed," he rather ominously adds, "to an existence on the fringe" (30–31).[20]

Yet it is precisely on the fringe that Bloom wants to place those who refuse to assimilate. Assimilation here means the erasure of "particularities" in favor of a putatively unmarked universalism. While there are many ways to understand the failure of universities to fully integrate black students and/or black students' resistance to assimilation, Bloom's ideal of assimilation depends on the possibility of blending in, a possibility very much dependent, in turn, on whiteness. Whiteness and masculinity are not generally assumed to *be* "particularities," and this freedom from the particular enables a degree of what Michael Warner calls "self-abstraction." Drawing on what he takes to be the intentions of "the Founders," Bloom baldly states that "minorities are in general bad things" for a country that should be directed toward unity and the realization of the "common good" (31). But, as Warner notes, the "utopian universality that would allow people to transcend the given realities of their bodies" can also be a major source of domination, for "the ability to abstract oneself . . . has always been an unequally available resource." Using "positivity" instead of Bloom's "particularity," Warner explains what it is that Bloom fails to note in the Founders: "Access to the public came in the whiteness and maleness that were then denied as forms of positivity, since the white male qua public person was only abstract rather than white and male" (Warner 382–83). The logic of Bloom's argument might be persuasive in the abstract, but such abstraction depends on "specific rhetorics of disincorporation" that provide a "privilege for unmarked identities: the male, the white, the middle class, the normal" (Warner 383). But neither in the past nor in the present do "minorities" exist only in the abstract, nor does Bloom content himself with leaving them there.

As it turns out, despite his desire to retain the abstraction that will keep his argument from appearing like a call for the literal extermination of "minorities," he draws on exactly the vocabulary most likely to invoke that literalness: the language and metaphors of sociobiology and social Darwinism. Resurrecting notions of "fitness" to replace what he sees as the unfortunate reliance on egalitarianism in American culture, Bloom laments the ways in which "the failure to read good books both enfeebles the vision and strengthens our most fatal tendency—the belief that the here and now is all there is" (64). Not everyone, however, is "fit for bookish adventure" (65), and those who refuse to jettison their particularity are necessarily excluded from such an adventure. Yet such exclusions are necessary, because the entire point of a liberal arts education is to *discriminate*, to recognize "the good" and to reject the spurious, the contemporary, the faddish. Because Bloom insists, somewhat improbably, that racism is no longer a force in American culture and society and that all "outsiders" can become "insiders" by adhering to the doctrine of "natural rights" crafted by the Founders, he means "discrimination" to be taken as a matter of taste and aesthetics (65). Yet "taste" takes on another meaning when Bloom is talking about black students' failure to assimilate: using an old metaphor that somehow manages to look more sinister because Bloom appears to take it so literally, he complains: "the heat is under the pot, but they do not melt as have *all* other groups" (93). Taking the metaphor even further, Bloom writes that black students have "proved indigestible" (91).[21] The metaphorical veers into the literal, the abstract into the material, in inadvertent testimony to the impossibility of keeping them separate, as "assimilation" begins to look uncomfortably like cannibalism, and its failure to look like the survival strategy it perhaps more accurately is.

Despite his professed belief in assimilation, in any event, it's not at all clear whether the educational system for which Bloom speaks is more threatened by racial and gender difference *or* by the sneaking suspicion of racial and gender sameness.[22] Positing essential and "instinctive" differences between black and white, as between male and female, sociobiology both enables the cordoning off of difference and relieves the burden of guilt that might otherwise accompany the acknowledgment of a failed racial or gender reconciliation. The norm of an unmarked white masculinity depends for its power and its position on the existence of others kept outside that norm. Bloom certainly argues for the value of exclusivity and criticizes the "relativism" that makes such exclusivity appear bad. Indeed, Bloom's attack on "relativism" is, in part, an attempt to save the white male "tradition" from the relativism that has been imposed on it by feminists and others who have claimed that being white and male means being marked by racial and gender "particularity." Bloom's recourse to sociobiology might work to bolster his more abstract arguments, but it also brings along with it a materialist, bodily emphasis that subtly undermines the claims Bloom makes on behalf of the abstract universal. In these parts of the book, the material trumps the abstract in what I want to argue is an ingenious, and probably not entirely conscious, strategy for ejecting women from participation in the kind of educational endeavor he prizes. Bloom's defense of the elitism of a now delegitimized liberal arts education rests on an argument for an exclusively masculine mode of relating intellectual endeavor to sexuality; what emerges in *The Closing of the American Mind* is an argument against the "domestication" both of male sexuality and of the rigors of intellectual work. He asks us to mourn the passing of a homoerotic model of education that has been destroyed by the influx of "barbarians" whose presence destroys the delicate balance on which that model depends.

The Closing of the American Mind is surprisingly taken with sexuality, and it fractures sexuality into two distinct categories: a bodily, female, "naturally" heterosexual, reproductive sexuality; and a vibrant, "spiritually tumescent,"[23] sublimated male sexuality, expressed through intellectual endeavor but nevertheless fully potent. The limning of this latter kind of sexuality is, in my view, the topic that most fully compels Bloom's attention. On the whole, and somewhat covertly, *The Closing of the American Mind* works to resuscitate a homosocial and highly eroticized conception of education and learning, one that depends on certain kinds of exclusivity for its power. But, as I said at the outset, Bloom believes that such a conception has been fatally wounded by the events since the 1960s. The effect that he is aiming at here is an emotional effect that will touch men who, like Bloom, mourn the death of the university as they knew it. I will return to this effect in a moment, but first I want to detail how Bloom disqualifies women from participation in the eroto-educational world he yearns for. Having eliminated "minorities" as minorities, it remains to get rid of those bothersome females who, though necessary to the perpetuation of the species, are a real drag in a university setting.

Time and again, Bloom returns to reproductive questions—not only in sections on "Relationships," where we might at least expect them, but also in sections on "Nihilism, American Style" and "The University." In each case, Bloom argues that feminists' attempts to "liberate" women from the tyranny of reproduction, childrearing, and the nuclear family, are doomed to fail because women are naturally predisposed to perform these functions. Appropriating sociobiology in service to an argument about the materiality of gender difference—that is, woman's difference from man—Bloom claims that feminism has destroyed the family, made male sexuality "sinful" again, and made women feel torn in two competing directions: "women are pleased by their successes, their new opportunities, their agenda, their moral superiority," Bloom begins; "But underneath everything lies the more or less conscious awareness that they are still dual beings by nature, capable of doing most things men do and also wanting to have children" (131). In a book purportedly devoted to matters of the mind, Bloom expends quite a lot of energy worrying about reproductive arrangements, but this is energy well spent, for two reasons. He uses sociobiology in a backhanded slap at those feminists who claim that gender differences are irreducible. What is the difference, he seems to ask, between a sociobiological, conservative insistence on the salience of essential differences between men and women, and a leftist, feminist insistence on the salience of socially constructed differences between men and women? Bloom's arguments against feminism (and against the "separatism" of black students) are bolstered by an essentialism strikingly similar to, if ideologically distant from, the essentialism he decries in an identity politics that grounds ideas in bodies. The discourse of sociobiology brings Bloom within the universe of identity politics, even as he argues that a focus on gender and racial difference inhibits academic freedom. Politically, arguments for seeing race as determinant of perspective have nothing in common with arguments for seeing race as determinant of intelligence, for example; but, as arguments, and as rhetorical strategies, they share a number of assumptions.[24] What Bloom's book has in common with the identity-based politics he now sees ruining the university is a concern with the location and meaning of difference, and an ambivalence about whether to emphasize or minimize that difference.[25]

Because Bloom's quasi-Darwinist argument has to be seen to be believed[26]—what does all this talk about species preservation and biological imperatives have to do with his professed subject, "How Higher Education Has Failed Democracy and Impoverished the Souls of Today's Students"?—let me summarize it here: While it is man's "instinct" to care for his property, it is not in his best interests biologically to care for his wife and children. It is women's "instinct" to do so and, thus, in the interests of family/community/nation, it makes sense for men to think of women and children as property. Men, given the choice, would spread their seed around, having no interest in buying the cow, having gotten their milk for free and done their duty for the preservation of the species/family of man/nation. Women must, thus, practice feminine "charms and wiles" (115) to make men toe the line, and those wiles are best understood as practices which preserve what Bloom refers to as "female modesty." Modesty is opposed to sexual display and machismo as *the* sexual difference, much like it is with birds and other species in which the pallid female blends into the landscape while the flamboyant male struts his stuff. Feminism has destroyed this delicate balance, sanctioned by nature and in the interests of the nation, and Bloom means to resuscitate that tired old notion that biology is destiny but it's culture, too, and anyone who claims otherwise is the "rankest [of] ideologues" (130). After all, warns Bloom, "Law may prescribe that the male nipples be made equal to the female ones, but they still will not give milk" (131).[27]

While we might pause here and sing the praises of a lovely little invention called infant formula, other questions press: Why does Bloom argue so strenuously for the reproductive imperative constraining female sexuality? Clearly, he's invested in arguing against feminism, perhaps seeking revenge for the violence feminists have perpetrated on his beloved "classic texts" (65); but something else is going on here. Throughout these arguments, male sexuality lurks in the background, awaiting its liberation from the reproductive imperative and the domestication of family life. In insisting that female sexuality is organized around reproduction, Bloom is also insisting that male sexuality is *not* so organized; in fact, male sexuality must be channeled, schooled, and domesticated if men are to participate in the family and in childrearing. Feminism has, ironically, liberated men from that domesticity by making male protectionism the sign of male chauvinism; "why should a man risk his life," Bloom asks (rhetorically, one assumes), "protecting a karate champion who knows just what part of the male anatomy to go after in defending herself?" (131). But there's another option for men, and one closed to women: men can *sublimate* this eroto-energy into the intellectual life. Women are banished from Bloom's ideal, eroto-educational world because, unlike men, their sexuality is directed toward reproductive ends. No sublimation is necessary or, indeed, possible for female sexuality—and, as we will see, sublimation is the primary value, and privileged expression, of a liberal arts education according to Bloom. "Feminism acted as a depressant on the Bacchanalian mood of the sexual revolution" with the result that "male sexual passion has become sinful again" (100–101), something to be rooted out rather than sublimated. Feminists *deserve* to be banished for this sin because the entire Platonic educational enterprise depends on what Bloom terms a Nietzschean, as opposed to Freudian, conception of sublimation.

The difference between Nietzsche and Freud is that while Freud saw sublimation as a pallid substitute for sexual expression, Nietzsche saw sublimation as a *higher* form of sexual expression. Freud's account, Bloom contends, "cannot help making the careful observer regret civilization and long for direct sexual satisfaction" (231). This, of course, is anathema to Bloom; but in the (particularly American) turn from Nietzsche to Freud, Bloom finds the "crisis of a civilization": "Sublimation has lost its creative or molding power, and now there is desiccated culture and besmirched nature" (231). The "man who said all greatness requires 'semen in the blood'" would have only "contempt" for "men obsessed by sexual repression, who could not make something sublime out of their eroticism, who longed for 'natural' satisfaction and public approval to boot" (232). Clearly, Bloom shares Nietzsche's contempt and, indeed, at other points in *The Closing of the American Mind*, he laments the American "sexual revolution" as the "recognition that sexual passion is no longer dangerous in us" (99) because it can be expressed so directly, because people nowadays take sex so lightly and so *literally*.[28] The "semen in the blood" fuels intellectual greatness and removes sex from "nature" (that is, from women and reproduction); but it needs to remain *in* the blood, circulating as a "powerful tension," a "literal lust for knowledge" (135). Man's learning is "for the sake of sexuality" and, "[r]eciprocally, much of the energy for that learning obviously comes from his sexuality" (133). The "measure of our crisis," Bloom argues, is that men no longer connect the *Symposium* to their experience, no longer look from the "two peaks" of "intense pleasure," "sexual intercourse and thinking" (137). "Are we lovers anymore?" Bloom asks rhetorically; "This is my way of putting the educational question of our times" (133).

Now, this is no simply "conservative" attack on the sorry state of higher education. Bloom imagines himself as a kind of brother-teacher (and, dare I say it, lover?) to his students, and the language he uses to describe this relationship borders on the ecstatic.[29] Indeed, those who position Bloom with the Moral Majority have, apparently, not read *The Closing of the American Mind* very carefully. This is racy stuff. Had this book come out after the Clarence Thomas confirmation hearings were televised, and the public discourse on sexual harassment become a further irritant to conservative dyspepsia, Bloom might have taken a slightly different tack here. As is, the frankly eroticized descriptions of student-teacher relations serve a different purpose. Against the "lame eroticism" he sees in his students' *sexual* lives (132)—and Bloom claims to know an awful lot about his students' sexual lives—he poses the powerful eroticism of the *intellectual* life. Erotic and sexual feeling should point us toward the *higher,* not the lower, spheres; should point us toward the soul and not the body. Before the sixties came along and liberated sexuality and shackled liberal education—the two effects are essentially the same as far as Bloom is concerned—teaching and being taught were the most direct routes to ecstasy. Bloom mourns the loss of a time when students came to the university "physically and spiritually virginal, expecting to lose their innocence there." The teacher, charged with the weighty and pleasurable task of "deflowering" and satisfying these virgins, participated in a sexual exchange with them; "His own satisfaction was promised by having something with which to feed their hunger, an overflow to bestow on their emptiness. His joy was in hearing the ecstatic 'Oh yes!' as he dished up Shakespeare and Hegel to minister to their need. Pimp and midwife really described him well" (136). While Bloom speaks for the authority of the classics, no one who reads this passage could indict him for a will to dominate his students; the sexual exchange here is quite different, with the teacher serving (servicing?) the students. As a "midwife," he delivers them into the sexual life; as a "pimp," he delivers them over to others who will use that sexuality. While nowhere does Bloom explicitly state that such an exchange is dependent on all participants being male, his language, coupled with the sustained attack on feminists' antisex stance, point toward that conclusion. Noting that today's students are "spiritually detumescent" and today's humanists are "old maid librarians," Bloom poses a phallic past against a limp and feminized present (136). Vital to that phallic past is sublimation of male erotic energies into literary or philosophic endeavor; having women about would, perhaps, focus attention too fully on a material and unsublimated expression of sexuality and, thus, divest this homo-eroto-educational endeavor of its very power. And having feminists and "minority activists" in the classroom would puncture the Platonic bubble, forcing a materialist and political analysis onto what Bloom aims to keep abstract and, really quite oddly, disembodied.

DEAD POETS AND THE PATHOS OF WOUNDED WHITE MASCULINITY

A very similar homo-eroto-educational endeavor is enshrined in another vastly popular late eighties text: Peter Weir's *Dead Poets Society* (1989). Like Bloom's book, Weir's film is fueled by the painfully pleasant nostalgia for the days when higher education was an exclusive white male club, and the classroom a space for a homosociality animated by sublimated sexual desire. Set in an exclusive boys' preparatory school, at the cusp of the decade which would forever change the meaning of elitist institutions, the nostalgia that pervades this film can be traced to the decentering of an elite white male class which is just around the corner. This film does the cultural work that Bloom's book could only dream of: it fixes forever in the American popular imaginary the pathos of wounded white masculinity at the origins of the sixties rebellions. The threat to this idyllic world of poetic rebellion, within the narrative frame of the film, is the middle-class prescription for conformity to a normative, protector-provider masculinity. But from a retrospective 1989, at the height of *The Closing of the American Mind*'s celebrity, another threat becomes visible: the threat posed by a liberationist culture and its emphasis on the egalitarianism that would disrupt the homosocial and homogeneous space of elite educational institutions. Because this threat has already been realized, and the elitism of those institutions already compromised, *Dead Poets Society*, like Bloom's book, becomes an elegy for the losses suffered in post-liberationist culture. As we will see, the suicide of one of the film's main characters literalizes and materializes this more metaphorical death, and adds to the film's emotional power. That power, I want to insist at the risk of alienating readers who are fond of Weir's film, depends on the viewer's acquiescence to the conservative nostalgia so apparent in the late 1980s.[30]

The film indulges in the language of rebellion, and even of culture war, as the quirky, "dangerous" Mr. Keating (played by Robin Williams) enjoins his "lads" to "seize the day," and resist authoritarian educational dicta: "This is a battle, a war, and the casualties could be your heart and soul," he warns. As in Bloom, the ideal space of a great books education demands that the material details of everyday life—including those represented by women and the "female drama"—be jettisoned in the interests of an abstraction that is not, however, therefore de-eroticized. On the contrary, as we saw in Bloom, eroticism and sexual expression get sublimated into the study of—in this case—the works of dead white male poets, mostly Romantic. The goal of a literary education, according to Mr. Keating, is to transcend the body, for our bodies are only the shells of our "souls"—"we are food for worms, lads," Keating says. The only true life is the life of the mind, embodied, paradoxically, in those dead poets who "were dedicated to sucking the marrow out of life." It is with "poetry dripping from their lips" that the lads can commune with the world of the body and desire. This eroticization of poetry (and of the poetry classroom) is based on just the educational model that Bloom celebrates in *The Closing of the American Mind;* Keating sees poetry as the route to "passion" and the "powerful play of life." The dead poets, who by the late 1980s had been pushed out of the cultural center not only by a changed educational system but by the rise of mass culture, "let poetry work its magic" with the result that "spirits soared, Gods were created, women swooned." Against this passionate vision, Weir poses the wet-blanket conservatism of the school's elder teachers, who warn that Keating's methods and his message will set the students up for disappointment: "They'll find they can't all be artists," says Keating's one-time mentor, "and they'll hate you."

The film insists that performance of poetry, and Shakespearean acting, are truly subversive acts in this world of future bankers, lawyers, and doctors. In this boot camp for the ruling class—75 percent go on to the Ivy League, the headmaster boasts—the liberal arts represent the antithesis of male responsibility. For the middle classes, in the mid- to late 1950s, this meant conformity, represented in this film by the august headmaster, but above all by the tortured Neil's father, who constantly eggs his son on to succeed in the narrowest of terms. But, as we will see, while this conformity does, in fact, destroy the most sensitive of the film's poetic souls, it is also the case that the cynical realist is also right: the boys *do* end up, if not hating Keating, then at least having some good cause to regret that they took his teachings so seriously.

While Neil's father, an authoritarian paternal figure if there ever was one, is the apparent villain of the film, the denouement of Neil's story actually works to support the ideology for which his father speaks. This happens because, as Tania Modleski points out, the film seems incapable of acknowledging what is so painfully obvious to its viewers: Neil rebels against his father and the normative, domesticated, virulently heterosexualized masculinity he represents by "playing a fairy" in *A Midsummer Night's Dream.* For Modleski, the film pivots on what must remain unspoken within it, making it a "'hysterical' text, in which the weight of the not-said, that which is again rapidly becoming 'unspeakable,' threatens to capsize the work's literal meaning" (137). The film simultaneously offers and disavows homosexuality as the route toward male rebellion and, in doing so, more or less accurately reproduces a dynamic that characterized hegemonic masculinity in the 1950s, one that pitted the mature, fully heterosexualized male against the immature, more sexually indeterminate male. The "immature male," as Barbara Ehrenreich notes, was understood to be the man who had not yet taken up the burden of familial obligation, work, and respectable citizenship. In 1950s psychoanalytic accounts of adult sexuality, homosexual desire and activity signify a refusal or failure to take up a mature masculine position. The threat of homosexuality was a potent weapon against male rebellion, understood primarily as rebellion against the breadwinner ethos. Significantly, the category of "pseudohomosexual" was created in order to account for exactly the kinds of rebellion represented in *Dead Poets Society*.

In psychiatric theory and in popular culture, the image of the irresponsible male blurred into the shadowy figure of the homosexual. Men who failed as breadwinners and husbands were "immature," while homosexuals were, in psychiatric judgment, "aspirants to perpetual adolescence." So great was the potential overlap between the sexually "normal," but not entirely successful man, and the blatant homosexual that psychoanalyst Lionel Ovesey had to create a new category—"pseudohomosexuality"—to absorb the intermediate cases. There was no "sexual component" to the pseudohomosexual's deviance, at least not if caught at an early stage. Rather, he suffered from some "adaptive failure" to meet the standards of masculine conformity, and had begun a subconscious slide toward a homosexual identity.

(Hearts of Men 24–25)[31]

"Pseudohomosexuality" is the "homo" without the "sex"—in other words, homosociality. In fact, except for the stigma which Ovesey and others tried so hard to attach to the nonconformist white male, the appeal of a world without women and the responsibility of marriage and family was too strong to be so easily dismissed. The world of the "pseudohomosexual" is the world of male bonding, in which it is possible to indulge in the exclusive pleasures of a privileged homosociality: the leather couches, the great books—in short, all that is evoked both in *Dead Poet's Society* and in Bloom's vision of paradise lost. Where better to locate "perpetual adolescence" than in an all-male prep school? With the phrase "adaptive failure," we are back in the language of social Darwinism; as expected, homosexuality represents the complete failure of adaptation, an opting out of the great drama of natural selection and the reproductive imperative. But, perhaps, the greater threat is that homosexuality offers a secret way out of what Bloom calls the "female drama." As John Updike, that most astute chronicler of normative masculinity, puts it, straight men can easily admire "the peculiar charm queers have, a boyish lightness, a rising above all that female muck, where life breeds" (*Rabbit at Rest,* 182). Needless to say, this admiration does not obviate homophobia.

As if to ward off the threat that the film so irresistibly invites, *Dead Poets Society* obsessively masculinizes poetry and does so by framing it as a privileged expression of heterosexual courtship and of male virility. Keating has the boys recite lines of poetry as they kick balls around the school fields, and utters injunctions like "seize the day." Keating tells of the time when he was a "98 pound weakling" with "bullies kicking copies of Byron in his face." But he learns, and teaches, that poetry, if rescued from a desiccated intellectualism to which academic readers want to assign it, is the route toward passion, bliss, and a masculinized expression of desire and action. Indeed, several of the boys learn to use poetry to "woo women" as Keating instructs and this emphasis in the film goes a far distance toward obscuring or at least diluting the homoeroticism of these all-male bands of randy poets and students reciting their verses to each other. The fact that Neil's rebellion comes from "playing a fairy," rather than exploring the scandalous but fully masculinized countercultural world of lower-class women, booze, and rock music—as the other students do—suggests not only his difference from the norm of the hegemonic masculine but his failure to rebel in an *authorized* way. His death indicates that homosexuality, even if only latent, is *too* rebellious, a nonconformity that endangers not only his own future but the world that the film, ultimately, is invested in saving: the world of sanctioned, safe rebellions that disturb but do not significantly disrupt the system of patriarchal power that feeds Welton and that Welton, in turn, perpetuates. The safe space of male rebellion is the Dead Poets Society, where white masculinity is made "different" by incorporating signs of otherness into itself. This is done, as we might have expected, by exploring women and the "savage" masculinity of nonwhite males.

Charley, who stands by rebellion to the end and whose manly honor is paradoxically secured by his dishonorable discharge from Welton, writes these privileged lads into narratives of dispossession and powerlessness. It is Charley who stresses the fact that the Dead Poets Society meets in an "Indian cave," and Charley who insists on being called "Nuwanda" after he paints an "Indian symbol for virility" on his face. White male rebellion here is imagined through the symbols, stereotypes, and clichés of racial otherness, a tried and true strategy. As David Leverenz points out, "white flight from civilized unmanliness to Native American traditions of patriarchal comradeship" is a staple of American literary representation, from Natty Bumppo to Robert Bly (23). Plugging into Native American tradition means getting a jolt of "savagery," and thus further distance from white middle-class conformity. But Charley is an equal opportunity expropriator: he also borrows from "beatnik" culture (that absolute an-tithesis of Welton culture), which, in turn, borrows from black urban culture. The true savages, we're led to believe, are those sheeplike men who blindly fol-low the prescriptions for normal adult male behavior, such as the white, mid-dle-class, vulgar public school boys Knox meets in his sojourn into the jungle outside of Welton. Finally, Charley speaks up for women's "equality," by de-manding unto expulsion that women be admitted to this bastion of male priv-ilege.[32] As is relatively obvious, the presence of women in the film merely serves to (inadequately) heterosexualize the male characters, as in the scene where Keating gazes longingly at a phantom fiancée, whose existence is nowhere else alluded to in the film.

Dead Poets Society's hysterical erasure of homoeroticism can be seen as part of its overall ambivalence toward rebellion as practiced by an elite group of white men who would seem to have little to gain from rebellion against the sys-tem which perpetuates their power. But, as we have seen, powerlessness carries its own attractions, and the spectacle of suffering white masculinity offers plea-sure as well as pain—pleasure, indeed, through pain. As Modleski points out, the film's hidden or repressed homosexual meanings are all in the neighbor-hood of the punitive; while the film appears to be "endorsing rebellious anti-authoritarian modes of behavior," she says, it is "actually evoking a longing for a closeted world in which such behavior would only serve to perpetuate a pow-er structure that would ceaselessly punish it" (138). In this entirely convincing reading, the film displaces its homoeroticism onto scenes of punishment and a kind of masochistic pleasure to be found in "lyriciz[ing] life in the closet" (140). The film preaches the virtues of repression and sublimation, as does Bloom in both *The Closing of the American Mind* and *Love and Friendship*. As Eve Sedgwick suggests, Bloom is "unapologetically protective of the sanctity of the closet, that curious space that is both internal and marginal to the culture: centrally representative of its motivating passions and contradictions, even while marginalized by its orthodoxies" (*Epistemology* 56). The sanctity of the closet insures that true pleasure is to be found in channeling erotic energies into readings of dead poets, most notably Walt Whitman. Neil's very poetic death—he strips, puts on his Puck crown of thorns, and opens his windows to the pure, white winter landscape—is a self-wounding whose pathos is depen-dent on what is never expressed in the film. Neil's death is the necessary con-clusion in this pleasurably punitive narrative economy, and the theatricality of that death—and the lyrical and loving grief displayed so excessively by the oth-er lads—serves as an appropriate finale to the film's ambivalent attitude toward white male rebellion against normativity.

That death is romantically eroticized in the film, not only because Weir films it as an eerie return to nature and a more elemental, less culturally restrictive, male subjectivity; but because Todd, whose story *Dead Poets Society* truly is, finds in Neil's death both the expression of his own "passion" and what the film takes to be the far more eloquent articulation of his loss. Running out into a purified, white, snowy landscape, Todd at last finds his "barbaric YAWP," a Whitmanesque expression of release and loss rolled into one. Todd's "YAWP" is a protest against the pain of Neil's loss, but it is not a protest against the forces that killed Neil—what the film wants to suggest is a coldly authoritative masculinity. For, having killed the rebellious "fairy," the film weirdly fails to punish that authoritative masculinity. In fact, after the suicide, white patriarchy reconstitutes itself by scapegoating Mr. Keating and his nonconformist ideas. As the most straight-laced of the in-group says about the powers-that-be at Welton, "They're not after us. *We're* the victims, us and Neil." These privileged young white men are the victims *both* of patriarchal authority *and* of its "subversion." Neil's dead body stands as testament to the pain of this victimization, a spectacular "lesson" about the cost of defying authority—or, is it the cost of accepting authority? Does Neil kill himself because he cannot force himself to defy his father? Or, does Neil kill himself in defiance of his father? What kills Neil? Conformity? Respectability? Upward mobility? Homophobia? Patriarchy? The film does not answer these questions, but instead, finesses them by ending with the emotional display of young white male loyalty and love for the Whitmanesque teacher, Mr. Keating. The lads conform to nonconformity and, with Keating's exit, business returns to usual.

And why shouldn't it? These boys are, after all, the future rulers of their world—no one, not even Keating, questions their rights nor the naturalness of the social order that safeguards those rights. Neil's sacrifice facilitates Todd's passage into manhood and, as Mike Hammond points out, enables the previously mute Todd to find his voice.[33] But it is not only Todd's passage into manhood that is facilitated by Neil's death, for this is not simply a story of distinct individuals confronting the challenges of their time and place; Neil's death also works to reconstruct dominant masculinity and to secure the other boys' position within it. That is, because these young men experience the loss that Neil's death represents—including the loss of "youthful," rebellious, and homoerotically charged masculinity—and then go on to themselves occupy the authoritative, patriarchal positions Welton opens up to them, the film reconstructs hegemonic masculinity as internally *wounded* but made fuller and more legitimate by that wounding. Such a scenario plays out, of course, against the *historical* context of the film, both its narrative time and place, and the time and place of its production. Wedding 1959 to 1989, the film simultaneously erases and reconstructs thirty turbulent years, anointing the privileged white male as the legitimate heir to both power and victimization. Neil, wearing a crown of thorns, is sacrificed so that the narrative of white male victimization can find legitimacy.

Dead Poets Society might, on one reading, appear to endorse an antiauthoritarian mode of education and, by extension, an antiauthoritarian mode of masculinity. Certainly, the headmaster represents a stuffy, life-denying conservatism that would crush out the very individuality on which hegemonic masculinity depends. In the 1950s, particularly, with anxiety over the "organization man" at its height, conformity to rigid rules impedes the expression of individual identity and creativity. But the seemingly progressive ideology masks a much more conservative stance in the film; or, rather, the film, in erasing the very fraught, political contexts in which it exists, also erases the differences between the progressive and the conservative, rescripting rebellion as a minor skirmish within a limited and homogeneous sphere. When the headmaster explains that the curriculum should not be changed—it's "set, it's tested, it's Tradition"—he sounds like Allan Bloom, and there's the rub. Keating *also* sounds like Bloom. "Being in the club," Neil explains, "means being stirred up about things"—poems, philosophy, great men. Being "stirred up" also nicely describes Bloom's vision of higher education and of intellectual and literary discourse as sublimated. Sublimation serves the needs of the dominant order as long as elemental energies don't get channeled into political action. In this as in many other respects, *Dead Poets Society* dovetails with Bloom's and other conservative critiques of a post-liberationist American culture.

For Bloom, the death of the homoerotic, sublime educational endeavor occurs in the sixties, when black power, feminism, and sexual liberation rose up against the established, liberal order and insisted on taking everything so literally, insisted on de-sublimating and materializing the tradition and its transmission. What makes the sixties a particularly destructive decade, according to Bloom, is that the revolutionary movements, in promoting "liberation," destroyed the intellectual, emotional, and sexual energy that is preserved through a closed circuit of educational and erotic exchange: "The students' wandering and wayward energies finally found a *political* outlet. By the mid-sixties universities were offering them every concession other than education, but appeasement failed and soon the whole experiment in excellence was washed away. The various liberations wasted that marvelous energy and tension, leaving students' souls exhausted and flaccid, capable of calculating, but not of passionate insight" (50–51, emphasis added). The "political" is a code word for an entire range of meanings, and it is the "political" that both the cultural warriors and Weir's film want to evacuate from the educational scene. The "political" means not only a focus on the relevance of gender, race, and class in the study of society and culture; it also means a focus on the material, rather than the abstract.

The body is welcome, but only as a metaphor that enriches our apprehension of the soul, the mind, and intellectual endeavor. Women and people of color are kept out of this exclusive educational scene—not because Bloom is a sexist or racist, but because the particularities that the dominant culture assigns *only* to its "others" necessarily impede communion with universals.

The real crime of feminism and multiculturalism is not that they make *truth* relative, but that they make *white masculinity* relative, by placing white men within the field of identity politics, by marking them as the embodiment of a particularity that "just happens" to coincide with the normative, and putatively, unmarked self. The culture warriors position themselves as beleaguered but heroic rebels, replacing other heroes in the annals of American liberation. It is much more compelling to represent this authority as beleaguered than as empowered, especially in a culture so enamored of the idea of the underdog. While there is ample evidence to suggest that white and male power reproduces itself through cycles of crisis and resolution, the rhetoric of crisis fueling the discourses of the culture wars produces other effects, as well. Announcing crisis is risky, in that it acknowledges the vulnerability of white masculinity; at the same time, that vulnerability can produce new kinds of power, the power of the wounded, the disenfranchised, the maligned. In the next chapter, we will continue our investigation into these paradoxes by tracing the fate of that most spectacularly endangered, powerfully vulnerable, of contemporary figures, the "dead white male author."

CHAPTER 3

TRAUMAS OF EMBODIMENT

White Male Authorship in Crisis

In *The Absent Body,* a phenomenological exploration of the hypothesis that "one's own body is rarely the thematic object of experience," Drew Leder remarks that "a certain telos toward disembodiment is an abiding strain of Western intellectual history" (1–3). This is nowhere more evident, perhaps, than in what until recently has passed for literary history.[1] While different eras have evinced more or less interest in the details of authors' lives, constructions of elite or highbrow authorship have generally tended toward the disembodiment of the writing subject. Much cultural work was done in the Romantic period, for instance, to insure that the Author occupied an ideological space explicitly outside the marketplace and, thus, implicitly outside the demands of bodily subsistence.[2] While the Romantic notion of the Author is by now thoroughly demystified as an ideological construction, the "death of the Author" announced in 1968 by Roland Barthes has, in some ways, further disembodied authorship. No longer even existing under the mask of "genius," writing becomes "that neutral, composite, oblique space where our subject slips away, the negative where all identity is lost, starting with the very identity of the body writing" (Barthes 142). Despite the deconstructive impulse at the heart of Barthes's project and those spawned by it, the Author, even through death, gets remystified as a disembodied force under the sign of "writing." Ironically, in one of those strange bedfellows moments of postmodernism, the anti-deconstructivist Dinesh D'Souza says much the same thing when he notes that "[t]here are disagreements and debates among these various new schools of criticism, but they are united in a general effort to capsize the author and his work in order to shift semantic authority to 'imperial readers'" (179).

D'Souza's lamentation—central to his scripting of the culture wars as a battle between the forces of unmarked and disembodied thought or creativity and the forces of an identity politics reducible to body politics—suggests that more is going on in the deconstruction of the Author than mere theoretical retrench-ments. Threatened by "theory," "politics," and the rise of popular culture, the white male author is suffering a second kind of death; as D'Souza and Barthes, writing from radically different political and intellectual traditions, both sug-gest, a language of violence and violation characterizes the shift in thinking about the "imperial" author. The emblem of this crisis is the figure of the Dead White Male author, whose fantasized disappearance has caused so much an-guished browbeating, narratives of victimized geniuses, and what now looks like a hysterical displacement of cultural angst onto the bodies of white men. The death of the Author and all the jokes about dead white males might be meant metaphorically; but it is also the case that the abstract meets the materi-al in such formulations, the impulse toward disembodiment competing with a barely acknowledged desire for reembodiment. This desire, always shot through with fear about the consequences of a focus on white male bodies, can be read within narratives about white men being *forced* to inhabit marked, and thus endangered, bodies. In this chapter I will look closely at how the emer-gence in contemporary fiction of a surprisingly literalized, materialized white male authorship in crisis challenges the myth that the body is somehow outside of, if not inimical to, intellectual and creative operation (and that the body be-longs to the "lower" depths of humanity and the mind to the "higher"), and thus challenges the gender dichotomies on which this oppositional structure rests. Wounded bodies replace abstracted minds, as the image of a disembod-ied genius gets replaced by a white male body and psyche in imminent danger. If, as Kaja Silverman remarks, the construction of disembodied authorship is a primary site for the reproduction of normative masculinity (*Male Subjectivity* 11), then literalizing and materializing the wounds of cultural, social, and polit-ical trauma threatens the very terms of that construction.

I have chosen to look at three novels that displace the anxiety provoked by the decentering of the white male author onto what I will call author-surro-gates, characters who play out, with varying degrees of literalness, the wound-ing of white male cultural authority: Philip Roth's *My Life as a Man* (1974); John Irving's *The World According to Garp* (1978); and Stephen King's *Misery* (1987). While the novels by John Updike discussed in chapter 1 register anxiety over the *political* decentering of white men, these novels worry over an analo-gous *cultural* decline. The "death of the Author" and the demise of a particular order of cultural politics get worked out in these fictions as bodily traumas. The somatization of the cultural anxiety produced by the feared decentering of the white male author gets literalized in this group of fictions that feature wounded, mutilated, and physically threatened white male authors. The dis-placement of cultural trauma onto the body, and the representation of social disempowerment by physical wounding, functions to recenter dominant masculinity even as it appears to evidence its decentering. As a group, the novels present an escalating sense of crisis afflicting the white male author in post-liberationist America: Roth's representation of a hysterical male body gives way to Irving's host of mutilated male bodies, which in turn predicts King's "raped" white male author kept captive and in pain. The increasingly literal, visceral, embodied nature of these traumas testifies to the ongoing process I'm analyzing throughout *Marked Men*, as personal, bodily injury overwhelms and replaces in importance collective hurts or oppressions, and the figure of the personally, individually suffering victim comes to stand in for cultural, social, and political hurts. As we will see, however, the bodily wounds on which these novels dwell also threaten to "feminize" the white male authors who suffer them, and the novels are thus full of contradictory representations of the relationship between their protagonists and a normative masculinity. In each case, the novels explore masochism, hysteria, and other so-called feminine afflictions, as a way to work out some of these contradictions. In doing so, they manage to ward off the cultural death of the white male author, even as they detail his physical and psychological deterioration. In fact, and in consonance with the logic we've already seen many times in this study, that deterioration is necessary to the cultural recuperation of white masculinity—*not* because wounds are the necessary condition for recuperations, but because those wounds and the impossibility of their full healing are the basis of a new, post-liberationist white masculinity. Objectified by cultural and political attacks on the authority of white masculinity, these author-surrogates suffer a savage embodiment forced on them by women, feminism, and the forces of cultural change in post-liberation America. At the same time, this embodiment, and its savagery, pave the way for a reconceptualization of a white masculinity and white male cultural authority.

THE "MYTH OF MALE INVIOLABILITY": SOMATIC DISINTEGRATION IN PHILIP ROTH'S *MY LIFE AS A MAN*

Philip Roth's *My Life as a Man* covers some of the same ground as *Dead Poets Society* (see chapter 2) as both texts place individual white male subjects in anxious opposition to a normative masculinity—*anxious*, because a rejection of that normativity threatens both to "feminize" and "homosexualize" the male subject. The film attempts to ward off those threats by tapping into a primal maleness found in various "primitive" traditions; but such a strategy never fully heals the anxiety at the heart of the film.[3] The production of a wounded male body—feminized and, arguably, homosexualized—both evinces and obscures the political and cultural stakes involved in 1950s male rebellions. The crisis of a masculinity divided against itself, thus, gets perpetuated rather than resolved as, in Tania Modleski's reading, the film offers a poetic male masochism as the emblem of that crisis: appearing to endorse "rebellious anti-authoritarian modes of behavior," the film actually "evok[es] a longing for a closeted world in which such behavior would only serve to perpetuate a power structure that would ceaselessly punish it" (138). The frantic disavowal of the feminization and homosexualization on which 1950s rebellion appears to depend makes of this film a "hysterical text" (Modleski 137). Roth's *My Life as a Man* is also a hysterical text, its meanings always threatening to spin out of control of the dominating authorial consciousnesses it both depicts and expresses. This novel about white male authorship under siege shares with *Dead Poets Society* an ambivalence about rebellion against normative masculinity, as well as an anxiety about (dead) white male authors and the waning of a masculine cultural authority. Its protagonist, Peter Tarnopol, is the wounded, victimized embodiment of a masculinity and authorship in crisis, a white male subject whose "rebellion" against the normative masculine leads to a masochism whose perversity threatens to both feminize and homosexualize him.

The novel is divided between "My True Story" by Peter Tarnopol, author and suffering spouse of the crazy and proto-feminist Maureen; and "Useful Fictions," also authored by Tarnopol but featuring surrogate author-protagonist Nathan Zuckerman.[4] Roth frames Tarnopol's literary production as a therapeutic enterprise that fails to work out and relieve the crisis of authorship and subjectivity produced by Peter's horrific marriage to, and divorce battle with, a wife who embodies a veritable catalogue of feminine (and feminist) sins. When the novel begins, Maureen is dead, but her ghost haunts Peter and the novel from the very first page, on which this dedication appears: "I could be his Muse, if only he'd let me." Maureen *is* Peter's Muse, but the literary production she "inspires" is as chaotic as the reversals her dominance over him set in motion. This battle between the sexes is both political and personal; but it is also *cultural* in ways that echo the culture wars we anatomized in the last chapter. The novel poses authorship, creativity, and masculinity against mass culture, the body, and femininity. Roth offers a new, post-liberationist twist on this oppositional structure that has been common since at least the nineteenth century:[5] mass culture, the body, and femininity are linked, as well, with politicized culture, particularly an emergent feminism that threatens to "mark" men as the spokesmen for, and patriarchal culture as the embodiment of, a politics of domination. Thus, a fiction of disembodiment gives way to a representation of a savagely embodied male subject, who is traumatized by the fact that he is "marked" socially as the bearer of a physically and symbolically apprehended power.

The novel aligns the creative subject of a masculinized high culture with a proud individualism, and the politicized subject of a feminized and proto-feminist mass culture with a vulgar collectivism. Published in 1974, the novel is set in the late fifties and early sixties, in an era that Roth represents as suffering the death throes of an earlier, more stable order of cultural politics. The novel almost hysterically evades its own historical and political contexts, representing social change as the mere backdrop to its protagonist's personal traumas. Roth makes this explicit and, in doing so, both ironizes and rationalizes the construction of authorship and of wounded masculinity at the heart of this novel. In one of the only references to the social world in which his troubles unfold, Tarnopol surveys the upheavals of the early 1960s (including assassinations, war and its protestors, racist violence in the South, and racial uprisings in the North), and concludes, "And so those eventful years passed, with reports of disaster and cataclysm continuously coming over the wire services to remind me that I was hardly the globe's most victimized inhabitant" (273). While Roth makes Peter self-conscious about his own claims to victimization, such passages are proleptic in that they simultaneously entertain and disable a critique of a solipsism that subordinates the political to the personal, the collective to the merely individual. When Roth has Peter admit that "news of bitter struggles for freedom and power . . . made my personal difficulties with alimony payments and inflexible divorce laws appear by comparison to be inconsequential" (268), the effect is *not* to consolidate a representation of Peter of a whiny, privileged man; rather, the effect is to authenticate his trauma by analogizing it with the "highly visible" social dramas he cares little about. The analogy "works" because Roth positions Peter as the wounded victim of another "drama of social disorder": the chaos produced by an insane feminist reversal of the established hierarchy which, in turn, threatens to destroy the very principle of hierarchy at work within American culture, particularly literary culture.

Maureen's feminism is based on the "myth of male inviolability" and the myth of female victimization, sanctioned by a legal and economic system that threatens not only male health and sanity but culture and art, as well. Maureen, and the entire "system of sexual justice" (131) for which she stands, insists on turning Peter into a figure for a dominant masculinity, erasing his individuality and endangering the image of the disembodied creative spirit he prizes so highly. When Milan Kundera describes Maureen Tarnopol as a woman who "embodies that part of being which, freed from every achievement of history and culture, belongs to the eternal interests of our bodies and of our animality" (161–62),[6] he does so not only because she, as a woman, is tied to the body, but because she forces an embodiment onto Peter, as well. Like the discourses of culture war I analyzed in chapter 2, Roth's depiction of a war between the sexes fantasizes a conspiracy between women, politicized responses to personal issues, and a debased and debasing popular culture. Peter rebels against Maureen's emergent feminist consciousness, represented by Roth as oddly in sync with the system that normalizes a protector-provider masculinity.[7] This rebellion positions him as a "feminized" figure whose vulnerabilities and weaknesses are metaphorically linked with an order of cultural politics at risk. Paranoid in the extreme, Tarnopol's pathological response to the failures and frustrations of his personal life veils the social and political contexts of those failures and frustrations. Key among these contexts is the renegotiation of both gender and culture, produced through women's liberation on the one hand, and the rise of consumer culture and mass media on the other. Roth finds a perfect emblem for Peter's crisis in his battle with Maureen over alimony: in one stroke, Maureen's demands commodify and vilify him, displacing him from an exalted position above the consumerist and social fray, and plunking him right down in the thick of contemporary struggles. In suggesting that Peter could pay alimony if he were to sell more stories, increase his output, and thus command more capital, Maureen dishonors the artist by locating him as an economic actor in a marketplace, rather than as a creative spirit in an isolated garret. Horrified by the prospect of producing literature "*on demand!*" (267), Peter retreats into the posture of wounded spirit, bravely fighting against the crazy Maureen, the dominance of women, and the commodification of literary production. He refuses, in other words, to "be a man," which means conforming to the prevailing spirit of the era. As any number of cultural commentators in the late fifties and early sixties suggested, conformity signals not only an abandonment of masculinity understood as uniqueness and individual will but also capitulation to the imperatives of a mass, mechanized culture.[8] In *My Life as a Man*, mechanistic and sham modes of production are embodied by Maureen, whose aspirations toward art are as degrading to the cultural sphere as her faked pregnancy is to the personal sphere. Active, disembodied masculine production is thus posed against a bodily reproduction that, itself, turns out to be inauthentic.

Yet a certain amount of male trouble comes with the artistic vocation, not only because the artistic realm has long been associated, somewhat illogically, with femininity, but also because Peter's opting for a less normative form of patriarchal power places his masculinity at risk. While masculinity might be secured through a distance from a feminized mass culture and everyday life, as Andreas Huyssen has convincingly argued, the modernist aesthetic through which a Romantic notion of authorship finds its apotheosis also carries within it a threat to the masculinity both of the artist and the cultural realm for which he claims to speak. The very terms of heroic alienation from bourgeois culture require that the male artist take up what we might consider a "feminine" position vis-à-vis that dominant culture. That is, the male artist must appropriate to himself, or manufacture, a symbolic outsider status that obscures his own comparative social advantages, crafting what Huyssen calls an "imaginary femininity" that "can easily go hand in hand with the exclusion of real women from the literary enterprise and with the misogyny of bourgeois patriarchy itself" (189). This imaginary femininity assures the male artist of an oppositional stance and does so by debasing the femininity associated with mass culture, with women, and with "everyday life": "Only by fortifying its boundaries, by maintaining its purity and autonomy, and by avoiding any contamination with mass culture and with the signifying systems of everyday life can the art work maintain its adversary stance: adversary to the bourgeois culture of everyday life as well as adversary to mass culture and entertainment which are seen as the primary forms of bourgeois cultural articulation" (Huyssen 197).[9] Roth's novel offers a nearly literal defense of this aesthetic, complete with its representation of Peter as "the suffering loner who stands in irreconcilable opposition to modern democracy and its inauthentic culture" (Huyssen 194) and the lionization of Flaubert as its icon.

But while fortifying boundaries is certainly the most time-honored remedy for an ailing masculinity, Roth's novel suggests that it is through the entertainment of disempowerment, the literal and metaphorical breakdown of the borders of the masculine, that the white male author can restore his cultural legitimacy and personal power. The *suffering* of the artist, in other words, is as important as his detachment. While the male author might position himself against the everyday, including the bodily details of gendered and racial experience, the image of the suffering artist brings the body back, and in Roth's novel, with a vengeance. Indeed, as David McWhirter points out, in a reading of the artist as masochist in Henry James, there is ample evidence to suggest that the modernist male artist's ambivalent positioning vis-à-vis normative gender constructions is constitutive of both the modernist aesthetic and the infamous misogyny that seems to go with it so perfectly.[10] As McWhirter notes of the modernist writers with whom Peter claims fraternity, the seemingly irresistible representation of the wounded artist explores "the problematical status of the artist in [a] 'feminized' American culture," and points toward "the masochistic self-authorizing strategies increasingly employed by high-modernist male writers in response to their real or perceived cultural and social marginalization" (469).[11] Such strategies are fully evident in *My Life as a Man* where, as we will see in a moment, even the title itself announces a crisis in the meanings and status of a masculinized, fully legitimized construction of cultural authority. Peter's masochism stages that crisis, but it also is meant to *manage* it; as we've seen before, it is through the performance of crisis that white masculinity both expresses its disempowerment and works toward a new conceptualization of power. Masochism, as a psychological and artistic strategy, is perfectly suited to express this doubleness (see introduction).

The imaginary and violable femininity of the male artist—his introjection of a victimized and submissive other into himself—produces a split subjectivity that David Savran associates with the masochism of the Beats, whose rebellions (roughly contemporary with the narrative time of Roth's novel) reach both backward into the modernism that Huyssen anatomizes and forward into the postmodernism they predicted. While, on the one hand, the Beats are worlds apart from Roth in their negotiation of the social and cultural shifts of postwar American society, Savran's discussion of them suggests that the much more mainstream Roth performs a similar rebellion through his author-surrogate. The rebellious, literary male, Savran writes,

> both identifies with and is possessed by a feminine other, an "invader." But insofar as he also self-identifies as a man, he must continually do battle with the femininity that has invaded him and inheres within. For as a subject, he is always split into a masculine—and sadistic—half that delights in displaying his prowess and his marksmanship, and a feminine—and masochistic—half that delights in being used as a target. His (impossible) project, as man and as writer, is to master the femininity at which he aims and does not aim, to write his way "out."   (45)

While Peter's respectability might make him an unlikely candidate for fraternity with the Beats and their "feminine" masochism, his ambivalent embrace/rejection of what passes for normative masculinity positions him in close proximity to a moral masochism that is first cousin to the "perversions" Savran reads in the Beats. Tarnopol's main characteristic appears to be his inability to do what will bring him pleasure, not pain; and this inability, in Roth's estimation, stems from a wrongheaded belief in the "rightness" of social convention, that is, in the value of the normative masculinity Maureen (and society) seems to demand of him. In his ineffectual but perpetual rebellion against the conventional wisdom that requires him to "act like a man," Roth dooms Peter to repeatedly perform masochistic scenarios in which he is both humiliated by his failure to "be a man" and gratified by the freedom from normative masculinity that humiliation announces. Thus, Peter wavers between violence and victimization, in one moment wanting to kill Maureen, in another parading around the apartment in her bra and panties.

But, while the Beats clearly positioned themselves as cultural outsiders, Roth's author-surrogate yearns to be on the inside of the literary establishment. Tarnopol, likely speaking for his creator, admits that he is "not a renegade bohemian or cutup or any kind" (229), but a mainstream writer who has absolutely no pretensions toward any kind of rebelliousness. Roth certainly has an interest in how difference from the norm positions the writer, and as both defenders and critics have suggested, this fantastically successful Jewish writer has more than a little riding on his ambivalent stance vis-à-vis the dominant culture and its "others." Writing about a later incarnation of author-surrogate Zuckerman (in *Zuckerman Bound*), Eric Zakim notes Roth's dependence on an ambivalent ethnic and cultural marginality that hinges on an impossible positioning: Roth and his author-surrogates depend on the marginality of the Jews even as they cash in on their own marginality to *that* marginality. Critical consciousness comes from being both inside and outside the marginalized community, and it is replaying that self-contradiction that keeps Roth (and Zuckerman) repeating the same stories. As Zakim puts it, in terms appropriate to my analysis here, "Zuckerman can't write about anything else because nothing else creates the type of hurt that the Jews elicit in him, and this hurt in turn becomes the arousal" (23). Aroused and hurt by his insider-outsider position, Tarnopol, too, obsessively returns to the narrative that marks so many of Roth's fictions, in which the Jewish writer works out his ambivalent marginality in sexual relationships with gentile women. Here, as elsewhere, that obsession fuels the fiction and shipwrecks the life; key to this dynamic are the *wounds* that Tarnopol/Zuckerman suffers from his association with, and distance from, the normativity oh-so-destructively promised by these gentile women, Tarnopol's Maureen and then Susan, and Zuckerman's Lydia. Being "a man" in *My Life as a Man* means occupying two positions at once; it means being both a victim and the boss.[12]

Vital to this paradox is the fact that it is Maureen's "feminist" marking of him that precipitates his crisis: it is by offering himself to Maureen's attack on his privilege *and* his inadequacy that Peter finds himself stuck in an impossible position. Peter is wounded both by his proximity to, and distance from, normative masculinity. What Roth construes as the "dominant fiction" of masculinity, to borrow a phrase from Kaja Silverman, interpellates men as all-powerful and malicious guardians of male power, so that despite his experience of his own disempowerment, Peter has been seduced by "the myth of male inviolability, of male dominance and potency" (Roth 172). Being an artist and, thus, refusing to "be a man" marks him as less than fully masculine; at the same time, embodying the sins of the patriarchal culture, as Maureen would have it, Peter is marked as all too fully masculine, the figure for a dominant, violent, and self-centered maleness that endangers everything from individual women to world peace. And this is the crux of Roth's representation of Peter's masochistic masculinity: according to the novel's gendered logic, Maureen's alignment with the forces of anti-art (that is, commercialism, commodification, and feminism) places her in the *dominant* position in an American culture that recognizes only collective, and not individual, suffering, and pursues only a commercialized or vulgar "culture." Peter's claims to artistic singularity ("distinguishable from the mass of my contemporaries, I read books and wanted to write them.

My master was not Mammon or Fun or Propriety, but Art, and Art of the earnest moral variety" [174]) allow him to occupy the space of difference, and to position himself as the wounded, oppressed, *marked* victim whose refusal to "be a man!" makes him both masochistic and heroic.

While Maureen claims to be Peter's "victim," and the victim of patriarchal institutions, it is something of an understatement to say that Roth undermines her claims. The novel delegitimizes a feminist narrative of social disenfranchisement and replaces it with a narrative centering on the psychosomatically wounded white male subject and the endangered cultural order for which he speaks. What Peter suffers are not only the wounds of a creative singularity doomed by and in a commodified cultural realm but also the effects of "modern democracy," to recall Huyssen—or, to use a more current vocabulary, identity politics. Peter is "marked" by Maureen and the "fifties-feminese" (170) that constructs men as having all the social and political advantages that women lack, at the same time as it constructs an artist as less than a "real man." The novel empties out the woman's position and installs Peter in it. Maureen marks Peter as the embodiment, quite literally, of a dominating and destructive masculinity, even as she criticizes him for being less than a man. Damned if he does, and damned if he doesn't, Peter is paralyzed, stuck in a state of crisis for which there is no way out. Doomed to repeat performances of masochistic desire and the pains that desire inflicts, Peter experiences not only a profound psychological hurt but an aesthetic blockage, as well. Wounded both by Maureen's hysterical and wrongheaded "marking" of him as phallic man, and the patriarchal institutions that actually serve women's interests at men's expense, Roth represents Peter as engaging in displays of bodily and psychic traumas, reveling in the pleasures and pains of spectacular disempowerments. Roth's novel, like Updike's *Rabbit Redux,* more or less explicitly announces and enacts a crisis in masculinity: the title, its meanings repeatedly ironized within the novel, sets in motion a clash between two ways of "being a man," or perhaps more precisely, two socially constructed masculinities that are each against men's interests. The words "my life as a man" snidely *and* self-pityingly announce the impossible position of middle-class white masculinity in this era. And because the crisis the novel represents is primarily artistic, *My Life as a Man* is about more than one man's inability to come to terms with the shifting social terrain on which is played out dramas about gender and power; it is also about the crisis afflicting the entire *cultural* identity of the United States, with the question of literary value and individual creative autonomy hanging in the balance. While Roth invites us to snicker a bit at his beleaguered author-surrogate, he never asks us to question the validity or sincerity of his valiant fight against the forces of commodification, feminization, and feminism.

"Being a man," is entirely at odds with being an artist in this novel and, while this opposition enables Roth to critique a normative masculinity ruled by the imperatives of domesticity and commodity culture, it also produces a good deal of anxiety about masculinity and heterosexuality. Roth flirts with the feminization and homosexualization of his author-surrogate: Peter fails to satisfy his sexual partners despite seemingly "heroic" efforts, a failure that Maureen attributes to latent homosexuality; Dr. Spielvogel, his Freudian analyst, reads a latent homosexuality in Peter's narcissism and obsessive repetition of disabling relationships with women;[13] and Peter's hysterical outbursts, in which he tends to rend apart his clothing and, sometimes, his skin, point to a feminine, masochistic desire to destroy the self instead of his antagonist Maureen. Peter is feminized by his failure to "be a man," "pussywhipped" (126) by a crazy feminist who nevertheless insists that he has power over her, and decentered in a culture in which he can only appear as a pathetic oddball, a "hysterical Jewish poet" (141, 148).

But, paradoxically, being a "real man," like his father, for example, leads to the same "feminization" as failure to do so; for, the "real man," "the aggressive entrepreneur and indestructible breadwinner" (214) finds himself weakened, "harassed" by "his overpowering commitment to the idea of Family and the religion he made of Doing A Man's Job!" (241). In an energetic, hysterical outburst, Peter claims for himself what a "growing body of opinion" on marriage and sexual politics claims for women: this new ideology holds that "there are the dominant and the submissive, the brutish and the compliant, the exploiters and the exploited. What this formula fails to explain, among a million other things, is why so many of the 'masters' appear themselves to be in bondage, oftentimes to their 'slaves'" (172). Peter is, indeed, "mastered" by Maureen; but, as his psychoanalyst, his brother, and virtually everyone else tells him, he *enjoys* the complicated mix of pleasure and pain, power and vulnerability, that comes from subjecting himself to Maureen's abuse. As he puts it, in a typically overwrought discursive outburst (Roth's prose is nothing here if not wildly incoherent and emotionally saturated—in a word, hysterical), he has "[n]ailed [him]self with [his] romantic morality to the cross of her desperation!" (243). Martyred on the altar of normative masculinity, with its skewed morality, Peter returns again and again for more punishment. That his humiliation at Maureen's hands is mixed with his violence against her suggests that, like the feminine masochism Savran analyzes in the Beats, Peter's pathology, his masculinity, is characterized by an "obsessive oscillation between feminized and masculinized positionalities, between victim and street tough, martyr and tyrant, aesthete and proletarian" (Savran 67). Peter viciously beats up Maureen, then dons her underwear; he physically attacks her lawyer while sobbing uncontrollably. The specific, historical configuration of masochism here owes to the dominance of a particular construction of masculinity against which Peter battles. That he willingly submits himself to that battle, and willingly opens himself up to the "analysis" of Spielvogel and various others, suggests a desire to keep that oscillation in suspension, to refuse to choose one positionality over the other.

Like other masochistic male figures in this study, Peter's crisis is characterized by the fact that it cannot be resolved; Roth represents him as a subject perpetually in crisis and, as such, akin to the subjectivity of the moral masochist. As Kaja Silverman argues (reading Freud on moral masochism), the moral masochist must live in unabated suspense, both the "cure" for, and expression of, his perverse pleasure forever deferred; this suspense "has a double face. It signifies both the endless postponement of libidinal gratification, and the perpetual state of anxiety and apprehension which is the result of that renunciation and of the super-ego's relentless surveillance" (Silverman, *Male Subjectivity* 200). The moral masochist, according to Freud, "must do what is inexpedient, must act against his own interests, must ruin the prospects which open out to him in the real world and must, perhaps, destroy his own real existence" ("The Economic Problem of Masochism" 169–70). As Silverman and others have noted, this description of masochism sounds an awful lot like a description of the everyday bargains made by the individual subject in the interests of civilization and society, particularly in a culture, like ours, where self-denial often bestows a kind of heroism on its practitioners. But, within the culture that Roth describes—a culture dominated by a consumerist ethos and the production of normative masculinity as the sole provider of the economic resources that fuel that ethos—Peter appears as singular, special, uniquely traumatized by his rebellion against its norms. Again and again, Peter flogs himself with his inability to "be a man," and his failures thus become evidence of his rebellion and his wounds.

The two stories Roth has Tarnopol write are the sole literary production of this paralyzed author, whose emotional and psychological traumas constipate his literary production. Tarnopol, often referring to himself as "hysterical," endures a writer's block which produces the somatic symptoms that bleed over from his "True Story" into the "Useful Fictions" he writes as a kind of therapy. At the apex of his author-surrogate's hysterical collapse, Roth has Peter's body somatize his frustrations over his creative constipation by afflicting him with a bout of diarrhea; all bodily fluids released in a torment of an inevitable expressivity, Peter is humiliated, sickened, and soiled: "I was sitting on the seat, watery feces running from me, sweating and simultaneously trembling as though I were packed in ice; every few minutes my head rolled to the side and I retched in the direction of the sink" (106). As his older, paternal, and leftist brother Morris diagnoses him, Peter is a "poor, pussywhipped bastard" (126), a "frail flower" (124) whose "hypersensitivity" makes him incapable of resisting the pull of victimized women. For, what produces his writer's block and its somatic symptoms is his wife Maureen, and her desire to embroil Peter in a masculine normativity that Roth represents as dangerous not only to his creative imagination but to his psychological and bodily well-being as well.

The trauma Roth represents here is both political and personal, as Peter rebels against a dominant construction of masculinity and expresses a resolutely antipolitical aesthetic dysfunction. Ingeniously, Roth uses Peter's writing to work out these contradictions; but rather than resolving his crisis, the two stories he writes instead perpetuate it. Displacing his economic, social, and political angst onto a textual realm, Peter's stories express his trauma as a literal, bodily wounding, which works to further consolidate his position as the victim of a "sexual system of justice" and the "myth of male inviolability." Under the guise of exploring why it is that Peter is drawn so inexorably and masochistically to wounded and difficult women, the stories actually undermine women's claims to victimization. Further, in a dynamic that should by now be familiar, the stories reproduce the very conflict between "real men" and feminized artists that they might be meant to resolve. The protagonist Peter creates, Nathan Zuckerman, condenses his creator's story down to its key elements.

"Courting Disaster,"[14] the longer and more interesting of the two stories, plays around with the cultural image of the effete Jewish intellectual/artist, whose unmuscled and pale body signifies a life of the mind far removed from the pleasures and problems of material existence. Laboring to differentiate himself from this haunting image, Zuckerman exercises his body as well as his mind, having learned in childhood the humiliations attendant upon bodily deficiency.[15] Instead of facilitating an integration of body with mind, however, Zuckerman's anxieties work to reproduce a construction of creativity, mind, and authorship as disembodied—and it is this that guarantees the "masculinity" of the artistic endeavor. Associations with the flesh, like associations with "poetry," threaten to feminize Zuckerman, and, thus, the story repeats the main narrative's anxieties about the opposition between "being a man" and being an artist. Zuckerman works out and, when in the army, joins the MPs, in order to make himself over into a "humanist with a swagger, an English teacher with a billy club" (51). Not unlike *Dead Poets Society,* in which poetry is insistently associated with action, heterosexuality, and virility, here the male author who is "feminized . . . by the practice of writing itself, that is, by his association with the cultural and artistic sphere" (Savran 67) must be remasculinized in the most hyperbolic terms. But the very fact of Zuckerman's hypermasculinity ("they did not make sissy invalids into MPs, that was for sure" [51]) marks it as an absurd overcompensation. Further, as if Tarnopol's own hysteria must necessarily spill over into his textual productions, Zuckerman's fragile bargain with his gender identity gets shattered by the unexplained arrival of migraine headaches, an illness that the story pretty clearly diagnoses as hysterical. These psychosomatic pains confirm what Zuckerman fears (in typical Roth fashion) is his "true" identity, as a "college genius (and Jewboy)" (51).[16]

The headaches in "Courting Disaster" represent a somatization of the despair and pain Peter suffers in his marriage: they are the displaced bodily manifestation of the creative and psychic wounds Maureen inflicts upon him, and are meant to materialize and make more convincing those wounds. Tarnopol's offering of these stories to various readers enables him to stage a kind of masochistic spectacle for those to whom he appeals for sympathy. In "My True Story," the painful pleasure such wounds and humiliations afford culminates when Peter dons Maureen's underwear, and then furtively leaves deposits of his sperm in locations all over town. Resisting Maureen's marking of his subjectivity and body as male, he uses that body to mark objects (books, friends' homes, phone payments) as extensions of himself. Spraying like a cat, he literalizes the metaphor of writing the male body, the penis substituting for the pen he can no longer wield successfully. He then produces this tale for his psychiatrist, in an effort to represent himself as vulnerable, wounded, victimized. Playing Dimmesdale to Spielvogel's Chillingworth (203), Peter's analysis is more like a self-flagellation than a cure, as the weakened and feminized artist ("unmanned" by Maureen [212]) faces the paternal authority, confesses to a "bloody scourge" (to quote Hawthorne), and collapses into a masochistic heap.[17] Not surprisingly, Peter finds himself drawn to masochistic narratives, as when he realizes that the syllabus for a course he's teaching, which includes *The Scarlet Letter* among other texts, "derived of course from the professor's steadily expanding extracurricular interest in the subject of transgression and punishment" (233).

As the age-old image of the suffering (male) artist suggests, the mythology of a powerful-vulnerable male author is nothing new, but Roth (along with Irving and King, as we will see) gives it a new spin, clothing this old image in the language of collective injuries publicized by the liberation and countercultural movements of this era. Exploring the pains of his author-surrogate's fall from disembodied creativity into a forced materiality, Roth's novel laments the loss of an older political and cultural order, without, of course, exactly acknowledging that culture and politics have anything to do with one another. But, along with mourning the passing of a particular construction of authorship, and the masculinity it figures, the novel also gives the devil his due by dwelling on the seemingly irresistible spectacle of a male body and male mind in pain. In this way, the novel surprisingly admits that disembodiment and a dematerialized life of the mind might carry its costs in social and political visibility; with the rise of identity politics and new attention given to the body writing (from feminists among others), the fiction of disembodied creativity appears as an anachronism, a nostalgic and hopelessly outdated desire for the truths of a bygone era. It is this anachronistic quality that, in my view, is at the center of Roth's own relationship to his author-surrogate, what enables him to simultaneously identify with and distance himself from Tarnopol. Finally, in Roth's representation of Peter Tarnopol, the hopelessly nostalgic pales in comparison to the appealingly masochistic, and what emerges from the novel is a new construction of the white male author as wounded by the social and cultural shifts of his era, but newly energized by those wounds. By the end of the novel, Maureen is dead, and Susan is recovering from a suicide attempt. Peter is writing and revitalized, precisely by what might be considered his "feminization": his sojourn into the bodily, the victimized, the wounded. He might remain haunted by Maureen, but her blood fuels his art: he has *incorporated* her.

RAPISTS, FEMINISTS, AND *THE WORLD ACCORDING TO GARP:* INAUTHENTIC VERSUS AUTHENTIC TRAUMAS

The scene in *My Life as a Man* in which Peter retches over the toilet while "watery feces" run down his leg (106) is juxtaposed with a description of literary production out of control. Peter confesses that "the pounds and pounds of pages" he has produced trying to express the emotional trauma of his marriage to Maureen have amounted to little more than wasted effort, a kind of literary diarrhea through which his creative energies are sapped. Peter's problems with writing stem from his obsession with, and victimization by, Maureen, who is represented as a brute fact of material life that impedes the expression of his "soul." In *The World According to Garp*, the white male author, far from spewing out worthless pages in a futile therapeutic effort, suffers a constipation of authorship. Garp's anal-retentive attitude toward literary production stems, in large part, from his ambivalent relationship with his mother, the famous feminist author, Jenny Fields. Jenny's fantastically successful feminist tome, *A Sexual Suspect,* is represented more as a bodily outpouring than a creative endeavor; Garp jealously carps that he, unlike his mother, "had no subject that could spill out of him in this fashion. Imagination, he realized, came harder than memory" (124). *A Sexual Suspect,* in Garp's opinion, had "the same literary merit as the Sears, Roebuck catalog" (13).[18] As this comment suggests, mass-produced feminist writing is aligned with commodity culture and posed against the scarce, and thus infinitely more valuable, literary production Garp ekes out. The fact that Jenny's words just pour out of her without her rational or creative control is linked in the novel with the more general connection between women, materiality, and bodily production, and its complementary connection between men, abstraction, and creative production. Like Maureen Tarnopol, whose faked pregnancy Peter reads as "*her* art of fiction," her " 'creativity' gone awry" (Roth 191), women in *The World According to Garp* are allowed expression only through the material body; for instance, in order to get over their son Walt's death, Garp's wife Helen is "delivered from the insanity of grief" by the birth of a third child, while "Garp's deliverance from the same insanity" is the birth of a third novel (443–44).

But not only are women disqualified from proper participation in the realm of masculine, abstract, creative production; they are often represented as poor readers, too literal-minded to appreciate the abstract and the creative.[19] Jenny gives up studying English literature for nursing, and sees the hospital environment as comforting because so starkly concrete: "She liked how the hospital reduced everything to what one ate, if it helped one to have eaten it, and where it went" (5). This lowest-common-denominator materialism represents a failure of imagination in Irving's novel, where life and art are kept resolutely separate, and "what was 'going on' " in the world "was never as important as what [Garp] is making up. . . . One of the things that upset him about his mother (since she had been adopted by women's politics) was that she was always discussing the *news*" (190). Like the subordination of the political—and, indeed, global history—to the personal in *My Life as a Man,* the battle between the news and the imagination in *The World According to Garp* articulates and develops the crisis in white masculinity as a struggle between a seemingly disembodied masculine individualism and a fiercely materialist feminist collectivism. In Irving's novel, this struggle over the social and symbolic priority of opposing epistemologies and aesthetics gets rather ingeniously displaced onto a textual battle. The novel focuses attention on the crisis in the *cultural* authority of white masculinity by representing the white male author, and the products of his creative imagination, as the wounded victims of a dangerous shift in aesthetic and interpretive norms.

While the novel is relentless in its attempts to save a masculine and dematerialized literary production from feminist attacks, it also is strangely pulled toward a literalized and materialized construction of the white male author.[20] Irving dwells so fully on the textual violations suffered by his wounded white male author that the novel is tempted toward a materialized and bodily construction of authorship even as it is invested in returning the masculine to the disembodied universal. The textual violations Garp suffers predict the physical violence that will follow from them, as Irving literalizes the effects of the wounding of white male cultural authority. Feminism, in league with commodity culture, makes the beleaguered author into a "marked man" and, indeed, paradoxically, makes dominant masculinity appear powerless. While feminists and other bad readers insist on reading literature as the embodiment of an identity politics, Garp insists on reading *criticism* as an almost physical violation of the author's work *and* his identity. Playing identity politics and the politics of victimization in a way similar to *Illiberal Education, The World According to Garp* insists that the death of the white male author (and of white male cultural authority) is literally, materially, and physically violent. The white male author becomes visible and embodied only through his wounding. Here as there, the desire to reinstate a disembodied, unmarked, and dematerialized masculine creativity competes with an impulse to position the white male author and thinker as the literally threatened and physically endangered spokesman for a passing social and cultural order. While Irving is intent upon critiquing the logics of victimization and identity politics motivating (mis)readings of Garp's fiction, the novel reproduces those logics and indulges in spectacles of trauma that rival those of the feminists Garp so violently disdains. Further, the novel's obsession with narrating scenes of bodily trauma belies the effort to separate the material from the literary, the bodily from the imaginative, the low from the high. As in *My Life as a Man, The World According to Garp* operates a series of reversals of the powerful/powerless binary and, in doing so, makes men into the wounded victims of not only feminism but of mass culture and liberationist ideology, as well.

The novel begins with the representation of a male wounding in the very first sentence, setting the stage for a lengthy exploration of the mutilations of the male body: "Garp's mother, Jenny Fields, was arrested in Boston in 1942 for wounding a man in a movie theater" (1). The death of the white male author is, quite literally, the story *The World According to Garp* tells, and it is no accident that the novel begins with a crisis in the paternal metaphor. Jenny appropriates the sperm of a critically wounded (and mentally destroyed) World War II ball turret gunner to produce the thus fatherless Garp.[21] Jenny raises Garp—mostly at the Steering School for Boys in New England, where she is school nurse—to become a writer and family man. Jenny writes a fantastically successful autobiography called *A Sexual Suspect,* which becomes a feminist classic and dwarfs Garp's own writing. Garp marries English Lit professor Helen, and they have two sons together. Garp stays at home, writing and cooking, until the death of his second son in a gruesome accident. From this death, others follow: Jenny is assassinated by a crazed redneck, Garp is assassinated by a crazed feminist. Irving treats us to the gory details of the soldier's wounding, as he will later represent in full color and detail a dog biting off Garp's ear; Garp biting off the dog's ear; Helen biting off "three quarters" of her lover Michael Milton's penis; the penetration (by Volvo gear shaft) of Duncan Garp's eye; and various less extreme mutilations. Roberta Muldoon, former tight end for the Philadelphia Eagles and current mediator between Jenny Fields and her son, has had a sex change operation, its own form of "wounding" and one that Garp can understand. What Garp, and Irving, cannot understand or countenance is the deliberate self-mutilations of the feminist women who cut off their tongues in sympathy with Ellen James, a young girl whose rapists cut off her tongue in order to silence her. These women, the novel insists, are "false" victims, their symbolic gestures empty of meaning, their wounds signifying nothing more than a wrongheaded and inhumane feminism. Against these false victims, Irving positions "authentic" male victims of bodily traumas, ending with the spectacular murder of Garp himself. These traumas are intimately connected to the novel's concern with the loss of value in literary culture: the novel represents the effects of a perceived crisis of white male authorship through the literal wounding of the author.

The textual violations Garp suffers from feminist readers and their relentless commodifications are the metaphorical precursors of the more literal, physical violations he eventually suffers at the hands of the Ellen Jamesians, Irving's contribution to popular cultural caricatures of radical feminism. Irving does feminism the dubious honor of equating it with a debased and cultish mass culture; while he grants feminism dominance over the contemporary cultural field, he also blames it for the corruption of that field. Echoing earlier anxieties over the rise of a feminized mass culture bent on destroying masculine singularity and art, Irving creates the Ellen Jamesians as a sinister embodiment of a faceless collective whose power manifests itself primarily through the self-mutilation that presages the mutilations of others.[22] The "literary" is posed against and threatened by the "material," with feminists and other "special interests" conspiring to destroy the unmarked and disembodied norm of an originary, creative, masculine individualism.[23] This is clearest in the narrative disasters fueled by the publication of Garp's third novel, *The World According to Bensenhaver*, a story of rape, retribution, and male paranoia, that is both appropriated and vilified by feminist readers. Irving uses this reception to signal feminism's ideological confusion, but also to set Garp up as a victim who must suffer the psychic wounds of misunderstanding, as well as the ideological violence done by readers who mistake fiction for "a *thesis.*" "It's a fucking *novel,*" says Garp about *Bensenhaver*, "it's a *story,* and I made it up!" (476).[24] Confusing representation with reality, such misreadings function to *mark* Garp as the embodiment of an identity (white and male), as well as marking him as the target for feminist violence.

Symbolic and real, interpretive and physical, the violence inflicted upon Garp suggests that feminists, and others who read all creative expression and indeed all identity in political terms, err by confusing the textual and the material. But *The World According to Bensenhaver* also offers the novel's most sustained representation of male violence and male pathology; it *is*, if not a thesis, then certainly a clear indictment not only of rapists but also of seemingly more benign forms of male dominance masquerading as protectionism. Further, as is characteristic of the novel's somewhat incoherent exploration of the relationship between textuality and materiality, this episode also underlines the contradictions at the heart of Garp's and, I would argue, Irving's desire to be both popular and "serious." To be popular means to cater to the debased tastes of the masses; but to be "serious" means to deprive oneself of an audience altogether. Although Garp has instructed his agent John Wolf to treat this novel as a hot property to be sold to the highest bidder on the vulgar marketplace—an excerpt appears in the porno mag *Crotch Shots*—he nevertheless positions himself as the victim of a mass culture Irving imagines to be in league with feminist interests. Jenny's book and the mass movement it immediately inspires represents the antithesis of everything Garp and Irving hold holy about fiction. As George Roy Hill's 1982 film has it—in the only nod to the novel's concern with such questions—Jenny's "a cult, not a writer," and her book is "timely." This verdict has more than a little in common with the oft-repeated indictment of academic feminism, and "theory" in general, as the latest fad, a passing fashion that will do little residual damage to the aesthetic and interpretive traditions it now threatens. Yet, as we saw in chapter 2, and as we can see here as well, there is a good deal of evidence to suggest that the crisis of white male authorship and cultural "standards" goes far deeper than that. Not only can we discern some uncertainty about the survival of the "tradition," but we can also glimpse some signs that announcements and enactments of crisis themselves work to remap the cultural and interpretive terrain.

Confusing the real with the symbolic, the personal with the political, the Ellen Jamesians are posed against the original Ellen James, the prototype of the innocent victim who is elevated to almost heroic status in opposition to those who claim to be her followers. The difference between Ellen James and the Ellen Jamesians is coded in familiar terms: Ellen's trauma is authentic because personal; the Ellen Jamesians' trauma is false because political. When Ellen James shows Garp an essay she has written entitled "Why I'm Not an Ellen Jamesian," Garp approves: the essay "made what the Ellen Jamesians did seem like a shallow, wholly political imitation of a very private trauma. Ellen James said that the Ellen Jamesians had only prolonged her anguish; they had made her into a very public casualty" (538).[25] The narrator, "to be fair," goes on and qualifies this disapproval, noting that there are "authentic" imitators of Ellen, as well as "false" ones. Again, the distinction rests on an opposition between personal and political: "For many of the Ellen Jamesians, the imitation of the horrible untonguing had not been 'wholly political.' It had been a most personal identification. In some cases, of course, Ellen Jamesians were women who had also been raped; what they meant was that they *felt* as if their tongues were gone. In a world of men, they felt as if they had been shut up forever" (538–39).

In articulating the social commentary of the Ellen Jamesians as an *imitation*, Irving more deeply entrenches the distinction between (artistic) originality and (political) sham. The genuine Ellen, it turns out, is a poet who expresses her outrage in the more acceptable and sublimated form of artistic creation.

The World According to Garp is no simply antifeminist novel, but its ambivalently feminist politics are complicated. Irving clearly wants to meet feminism on its own terms and articulate a critique that avoids throwing out the baby with the bathwater. What interests me so much in this effort—and why this novel is so central to the articulation of a feminist-produced crisis in dominant masculinity—is how the novel bumps up against a number of contradictions in the process. Those contradictions all have to do with the relationship between the symbolic and real, the imaginative and material, the political and the personal—binaries that *The World According to Garp* inherits to be sure, but reconstructs in striking ways. The extended analogy between rapists and feminists is the route toward this end. The novel is as compulsively concerned with rape as it is with feminism, and even goes so far as to suggest that feminism and rape are two symptoms of the same malady: the elevation of the collective over the individual, the political over the personal.

Both rapists and feminists are responsible for violations of the personal. Where rapists fail to respect personal, bodily boundaries, feminists err in reading all such personal, bodily boundaries through a political lens. Irving frames feminism as a crime of violence against men and against the authentic personal, a crime that is akin to rape, and one that reduces gender to a bodily essence: for Irving, both feminists and rapists turn bodies into the terrain of power struggles. Feminists obsess about the body, as they threaten to turn Garp into a gendered, embodied being in order to insert him in their narratives of rape, brutality, and domination. Men are lumped into one category by feminists, and a category defined *not* by a relation to social, political, or cultural power, but by the mere presence or absence of a penis. Rapists misread women as rapable, and feminists misread men as (potential) rapists. Both rapists and feminists, thus, reduce human beings to bodily essences—orifices and penises. For instance, one of the "wounded women" who seeks safe haven at Jenny's hospital misrecognizes the wounded and grief-stricken Duncan Garp as a phallic and threatening presence, even in his castrated state: "even little boys like to paw you over with their eyes—even with *one* eye. . . . This is just the kind of routine I had to get away from. Some *man* bullying me all the time, some ding-dong threatening me with his big-prick violence" (390–91). The reader is primed to savage this woman, and thus the text manipulates us into assenting to Garp's response, which is a sentence of rape: "Fuck you to death" (391). That this woman meekly goes when her redneck boyfriend comes for her just shows how shallow such "political" convictions are. This, perhaps, should come as no surprise in a novel in which the woman claimed as a feminist hero rejects the label: Jenny "felt discomfort at the word *feminism*. She was not sure what it meant, but the *word* reminded her of feminine hygiene and the Valentine treatment [for syphilis]" (185). Jenny confuses the political with the bodily, a movement for sexual equality with the treatment of a sexually transmitted disease. The great feminist heroine, then, manages to make nonsense out of the feminist slogan, "the personal is the political." For Irving, the political is the petty, and feminism's greatest sin is its misunderstanding of the personal.

Feminists are guilty of objectifying Garp, and this objectification endangers his relation to a masculine norm on several fronts. But Irving plays this objectification for all it is worth; rather than working to remasculinize Garp, the novel instead seems to move in the opposite direction, piling wounds and humiliations on top of each other and reveling in the textual and physical violations suffered by this marked man. While the novel clearly laments the forced embodiment of men in general (and Garp in particular), it, too, ultimately reduces male privilege to a question of body parts and physical "expressions" of male privilege. Rape is the *only* crime against women explored in this novel, and so Irving unwittingly reproduces the very logic he is intent upon displacing. We can see this in an editorial aside in which anger about rape mutates into dismay at the "all men are potential rapists" logic that marks all men as guilty: "Perhaps rape's offensiveness to Garp," the narrator editorializes, "was that it was an act that disgusted him with himself—with his own very male instincts, which were otherwise so unassailable. He never felt like raping anyone; but rape, Garp thought, made men feel guilt by association" (209). Rape is offensive because it makes all men feel guilty, because it *marks* all men as potential rapists. This comment suggests that rape bothers Garp not only, or even primarily, because it hurts women, but because it demonstrates that those "otherwise so unassailable" male instincts, whatever those might be, can so easily be perverted. In other words, rape is a crime against men because, like feminism, it points to the fact that the "unassailable male instincts" are directed toward power, conquest, and violence.

But more is at stake here, for the novel is invested in both acknowledging and disavowing the logic of the feminist claim that all men are potential rapists; that is, the novel entertains feminist thinking only in order to incorporate it into a more individualist and personalizing humanism. Like Michael Crichton's claim that (false) accusations of sexual harassment and rape produce a "fear that only men can know," and a fear as bad as, if not worse than, the fear of harassment itself (see chapter 2), Irving's representation of the "rape" of male bodies—their penetration by various phallic objects—projects onto men an equal status as victims of sexualized and gendered violence. The excess of wounded male bodies in the novel functions to divert attention away from male bodies as phallic weapons. The novel is as obsessed with the bodily traumas of white men as it is with rape. This is no mere coincidence; as we saw in the previous chapter, a perceived loss of male power precipitates an exploration of symbolic "rapes" of male bodies. Garp's father, for example, has been "penetrated" by shrapnel. The narrator describes the case of a man "whose head had been similarly penetrated. He'd been fine for months, just talking to himself and occasionally peeing in his bed. Then he started to lose his hair; he had trouble completing his sentences. Just before he died, he began to develop breasts[!]" (24). Once a penetration is suffered, then other attributes of masculinity—and, particularly, bodily signs of it—go the direction of femininity. In the elder Garp's case, he retains a bit of his masculine dignity as long as he is able to get his "especially large erection[s]" (21), and succeed in ejaculating—an activity with which he has been occupied since his wounding. In a move which anticipates King's representation of "crippled" prose in *Misery,* Irving has the ball turret gunner progressively lose the little speech he has left: when first brought to Jenny's hospital his only word is "Garp," which deteriorates to "Arp," then to "Aaaa." But his true deterioration comes when "he had no more erections" (29). The novel finds humor in this gradual but extreme emasculation, but the younger Garp seems intent on recuperating the masculinity so finally compromised in his father's story. Jenny has reduced Garp *père* to the lowest common denominator of his bodily existence—his sperm; and Garp *fils* will fight back with a good deal of energy. When told that his father died when Jenny was off duty, he replies: "When *else* could he have died? . . . With my mother off duty was the only way he could escape" (29). As Jenny describes it, the senior Garp regresses to infancy and then dies.

Technical Sergeant Garp and his fellow soldiers are authentic victims whose bodies (and body parts) are sacrificed for an identifiable and worthy cause. In the postwar world, however, such causes become increasingly rare, if the idea of a "cause" is not altogether vulgarized by the legions of inauthentic victims clamoring for attention. Janice Doane and Devon Hodges note that these mutilations speak to the fear of castration prevalent in the novel: "This fear is represented when Helen bites off Michael Milton's penis; but more threatening to Garp is the graphic equation of castration and silence in the figures of the Ellen Jamesians" (72). That these figures are, indeed, threatening to Garp is evidenced by his extreme hostility toward them—a hostility that is ultimately justified by the fact that he is "assassinated" by an Ellen Jamesian. But Garp's hostility has more to do with his disdain for their "sour" public imitation of a personal trauma than with fearing an identification with tongueless women. In fact, positing an identification between Garp and victimized women enables Irving to position his white male author figure as a true victim, despite (or even because of) his "natural" male impulse toward sexual domination, if not vio-

lence. In disqualifying the Ellen Jamesians as "authentic" victims, Irving simultaneously authorizes Garp, his sons, and even Michael Milton as the "real" victims. The spectacle of the white male body in pain, then, works to displace feminists (and, indeed, all "unraped" women) from a position of personal *and*
political authority, while installing white men (and boys) in the morally unassailable position of victim.

This move is even more fully evident in George Roy Hill's film based on Irving's novel. Weirdly, the film manages to both underline and under*mine* the
novel's engagement with feminism, with the effect that Hill retains the attack
on feminism but jettisons the novel's uncomfortable recognition of the need
for attacks on male dominance—at least as male dominance is manifested in
rape. The film mourns the death of the paternal metaphor far more compulsively than the novel does by extending into a general cultural trend Jenny's
cold-blooded reduction of the father to a biological essence unfortunately necessary for the production of children, but not significant in any other way. Not
only is the young Garp obsessed with his dead father, but the only jokes anyone
ever tells in the film have to do with the reduction of fatherhood to the biological. Where the novel suggests that Garp does, in fact, resent his mother's un-
conventional reproductive strategy, the film makes Jenny (played by the daunt-
ing and often scary Glenn Close) even more of a villain in this scenario. Garp
balks against Jenny's reduction of his father to a sperm delivery system, and the
battle over the dead father's place in the family produces all the strife between
mother and son. Obsessed with recovering some connection to the father,
young Garp gets into numerous scrapes in his attempts to approximate that father's mysterious and romantic identity as a "Flyer." In one scene, where a
young Garp is grilling Jenny in what the film suggests is a habitual conversation, Jenny rather coldly mocks him for even wanting a father: "All the other
kids have trenchmouth, too," she says in response to his plaint that fatherless-
ness marks him as an oddball; "do you want that, too?" Garp's obsession with
his missing father is echoed and reinforced by the fact that, in several different
scenes, Steering boys are heard making jokes about fathering: "Why can't a basketball player father a child? Because he dribbles before he shoots." Repeated in
several contexts, with different examples of impotent fathers, these jokes reduce fatherhood to biological maleness and mock Garp's merely incidental pa-
ternity. Fathering is only a joke in this film, and the pathos of Garp's desire for
the missing father—coupled with his own virtuoso performance as a sensitive
and devoted, if slightly obsessive, father—suggests that Jenny's particular
brand of feminism, like the demonized Ellen Jamesians, is responsible for the
general cultural condition that favors women over men, mothers over fathers.

Equating fatherhood with trenchmouth is only one of the ways in which the
film stresses Jenny's strident and reductive feminism as the sum total of her

character. When Jenny tells Dean Bodger of the odd circumstances of Garp's conception, he bursts out with "You raped him! You raped a dying man!" Now, while what Jenny did with and to Garp *père* might conceivably be considered a "rape"—particularly in a story that returns compulsively to representations of rape—the film does not, in fact, dwell on rape. What is most striking about the film's rescripting of Irving's novel is its almost total erasure of rape as an issue and, with it, any evidence of the *need* for feminism. As I've said, the novel trips over the question of whether male dominance is expressed socially or biologically, politically or physically, concluding (more or less) that rape is the only evidence of male dominance. In the process, the novel makes feminists appear as guilty of physical "dominance" as rapists, and more guilty by far than men who are not rapists. But the film offers absolutely no evidence in support of Jenny's feminist views: women hold all the cards in this film and, except for the real Ellen James, no women are raped, beaten, or otherwise traumatized by men. Instead of writing *The World According to Bensenhaver,* Hill's Garp (played by a cute and cuddly Robin Williams) writes a nonfictional, book-length polemical attack on the Ellen Jamesians called *Ellen;* no girl gets raped in the park; no men threaten Roberta Muldoon by wishing that she be "gang-raped" in payment for her "perverted" and treacherous abandonment of male privilege via "castration." The film reserves the word "rape" as a stick with which to beat feminists who, against all evidence, insist on reading men as the embodiment of violence and power.

And beat them it does. Jenny is represented as not only asexual but violently antisexual, while Garp's desire to sleep with any woman who happens along is represented as "natural." Jenny's tirades against male lust, moreover, are here rewritten to point toward lust as a *human* and natural impulse—experienced equally by men and women. The human is opposed to the feminist, and feminist ideology is caricatured as a single-minded and life-denying obsession with rooting out lust, sex, and happiness wherever it grows. When Helen's father Ernie tries to assure Jenny that the developing attraction between their children is only natural, Jenny curtly replies, "disease is 'natural,' too, but that doesn't mean we have to give in to it." As we will see in more detail in chapter 5, the opposition between the feminist and the "natural," particularly in sexual matters, experiences something of a resurgence in post-liberationist American culture; here, feminism is clearly positioned against nature much in the way that Irving's novel positions feminism against culture. Hill's rereading (misreading?) of Irving's beef with feminism makes the film far more of a "backlash" against feminism than the novel is. In fact, as I've suggested, the novel is less symptomatic of a backlash than it is of a desire to remake masculinity in a postfeminist mold. The film sanctifies Garp until all evidence of Irving's complex portrayal of white masculinity in crisis disappears. Garp indulges in only

one minor infidelity—with a babysitter whose age (a legal eighteen) he's careful to establish—an infidelity represented as spontaneous, impulsive, the "natural" expression of a rowdy but somehow innocent male sexuality. Helen, on
the other hand, engages in a lengthy and calculatedly cold affair with Michael
Milton which contrasts with Garp's fling in a number of ways. Helen appears to
take no pleasure whatsoever in this affair—Helen, along with Jenny, is pretty
cold and lifeless throughout the entire film, in any event—and the film offers
no explanation for why she strays. In the novel, Irving represents Helen's affair
as a payment in kind for Garp's numerous infidelities (he titles one chapter "It
Happens to Helen"), and distributes blame equally between Helen and Garp
for what happens in the horrifying car accident in which Walt dies. The film
lays the bulk of the blame on Helen, in part by contrasting the sexual exchange
in Michael's car with the earlier and far more bucolic sexual exchange between
Garp and the babysitter, also in a car.

We see no men treating women badly in the film; we only hear feminists
claiming that men treat women badly. In contrast, we see women behaving
very badly indeed, from Helen on down to the murderous Pooh Percy. Although Hill has cut out a massive portion of Irving's narrative, he retains nearly all the scenes of female violence against men, including the scene where Garp
is attacked at his own mother's funeral—to be rescued, in the film, by the mute,
delicate, and intensely grateful Ellen James who, clutching a copy of Garp's
Ellen, sanctifies the wounded writer even more. The film has little interest in
the cultural politics that occupy the novel, downplaying Garp's angst over his
mother's writing and the textual violations that come from the misreading of
his own work. What is so much more interesting about the novel—along with
the sheer force of its epic qualities not even attempted by the film—are the
ways in which Irving parallels the story of this one white male author with the
story of an order of cultural politics in crisis. The four years between the publication of the novel and the release of the film might go some distance in ex-
plaining the film's failure to engage more actively with the feminist discourses
and positions the novel grapples with; by 1982 a backlash against feminism was
already becoming evident, and by 1987, Glenn Close's Jenny would mutate into
Alex Forrest, that quintessential figure of frightening and homicidal feminism
in *Fatal Attraction*. The film makes the novel appear positively, rather than ambivalently, feminist, and this is one instance where it seems that Hollywood
seems intent upon orchestrating a backlash against feminism. As I've suggested, Irving's middlebrow novel is far more torn than this.

As in Roth's novel, the traumas of embodiment narrated by Irving all stem,
directly and indirectly, from feminism's critique of masculinity as a gendered,
embodied category, rather than as the category of humanity per se. In the later
novel, the opposition between the material-feminine and creative-masculine

gives way to an opposition between the political-feminist and personal-humanist in a move that attempts to erase masculine specificity entirely. Such an attempt was bound to fail in a novel so concerned with bodily traumas which are all, in one way or another, *gendered*. Indeed, it is gender per se—or, rather, the politicization of gender—that wounds in this novel. As Irving has said, "I wanted to make [*Garp*] a sort of fierce sexual argument, in favor of individualism really, saying that we are a society beset with groups and group misunderstandings" (Priestley 493). Yet why is it that the only "group" Irving ends up criticizing is feminism, and a feminism of the most caricatured sort? Like the conservative critics of the academy who arrogate to themselves a space *outside* of struggles over identity and cultural value by laying claim to a universalized and seemingly disembodied creative or intellectual tradition, Irving's novel attempts to erase the marks scripted (by feminists and others) onto the body of the white male author. But, as we've seen, such attempts almost irresistibly plunge white men back into the crisis that that erasure was meant to resolve. In other words, if white masculinity has been placed in crisis by making white men feel and act as if they are "marked men," then the very announcements and enactments of crisis that are meant as a first step toward recuperation and resolution actually function to perpetuate that crisis.

Moreover, there is clearly a payoff that comes from the representation of white male bodies, minds, and psyches at risk; masochistic or otherwise, such representations offer a pleasure that is partly dependent on occupying the coveted position of the beleaguered individualist, and partly dependent on occupying exactly the position claimed by the white man's "others": the position of oppressed, minoritized, and embodied difference. Marked men are made visible not only as the gendered and racialized embodiment of a cultural tradition under attack; but visible, as well, as the wounded and empathic embodiment of oppression itself. There is more going on here than a simple "appropriation" of a position that belongs to, is the rightful property of, someone else; indeed, the very idea that some subjects or some collectives "own" victimization or wounding makes it difficult to see how white men are fully engaged in, rather than outside of, the identity politics and politics of victimization that Irving and others might claim. Reading against the grain of such texts, I am insisting that the paradoxes and contradictions that characterize "backlash" against feminism and other liberationist discourses and movements make of the current crisis in white masculinity the ground for new, rather than the effect of old, configurations of gender and racial centrality/marginality in American culture. The use of the metaphor of "rape" to connect wounded minds, the violence to free expression caused by politically correct speech, and the actual physical violence of bodies in pain suggests quite forcibly that the literal and the metaphorical, the somatic and the social, the personal and the political, the material and the abstract are all mixed up and perhaps inevitably so. Irving's attempt to separate the authentic from the political, the individual from the collective, and the feminist from the humanist crashes against a seemingly irresistible pull in the other direction: to claim the imbrication of the personal and the political, and to reembody white masculinity despite the threats to cultural priority that embodiment heralds.

"EXERCISING EDITORIAL AUTHORITY OVER HIS BODY":
THE CRIPPLING OF BODY AND TEXT IN STEPHEN KING'S *MISERY*

Stephen King's *Misery* takes the wounding of the white male author to a materialized extreme and, in the process, touches on most of the thematics I've explored in Roth and Irving. Although King arguably embodies the mass culture that both Roth and Irving position themselves against, it seems more accurate to say that the phenomenon of Stephen King and other "brand name authors" like him has altered the cultural landscape so fully and permanently that the very categories on which Roth and Irving stake their claims to cultural authority have eroded almost entirely—including the construction of autonomous, masculine authorship.[26] Now fully positioned within the middlebrow—his books habitually reviewed by the *New York Times Book Review* and criticism of his work a veritable cottage industry within the increasingly respectable subfield of popular culture studies—King has, over the course of his fecund career, worked indefatigably to reshape the middlebrow so that he could find a place within it. Endowing named chairs in English departments, sprinkling his novels with references to other middlebrow writers, and generally theorizing about the place of genre fiction in the American cultural marketplace, King has made his mark on the middlebrow in such a way as to erode the always fragile boundaries separating the "serious" from the "popular." *Misery,* published in 1987, is a pivotal text not only within King's career and his movement into the middlebrow, but within American middlebrow culture itself; for this novel articulates fully and explicitly the crisis of cultural politics as it is played out within a crisis of masculinity.[27] It is precisely the project of *Misery* to carve out a middlebrow space for King's author-surrogate, Paul Sheldon, and it is in line with the logics I've been attending to throughout this study that that position is one of vulnerability, crisis, and pain. The plot of *Misery* enacts Paul Sheldon's rise from a feminized mass culture into a more properly masculinized middlebrow, and it is, significantly, through the defeat of a bodily, devouring femininity that this ascent is accomplished. Yet the novel is full of the ambivalence that comes both from a rejection of mass culture *and* the surrendering of that culture to the feminine.

If *Misery* announces King's arrival into the middlebrow, he arrives as a marked man; like the beleaguered author figures in Roth and Irving, King's surrogate is traumatized by the textual and physical violations that attend the coming into visibility of the white male authorial body. As in *The World According to Garp*, the most urgent threat to white masculinity in this novel comes from the vulnerability involved in writing and the trauma produced by misreadings. While Annie Wilkes, a monstrous woman reader, is not represented as "feminist," it's clear that her victimization of Paul is a gendered violation, as well as a violation of gender. Where both Roth and Irving imagine a politicized discourse of gender as the main threat to a construction of disembodied, universalized authorship and masculine cultural authority, King's novel zeroes in on the other major threat: the rise of consumer culture and the consequent "feminization" of the cultural sphere. *Misery* represents a white male author held captive by and to a woman who threatens not only his life and his sanity but an entire order of cultural politics: Annie Wilkes, romance reader and psychopath, represents the revenge of the popular on the serious, and it is no coincidence that the "popular" is here represented as a debased and devouring feminine. Echoing Andreas Huyssen's characterization of an earlier construction of mass culture as feminine, *Misery* literalizes and materializes the threat of that feminized mass in a way perhaps not seen since Nathanael West's *The Day of the Locust*. King's author-surrogate Paul Sheldon meets in Annie Wilkes "the nightmare of being devoured by mass culture through co-optation, commodification, and the 'wrong' kind of success"; but, rather than "fortifying the boundaries between genuine art and inauthentic mass culture" (Huyssen 196), as Huyssen suggests the modernist artist does, King pushes further toward a full erosion of those boundaries. Like Peter Tarnopol and T. S. Garp, Paul Sheldon experiences a savage embodiment, as a crazed female reader insists on reading too literally his creative productions; but *Misery* is quite distinct from the other two novels in that King's investment in eroding the boundaries between the "serious" and the "popular" compels him to explore the parallel breach of the boundaries between the masculine and the feminine, the abstract and the material. In *Misery,* King enacts a battle between these seemingly opposing forces that, while ultimately destroying the feminine and, thus, masculinizing the "popular," also produces a good deal of male trouble in the process. Not only does Paul suffer spectacular humiliations and disempowerments as his female audience/captor subjects him to a forced and savage embodiment; but he also indulges in a good deal of *self*-flagellation in a display that works to perpetuate the pain caused by Annie. The crisis in white male authorship the novel literalizes never gets fully resolved; on the contrary, King uses the crisis to reembody white male authorship and to, somewhat indirectly, answer those critics whose feminist displeasure with his representation of wo-

men makes him both humble and, as we will see, defiant.[28] By launching a critique of a feminized mass culture from *within* that mass culture, King's novel
adds a whole new dimension to the debates over cultural hierarchy in America.

The plot of *Misery* ingeniously conflates the physical wounding of an individual white male author with the cultural trauma caused by a female audience
whose insatiable demands threaten to destroy authentic cultural value in their
relentless pursuit of the "fix" of popular romances.[29] Paul Sheldon, having just
finished his "real" novel, *Fast Cars*—a novel as far removed from his popular
Misery romance series as the masculine is from the feminine and art from
trash—is "rescued" from a car wreck by his "number one fan," Annie Wilkes, an
overweight ex-nurse whose joy in life is her rabid consumption of, and devotion to, Sheldon's *Misery* novels. Unbeknownst to Annie, Sheldon has killed off
the character Misery in what he planned as the last installment of the series.
Annie reads *Fast Cars,* determines it "trash," requires Paul to burn it by threatening to cut off his pain medication, then demands that he find a way to bring
Misery back to life in a new novel. As the writing of *Misery's Return* progresses,
Annie threatens to cut off a good number of other things. In the course of the
novel, Sheldon is subjected to a series of physical and emotional mutilations at
the hands of his "number one fan." Different in degree but not in kind from
other *Misery* readers—90 percent of whom are female—Annie suffers from the
kind of "radical reader involvement" (251) that, as in Irving's novel, confuses
the textual with the material. Like the feminist readers in *The World According
to Garp,* who forcefully impose their materiality on the author's textuality—by
making the "dead white male author" a reality—Annie Wilkes wants not only
to control Sheldon's creative output but to "exercise editorial authority over his
body" (287). But, while Irving remains at least partially faithful to an aesthetic
credo that valorizes the abstract over the material, and the "universal" over the
"political," King abandons that credo entirely. Perhaps because of his own materialist belief that what makes writing "serious" is the necessity of paying the
bills,[30] and perhaps because of horror's tendency toward literalizing the usually imaginary, King opts for materiality over textuality and, in the process, even
further entrenches the image of the wounded white male author as the victim
of more widely cultural and social forces. Coupled with his representation of a
seemingly "feminized," vulnerably embodied male authorship in crisis, however, is a newly reconstructed, oddly literalized masculinization of the writing
process. The savagely embodied, pain-wracked male author suffers countless
bodily and psychic humiliations; but his trials also work to remasculinize writing as an *embodied* process, a process embodied as male. It is in the gaps between these two mutually exclusive positions that the novel imagines a white
masculinity made culturally powerful, and appealingly vulnerable, in new and
somewhat surprising ways.

The vulnerability of the masculine is painfully evident from the first pages of *Misery*. The novel begins with an unconscious and severely wounded Paul "being raped into life by [a] woman's stinking breath" (6), a potentially feminizing experience, but one which (as we have seen in this chapter and chapter 2) can be expropriated by the masculine. Here, Paul comes into contact with evidence of Annie's rabid consumption, later tying the detritus of her eating binge to this experience of rape. King repeats the term "rape" several times in the opening pages, stressing the gendered and sexualized form of Paul's violation. Paul is completely and utterly abased in this transaction, and this scene sets in motion the novel's exploration of the gendered meanings of embodiment, physical vulnerability, and creative strength. Annie's resuscitation is both a rape and an "infection," her rank breath and gaping mouth signifying the horrifying abyss of female bodily orifices and functions which haunts this novel, beginning with the epigraph from Nietzsche: "When you look into the abyss the abyss also looks into you." As Paul begins to recover, he suffers other "penetrations" at Annie's hands: he is, for example, unaccountably traumatized by the presence of an intravenous needle in his arm, and fears Annie "giving him an enema with a handful of Ginsu knives" (164). He also must suffer through other looks into the abyss, experiencing extreme terror when faced with Annie's mouth. Indeed, as a number of the novel's critics have pointed out, what seems to make Annie so horrifying is that she is both penetrator and hole, masculine force with feminine orifice. She is the nightmare phallic mother, nursing Paul back to health while simultaneously threatening castration at every turn.[31]

King's use of rape to describe the resuscitation numerous times within the first few chapters points not only to Paul's complete and utterly feminized disempowerment, and to Annie's arrogation of a "masculine" prerogative, but also to the strange mix of the metaphorical and literal that characterizes the novel's exploration of the textual and bodily violation of the white male author. *Misery* literalizes a number of metaphors traditionally used to distinguish (masculine) production from (feminine) consumption, and further, uses that literalization to explore the high-low cultural divide that, itself, is most often gendered. Annie is represented as a hungry consumer, whose avid desire for the next *Misery* novel is matched by her pathological appetite for unnourishing foods. Annie devours junk food and junk literature, and King represents her as a gaping hole that threatens to suck all life and substance out of Paul. What Paul recalls most about his "rape" is Annie's breath, a "dreadful mixed stench of vanilla cookies and chocolate ice cream and chicken gravy and peanut butter fudge" (5). He later witnesses, in shocked horror, the evidence of her binge eating: "A mound of lime Jell-O covered with a crack-glaze of dried whipped cream stood on top of the TV next to a two-liter bottle of Pepsi and a gravy-boat. . . . He saw her sitting in here and scooping ice-cream into her mouth, or maybe handfuls of half-congealed chicken gravy with a Pepsi chaser, simply eating and drinking in a deep depressed daze" (177–78). This nightmare vision of a large woman indiscriminately eating unhealthy or simply vulgar foods has class as well as gender reverberations: Annie appears as nothing so much as the embodiment of a pathologically uncontrolled consumer, a "white trash" figure whose mixing of Jell-O with chicken gravy indicates both a lack of "class" and an inability to control her appetite.[32]

Annie's indiscriminate eating is linked with what Paul takes to be her passive consumption of his *Misery* novels; when she's depressed, she binges on junk novels, as well as junk food and, like the bulk of Sheldon's female readership, exhibits an insatiable appetite that keeps him away from producing his "real" work. King's representation of this pathological eater-reader rather uncannily echoes the language that Janice Radway has analyzed in attacks on the growing audience of the Book-of-the-Month Club in the early part of the century. Although, in Radway's analysis, the hostility evoked by the Club points to elite culture's paranoid desire to quash an emergent middlebrow culture in part by brushing it with the taint of feminization, the language of these attacks is nearly identical to the language in which *mass* culture is demonized. As Radway describes such attacks, it becomes clear that part of what irks the elites about the consumption of popular culture is the sheer quantity of that consumption. The assumption that quantity and quality are mutually exclusive— as we saw in *The World According to Garp*—functions here to separate the connoisseur from the consumer, and to separate the masculine individual from the feminine collectivity. Pointing to the prevalence of bodily metaphors to describe the consumption of "culture," Radway notes:

In virtually all of their manifestations, these metaphors rhetorically constructed an opposition between the individual, independent reader capable of actively seeking out *real* literature and an undifferentiated mass of passive "consumers" who were satiated by their indiscriminate absorption of a wholly undifferentiated substance. Usually compared either to unnourishing food or to food considered particularly distasteful, mass-distributed, middlebrow culture was thereby demonized by its metonymic association with those who would force-feed their docile charges, that is, with women. . . . Hence, the critics' characteristic emphasis was on the book club exchange as an activity dominated by the indiscriminate distribution of pabulum (the 1920s metaphorical equivalent of today's fast food) and on the correspondingly passive consumption of distasteful, undifferentiated, oozing substances. It seems highly likely, then, that the not always faint echoes of maternal force and infantile regression encoded in these metaphors betokened the critics' deep-seated worries about the threatening surge of social and materi-

al forces that posed a challenge to the survival of the separate, elevated, purified, rational, bourgeois *male* body.   (*A Feeling* 210, 212; Radway's emphasis)

This description is so consonant with King's representation of Annie and the
cultural group for which she stands that two things become clear: first, that
the struggle over cultural hierarchy has remained gendered throughout the
twentieth century; and, second, that the struggle over cultural legitimacy continues to be analogized in bodily terms that pose creative, masculinized production against "passive" female consumption and an equally passive female
reproduction.

Like the fantasized, abject maternal body Radway invokes here, Annie figures a "terrible bogus maternity" (King 94). Force-feeding Paul food and drugs,
Annie also disciplines the author-son, teaching him to associate his transgressions with bodily pain. She is a horrible embodiment of the maternal function,
a body that is "big but not generous," with a "large but unwelcoming swell of
her bosom." "There was a feeling about her," King writes, "of clots and road-
blocks rather than welcoming orifices or even open spaces, areas of hiatus" (7).
Annie's body signals a perversion of "proper" femininity—generous, welcoming, full of holes to be filled—that threatens Paul's certainty about what constitutes proper masculinity. The "feminization" of Paul and the "masculinization"
of Annie—clear, of course, in the initial rape scenes—is far more interesting
and complex than it appears at first. While images of castration and other conventional tropes of demasculinization do appear in the novel, what pushes
Misery toward a more nuanced exploration of masculinity in crisis is its interest in Paul's experience of a new and unaccustomed embodiment. Annie's
power (and monstrousness) does not come simply from her unruly and threatening body, nor from *her* violation of the norms of gendered embodiment: she
is also monstrous because she forces *Paul* to experience a savage embodiment
and, thus, forces onto *him* a crisis in gender identity.

Annie forces Paul to live in his body, first by giving him pain killers to which
he becomes addicted; and, later, by teaching him to identify his bodily traumas
with his failures of will. In the course of the novel, Annie chops off a foot, and
a thumb; she rebreaks his legs with a hammer, and "rapes" him again with a
bucket of dirty, soapy water—in a horrifying parody of a mother washing her
child's mouth out with soap. He suffers hunger and thirst, addiction and withdrawal. He is so reduced to his bodily materiality that he willingly burns the
only copy of his manuscript of *Fast Cars* when the pain of Annie's withholding
his medication becomes too much for him. The author is savagely reembodied
in this novel, "turned into a painwracked animal with no moral options at all"
(86). Paul's gender crisis is mapped onto the crisis in authorship, and this is
where this metafictional novel gets really interesting: Paul's mutilations of

body are continuously linked with his creative impasses, as the textual and bodily merge nearly seamlessly in a portrait of white male authorship under siege.

King most ingeniously links Paul's bodily wounds with his creative impotencies through the typewriter on which Annie forces him to write *Misery's Return*. As if it weren't enough for him to have to write at gunpoint—or, in this case, axe blade—he must do so on an outmoded and extremely hostile instrument. Annie chooses for Paul an old Royal manual typewriter, signaling her isolation both from contemporary technological society and from the tools of the writing trade. Paul perceives the typewriter as an extension of Annie, describing it in almost the same terms with which he describes her: The typewriter is "as solid as the woman and also damaged; it sat there grinning with its missing tooth, promising trouble" (60). Annie creates for Paul "a kind of cripple's study" (61), and throughout the novel, we see how Paul's *prose*, as well as his body, becomes crippled. The agent of this crippling is the typewriter, as atavistically female as Annie herself. When Annie first brings it, it is missing its "N," and as the writing of *Misery's Return* progresses, it loses numerous other letters, and finally gives up the ghost entirely, forcing Paul to finish the novel in longhand. Because King "reproduces" Paul's output within the pages of his novel, mimicking the font of such a typewriter, the reader is able to witness the crippling of his prose. To further the humiliation, and to highlight his impotence and dependence, Annie is charged with filling in the "N's," completing his text, collaborating on it. After Annie chops off his thumb (the symbolism is too obvious to dwell on), Paul experiences a general impotence, of body as well as imagination. Suddenly unable to write, he "seemed to have lost some vital ingredient, and the mix had become a lot less potent as a result. He tried to blame it on the missing n, but he'd had that to contend with before, and, really, what was a missing n compared to a missing foot and now, as an extra added attraction, a missing thumb?" (256). After the Royal throws off its T and E, Paul's prose must hobble along, just as crippled as he himself is. Amputated prose follows from amputated members, and a general castration is the order of the day. When Annie tells Paul, "You're lucky I didn't cut off your man-gland. I thought of it, you know" (272), both Paul and the reader are forced to acknowledge that, in all senses except the literal, Annie has indeed cut off Paul's "man-gland." But Paul's "man-gland" is essential to his creativity, for the novel insistently embodies the male author as a phallic, if now failing, force. The pen stands in for the penis, and vice versa, and Annie would no more cut off Paul's man-gland than she would burn *Misery's Return*.

Misery so fully literalizes the "pen is penis" metaphor that it plunges Paul Sheldon into a bodily materiality that threatens to capsize a construction of masculine authorship based on abstract, disembodied "creativity." Literally comparing writing to masturbation—you "beat the typewriter instead of your meat" (244)—the novel constructs authorship as inevitably male; but this construction also works to reembody that authorship, to materialize the authorial body in such a way as to undermine the construction of disembodied authorship at the heart of elite literary culture. The phallic author, whose "writing bone" is used to "please" his female audience (112), has a power that no woman can command; but in dwelling on the embodiment of the creative imagination—the dependence of creativity on the penis—the novel paradoxically risks undermining the ideological foundations of the "natural" fit between masculinity and creativity. The visibility of the penis in these scenes of writing, if only metaphorically, makes that penis vulnerable. As a number of recent analysts of masculinity have argued, the mystique of the phallus is dependent on keeping the penis invisible; as Maxine Sheets-Johnstone puts it, "a penis remains shrouded in mystery. It is protected, hidden from sight. What is normally no more than a swag of flesh in this way gains unassailable stature and power" (quoted in Bordo, "Reading the Male Body" 698). The metaphor of author as (pro)creative god safeguards this power and stature; the representation of a flaccid and failing male body does not. Paul's writing bone is broken, his mangland on the line, and the novel's focus on these creative and sexual impotencies approaches the masochistic.

On a meta-level, as well, a good deal of masochism is evident in King's exploration of the gendering of mass culture as feminine. Paul Sheldon positions himself against a feminized mass culture, but he is so fully a *part* of that culture—indeed, one of its most valued producers—that this attitude inevitably undermines the very cultural hierarchy it was meant to uphold. King's insistence in *Misery* on representing mass culture as the place of the feminized, materialized, debased body pushes his author-surrogate into the realm of masochism. Indeed, Paul flagellates himself both for his failure to fully enter elite culture, and for his pretensions in upholding the high-low culture divide. Like Annie, who cuts and scratches herself in a classic symptom of a feminine masochism, Paul picks away at the wounds to his status as privileged bearer of an intellectualized and disembodied "art." This is clearest in a passage toward the end of the novel, where Paul ventriloquizes King's anxieties over status and bestsellerdom, mocking himself even as he mocks the institutions that perpetuate cultural hierarchy: "the increasing dismissal of his work in the critical press as that of a 'popular writer' (which was, as he understood it, one step—a small one—above that of a 'hack') had hurt him quite badly. It didn't jibe with his self-image as a Serious Writer who was only churning out these shitty romances in order to subsidize his (flourish of trumpets, please!) REAL WORK!" (286). If, as Janice Radway has argued, the "middlebrow" in American culture mediates between the "literary" and the commercial, and is defined by that me-

diation, *Misery* can be seen as enacting within the pages of one book the contours of the struggle that mediation produces—from the perspective *not* of the
elite critics of middlebrow culture, but from an author invested in finding cultural authority and legitimacy within it.

The cultural crisis the novel explores is, really, a *bookish* crisis, that is, a crisis
over the meaning of the "literary" and the "commercial," a crisis in the middlebrow. Because of this, it's interesting to note that Rob Reiner's 1990 film *Misery*
fails to register the battle over cultural legitimacy, seeing King's novel as more
"cinematic," that is, visually centered on the more easily filmable battle between Paul and Annie. Where King's novel interrogates the high-low cultural
divide, and the gendering of that divide, Reiner's film rescripts King's story as a
narrative about failed femininity and resurgent masculinity. Paul's writing is
key to the plot, but the film's thematic interest lies elsewhere. The battle between Annie (Kathy Bates, in her Oscar-winning performance) and Paul
(James Caan) is not a battle over the production and consumption of culture
and the gendered meanings of authorship; it is a battle between an inadequately feminized woman with pathetic romantic aspirations and the fully masculine cultural authority that is the object of her desires. Annie is a wide-eyed innocent, whose performances of self-effacing femininity sometimes give way to
a different kind of femininity, a homicidal, maternal femininity. The film does
not stage Paul's experience as a crisis in masculinity for it pays no attention to
the forced embodiment of the white male author and the attack on his cultural
authority produced by that forcing. While Paul is certainly wounded by Annie,
the film does not represent this wounding as a feminization or a demasculinization. Where King has Paul become addicted to pain medication—in a clear
parallel to the ways in which readers become addicted to his *Misery* novels—
Reiner has Paul secret his Novril away, saving it up to drug his captor.[33] Paul
takes his pain like a man, manfully enduring it in pursuit of a rational plan, a
larger objective. Where King's Paul "would have burned *all* his books for even a
single Novril" (50), Reiner's Paul burns his manuscript only because Annie has
doused his body with lighter fluid. No rape requires Paul's eventual remasculinization; in fact, James Caan's Paul is never in *need* of remasculinization
because he remains throughout the whole film, broken bones notwithstanding,
the very image of tough masculinity, able to withstand any pain or trauma Annie throws at him. Paul does not experience a gender crisis; rather than using
the wounded white male author to explore the crisis of cultural authority that
is the subject of King's novel, the film settles for a conventional "role reversal"
and the eventual and inevitable restoration of the "natural" order that reversal
threatened.

At times playing Paul's lover, at times playing his mother, Annie never even
approaches the status of collaborator that King's novel suggests. Annie is mere-

ly an individualized lunatic rather than an embodiment of a certain dynamic of cultural consumption. Reiner's Annie does not, in King's words, "really chow down" (177); the only scene where we see her consuming the junk food that is her trademark in the novel is when she is eating out of a bag of Cheetos, while watching "Love Connection" on TV. This scene, rather than offering an analogy between Annie's consumption of junk food and pulp fiction, instead serves to underline her failed femininity: unlike the women who win dates on "Love Connection," and unlike the women who populate romance fiction, Annie has no hopes of romance. Her pathetic confession to Paul—"When you first came here, I only loved the writer part of Paul Sheldon; now I know I love the rest of him"—works to reinforce Paul's unimpeachable masculinity and make more pathological Annie's failed femininity. While King very deliberately does *not* represent Annie as the stereotypical romance reader—the frustrated, bored woman who yearns for romance—Reiner's film has Annie waltzing around the room bubbling, so pathetically, "Misery's alive! Isn't it romantic? This whole house will be filled with romance—I'm going to put on my Liberace records!" The joke here is at Annie's, not Paul's, expense: where King implicates Paul in the production of the mass culture he's so ambivalent about, the film portrays him as somehow magically removed from that culture, as if the *Misery* novels do, in fact, spring fully formed from Paul's brow (King 56). That Reiner has Paul actually burn the completed manuscript of *Misery's Return* with the same glee with which he kills Annie further confirms the film's lack of interest in the cultural issues the novel explores. Where the novel has Paul jealously guarding the product of his "collaboration" with his insane muse and editor, the film sidesteps Paul's doubts about gender and cultural hierarchy, further entrenching the binaries the novel pulls apart: between high-low, good literature–trash, masculine-feminine, intellect-body.

The deconstruction of these binaries is central to King's entry into the middlebrow, for they are what keeps the "popular" writer outside the gates of culture. One of the most striking shifts in the novel has Annie and Paul, reader and writer, consumer and producer, moving closer together, until Paul's production of *Misery's Return* becomes not only a kind of collaboration with Annie but also precisely the kind of "escape" for which consumption of genre fiction is so often vilified. Exploring the author's "addiction" to writing, as well as the reader's addiction to reading, *Misery* works toward an erosion of the dichotomies on which cultural hierarchy depends. While, on the one hand, making Sheldon a *romance* writer rather than a horror writer creates some distance between King and his surrogate (a distance that has as much to do with gender as it does with genre), on the other hand the insistence on the feminization of mass culture causes a certain amount of male trouble for this surrogate-author and his creator. That the novel Sheldon writes under Annie's tutelage is more like a horror novel than a romance—more violent, more adventurous, arguably, more "masculine"—suggests a masculinization of mass culture, such a move does not manage to remedy the wounds to his cultural authority suffered by this aspiring middlebrow author-surrogate kept mired in the popular by his demanding female audience. Rather than simply masculinizing the text, King must also remasculinize the author—not just Paul Sheldon, but the capital A Author, the location of autonomous, creative subjectivity and, as Silverman argues, a primary site for the reproduction of normative masculinity. It is in this attempt that *Misery* both succeeds and fails, resolving the individual crisis suffered by this beleaguered and wounded white male author, but leaving the larger cultural crisis in suspension. The individual crisis of the author-surrogate parallels the larger crisis stemming from shifts in cultural hierarchy: what is at stake in struggles over cultural value, and "brow" level, is a set of distinctions separating not only the masculine from the feminine but also the disembodied, falsely universalized abstract individual from the marked, differentiated, fully embodied other. As Radway notes, the erosion of cultural hierarchy prompted by changes in the relative visibility and power of elite versus mass culture "threaten[s] to obliterate the fundamental distinction that under[writes] this entire system of privilege, that is the distinction between the material and the immaterial, between the particularities of the body and the universality of the intellect" (*Feeling* 245–46). *Misery* registers the undecidability of these oppositions and, thus, evidences a postmodern take on what is essentially a modernist problematic.[34]

Stephen King is perfectly positioned to register the ambivalences of the contemporary renegotiation of the high-low cultural divide, and *Misery* literally enacts the birth of the middlebrow out of a "collaboration" between the "literary" and the "commercial," the "serious" and the "popular." The collaboration between Paul and Annie results in a hybrid product, neither entirely "lowbrow" nor "highbrow," a gothic text that is as different from the previous *Misery* novels as it as from Paul's "serious" book, *Fast Cars*. While this new, somewhat monstrous form might appear, from the heights of the "literary," to shape the middlebrow as, in Radway's words, "an illegitimate quarter where authentic literature and true art were supposedly prostituted to alien and suspect powers" (219); from the realm of mass culture, things look slightly different. Indeed, while *Misery* does explicitly invoke the specter of "prostitution" in relation to Sheldon's production of the *Misery* novels, it does so only in order to suggest that such a view is wrongheaded to the extent that *all* literary production, within the latter half of the twentieth century, is subject to the laws of the marketplace, the laws of the body, the laws of material culture. The middlebrow produced by the collaboration between the feminized commercial and the masculinized literary is a middlebrow poised tenuously between the high and the low, kept in crisis by that tension. Who better than Stephen King to understand this dynamic, a writer who must repeatedly fight the battle over the meaning of the middlebrow and his place within it?

The ending of the novel, on one hand, appears to signify a remasculinization of the author who was earlier threatened by both a monstrous feminine audience and the feminization produced by his association with a debased mass cultural form. After all, Paul finishes *Misery's Return*, and "rapes" Annie with the burning cylinder of a manuscript that even further literalizes the pen as penis metaphor (317). Such an ending might represent King's desire to bury his own connections to mass culture and to give birth to himself as "serious" writer—much as Paul Sheldon plays Zeus to Misery (56) and later revels in his liberation from his enslavement to the popular (expressed in his jubilant *"I'm free at last! The silly bitch finally bought the farm!"* [15]). Yet, on the other hand, not only is Paul's "remasculinization" compromised by the fact that he remains haunted by Annie, but *King*, too, is marked by his encounter with a construction of mass culture that necessarily compromises his entry into the middlebrow. Why would a male writer who proudly claims to be the "brand name" of horror fiction risk a lengthy and powerful exploration of the essential femininity of mass culture? Why would King appropriate the metaphors used *against* him to rescript the high-low culture divide? The answers point toward a recognition of *Misery* as not merely contemporary but "postmodern," too—a designation most often reserved for a kind of fiction that is more intellectual, less materialized, more abstract.

In *Misery*, the death of the (white male) Author is narrowly averted, and his authority at least partially restored. But what of the undeniable fact that the novel lingers sadistically over the woundings of the white male body—so much so that it's tempting to argue that what we're seeing here is King's staging of male masochism, put on for readers who are primarily male?[35] What pleasures are derived from this representation of the savage embodiment of the white male author figure which, in a number of ways, significantly departs from King's previous work?[36] One of the clichés offered to explain response to horror fiction and film is that the genre gives "us" a scary pleasure by materializing "our" worst nightmares. In this reading, the pain and mutilations suffered by Paul might represent what "we" most fear from those dangerous and violent women who people "our" nightmares—much like Milan Kundera's claim that Roth's Maureen Tarnopol embodies such a force: "I know her by heart through my nightmares; from the time I was eighteen I have feared one day becoming her victim, and all my life I have constantly been defending myself against her dreaded attacks" (162).

Such nightmares are clearly gender-specific and, as such, suggest that there is something painful-pleasurable in not only seeing such "bitch-goddesses" die horrible deaths, but in vicariously experiencing the pain they cause, the bodily traumas they unleash. Carol Clover argues that, because male horror viewers want to experience a masochistic pleasure of bodily trauma, and because such masochism is gendered female, it is necessary to represent the victim/hero of slasher films as a woman. "Cinefantastic horror, in short, succeeds in incorporating its spectators as 'feminine' and then violating that body—which recoils, shudders, cries out collectively—in ways otherwise imaginable, for males, only in nightmares" (53). The violation is pleasurable *because* it is embodied on the screen by a female figure—but this is clearly not the case in King's novel, nor in Rob Reiner's film of it. What is the attraction of Paul's suffering, the multiple dismemberments narrated in *The World According to Garp*, and the bodily traumas of Peter Tarnopol's "Life as a Man"?

Clover argues that the increased visibility of women as hero-victims, presumably rather than simply as victims, can be explained, in part, as a "structural effect of a greater investment in the victim function. For whatever reason, modern horror seems especially interested in the trials of everyperson, and everyperson is on his or her own in facing the menace, without help from 'authorities'" (17). Perhaps this might explain the creation of a new category of narrative function/persona, that of the "victim-hero," and the necessity of embodying that function in female form; it is too threatening to represent a female figure as pure menace, Clover suggests. But it seems to me that the phenomenon of "everyperson" facing a menace without aid of authorities is preeminently a masculine one, cropping up everywhere in the Reagan era, for instance, in figures like Rambo, the later Dirty Harry, and the Terminator.[37] As I have been arguing, the post-sixties era witnesses a new white and male investment in the "victim-function," a desire on the part of those whose social and political dominance has positioned them as victimizers, not victims, to cash in on the symbolic value of victimization and to experience the pleasures and pains to be found in a new white and male embodiment.

While each of these novels ends with at least a partial recuperation of the masculinity seemingly lost through such bodily humiliations, symbolic castrations, and graphic mutilations, recuperation is not necessarily either the goal or the effect of these representations. Indeed, the sheer volume of words devoted to wounded bodies in these texts suggests that the woundings themselves, rather than the healing of those wounds, serve a particular purpose. The protagonists in these novels are not the Rambo figures of Hollywood action films who, as numerous critics have argued, figure a masochistic wounding of masculinity in order to retool that masculinity as bigger and better.[38] This is, in some ways, the project of Reiner's film. While clearly in distant brotherhood to these filmic representations, the novels here take different strategies entirely. That embodiment is only imaginable in these texts as bodily *trauma* is also connected to the "victim-function," to the implicit assumption that embodiment is only forced upon our attentions through the apprehension of the body as problematic. Women's bodies, and the bodies of people of color, have always been apprehended as problematic—walking down the street as much as in literary and scholarly representation. As we saw in chapter 2, bodies become visible through surveillance and objectification; the marking of white men as specifically embodied, gendered, and racialized subjects, functions as an objectification that, as we saw in this chapter, produces responses ranging from acceptance of material vulnerability to defiant reassertions of abstraction. Indeed, as I have argued here, the two responses work in tandem to produce a white masculinity perpetually in crisis.

Authorship is a particularly powerful scene of the crisis in white masculinity because not only has authorship come under attack in literary theory, but the authority of the white male author has been challenged in the academy *and* in the mass market. Because the "literary" has served as the sinecure of a particular construction of masculine individualism and subjective agency—while the "commercial" is linked with the vulgar and most often feminized demands of the marketplace—the middlebrow is also a key space for dramatizing the crisis of masculinity that follows, in part, from a remapped cultural field. The crisis of the "literary" is, in some sense, the crisis announced by the culture wars and, as I argued in chapter 2, that crisis evidences the anxiety that comes not only from the "marking" of the white male author but from his immersion in the marketplace. As was clear in both *My Life as a Man* and *The World According to Garp*, the commodification of a masculine literary production is always connected with feminization; and, the middlebrow, as Radway convincingly argues, is poised in tension between an entire series of binary oppositions, including that between the material and the abstract, between the bodily and affective and the intellectual. Authorship also functions as a potent metaphor to describe the cultural authority of the elite in American culture; this power, too, has been diffused by the commodification of authors and books, and the increasingly rapid shifts in publishing, information technology, and copyright law.

But, while authorship might signify power, it also can signify disempowerment, and the most common trope for that disempowerment is writer's block. In each of the novels discussed in this chapter, the white male author figure suffers at least one battle with writer's block. The trauma endured by these author-figures originates in a troubled sense of masculinity: Peter Tarnopol, T. S. Garp, and Paul Sheldon all experience writer's block as a response to attacks on their power and privilege by women. Writer's block constrains creative expression, makes it impossible to let creative energy out, and, in the case of Roth, that energy gets channeled into somatic symptoms. Peter's diarrhea and vomiting can be read as a bodily response to the blockage of his creative and emotional energies, as the body forces out substances imagined as polluting or corrupting. It is as if he is vomiting and shitting Maureen out of his system in order, then, to be able to write. Garp's writer's block can be traced to a masculine self-control that threatens to veer into a dangerous repression; unlike Jenny, who appears to "emit" her book without much conscious artistry or even control, Garp's more constipated literary output is a sign both of his power and the control of that power. Paul Sheldon's writer's block is analogized to a sexual blockage, and he breaks out of it when he recaptures his sense of sexual potency and goes on to "beat the typewriter" as he would "his meat." The power of his output, thus, is dependent on the earlier blockage. Masculine literary talent resides in the power to hold back, to practice continence, and it is this power that can so easily mutate into writer's block. Writer's block is a perfect metaphor for the condition of contemporary masculinity, for while a powerful masculinity is often secured by inexpressivity—as in the strong, silent type of the powerful man—it is also true that certain kinds of blockage impede the true expression of masculinity. It is to this paradox that I now turn.

CHAPTER 4
MASCULINITY AS EMOTIONAL CONSTIPATION

Men's Liberation and the Wounds of Patriarchal Power

In *The Water-Method Man,* published six years before *The World According to Garp,* Irving created a protagonist who literally embodies the emotional and social crisis afflicting straight, white, middle-class men who, in an America drunk on "liberation," are desperately trying to come to terms with that intoxication. While much of American culture is celebrating the free flow of released energies, Fred "Bogus" Trumper is a study in repression. Unable to "commit" to a long-term relationship, he is emotionally stunted, seemingly incapable of expressing his desires and emotions honestly, and, consequently, tends to engage in self-destructive behavior. He can't finish his Ph.D. dissertation, can't commit to his new girlfriend (having virtually begged his first wife to leave him with their young son), and can't quite settle into his new career. He is stuck, blocked, and paralyzed. But it is not only his psychology that militates against the flow of emotion, life, and affiliation; Irving creates a somatic equivalent of Bogus's emotional state by giving him a penis that doesn't work properly. It, too, is blocked, making urination painful and sex, "typically, unmentionable" (12). After years of balking at having an operation to unblock what his urologist refers to as his "narrow and winding road" (12), Trumper has the operation and, miraculously, finishes his dissertation, agrees to marry his girlfriend (who has just had his child), settles into a job, and makes peace with his first wife and his son. Having gotten his plumbing unblocked, his emotional passages follow suit.

Irving's somatization of Trumper's emotional blockage is based on a construction of masculinity that has a long history in American culture and one that is epitomized in the apparently unimpeachable truth that men aren't permitted to express their emotions. This truth, rarely contested, is linked by a complex and fascinating logic to the equally uncontested truth that male sexual energies must be released lest men implode from the force of their suppression. To some degree, these truths are gender-neutral: sexual energies, in gener-al, are understood in post-Freudian American culture as bodily material that will seek their "outlet" in one way or another, just as crying is imagined as pro-viding an almost literal release of emotional energies. But, whereas women are popularly understood to cry at the drop of a hat—or at the drip of a hor-mone—popular representations of masculinity are nearly uniformly intent on ratifying the idea that men suffer because they aren't allowed to cry. Similarly, while most popular books on sexuality at least pretend to grant women the same range and intensity of sexual desire as men, certain mythologies persist which hold that men suffer far more deeply when forced to bottle up their sex-ual energies. Indeed, the very idea that male sexuality is *automatic,* a natural force that must not be dammed up, is remarkably persistent, despite the wealth of scholarly and even popular attention paid to the social construction of sex-uality. Male heterosexuality remains *unmarked* by culture—or, at least, the power of certain commonsense ideas about male heterosexuality is secured by keeping male heterosexuality invisible.

Based on a still-dominant model of emotional and sexual economy, con-structions of a masculinity torn between the imperatives of blockage and re-lease construct the male body as a fragile vessel full of simmering impulses and thwarted desires. Competing imperatives toward blockage and release are evi-denced throughout the history of American masculinity, but come to the sur-face with particular force in the mid- to late 1970s, when questions about the future of straight, white masculinity became urgent. As Glenn Bucher put it in his 1976 call to arms, *Straight/White/Male,* "we are headed for a crisis of sub-stantial proportion. We will be forced to consider our own self-identities long before we are liberated from them. Why, then, has an inquiry about the libera-tion of straight white males now seen the light of day? Because these persons are in trouble!" (6–7). The rhetoric of crisis that marks this and other calls for "male liberation" invokes images of white male minds and bodies at risk, even as it springs from a recognition of white and male privilege. Popular studies of, and novels about, men trying to come to terms with a masculinity recently at-tacked as dangerous, rely on a set of rhetorical figures to negotiate between the privileges of patriarchal power and the guilt induced by the feminist critique of that power.[1] These rhetorical figures all have to do with blockage, and the pre-vailing diagnosis of what's wrong with masculinity is that men have been forced to repress, suppress, and even oppress; and, as a result, male bodies and male minds are on the verge of shutting down.

More than the novels by Roth, Irving, and King, these fictional and nonfic-tional texts enter into a dialogue with feminism. Nonfictional prescriptions for the "liberated man," self-help manuals with titles like *The Male Dilemma: Sur-viving the Sexual Revolution,* and fiction about emotionally, sexually, and physically wounded straight white men all take their cues from feminist critiques of white and male power. But, as we have seen throughout this study, the marking of white men as victimizers can easily produce its opposite: an understanding of white men as victims of that feminist critique. As in other instances of wounded white masculinity, these claims rest on an erasure of the institution-alized power of white men, and on an individualized and personalized idea of victimization. The construction of masculinity as dangerously blocked com-petes with an increasingly visible, post–women's liberation understanding of masculinity as dangerously expressive of violent emotions and sexuality. "Every man is a potential rapist," writes Marilyn French in *The Woman's Room* (1977), a diagnosis that ratifies the construction of masculinity as always on the verge of explosion, even as it argues *for* the blockage of male emotional and sexual energies. Contemporaneous with the radical feminist critique is a "masculin-ist" critique offered in books like Herb Goldberg's *The Hazards of Being Male: Surviving the Myth of Masculine Privilege* (1976), Warren Farrell's *The Liberated Man: Beyond Masculinity—Freeing Men and Their Relationships with Women* (1974), and Marc Feigen Fasteau's *The Male Machine* (1974). In part based on a limited understanding of women's liberation as a program for personal growth, rather than a movement for social justice, men's liberation discourse focused on the psychological and bodily harms suffered by men whose health was endangered by the blockage of emotional expression.[2] The male libera-tionists represent white, middle-class heterosexual men as both literally and metaphorically wounded; but *not*, as we might expect, by women, feminism, or even the radically shifting social terrain of gender. Instead, these texts give us men who are wounded by their power, their responsibilities, and indeed, by pa-triarchy itself.[3]

In their representations of a dominant masculinity in crisis, the male libera-tionists substitute a bodily economy of emotional and sexual "energy" for a so-cial system that prohibits and permits certain kinds of emotional expression based on gender. The image of a powerfully vulnerable male body perpetually in crisis becomes the emblem of a new masculinity. As with other representa-tions of white male woundings we've attended to in this study, the texts I will look at here prompt a doubled reading of the desires fueling an ideology of male release and the possible feminist effects of that ideology. On the one hand, the seemingly unimpeachable assumption that emotional and sexual forces *must* be released constructs a blocked masculinity in order to legitimize various forms of release and, thus, to recuperate a masculinity that has suffered from the feminist critique of male power and privilege. Appealing to nature, these texts advocate the release of male energies to heal a masculinity wounded by "unnatural" blockage. On the other hand, however, the entertainment of male bodily and psychic vulnerability points toward a new, specifically post–women's liberation masculinity. The masculinity promoted within men's liberation discourse is based on a willingness to abdicate a good deal of power—or, more precisely, a willingness to renegotiate the terms of patriarchal power. Men's liberation discourse of the seventies is the first, and at this point hopeful, sign of the much derided "sensitive man" who, by the mid-eighties, had become the butt of so many jokes—both feminist and antifeminist. By the late eighties, the sensitive man had become the *enemy* of male liberation and well-being, as the "soft male" enters the public eye via Robert Bly's diagnosis of the current crisis in dominant masculinity. But, while Bly argues that men need to get in touch with the "deep masculine" signified by the Wild Man, he, too, leans heavily on both an ideology of emotional and sexual release and the therapeutic power of the male wound.[4]

As we have seen throughout this study, claims that white men suffer a loss of political, social, and cultural power are buttressed by images of white male bodies at risk. The spectacle of a suffering body gives to claims of white male disenfranchisement a rhetorical force that would otherwise be lacking. As Leonard Michaels suggests in his 1978 fictional satire of men's liberation groups, *The Men's Club*, men lacked what made "liberation" necessary: oppression. "I thought about women again," the narrator says. "Anger, identity, politics, rights, wrongs. I envied them. It seemed attractive to be deprived in our society. Deprivation gives you something to fight for, it makes you morally superior, it makes you serious" (13). Lacking the social grounding for a collectivized and politicized call for rights, white men in post-1968 American culture enthusiastically begin to elaborate wrongs, constructing narratives about individualized psychological and bodily wounds. While women, people of color, lesbian and gay men were able to argue convincingly that they had been disenfranchised socially by their marginalized position in U.S. society and culture, the middle-class white men most likely to join men's lib did not attempt to claim a social disenfranchisement; instead, they increasingly began to argue that they were personally and individually wounded by a vaguely sketched "society" which, while awarding them power and privileges, produced psychological and bodily symptoms of powerlessness. Not only are visibly victimized groups increasingly considered morally superior, but, arguably, a narrative structured around victims and victimizers becomes *the* national narrative in the post-liberation era. Irresistibly, perhaps, white men begin to be drawn to a rhetoric of crisis and wounding that, paradoxically, *re*centers white masculinity while announcing its *de*centering. Trumping women's blocked opportunities with men's blocked emotional expression, the men's liberationists substituted the personal for the political instead of forging a link between them.

The emerging construction of vulnerable masculinity risks a metaphorical femininity through its emphasis on weakness, bodily vulnerability, and wounds. One way this risk is managed is by "masculinizing" emotion, making release look violent, like "hurricanes" gathering force and "volcanoes" threatening to erupt. But rather than simply reconstructing a phallic masculinity in backlash against the crisis caused by women's liberation, these discourses instead move professional white men firmly into the arena of liberation—not as the unmarked norm against which others must struggle, but as another group struggling against a vaguely sketched social order. A wounded white male body becomes the emblem of the crisis in masculinity and a virile victim emerges as the figure for post-liberation American normativity. While I will focus on the patriarchal ends served by prescriptions for male release, I do not take these seventies texts as antifeminist; compared to the most recent round of books on the "masculine mystique," the "myth of male power," and the "soft male," these texts are positively revolutionary in their gender analysis.[5] In the remainder of the chapter, I will return to the Irving and Michaels novels and read in them an incipient, but highly ambivalent, critique of the therapeutic value of male release for resolving crises in masculinity. Both therapeutic narratives in one way or another, these novels offer a more nuanced view of what is at stake in prescriptions for male release, and suggest that both blockage and release can serve to "liberate" men. It remains to be seen whether this will be good news for women.

THE HAZARDS OF BEING MALE

In *The Liberated Man,* Warren Farrell argues that men are "emotionally constipated" and that "real emotions are stuck in [man's] system" (71). Using a bodily metaphor to describe an emotional blockage, Farrell here travels a rhetorical path characteristic of texts interested in critiquing the "straitjacket" or "harness" or "machine" of traditional masculinity. Blurring the boundaries between the emotional and the physical, and between the metaphorical and the literal, Farrell suggests that men's emotional constipation actually *produces* ulcers and other somatic symptoms: "In [the standard workplace] atmosphere, men cannot help but be either emotionally incompetent (unable to handle emotions expressed by others) or emotionally constipated (unable to express their own emotions) or both. His emotional constipation leaves no outlet for his stomach but ulcers" (71). Farrell means "liberation" literally, as well as figuratively, and the dominant trope of his and other studies of "constipated" masculinity is *flow:* if masculinity and men are to be liberated from the "harness" of the male role, emotional energies must be released, the tears must flow. Men are "maimed" by their own power and by the "male role" that requires blockage of emotional energies: expression is the cure for what ails men.

Bodily wounds have a persuasive power that does not depend on the social; and images of male bodies at risk work to legitimize a discourse that often veers into the apolitical and asocial. It is a function of the psychologized representation of the costs and benefits of male privilege that Farrell's account, antisexist and women's liberationist in intent, ends up appearing like an opportunistic appropriation of the "victim" position for successful white, heterosexual men.[6] Banking on the appeals of male pain, Farrell invites his groups to focus on how patriarchy wounds them; "consistently," he says, "*the technique of asking 'How is this also hurting us?' enabled us to discover how our own self-interest was being threatened by the same phenomenon that threatened women*" (239, Farrell's emphasis). The assumption here is that men suffer identical, or at least identically traumatic, hurts from the patriarchal system that channels women and men into narrow forms of personal expression. If all that is threatened by patriarchy is "self-interest," or fulfillment of individual goals, then a therapeutic solution is adequate, and social revolution becomes unnecessary.[7] Substituting the bodily for the social, and conflating emotional constipation with political powerlessness, Farrell wonders "if there is such a thing as a liberated top executive, or does the trip through the bureaucracy maim them all?" (71). Implying that successful white men are maimed by the exercise of their own power, Farrell offers an image of wounded white masculinity as the emblem of a post–women's liberationist age.

The men's liberationists take from contemporary feminism a validation of emotional release, a sanction for airing pain and grievances, and most importantly, a permission to express rage. According to Herb Goldberg's *The Hazards of Being Male: Surviving the Myth of Masculine Privilege,* men should take women's lead, open the floodgates, and express a heretofore "heavily repressed male rage" (17). Goldberg represents men as casualties of patriarchy who must be taught "how to survive the myth of masculine privilege," a myth that covers over the reality of white male bodies at risk. Like Farrell, Goldberg begins from the premise that feminism has the potential to liberate men because, having given women the license to be "strong" and independent, men can abandon the many onerous tasks and ways of being that patriarchal culture has forced on them; but the analysis quickly shifts ground, as men become the victims, *not* of women or feminism, but a vaguely sketched and nonagential "society" that forces men to take up dangerous, dominating positions. Even while lamenting the fact that men aren't "allowed" to be passive, the male liberationists construct men as the passive targets or recipients of a gender ideology in which they "are directly denied the freedom to experience and express emotion in all but the most narrow channels" (Fasteau 31). Passive verbs abound in men's liberation discourse: men are "forced," "not permitted," "not allowed," "excluded."[8]

This is particularly true of *The Hazards of Being Male,* where men emerge as the wounded and surprisingly passive victims of their own self-control. The key term in Goldberg's diagnosis of the crisis in masculinity is "blockage," a trope he uses repeatedly to describe man's general and specific "inability to respond to his inner promptings both emotionally and physiologically" (16). Men "block" their "conquering" impulses (56); they "block the flow of tears" (60); "emotional upsets and disturbances" are "blocked out of awareness," endangering man's mental health (69); men's genuine fears of marriage and economic "slavery" are "blocked out" (73); the contradictions between the male's different roles are "blocked out and repressed for self-protection" (106); and, finally, men "block out the symptoms of malaise until the illness is so overwhelming that it disables them completely" (112). Self-control and control of others is not the route toward social power; it is, instead, a certain path toward ulcers, cancer, mental breakdown and pain.[9] The literal and figurative merge here, as the bodily and emotional work entirely in tandem: If men continue to control themselves, Goldberg warns, "emotional starvation" will eventually produce "drinking binges, wild driving, a blatantly destructive affair, or a violent outburst, among other [problems]. All are spoutings of the inner, hidden volcano" (69). This language, typical of men's liberationists' description of the evils of male blockage, carries a barely veiled threat: placing limits on the expression of male impulses will lead men not only into the self-destruction of ulcers and cancer but also into the very modes of male destructiveness and power against which women's liberation had so recently and powerfully taken a stand.

While Goldberg might be read as prescribing the abdication of male power—he is, after all, in favor of the liberation of women, too—his idea of wounding and "liberation" is asocial, grounded in the body and dependent on the idea that there are "natural" impulses that men have been schooled into repressing. The language of blockage and release, and the analogy between physiological and affective economies, is most fully evident in the following passage describing the endangerment of the male:

It is very much in style today to urge men to feel. However this urging is partially reminiscent of taunting a crippled man to run. . . . It is unlikely that a mere act of will on his part can unlock the hurricane of repressed feelings within him. Today's man is the product of massive, defensive operations *against* feelings. These defenses are geared to protect him for survival's sake by transforming the host of powerful, socially taboo impulses, needs and feelings into acceptable male behavior. To survive and contain these repressed feelings he must detach himself increasingly from all relationships that might stimulate or provoke him into an uncontrollable response. . . . Because feelings are not permitted free expression the male lives in constant reaction against himself. What he is on the outside is a facade, a defense *against* what he *really* is on the inside. *He controls himself by denying himself.*

(68–69, Goldberg's emphasis)

Although slightly overwrought, this passage is fairly typical of analyses of men's emotional blockage, in that it assumes the existence of an array of "uncontrollable responses" and natural if taboo impulses. Marc Feigen Fasteau, far more feminist than Goldberg, also subscribes to this watered-down Freudianism when he describes men as suffering from "crippling" emotional constraints (31). Male bodies in pain haunt these pages, as men's liberationists evoke the language of victimization and handicap to image the condition of dominant masculinity.

This new construction of a wounded white masculinity depends on a literal, materialist understanding of "liberation" that depends, in turn, on a construction of emotional "energy" as a bodily fluid that must be released. Repressed emotions are here understood as material, physical entities, and the language of flow and release, blockage and outlet, invokes what anthropologists Lila Abu-Lughod and Catherine A. Lutz argue is the dominant construction of emotion across disciplines: "Emotions are psychobiological processes that respond to cross-cultural environmental differences but retain a robust essence untouched by the social and cultural" (2). Constructions of masculinity as dangerously blocked imply that the release of emotion is *inevitable:* in a construction of emotion as "psychophysical" product, rather than socially situated process, the men's liberationists insist that blocked emotions *will* come pouring out in one way or another. The prevalence of liquid metaphors buttresses this construction: emotions are blocked, pent-up, bottled up, and must flow, be channeled, find an outlet. The truism that men aren't "allowed" to cry and thus to release pent-up emotions is central to the men's liberationists' construction of blocked masculinity.[10] Tears are represented as liquid emotions that, when released, facilitate the "softening" of a rigid masculinity. Most work on gender and emotion has stressed how a gendered rhetoric of emotional control reinforces women's subordination within societies that privilege rationality, self-control, and the stable boundaries between interiority and exteriority that emotions appear to breach.[11] But the men's liberationists' emphasis on emotional expression, not control, as the sign of healthy masculinity prompts us to ask *not* how emotional *control* serves patriarchal ideology, but how a rhetoric of *expression* and letting go does. Prescriptions for emotional "release," like rules about emotional control, require that emotion be conceptualized as a psychophysical essence; whether a society requires control or liberation of emotion, emotions are figured as material, even liquid, substances that flow or not—rather than, for example, a state of mind.

Why are emotions conceptualized in this way? This question is related to the question of why it is that "blockage" is always unhealthy, particularly for men. The answers must be sought in the slippage between "emotion" and "sexuality." For, isn't it the case that the ideology of emotional thrift and spending, blockage and release, runs parallel to an ideology of sexual thrift and spending, blockage and release? If affective energies are constructed as psychobiological material—released through the shedding of tears or the outbursts of physical aggression—sexual energies are construed as even more literally fluid. Prescriptions for the unimpeded release of male sexual energies enter through the back door, as it were, piggy-backed onto prescriptions for the release of emotional energies. Indeed, as Lutz has argued, in contemporary American culture "a popular discourse on the control of emotions runs functionally parallel to a discourse on the control of sexuality; a rhetoric of control requires a psychophysical essence that is manipulated and wrestled with and directs attention away from the socially constructed nature of emotion" (72). The functional parallel Lutz identifies between popular discourse on emotion and on sexuality is no coincidence; a popular conceptualization of emotion as a *bodily* material which always seeks its outlet (despite personal or social attempts to block its flow), takes its meaning and force from an analogy with sexuality. And, conversely, a construction of sexuality as a *material* force that always seeks its outlet (despite personal or social attempts to block its flow) finds support in the less obviously interested masculinist construction of emotion as psychophysical essence. The idea that men are emotionally blocked owes its sense and its dominance to a particular construction of male heterosexuality and the male body: male sexual energies are constantly flowing, sexual arousal "automatic" and uncontrollable, and any blockage of these energies, and the substance through which those energies are expressed, leads either to psychological and physical damage or to violent explosions. "Emotional discharge," in Goldberg's terms, is meaningful only in analogy to sexual discharge, and the blockage of male sexual and emotional energies becomes identically dangerous. Neither emotion nor sexuality needs to be thought of in these terms, and the dominance of the model of emotional and sexual blockage and release works to naturalize a particular construction of blocked masculinity that is violently at odds with the spirit behind women's demands that men "open up," express themselves honestly, and release their repressed emotions.

Importantly, the emotions most often identified as dangerously blocked are anger and resentment, rather than, say, love and fear. Because the men's liberationists take their cue from women's liberationists, it perhaps makes sense that anger and resentment would be the dominant emotions. Yet what are men angry at, or resentful of? Where women are angry at blocked opportunities, the men who seek Goldberg's or Farrell's help appear to be resentful at the mere fact of blockage. Because American masculinity has always been about the free-dom to move forward (into the frontier or up the career ladder), blockage is, by definition, a threat. For those who have been nurtured on inalienable rights and "natural" entitlements, blockage must appear particularly threatening.[12] But, further, in focusing on the blockage of anger, for instance, the male libera-tionists "masculinize" emotion, making release look violent, like "hurricanes" gathering force and "volcanoes" threatening to erupt. In framing sensitivity *as* repression, Goldberg's analysis subtly constructs true, unrepressed masculinity as the antithesis of the sensitive male—invitations to cry notwithstanding. In doing so, he cements the analogy between violence and male "liberation"; vio-lent impulses are psychophysical essences which naturally seek an outlet. As we will see in the next chapter, a particular construction of male sexuality is the glue that holds this analogy together. Here I simply want to make the point that, for the men's liberationists, the line between "emotion" and "sexuality" is, in any event, a tenuous one; because of the association of emotion with the feminine, invocations of a phallic sexuality works to ward off the feminization that a focus on "soft" emotions might risk.

An undeniable phallic emphasis on "release" diffuses anxieties about femi-nization, as emotions get reconceptualized as virile, and male expressivity as the right of all men. This argument, drawing on a liberationist discourse of rights and entitlements, works by a sleight-of-hand: springing from a feminist discourse that had reason to criticize male emotional inexpressivity as a behav-ior that perpetuates male power, men's liberation discourse now claims that men have been deprived of their right to express themselves.[13] What ails the emotionally repressed man is not his failure to experience or understand a range of emotion; rather, the failure can be attributed to a vaguely apprehend-ed social order that "requires" men to block the *expression* of emotion. It's im-portant to stress here that, for Goldberg, whose notion of "repression" is decid-edly un-Freudian, direct expression is the only healthy thing that can be done with emotions. No theory of sublimation puts the reins on Goldberg's desire to allow men the uninhibited expression of impulses; no theory of the part re-pression plays in the formation of the subject is evident here either. Men be-come conscious of their emotions and impulses *only through expression,* and thus, release is the only way that men are to be "liberated" from their bonds. This is true of Farrell as well, who acknowledges a difference between having and showing emotions only to say it doesn't matter. Male introspection is un-derstood as a possible good, but only when it is tied to *expression.* The empha-sis on the blockage of *expression* over the blockage of awareness works, subtly in Farrell's case, to legitimize various forms of release as the goal of male liber-ation and to construct the male body as a fragile vessel full of simmering im-pulses and thwarted desires. While Farrell appears to contest the ideology of male release animating Goldberg's book, he ends up reinforcing a romanticized image of dominant masculinity as hurt by its own power and the necessary blockage of its "natural" impulses.

While an emphasis on release can be read as simply part of the antirepression orientation of popular seventies therapies, what distinguishes a men's liberation approach to healthy masculinity from, say, a Human Potential approach, is that it is piggy-backed onto a *political* movement for equal rights. A program for personal growth and freedom from restraint thus cashes in on the moral currency attached to political movements—*and* at a moment when Goldberg's and Farrell's clients (successful white men) belonged to precisely the category that was being "marked" as the *enemy* of liberation. Rather than confronting the gap between the personal and the political, the men's liberationists instead draw on a rhetoric of personal injury and pain and, thus, enter the field of "liberation" both acknowledging and disavowing the political. The discourse on men's liberation operates within a therapeutic model which, as many cultural analysts have pointed out, works to evacuate the social, "translat[ing] the political into the psychological" (Peck 152).[14] This is perhaps most clearly demonstrated in Warren Farrell's *The Liberated Man*. Farrell anatomizes the hurts caused by adherence to a rigid patriarchal script and even offers a blueprint for male liberation: radically, Farrell calls for flexible work schedules, payment for housework, better affirmative action programs, and better childcare to bring men into childrearing and to free women for work. But, strangely, this part of the book exists entirely in isolation from the second half, in which Farrell describes his work with men's consciousness-raising groups and offers aid and advice to those men who wish to participate in such groups. Farrell counsels the men to *feel*, rather than "intellectualize," and to stress the personal over the political. For Farrell, "liberation" means "psychological freedom" (4), and the revolutionary social programs he describes seem merely tacked onto the program for personal liberation. In comparison to the rather dramatic narratives of consciousness-raising at the center of Farrell's project and his interest, the feminist analysis appears positively tepid, vague, and unsatisfying—including the hopeful if not altogether convincing "twenty-one specific areas in which men can benefit from women's liberation" (175).

Nowhere does the slippage between the personal and the political become clearer than in the arena of consciousness-raising, a process for which Farrell evinces an almost religious devotion. The consciousness-raising sessions Farrell details in *The Liberated Man* bear little resemblance to Goldberg's vision of men's consciousness-raising groups as just another agent of male blockage, devoted as he imagines them to be, to rehearsals of guilt and self-flagellating analysis of male privilege and power.[15] But neither do Farrell's groups resemble women's consciousness-raising groups which, as Alice Echols argues, were devoted to discussion of social, not self-, transformation. While some mocked feminist consciousness-raising as therapy, Echols notes that "proponents of consciousness-raising made every effort to distinguish it from therapy. They argued that the purpose of consciousness-raising was to analyze male supremacy in order to dismantle it, while the purpose of therapy was to carve out personal solutions to women's oppression" (87). The rise of more psychological and personal, less theoretical and political, types of consciousness-raising would coincide with the rise of cultural over radical feminism in the mid-seventies; but the initial impetus for consciousness-raising was quite distinct from the therapeutic impulse evident in the men's groups Farrell describes. That therapeutic impulse is made visible by an opposition between liberating "feelings" and the "intellectualization" which stanches the flow of feelings. "Intellectualization" means overanalysis, but in the context of the liberation movements from which these discourses spring, it also means *politicization*. Goldberg even goes so far as to claim that the "three basic processes that contribute to the physical deterioration of the male body . . . are intellectualization, macho rigidity, and guilt" (107). Guilt and intellectualization are both legacies of the women's movement: guilt for the exercise of male power and privilege, and intellectualization as the political analysis which produces that guilt. True to the spirit of the therapeutic, Farrell sees consciousness-raising groups as focused on self- and not social transformation: the goal is to "develop each other's awareness of alternative ways of overcoming the limitations on our lives that have evolved from our view of ourselves as masculine or feminine" (217). Rather than focus on guilt or theorize the social construction of gender, these men are encouraged to express their pain.

Because of the psychologized, therapeutic solution favored by the men's liberationists, this new construction of masculinity ultimately works to reinforce, rather than contest, male dominance. The cure for what ails these men is not, as we might have hoped, the abolition of patriarchy, but rather the uninhibited release of emotional energies and "natural" impulses. The construction of male sexuality as *naturally* resistant to repression or control is the foundation of the idea that men are "damaged" by the *cultural* or *social* suppression of emotions and expressivity. The intertwining of the natural with the social, and of the somatic with the affective, works to authorize two seemingly contradictory perspectives on men and power: the idea that men are wounded, weakened, and "oppressed" by patriarchy, male privilege, and power; and the idea that men are naturally prone to expressions of sexual power and sexual violence. In both respects, emotionally and sexually, men are urged to "let it all hang out," or else suffer the consequences, which include heart attacks and impotence. As Herb Goldberg puts it in *The Hazards of Being Male*, "the price of macho rigidity—including the resistance to asking for help, the fear of dependency, the resistance against passivity, notions about what constitutes 'masculine' foods, reluctance to pamper oneself and the bottling up of emotions—is high indeed in terms of the damage done to the body" (118). In dwelling on a wounded white male body, these men's liberationists work to erase the social and political contexts of the crisis they are keen to resolve. Yet these texts do not resolve that crisis; instead, they present white men—recently marked by a feminist critique of their power—as heroic but ineffective rebels against an oppressive gender system. Fighting against the status quo, these displaced white men draw on the rhetorical power of "liberation" at the same time as they subtly work to undermine the bases of other liberationist claims. Wishing themselves out of the category, "straight/white/male," the men's liberationists and their clients remake that category as itself in need of personal and political liberation. One way this is accomplished is by isolating white men from those others who have marked them as unfairly privileged; what emerges is men's liberation as a kind of male bonding experience that, unsurprisingly, ends up indifferent, if not hostile, to women. The novels to which I now turn also explore the paradoxes of blockage and release, but because they place men in proximity to women, they are more concerned with the ways in which the personal and the political coincide. These novels suggest that male power is expressed through cycles of blockage and release, and so foreground, somewhat ironically, the impossibility of translating the individualistic, personal, and bodily vision of male wounding and health to the social and political realms.

THE WISDOM OF THE PENIS

Like men's liberation discourse, John Irving's *The Water-Method Man* is obsessed with images of blockage and flow. The novel uses a network of plumbing metaphors to explore the paradoxes of blockage and release, linking Trumper's obstructed physiology, unexpressed emotions, blocked creativity and, even, clogged toilets. Emotional release is metaphorically dependent on sexual release, and both are premised on a construction of male energies as liquid, material forces that flow through the body. The body resists efforts to curb or shape its "natural" impulses, and Trumper's physical blockage signifies blockages elsewhere. But while the men's liberationists ultimately offer a therapeutic solution to a political problem, Irving's novel suggests that therapies aimed at "liberating" men from macho rigidity actually work to legitimize the very forms of "release" that feminists were reading as the "expression" of male privilege. At the same time, he cautions men that calls for emotional expressivity can lead men right back into the "harness" of responsible manhood the "liberation" of emotional energies was meant to destroy. Advocating neither women's liberation nor men's liberation, the novel reveals further reasons to doubt the therapeutic value of "release" for solving the crisis in masculinity.

Irving sets up two competing versions of male blockage/release and does so by creating a cast of male characters whose differing responses to the damaging demands of mature manhood complement Bogus's and together create a map of male liberation. The late Merrill Overturf haunts Bogus and the novel, an adolescent characterized mainly by his incontinence—in both literal and metaphorical ways. Bogus romanticizes Merrill as the essence of male liberation, and his early death in mysterious circumstances functions to martyr him as a free spirit who is simply too much for the middle-class world to which Bogus ultimately swears allegiance. Trumper is clearly hurt by the "blockage" of the energies that Merrill represents. Not able to accept the "harness" of a traditional masculinity, Bogus's blocked energies find more self-destructive, if also self-indulgent, outlets. Ralph Packer speaks for male liberation, too, as he helps Bogus "escape" from his wife Biggie and, later, gives him sanctuary in New York. There is the never seen but often remembered Harry Petz, a graduate student in Comparative Literature who is mythologized as the man who cracks under the stress of what Warren Farrell calls the "straitjacket" of masculinity (9). Petz haunts the narrative as a warning of what will happen to Bogus if he allows himself to be trapped by women and by the familial obligations which can staunch the flow of healthy male energies. Finally, there is Couth, who has managed to evade the "professions" that Warren Farrell suggests might "maim" the hapless if successful middle-class man. Couth is a photographer, a handyman, and an entirely free-flowing spirit: he is, in short, the epitome of liberated manhood. Rather than intellectualize, like Bogus, or stress out, also like Bogus, Couth goes with the flow. Where Bogus freezes with anxiety "contemplating the horror of having to look for a real job" (162), Couth just goes about the pleasant business of living on an island off the coast of Maine. Not worried either about owning property or making a mark on the world, Couth is the antithesis of the never solvent but always obsessing Trumper. There is nothing wrong with Couth's penis, either; he's not a member of that "rare fraternity," "the urinary-wounded" (165).

But Couth is not the hero of this novel. Bogus commands our interest because he is the wounded man who nevertheless manages to express a good deal of power. The novel represents Trumper as the epitome of silent and "blocked" masculinity; he refuses to express his emotions and this inexpressivity produces exactly the types of violent explosions and bodily wounds that the men's liberationists predict. In one scene, for example, in which his girlfriend Tulpen accuses him of not "coming across" (94), Trumper's repressed emotions eventually find an outlet in a physical expression of violence. In response to Tulpen's desire to have a baby and thus, in Trumper's view, tie him down to a domesticity that would impede his "flow," Trumper explodes, breaking Tulpen's prized fish tank, and "releasing" a torrent of water in the bedroom. It is only through a physical expression of his emotions that Trumper realizes what he is thinking and feeling. What was mostly implicit in men's liberation discourse becomes explicit here: men can only experience and express their emotional impulses by transforming them into physical impulses. The scene ends with a guilty and triumphant Trumper announcing, "I guess I *don't* want a baby" (95). Being blocked is a form of self-*preservation* for Bogus, since the women in his life are constantly trying to acculturate him into mature and responsible manhood, a project for which they require his consent. His resistance to giving it remains fierce until the end of the novel, but instead of exalting in his triumph, Bogus revels in his own inadequacy as husband and father and, later, lover. His failures *are* his triumphs, and Irving's representation of Bogus's emotional state suggests that he is pleasurably wounded by his failure to become what his stuffy father calls a "professional man." For much of the novel he is liberated from his familial responsibilities and the financial stresses they entail; and the bulk of the narrative leaves him wallowing in his painful-pleasurable state, guilt and triumph coming together in the portrait of a happily humiliated and failed man. The therapeutic "cure" that Trumper will eventually choose, in fact, proves far less satisfying a resolution than his display of wounded masculinity.

The Water-Method Man spends a good deal of narrative energy dwelling on Trumper's physical and psychic wounds and exploring the pains that accompany his attempts both to be responsible and to evade that responsibility. In Iowa City, for example, Trumper follows his aroused penis into a ridiculously ill-planned encounter with a student, which ends with him naked and abandoned in swampy and rugged terrain. Rather than put on his shoes—or, for that matter, remove the condom from his exposed penis—Trumper tramps barefoot through frozen broken corn stalks and other debris, ending up with "festering foot wounds, chiefly punctures and lacerations" (208). These wounds signal Trumper's martyrdom and offer a corporeal equivalent of the psychic pain Bogus suffers when Biggie throws him out—after he forgets the condom and urinates into it while Biggie watches. Lurching around the house seeking scissors (for some unaccountable reason), Bogus presents a spectacle of humiliated masculinity, "banging along on his knees, cradling the bulbous rubber in one hand" (191). Importantly, it is Trumper's anatomy that expresses, and clues him into, his emotional and psychic blockages. Trumper, in other words, exhibits "penis wisdom": the ability of the heterosexual male body to signify problems of gender identity in ways often "more perceptive than conscious thought" (Goldberg 37). The physiological condition and activity of the penis expresses his repressed emotions. Forgetting the condom is a way for Trumper to force

Biggie's hand, to "act out" his desire to get out of the marriage, since Bogus is unwilling to express his emotions in language and other direct forms of communication. Specifically, the condom blocks the flow of urine and also presents evidence of Trumper's unacknowledged desire to leave Biggie. The dominance of a liquid model of emotional and sexual energies is underlined in this novel by the plumbing allusions that flow as freely as the energies male liberationists would release.[16]

In Irving's novel, as in men's liberation discourse, a construction of emotion as a liquid, material force that flows through the body parallels the construction of sexuality and makes emotional release metaphorically dependent on sexual release. *The Water-Method Man* really runs with these metaphors, as the novel is nearly obsessed with plumbing, blockage, and flow, and full of vignettes of painful or problematic urination. The diabetic Merrill Overturf looks with "bewildered pain" (125) at his own uncontrolled acts of bodily "expression," and Bogus experiences excruciating pain when, with an adolescent case of the clap, the "tip of his life" (146)—that is, his penis—is blocked. Irving does not spare us the details of this pain, as Bogus remembers how he "straddled the hopper and peed what felt like razor blades, bent bobbypins and ground glass" (145). Metaphorically, too, the novel is full of references to blocked and freely flowing plumbing; in an early chapter entitled "Old Tasks & Plumbing News," for example, we hear that even Trumper's *toilet* is clogged. In each of his letters to Couth, Trumper asks his friend to "flush all seventeen of the johns for me" (26, 37) at the Pillsbury mansion in Maine where Couth is caretaker, and to which Biggie eventually moves after the breakup with Trumper. Finally, the "water-method" of the novel's title refers to the urologist's advice that drinking mass quantities of water before and after sex might literally flush out the pain that normally accompanies both sex and urination. All of these literal and metaphorical references to blockage and release converge in the novel's representation of Trumper's physiological and emotional "therapy," the end toward which the novel inexorably tends.

The novel is structured as a therapeutic narrative, but subtly offers a critique of that therapeutic model.[17] Irving's critique is emphatically "apolitical" and, thus, is quite different from the critique I offered in the first part of this chapter. Far from criticizing therapy for offering a personal solution to a political problem, Irving instead criticizes therapy for offering a one-size-fits-all model of psychological and social adjustment—particularly to norms of masculinity. As is true of Irving's entire corpus, *The Water-Method Man* eschews the collective in favor of the individual, the political in favor of the personal, as we saw in the case of *The World According to Garp* in the last chapter. What the novel is interested in is conceptualizing a male liberation that evades both the pitfalls of therapy as a process of adaptation,[18] and the pitfalls of a female-sponsored (and possibly feminist) attempt to put the brakes on male "expression." Trumper's physiological therapy, the unblocking of his penis, is accompanied by a psychological therapy, as he reluctantly participates in the making of "Fucking Up," the film about his life that his friend Ralph writes and directs. Together, the film and the operation enable—or, rather, force—Trumper to own up to his responsibilities. As he sardonically tells Dr. Vigneron, his suave French urologist, "I'm a new man. I'm not the old prick I was" (318). But while the ending of the novel signifies the liberation of Trumper's emotional and creative energies, it also signifies his acceptance of the "male role" that men's liberationists warn will produce blockages of all kinds.

After the operation he goes back to Iowa City and to his "blocked" dissertation, and embarks on a different kind of "therapy" (349). Swearing off the self-destructive habits of his youth, he becomes a kind of monk-scholar and finishes his degree. It is seeing "Fucking Up" that does the trick, a therapy after all, in the viewing if not the making. Returning to Tulpen—and new baby Merrill—he admits that his "straight, honest feelings were a long way down in a bog"—more metaphorical liquidity—"a bog he had been skirting for so long that now it seemed impossible to dive in and grope" (365). But dive in he does, and the last scene in the novel gives us a male liberation into emotional commitment, freely flowing friendship and love, and babies popping out everywhere. We know Bogus has fully taken the therapeutic plunge when we're told that a niggling little snake in this paradise found will be "processed": "He knew that back in New York there'd be a week of trying to understand" the jealousy that Tulpen feels for Biggie (378). The artificiality of this ending points to some ideological confusions that are sutured over in the interests of closure.

While *The Water-Method Man* ends in a conventionally happy way, the novel is nevertheless bathed in a nostalgia for the adolescent male liberation modeled by Merrill Overturf. Because Merrill haunts this novel so fully, the ending is compromised by the suspicion that love-fest aside, it's no fun being "straight"—a term that, in the late sixties and early seventies, equated male heterosexuality with the "establishment." As Charles Gaver puts it in his contribution to the heady *Straight/White/Male*, "the term *straight* refers to a bland, bigoted manner of existing, as in the phrase *straight and narrow*. Part of the problem with un-gay people is just that: they are too inhibited to enjoy and celebrate the gay things in life" (62). "Inhibition" is another word for inexpressivity, and the straight man is a blocked man, not only by individual temperament but by belonging to a normative category.[19] Trumper does, in fact, go "straight" by the end of the novel and, not surprisingly, this is the language in which his penile problems are described: his narrow and winding road gets "straightened out" by the operation and, despite the fact that Trumper is obviously thrilled to be cured of his physiological problem, he is at least a little bit regretful at having become "normal": "compared to what he had been used to, he now had a bathtub drain." When assured that his new penis is perfectly normal ("That's a beautiful meatoplasty," a doctor tells him), he becomes aware of "how abnormal he must have been" (347). But this is not a novel in which "normal" is a badge of honor or authenticity, and the happily heterosexual if slightly hippyish spectacle of family life and responsible adulthood with which the novel ends cannot erase an evident nostalgia for Trumper's earlier "blockage." While the therapeutic narrative ends with a "cure," a good deal of uncertainty attaches both to the efficacy of that cure and, indeed, the nature of the disease: "He had an image of how he'd *like* to return—as someone triumphant, like a cured cancer patient. But he couldn't decide what disease he'd had when he left, so he hardly knew if he was cured" (356–57). Tulpen is serene—she has what she wanted in the baby Trumper emphatically did not want; Biggie, Couth, and children are blissfully happy; even Ralph Packer has settled down with a wife and baby. But what about Trumper? Is he healthier, having been unblocked? Or, has he just conformed to a therapeutic culture that requires emotional, as well as physical, "flow"? Has he simply been acculturated into being the "mature" adult, accepted the "harness" that will eventually necessitate another unblocking? While the narrative *wants* to end with the image of a healed Trumper, doubts persist, including the doubt that, in post–women's liberation America, these women will be content to be the earth mothers of male fantasy, flaunting breasts that "lolled free" with "nipple-glued" children "riding on each busy hip" (381). The women's desires aside—the women in this novel are not particularly well developed in any event—Trumper begins to feel just a little bit suffocated by all this fecund femaleness: "Bogus wondered what he could have thought he wanted. But the kitchen was far too flurried for thinking; bodies were everywhere. So what if dog puke still lurked unseen in the laundry room! In good company we can be brave" (381). Not thinking is a positive good within the therapeutic milieu of men's consciousness-raising or men's liberation groups; but here, the emphasis on the emotional and the bodily as the antitheses of the intellectual carries a hint that Bogus will someday want to break free of all this "liberation." The happy ending cannot erase an evident nostalgia for Trumper's earlier "blockage."

THE EMBARRASSMENTS OF EMOTIONAL INCONTINENCE

The women in Irving's novel aim to block the free flow of male sexual energies, and to acculturate the men into mature and responsible manhood. But they also require that the men "communicate" openly, experience, express, and share their emotions—as long as those emotions are "soft" and "safe" and *not* an expression of male priority, privilege, or power. What Irving represents as women's contradictory demands is also evident in men's liberation discourse; but, there, such contradictions are studiously repressed in the interest of emphasizing the importance of flow and the dangers of blockage. These contradictions are even more marked in Leonard Michaels's *The Men's Club*, where the representation of a feminist-inspired men's consciousness-raising group leads subtly but inevitably to a warning against the a priori privileging of male release. The novel suggests that if women, and the "feminized" therapeutic culture to which they want to acculturate men, invite male release, then men cannot be responsible for the consequences. Satirizing the men's liberationists, Michaels's novel foregrounds how calls for the liberation of men are based on a misreading of feminism as a program for personal growth, rather than a demand for political change. The novel goes even further, warning that the version of male dominance we have now is positively benign compared to the version that will be unleashed if men actually take up the call to unblock their impulses. Metaphorical desires and feelings get translated into literal, physical needs as this men's consciousness-raising group devolves into a quasi-Darwinist spectacle of animalistic masculinity.

The entire novel takes place in the first session of a "men's club," where a group of emotionally inexpressive men get together to talk about their lives in an effort to reproduce the dynamics and outcomes of women's groups. Predictably, the talk immediately turns to sexual experiences, and the men in the club take turns narrating tales of bizarre transactions with what quickly turns out to be an alien and incomprehensible "opposite sex." The novel plays on the stereotype of emotionally repressed masculinity, but rather than making fun of men or critiquing masculinity, Michaels ultimately targets the therapeutic culture that requires men to participate in the touchy-feely emotional expressiveness of consciousness-raising. Kramer, the host of the men's club, is a practicing psychotherapist whose language comes under sharp and biting critique by the narrator, the club's members and, finally, his wife Nancy. The narrator, for example, mocks the ethos of free and open communication touted by popular seventies therapies: "It was time to be supportive, as they say. Go out of oneself feelingly. Leap the psychic fence. Stand in Cavanaugh's space. Let him know I feel what he feels" (60).

Here, as elsewhere, Michaels is simultaneously mocking the men and legitimating their understanding of the "truth" of masculinity. Unlike women's consciousness-raising groups, focused on "anger, identity, politics, rights, wrongs" (13), the men do not attempt to generalize from their experience nor to theorize the route to social (or even personal) change. Instead, they nervously engage in aimless and opaque conversation, warding off any insights that might prompt them to change the way they perform their masculinity. Instead of liberation, the men find themselves "embarrassed by [their] own incontinence" (107). Performance of masculinity is the best way to describe what happens in the men's club, but it is a performance that seems inevitable. While lampooning a therapeutic culture of manly sensitivity, the novel keeps intact a construction of dominant masculinity as emotionally blocked and, further, naturalizes that construction by making men appear constitutionally incapable of expressing "genuine" emotion. At the same time, in the many stories of sexual conquest and/or wounding that the men tell, the novel naturalizes a construction of male sexuality as automatic and unstoppable: men risk bodily and mental health by acceding to women's demands that they curb their sexuality. While individual men might blame women for forcing them to curb their "primitive" manly impulses, the true target of scorn is the soft and feminized therapeutic culture and its futile efforts to tame dominant masculinity.

The novel naturalizes male emotional *in*expressivity at the same time as it naturalizes male sexual *ex*pressivity. This becomes clearest in the story of Cavanaugh, who embodies a masculinity always on the verge of explosion but even more powerful for its ability to rein in emotional and other energies. A former professional basketball player, Cavanaugh represents a primitive and volatile masculine force kept in check and "blocked" by the civilizing requirements of social and family life. "He descended from heroes. Invincible, murderous, rapacious stock" (60), but is now domesticated by the "symbolic manacle" of family life and white-collar work. Cavanaugh is the figure for an emotionally blocked and sexually explosive masculinity: he doesn't communicate with his wife, and the force of his unexpressed emotional and sexual needs produces bodily trauma, paralyzing him under the force of his unexpressed emotions: "Soon there was nothing in my body but anger. I got into fights with my own teammates. I couldn't shave without slicing my face. I was smoking cigarettes. I had something against my body and wanted to hurt it" (25). Cavanaugh opens the valves of his emotional system inward rather than outward, engages in a form of self-mutilation, and offers his bodily wounds as evidence of his disempowerment. Such masochism, as we have seen, does little to challenge male power, as the self-inflicted wounds are used to evince the need *not* for a changed social order but for the "liberation" of individual men. Speaking for the ideology of male sexuality that undergirds the representation of dangerously blocked masculinity, Cavanaugh later tells of an argument with Sarah in which he is obviously aroused by her anger, in a story that reinforces both the wisdom of the penis and the man's "innocence" of the penis's designs: "My dick was pointing at her like she'd been out of town for a month. I tried to concentrate on what she was saying. She said I made her feel like throwing up. Like

I was my dick" (53). Not responsible for the "natural" expressions of his body, Cavanaugh is wounded by his wife's marking of him as a "typical man": her anger and her pain pale in comparison with his.

The narrator's admiration for the dammed masculine force circulating and recirculating in Cavanaugh's powerful body predicts the physical release toward which the narrative inexorably tends: Cavanaugh's blocked rapaciousness will eventually find an outlet in the novel's crescendo, where we learn that the true "release" comes only when the men "express" themselves physically. The first step toward this release is a highly mediated attack on women's groups and on feminist attempts to curb male "appetites." The group of men "rape" the refrigerator and devour the food and wine that Kramer's wife Nancy has prepared for her women's group meeting the next evening. This is absolutely explicit, as the narrator describes the now violated appliance, source of food, and target of violence: "Standing alone, raped, resonant with humiliation. Our ice mother. We'd seized her food" (50). The men indulge themselves in a ritual of consumption that unites pleasure and pain, innocence and guilt. The "rape" of the refrigerator is both a violation of women's groups and an attempt to appropriate and literally incorporate women's claims of victimization. But it is also a dark celebration of male privilege, and it is in the context of this episode that Michaels articulates most clearly what drives these privileged men to believe in their natural entitlement. Comparing the seizure of the food to the pillaging of jungles from monkeys, the narrator implies that it's fine for animals to be made homeless, for refrigerators to be raped, for women's food to be stolen, and for forests to be devastated—all for men's pleasure. Acknowledging that they are "lucky to be men," the narrator revels in the privileges afforded to men, and notes that "number one has more fun. The preparations for the women's group would feed our club. The idea of delicious food, taken this way, was thrilling" (43). Michaels represents this episode less as a critique of a raping masculinity, however, than evidence of its inevitability. Granting truth to feminist critiques of certain forms of male "expression," then, the novel just leaves us to regret that truth.

The novel, thus, is less critical of the men who embody the stereotype of repressed and violent masculinity than it is of the culture that attempts to "liberate" men from themselves.[20] This is not to say that the novel does not articulate dominant masculinity as emotionally repressed; it is to say that the novel questions the ability of men to express emotion, and questions, as well, whether *anyone,* men or women, will want to deal with the consequences of male expression. Michaels suggests that if a healthy masculinity is an expressive masculinity, the only thing that men are going to be willing to express is power. The novel locates male power only in physical and sexual expression, and in emotional *repression.* The inevitability of physical release is predicted by Canterbury's homophobically nervous question, "Why aren't we doing anything physical?" (121) that follows up on his earlier comment that talking about feelings makes "[y]ou guys sound like a bunch of homos" (119). Indeed, the threat of being marked as homosexual wafts through a number of different conversations in the novel, and the narrator turns Canterbury's homosexual panic into evidence of homosexual desire: "I wondered if he was gay. . . . He'd eaten like the rest of us and sat there listening, but produced no credentials" (114–15). Against the claims of gay liberation, the narrator sees gay men as "grim" and "dismal," perhaps too intent on anatomizing the wrongs they've suffered to revel in the sexuality their liberation was meant to release.

Abandoning entirely the possibility of a verbal expression of emotional experiences, the men's violence escalates into a knife-throwing episode, quickly followed by the howling that turns this consciousness-raising group into a spectacle that predicts the Robert Bly-inspired return of the "Wild Man" in the late eighties. As with the rape of the refrigerator, the house is wounded as the men project their hostilities toward women and feminist demands that they "communicate" onto the domestic space that signifies femininity. Michaels presents this devolution into violence as inevitable and exhilarating, a welcome release of repressed energies that outstrips the tame and feminized remedies of psychotherapies, and one that is worth quoting in its entirety:

> The howling was liquid, long, and thick in the red room, heart of Kramer's house. His cherished table lay on its side like a dead beast, stiff-legged and eviscerated, streaming crockery, silver, wine, meat, bones, and broken glass. We sounded lost, but thought we'd found ourselves. I mean nothing psychological. No psycho-logic of the soul, only the mind, and this was mindless. The table's treasure lay spilled and glittering at our feet and we howled, getting better at it as the minutes passed, entering deeply into our sound, and I felt more and more separated from myself, closer to the others, until it seemed we were one in the rising howls, rising again and again, taking us up even as we sank toward primal dissolution, assenting to it with this music of common animality, like a churchly chorus, singing of life and death.   (161)

This epiphany, a moment of communion between men that has the power to lift them out of themselves, suggests that the men have expressed themselves in the only way that men can—and it's sheer poetry, a moment to be enjoyed and reveled in and not analyzed, a moment that recalls Warren Farrell's injunction just to "feel," rather than intellectualize. Do the men appear ridiculous here, or sublime? The novel does not allow us to dwell on this question for very long because Michaels chooses this intense moment of male bonding to reintroduce a feminine presence, and it's hard to imagine a choice more geared to frame the woman as an alien, invasive presence, and men as the misunderstood objects of feminist scorn.

Nancy errs in (mis)reading this masculine experience as an adolescent and ridiculous exercise in male dominance. Michaels deflects attention away from the mindless destruction and acting out of male entitlement that this scene signifies by shifting focus away from the behavior to Kramer's ridiculous therapeutic response to Nancy's anger. What looks silly is not the men nor the mindless masculinity they perform, but Kramer's attempt to water the spectacle down with psychobabble, to which Nancy responds with a vicious mockery that escapes no one but the hapless Kramer. In a dialogue almost painful in its mockery of the clueless "analyst" Kramer, Nancy parodies her husband's language. Appearing to buy Kramer's line that the devastated house is a form of "creative expression," and thus sacrosanct, Nancy disappears into the kitchen to return with a cast-iron skillet, and whales on Kramer's head. Meanwhile, the narrator is fantasizing about having sex with Nancy, and the other men are busily noting her appearance, clothes, hair, intent on either ignoring or trivializing her anger. When she hits Kramer, he is stunned for only a minute, and then returns to therapy-speak: "I feel you're feeling anger" (172), he says, as the blood runs down his face. Nancy retreats, and her behavior wonderfully metaphorizes the novel's satire of recipes for male expressivity: she flushes the toilet repeatedly, in what the narrator describes as "violent annihilations" (175).

Nancy's violence diverts attention away from the men's violence; after all, they hurt only inanimate objects, she wounded her husband. So, while readers might smugly sit by and say, of course, the men devolve into violent physical behavior, how typical of men; such a reading must come to terms with Nancy's display of physical violence, and the narrative does not shy away from representing it: "[Kramer] rocked slightly, absorbing the blow, letting force slip down spinal ridges to ass and legs and heels while his hair released blood; red genius, oozing from his mind" (172). In contrast, the men appear positively harmless. While the novel might be read as giving a respectful airing to a justified female rage ("Women wanted to talk about anger, identity, politics, etc." [3]) and articulating a critique of male entitlement, it ultimately works to justify male rage and to deauthorize the feminist critique of the male privilege hidden behind male inexpressivity. Nancy's violent reaction suggests that feminist consciousness-raising is more dangerous than it appears and, further, that while men might direct their anger and aggression inward in line with a cultural requirement that men repress, *women*, radicalized by feminism, will direct that anger outward. "It is true that women are not emotionally constipated," writes Warren Farrell; "they can get their emotions out of their system" (166). But *The Men's Club* warns that female anger can mutate into female violence and, thus, *should* be blocked lest men risk physical, as well as emotional, woundings.

The Men's Club suggests that if men are forced to participate in a feminized therapeutic culture which invites them to "express themselves," then it is inevitable that such expression will result in the release of those male energies that simmer below the surface of a "civilized" facade. Although articulated in slightly different terms, Michaels's representation of the inevitably physical expression of male needs and desires echoes the male liberationists' focus on the *bodily* effects of emotional repression and of patriarchal power. Both *The Men's Club* and *The Water-Method Man* point to the fact that the masculinity described by men's liberation discourse is so fully dependent on a naturalized construction of dangerous male energies that it is impossible to believe that the endpoint of male liberation would be the expression of those softer emotions like compassion, sympathy, and so on. Because the blockage-release model defines the male body as a cauldron of warring impulses and emotions, masculinity gets naturalized as powerful but vulnerably so, its power dependent precisely on the regulation of "natural" male energies. If men are to be "liberated," they must be liberated from nature; and such liberation almost always produces a new cycle of blockage. This was perhaps clearest in *The Water-Method Man*, where one kind of expressivity leads to another kind of blockage: Trumper learns to "come across," to open up, to his lover and others and thus proves himself ready to accept "the male role." Male liberation, as it is theorized in these texts, is an impossible goal—*not* because actual men cannot change, but because the model of blockage and release naturalizes a powerful-powerless masculinity that is, by definition, resistant to change.

The naturalization of a particular construct of male sexuality and of male violence becomes the fly in the ointment of men's liberation, and the novels I've looked at here focus attention on the central problems in men's liberationist discourse. Male expressivity is healthy, but what will be expressed once blockage is alleviated? The model of dangerous blockage and healthy release comes up against its opposite, a recognition that release itself can be dangerous, and blockage healthy. Are there male impulses that might better be blocked? Or, is male release an a priori good? Goldberg would answer no and yes, respectively, but I don't think the others would be so sure. The liberation predicted in Warren Farrell's *The Liberated Man* and in Marc Feigen Fasteau's *The Male Machine* did not come to pass because the terms in which this liberation were articulated made it impossible. Not only do the texts naturalize, and thus make resistant to change, the very construction of masculinity they mean to displace, but their agendas are also shipwrecked on a naive faith in the power of the individual and an underestimation of that individual's imbrication in the social. Patriarchy requires both blockage and release in men, and one of the main problems of men's liberation discourse is that it doesn't distinguish between the kinds of blockages that hurt men and the kinds that benefit them. The hazards of being male are set off by the benefits of being male, and the erasure of these benefits might work to imagine a new vulnerable, open, and more "feminized" masculinity; but it also works to authorize asocial, and thus apolitical, understandings of the supports of male dominance. The story of seventies male liberationists ends sadly with Warren Farrell who, in 1993, published *The Myth of Male Power: Why Men Are the Disposable Sex.* No longer feminist, Farrell believes that feminism, the rise of the "government as substitute husband," the continuation of an exclusively male combat force, the overrepresentation of men in the "death professions," and the shutting of men out of reproductive and childraising decisions—all of these forces have conspired to turn men into the "disposable sex." While Farrell does shed some light on why American men might be feeling pain at this particular historical moment, his goal seems to be to present the case that men suffer more than women. To do so, he draws on a rhetoric of bodily pain (as opposed to, say, economic pain) to challenge feminist assertions that men are in power.

But being in pain doesn't mean being disempowered. As easy as Farrell's arguments would be to contest, such a critique would do nothing to shed light on *why* male pain is so central to calls for male liberation. I cannot help but suspect that the male liberationists don't really want to liberate men at all; instead, they seem content to dwell on male pain both given and suffered. In so doing, Goldberg, Fasteau, and Farrell sketch out the contours of a new masculinity: a masculinity defined by the pain of emotional blockage, but one defined, as well, by the painful necessity of restraining the "primitive" impulses that always threaten to emerge. This image of a simmering male body whose psychophysical energies are always circulating and recirculating in an effort to avoid both destruction and self-destruction constructs a masculinity that embraces pain as a manly credential even as it threatens to release those natural male energies that cause pain to others. Men *must* restrain their dangerous impulses, but men *cannot* restrain them; men *must* release their blocked emotions, but men *cannot* release them. It is in the space between the "must" and the "cannot" that the physically and psychically wounded man emerges, *not* as a pathological, or even "failed" man, but as the norm of a masculinity that can only attempt to be "healthy." In the next chapter we'll see how this impasse produces a hysterical male body whose particular affliction is its inability to express an essential but dangerous masculinity—and whose pleasure in pain testifies to the desire to keep in suspension the crisis of dominant masculinity.

CHAPTER 5

EXPRESSION, REPRESSION, AND MALE HYSTERIA

Marked Men and the Wounds of a Dammed Masculinity

The devolution into a primitivist spectacle of male release at the end of *The Men's Club* leaves us with the image of a dominant masculinity set free from social constraints. Ironically, a men's club prompted by feminist political analysis ends by evincing the impossibility of political action. Trumping the social with the natural, Michaels's men end up reinforcing the inevitability of a "raping" masculinity. References to both Freud and Darwin grease the path toward this end, as instinct and survival replace consciousness-raising and analysis. The release of male impulses and energies gets naturalized through a discourse that roots social trauma in the body, and uses biology to explain emotional expressivity and inexpressivity. The substitution of the personal for the political gives way to a new celebration of the "primal," as Michaels does the men's liberationists one better. Yet even within the politically motivated if therapeutic discourse of men's liberation, a narrative charting the struggle between the primitive and civilized aspects of dominant masculinity can be discerned. It is, perhaps not surprisingly, around the concept of male sexuality that this struggle most fully emerges. In this chapter, I will further explore the effects of the naturalization of a construction of masculinity as torn between repression and expression, blockage and release, by focusing on a set of texts that place the current crisis in white masculinity within the context of a seemingly ahistorical battle between the forces of primitivism and the forces of civilization: James Dickey's *Deliverance* (1970) and the John Boorman film based on it (1972); Pat Conroy's *The Prince of Tides* (1986) and, more briefly, Barbra Streisand's film of it (1991). Like the texts I discussed in the last chapter, these narratives are drawn to an image of a white masculinity perpetually in crisis, and figure that crisis in bodily terms. As we will see, they do so by drawing on discourses of evolution, biological determinism, and natural instinct, discourses that work to validate male power even as they gesture toward an acknowledgment that that power is fragile, always under siege, always in crisis. The body that emerges from these texts is a body made vibrant by the warring impulses between blockage and release, a hysterical body on which is written emotional, social, and political trauma.

The suppression of men's impulses has occasionally been understood as a necessary evil, if not a positive good; but in the wake of the various liberation movements of the late 1960s, as we saw in chapter 4, blockage becomes synonymous with oppression, and a discourse on men's liberation begins to anatomize the "hazards of being male." The biologistic slant of men's liberation discourse, echoed by popular sexologies intent upon negotiating the feminist challenges to a particular construction of male heterosexuality, has the effect of naturalizing a set of social relations and a narrowly conceived construction of the male body and the male psyche. Men's liberation discourse conflates emotional, sexual, and violent "release" and suggests that men will suffer psychic and physiological wounds if no "outlet" can be found. Implicitly, if not explicitly, contemporary masculinity is diagnosed as hysterical, and the male body the canvas on which repressed trauma is written. The body "speaks" men's discontent, much as the feminist analysis of hysteria has suggested that the female body "speaks" the woman's oppression under patriarchy. The intertwining of the sexual with the emotional furthers such a diagnosis, as the men's liberationists represent men as torn between a "natural" imperative toward sexual expression and a social imperative toward restraint. A disturbance in the field of sexuality codes and thus obscures the political trauma that simmers below the surface of these texts. While in the last chapter I focused on how emotional blockage is linked by analogy to sexual blockage, here I want to look at how an explicit discourse on male sexuality works to reinforce and naturalize a construction of the heterosexual male body and male psyche as wounded by the impossibility of choosing between expression and repression. Behind this explicit discourse on sexuality is an implicit response to feminist critiques of a "raping" male sexuality, a political context that must be disavowed in order to represent dominant masculinity as wounded by its *own* power.[1]

After revisiting men's liberationist discourse, I will turn to *Deliverance* and *The Prince of Tides*, two narratives that metaphorically render the crisis in contemporary masculinity as the "damming" of masculine impulses and energies. As Marc Feigen Fasteau remarks in his 1974 study of the perils of the male role, *The Male Machine*, *Deliverance* (novel and film) exemplifies the American mythology linking the "release" of male violence to health, and the repression of violence to bodily harm: "basically, *Deliverance* celebrates the idea that the kill-or-be-killed situation, away from civilization and its artificial protections, is where men are most profoundly alive and, if they pass its tests, most profoundly masculine" (148). But while this assessment might apply to the novel, the film is far more ambivalent about the therapeutic value of male violence and the unhindered release of blocked energies. In contrasting the novel and film, I aim to chart the difference between two responses to the crisis of post-liberationist white masculinity: the novel resolves the crisis through a remasculinization of its central protagonist, while the film reconstructs dominant masculinity as a far more fragile identity formation, perpetually in crisis.[2] From here, I will turn to Pat Conroy's *The Prince of Tides*, a novel that renders a hysterical male body as the result of an irresolvable conflict between an inevitably violent and sexually predatory masculinity and a masculinity wounded by the repression of its emotional and physical energies. After analyzing the complicated ways in which the novel contextualizes its hero's crisis within a post-liberationist social, political, and psychic terrain, I will briefly discuss how and why Barbra Streisand's 1991 film *The Prince of Tides* erases the political contexts of Tom Wingo's crisis. The film envisions Tom's blockage and his wounds as the merely personal responses to repressed memories, and his sexual/emotional healing as a magical result of the therapeutic enterprise. Substituting the therapeutic for the feminist, the film, somewhat ironically, goes much further than the novel in dehistoricizing the battle between the repression and expression of male impulses and arguing for an a priori privileging of male release.

MEN'S LIBERATION REDUX: SEXUALITY, EVOLUTION, AND THE EMBODIED STRUGGLE BETWEEN BLOCKAGE AND RELEASE

As we saw in the last chapter, sexuality, like emotion, is framed as always potentially violent and explosive, a "natural" force that is endangered by any tinkering with elemental impulses. As we will see here, a discursive struggle over the meanings of "liberation" pits evolutionary imperatives against sexual politics. Drawing on a social Darwinist conceptualization of biological imperatives, Herb Goldberg and others naturalize and thus depoliticize a particular construction of male heterosexuality—recently come under attack, of course, by feminism. The politicized discourse on liberation gets replaced by a biologistic discourse on "survival," and the battle between men and women gets rewritten as a battle between the forces of "nature" and the forces of "society." Goldberg, for example, never directly blames feminism, women, or patriarchy for what ails men, sexually or otherwise; instead, he exhibits what can best be described as a survival-of-the-fittest approach to gendered liberation. *The Hazards of Being Male* unfolds across a cultural and social field in which power relations have been flattened, and individual men and individual women are left to fight out their own "liberation" and survival. The subtitle of Goldberg's book, *Surviving the Myth of Masculine Privilege*, invokes this battle, posing men not so much against women as against any social, political, or personal obstacle placed in the way of male liberation. While we might find it refreshing to note that women aren't blamed for this crisis in masculinity, this strategy enables Goldberg and others to avoid engaging with feminism and discussions of sexual politics. The reluctance to blame women or feminism for men's disempowerment, then, can be read as a reluctance to trace the crisis of masculinity to the political. Popular books on "the new sexuality" perform a similar rhetorical feat and do so by endowing Nature with a human agency that reduces both men and women to mere pawns in the unfolding of a fated design.

Like the men's liberationists who credit feminism with paving the path of male liberation even as they leave the political insights of feminism behind, popular sexologists applaud female sexual agency in the same breath as they lament the increased pressure on men produced by that agency. To negotiate these contradictions, these texts displace the battle of the sexes onto a seemingly ahistorical, apolitical stage on which is played out an age-old battle between man and society. "Society" is a more or less empty signifier in both popular sexology and men's liberationist discourse, and what it is emptied of is any specific, materialist conceptualization of how power flows and how rights and privileges are distributed. A straw man, "society" functions as a composite of shadowy forces that conspire to tamp down or regulate the flow of "man's" energies and impulses. The construction of sexuality as "natural" instead of social or political works to contest the increasingly visible feminist analysis of sexuality as an arena of power relations, albeit indirectly.[3] But because sexual politics gets replaced by sociobiology as an explanatory model, the necessity for remolding male sexuality in relation to the feminist critique is obviated. The use of "nature" as the agent of sexual conduct makes it possible to override the political critique of a normative male heterosexuality and to argue that men must reclaim their "rights" in the sexual realm. Nature and the language of natural law are used both to excuse the uninhibited release of male energies *and* to position men as vulnerable, subject to laws beyond their control. So, while the language of nature might appear simply to reconstruct male privilege and remasculinize men, things are actually more complicated than that: men are wounded by the convergence of competing imperatives within their fragile bodies and psyches, subject to both "nature" and "society," and left to fight for their own liberation.

This naturalist approach to the battle of the sexes requires that social constructions of masculinity be relegated to the "society" side of the "man" versus "society" couplet, and thus be understood in an adversarial relation to "man." On the one hand, this way of thinking owes to the feminist critique of the social construction of gender; on the other hand, however, it is utilized to justify and naturalize the "truth" of a primal masculinity allegedly untouched by the social. These contradictions are particularly evident in discussions of male sexuality, where a battle between the natural and the social gets embodied as a battle between the uncontrollable and the forces of inhibition. "Men tend," Bernie Zilbergeld notes in *The New Male Sexuality*, "to view sexual arousal as a runaway train; once in motion, it should not be stopped or deflected until it reaches its destination" (166). Although Zilbergeld undertakes to dispel the myth that male sexuality is automatic, not under a man's control, he nevertheless authorizes this construction when he counters the "bad press" that men (and penises) have had by saying that "the criticisms themselves are wrongheaded and destructive. Males can't help having their attitudes, which are probably due at least as much to physiology as to learning. Sex, after all, is life-affirming, and there's no point in feeling bad about that" (161). Male attitudes that might be understood as socially grounded and inflected by sexual politics are here framed as "physiological," based in biology and, thus, not subject to change.[4] It is just a short step from this claim to the slightly more overblown one penned by Kenneth Purvis, author of *The Male Sexual Machine: An Owner's Manual*.[5] Positioning women and feminism against an entire evolutionary history, Purvis argues that women are requiring men to go against nature in demanding that their lovers "suppress" the "primitive reflex" of speedy ejaculation; "in our modern, sexually emancipated society," Purvis laments, "men are under increasing pressure to overcome this reflex, which has taken nature millions of years to evolve" (77).[6] Sensitivity to female sexual needs equates with repression of natural male impulses and evolutionary needs. We see this, too, in Herb Goldberg's version of sexual reality. Claiming that "men invariably try to accommodate female [sexual] needs rather than fulfill their own" (40), Goldberg urges men to "forget all the old imperatives regarding male obligations to satisfy the female" (51). Men are counseled to reject the new "super-gentle and super-sensitive" feminized sexuality, diluted by "the defense against anger [which] will spell the death of spontaneous sexuality" (62). The body, the seat of the natural and the primitive, must go its own way; and, thus, the penis is posed against "civilization" and its attempt to channel male impulses. Women and feminism are located firmly on the side of "civilization," and an overwhelming sense of the male body under siege emerges.

Nowhere is this clearer than in Dr. Harvey Kaye's aptly titled *Male Survival: Masculinity Without Myth* (1974), which goes even further than Zilbergeld's defense of "physiological" attitudes or Herb Goldberg's account of "penis wisdom" in his claims that the brain, or a psychological orientation to male sexuality, has placed the penis in jeopardy. Drawing on the language of evolution and anthropomorphizing the penis—as does nearly every writer on the subject—Kaye endows the "humble organ" with a mind of its own, a kind of phallic knowhow that exceeds or is at odds with current thinking about male sexuality. Like Goldberg's arguments against monogamy,[7] Kaye's discussion of "The Sexual Life of a Penis" positions itself pretty directly against feminist attempts to reform or reshape the male sexual impulse, to channel male energies into limited and biologically unsatisfying outlets. Conceding that the brain might work with the penis by providing images and fantasies to enhance sexual pleasure, Kaye nevertheless worries that the cultural baggage which occupies brains—including "the guilts, and the assorted hang-ups which have been the lot of 'civilized' man for centuries"—will impede sexual release, and the "penis [will] pay the price" (71). In sections entitled "The Disenfranchised Penis" and "The Penis Under Siege," Kaye equates the penis with the phallus and argues that the "phallus appears as a principal casualty of our most recent social upheaval" (67). The penis/phallus emerges as wounded, but more importantly, always in danger of being wounded *again*. The male body is, thus, perpetually in crisis, and the "contemporary penis finds himself the focal point of converging imperatives" (74). Torn between the natural and the social—the latter represented by the forces of feminism, the patriarchal "Male Mystique," and the new validation of the "relational" over the "recreational"—the "disenfranchised penis" "may view itself as under a chronic state of siege" (79). Note that Kaye couches his defense of the biological in the language of the social: the penis is not "limp" or "forgotten" or even "wounded"—it's "disenfranchised." In representing the penis as the victim of the sexual and women's liberation movements, Kaye joins other writers in not only substituting the personal for the political but in *naturalizing* that substitution. What emerges from such conflicted accounts of male power/disempowerment is not a "remasculinization," despite the rhetoric of primitivism and natural instincts; central to these reconstructions is the image of a wounded masculinity always in need of "liberation," but inevitably poised against the forces of a "society" that insists on the "myth of male privilege."

All of this talk about penises, moreover, is bound to increase men's anxieties about sexual performance *and* male power. While frank discussion of male sexuality, the male body, and the penis might be meant to liberate men from disabling myths, such discussion also works to make visible male bodies and sexuality and, thus, to exacerbate the very crisis these texts want to sooth. The heterosexualized male body has been veiled by constructions of phallic masculinity that are endangered by the increased visibility of that body; for, while sexual power has long been central to these constructions, that power has often approached the mythic. This has kept the specific, embodied sexual experiences of men invisible, and hidden the penis behind the phallus.[8] Talk about the penis can work to demystify the phallus. As Antony Easthope puts it, "as a cultural object the phallus may attract immense force and charisma while the humble penis carries on as best it can with its usual bodily functions" (4). Peter

Lehman echoes this sentiment when he notes that "traditional patriarchal constructions of masculinity benefit enormously by keeping the male body in the dark, out of the critical spotlight. Indeed, the mystique of the phallus is, in part, dependent on it" ("In the Realm," 105). Perhaps more than any other time in American history, the seventies witness a hyper-visibility of the penis, as radical feminists, men's liberationists, and the chroniclers of human sexuality all turn their attention to the penis and its (dys)functions. As one commentator notes, the liberationist discourses of the seventies and the technologies of sexuality they ushered in might have demystified the penis and male power right out of existence: "Slowly but surely . . . the secrets that men have kept to themselves for thousands of years, their weaknesses, their sexual fears are being laid bare for all to scrutinize" (Purvis 72). While the revelation of these secrets might lead toward healthier attitudes toward male sexual (dys)functions, the language here reveals a good deal of anxiety about the mythic power that might be lost in the process.

Kenneth Purvis's *The Male Sexual Machine*, published in the early 1990s, can be used as an example of how this attention to male bodies and body parts has produced, over a period of years, an acute anxiety about male sexuality and male power. The marking of male sexuality as dangerous and predatory in the early days of the feminist movement has given way to a much more conflicted view of the penis as *both* powerful "weapon" *and* vulnerable organ. This conflict serves to keep masculinity and the male body perpetually in crisis, as experts and laymen alike attempt to come to terms with the contradictions produced through attention to bodies formerly kept out of the light of day. Purvis begins his book with a discussion that shares a language with recent academic studies of masculinity and the male body. "For thousands of years," writes Purvis with characteristic overstatement and a flattening of history, "man has kept his private parts too private. . . . The shroud of secrecy that surrounds the workings and structure of the male organs smells of a male conspiracy with long roots" (vii–viii). For Purvis, whose interest is in male sexual health rather than the abolition of male privilege, such secrecy has hurt men physically even as it has secured a certain powerful mystique. He goes on to note that the first "cracks in this shell of secrecy" appear "with the rise of feminism and the birth of the so-called permissive society," and thus argues that the new visibility of the penis and of male sexuality is a kind of "marking" imposed on men by women and "society":

> Women began to demand orgasms and to put the male's sexual performance under a microscope. They read letters in women's magazines about the sexual lives of other women and compared notes. The bluff that men had practiced so expertly for a thousand years was suddenly called. Words of derision

like "macho male" and "chauvinistic pig" appeared, as women for the first time dared to sneer at the animal within their mates. As cracks become chasms, men gradually become imperfect both to themselves and to the growing multitudes of interested female spectators. The myths and the stereotyped images have been cast aside, and the time has come for both women and men to discover the truth about maleness and find out what makes men tick.   (VIII–IX)

While Purvis is arguing that knowledge and visibility are good for men, there is a whiff of nostalgia here for the days before women threw around derisive words, before women forced into visibility the male body. Such ambivalence is evident throughout Purvis's and other books on male sexuality; indeed, the very presence of books on *male* sexuality at the bookstore or library proclaims loudly for all to hear that the patriarchal ruse of keeping the male body in the dark is no longer working. The gig is up. Or is it?

As I argued in the introduction to this book, visibility is a mixed blessing, both for the white men who have enjoyed the privileges of unmarkedness and those who aim to strip them of those privileges. As Purvis's and other books on topics like *The New Male Sexuality* or *Undressing the American Male*[9] indicate, the coming to visibility of the male sexual body—and, most importantly, the penis—means a perpetuation of the current crisis in masculinity, soothing words and the prediction of happy endings notwithstanding. There is a residual anxiety left at the end of such books, a slightly hysterical note that male liberation, sexual and otherwise, comes at a price that might be too steep. Images of wounded white men, victims of sexual dysfunction and the "unnatural" restraint of impulses and energies, ironically, work to manage the anxieties produced by the new visibility of the male body and sexuality by giving "normal" men a place within a zeitgeist that appears to privilege the disenfranchised over the enfranchised. But this representational strategy, deliberate or not, makes it nearly impossible to resolve the crisis in masculinity, since such images necessarily risk provoking yet another crisis. As we've seen throughout this study, representations of the bodily wounds of white men work to recenter white masculinity in a social terrain altered by the discourses of liberation and oppression, victimized and victimizer, even as such representations perpetuate the crisis of masculinity. If "[g]etting an erection is the essence of male dominance" (Purvis 106), the intense scrutiny trained on that dominance both reinforces it and places it at risk. What is at stake in such discussions is the question of the normative: what happens to the normativity of white, male heterosexuality when it becomes visible as a specific, embodied category?

The popular discourse on male sexuality in the late seventies necessarily unfolds against the backdrop of changes in racial and gender power relations and the massive shifts in the normative caused by the sexual revolution. While feminists were enjoining men to be more sensitive to women's sexual needs, black power spokesmen like Eldridge Cleaver were framing white masculinity as sexually enervated and effeminate.[10] Such public discussion serves to "sex" white heterosexual men, to mark these men as, alternately, sexual predators of women, feminized "fags," or the impotent "straight" men positioned on the margins of the sexual revolution. As Charles Gaver argues in his manifesto "Gay Liberation and Straight White Males," published in Glenn Bucher's heady *Straight/White/Male* (1976), gay liberation has liberated sex itself, freed it from the uninspired and mechanized formula, and the "ego trips over who is on top, literally or otherwise" (63). But while Gaver's goal is to argue that straight men should rejoice in this liberation, his construction of the "straight" contains a critique that is geared to produce anxiety in the very population he is trying to convince. He makes straight male sexuality visible and visible as a pathetic imitation of the gay sex which "treats the entire being as an erogenous zone": "Straight sex has too often degenerated into a mechanical process—genitally-centered, orgasmically-oriented. Heterosexual books are crammed full of position after position, a myriad of acrobatic stunts, all a variation of the same 'thing-hole' concept" (62–63). Gay liberation functions to publicize male sexuality, and in ways that were guaranteed to trouble a white heterosexual population schooled to associate homosexuality with effeminacy and male heterosexuality with power. These threats are managed through a decidedly masculine ideology of heterosexual release, and, as Warren Farrell's consciousness-raising groups suggest, one that deals with the threat of a demasculinized homosexuality by channeling overflows of sexual energies into a far less troubling bisexuality. Farrell narrates an encounter in which one of two visibly gay men "liberates" himself into bisexuality. This man goes from being a little too "open" about his homosexuality—Farrell confesses some uneasiness among the men for "being treated as a sex object"—to being "open" to the possibility of a heterosexual relationship (245–46). Openness, here as elsewhere, is the supreme good, and bisexuality becomes the ideal. Farrell's men gleefully announce "I'm a compulsive heterosexual!" as they discover their own repression at the hands of a vaguely sketched but nonagential "society"; but this insight is a purely personal one, compulsive heterosexuality understood as the very ideology of male sexuality I have been attending to here. In other words, these men find that they have been hurt, not by social interdictions against homo- or bisexuality, but by their adherence to a personally inhibiting idea that men should and must get aroused, and act on that arousal, whenever an appropriate female object appears. Compulsive heterosexuality in this sense is, as Dr. Zilbergeld puts it, "one of the ways in which males get a raw deal" (7); but it is also a "natural" justification for a construction of male sexuality that legitimates sexual release at all costs.[11]

Prescriptions for male heterosexual release, however, can have the unwitting effect of increasing anxiety about impotence, a central concern in men's liberation discourse and popular sexology. As Kenneth Purvis wryly notes, "with the rise of feminism many men prophesized the end of civilization as we then knew it. Books were written forecasting epidemics of impotence as women gradually took more and more control in the sexual act, taking away the male initiative and his hunting instinct" (108). With increased attention to women's sexuality, gay men's sexuality, and indeed, sexuality in general, the mystique of the penis/phallus falls into disrepute. While women and gay men are loudly proclaiming their sexual liberation, heterosexual impotence is on the rise and, according to Marc Feigen Fasteau, this is so in part because women (and the times) are demanding that men move away from just the kind of "straight" sex that Gaver ridicules. Fasteau suggests that men are made anxious by women being sexually assertive, by the performance ethic, by women's demands that men become more emotionally involved in sex, and in general by sexual experimentation: "Not being on top, in 'missionary position,' for example," he concludes, "is upsetting to many men" (29). While Fasteau, Farrell, and a number of popular sexologists see impotence as one of the consequences of *both* the male role and the feminist critique of that role, Goldberg takes the pressure off men by arguing that "so-called impotence" is not epidemic at all and is, in fact, simply a sign of "penis wisdom." Claiming that men would sooner admit to the medical condition of impotence than confess that their partners don't turn them on (36), Goldberg sees the failure of sexual release as a defense strategy to "save" the penis from an unwanted sexual encounter.

Understandings of impotence have long been based on models of blockage and release that shift in response to changes in medical and social constructions of male heterosexuality. In the American 1920s, for instance, as Kevin Mumford argues, a Victorian construction of impotence as caused by excessive sexual expression gives way to a construction that targets excessive continence or repression as the cause of impotence. This shift accompanies a larger shift in the understanding of the economy of male sexual desire and energy from a finite and closed system to an unlimited and self-replenishing one. In both cases, male sexual energy is imagined as *substantial,* a fluid that can be saved or released; what changes is the meaning of that release. Mumford concludes that "the scientific consensus on what caused impotence and how to treat it was shifting gradually away from a . . . model of scarcity, depletion, and saving toward a psychological model of abundance, repression, and spending" (49). By the 1920s, physicians were "more likely to prescribe therapies of sexual release, rather than restraint, while some psychologists went so far as to argue that restraint itself caused impotence" (50). Men's sexual problems stemmed more from the "psychological guilt" induced by sexual release than from the release itself. Not surprisingly, when physicians began to prescribe sexual release as a cure for impotence, medical attention turned to women as the erotic objects who did, or did not, arouse sufficient desire for that release to be accomplished (53)—a version of Goldberg's "penis wisdom."

While manly self-control was deemed a positive virtue of masculinity before the rise of the "sexualized society," self-control begins to be dangerous to manliness, and sexual release is prescribed as the cure for what ails a repressed and wounded masculinity. A new cycle of crisis in the meanings of male sexuality is evident in the 1970s, complete with renewed interest in impotence and anxiety about how to negotiate between two seemingly contradictory prescriptions for strong masculinity: self-control and abandoned release. As in the early twentieth century, discussions of the healthy effects of sexual release are based on a continuing misinterpretation of a Freudian theory of repression. This misunderstanding stems, in part, from a very American emphasis on individualism, and a conviction that larger social, cultural, or even "natural" forces exist entirely separate from the individual. "[P]opularizers of instinct theory" in the 1920s, Kevin White points out, "misinterpreted Freud's insight that psychological adjustment and heterosexual adjustment were one to mean that healthy psychological adjustment was facilitated by having lots of sex. An ideology that urged sexual expression in this way gained ascendancy over an ideology that emphasized repression"[12] and obscured Freud's "respect for the power and force of male sexuality and his awareness of its need to be controlled if civilization were to be preserved" (White 59). But this individualist understanding of sexual expression and repression also depends on the existence of male "others" onto whom white men could project the "darker" meanings of sexual release. Indeed, in some sense, the very notion of the liberal individual depends on the existence of those others, African or Native American, who, as Toni Morrison has suggested, "provided the staging ground and arena for the elaboration of the quintessential American identity," "the new white man" (44, 39).

References to "civilization," as in the discourse on manly self-control, necessarily invoke the complementary term "savagery," and with such terms comes a racialized discourse pitting white manhood against an array of "primitive" male others. The visibility of those male others—through widely promulgated narratives about virile black masculinity and savage Native American masculinity, for instance—brings an awareness of the potential for dangerous masculinity. Manly self-control for white men, thus, is predicated on the ability to control the expression of other, more dangerous masculinities.[13] But while projecting the most dangerous forms of uncontrolled male sexuality outside the self and onto a male other might work to contain the danger and envision routes toward its control, such strategies also justify the "release" of a primitive masculinity in *all* men. Obsessive interest in the figure of the black male rapist, a historically constant register of white male anxieties over sexuality and its control, testifies to a simultaneous attraction to, and repulsion against, those dangerous male others who are both different from, and the same as, the white male self. The visibility of "savage" male others—whose bodies are marked so that the white male can remain the paradoxical embodiment of the disembodied individual—offered evidence of a dangerous masculinity *and* enabled white men to practice modes of control. "By gaining the manly strength to control himself, a man gained the authority, as well as the duty, to protect and direct those less manly than himself—whether his wife, his children, his employees, or his racial 'inferiors'" (Bederman 48). White male sexuality *and* the violence needed to control the sexuality of others are sanctioned by the presence of the savage, racial male other who expresses a primitive masculinity and occasions the display of white male control. As Sandra Gunning notes, "[c]onveniently, the stereotype of the black rapist . . . helped to distance white men from their own sexual transgressions" (28) and to justify *white* male savagery; thus, "white male retaliation could be writ manageably as the protective concern for domestic spaces" (Gunning 24), enacted through lynching and other forms of racialized (and sexualized) violence.[14]

While the heyday of the convenient stereotype of the black rapist might have been in the Reconstruction South, such stereotypes continue to be resurrected in post–civil rights American culture. As we will see in a moment, the "redneck" or "hillbilly," a primitive but still white male other, comes to substitute for the black male rapist in narratives of a white masculinity in crisis; but the racialized dynamics involved in projecting a dangerous masculinity outside of the white male norm are still evident. This image of an uncontrollable, dangerous male other also meets up with more ambivalently masculinized images in the South, where the genteel aristocrat evinces a civilized and somewhat enervated masculinity and the tragically defeated Rebel a wounded one. While the southern gentleman is characterized by his desire to protect women and children from the dangerous others who might lurk in the shadows—and, as I've suggested, even within *himself*—the tragically defeated Rebel evinces the failure of chivalry and, indeed, a failure of masculinity that will haunt southern men far into the twentieth century. Because the Reb is the figure for an independent white masculinity idealized *as* defeated, he becomes a reservoir from which other white men can draw when seeking to image a victimized but still heroically fighting white masculinity. The Reb offers white men a powerful image of tragically wounded masculinity and, as is evident in refrains like "the South is going to rise again," provides the occasion for new narratives of male violence.[15] But, as we have seen in other instances throughout this study, remasculinization is not the only strategy used to recoup the losses suffered by white men who feel themselves to be displaced or decentered; claiming the po-

sition of wounded victim can also work to manage the crisis in white masculinity, not through a final healing but, instead, through a perpetuation of
that crisis. The South is, thus, figured as a space of an ongoing crisis in masculinity, one that can never be resolved but instead gets repeated again and
again; that crisis is given a bodily form, as southern white men experience the
vulnerability and wounds that come from repressing what is understood as a
natural male violence.

DAMNED IF THEY DO, DAMNED IF THEY DON'T:
DELIVERANCE AND THE HYSTERICAL MALE BODY

John Boorman's 1972 film *Deliverance* is, inevitably, most often remembered for
the humiliating scene of male rape at its center, with Bobby Trippe (played by
Ned Beatty) forced to "squeal like a pig" as he is sodomized by a hillbilly who
embodies a middle-class nightmare vision of "white trash." Watched by Ed
Gentry (Jon Voight), the central protagonist, Drew Ballinger (Ronny Cox), the
one who doesn't survive the trip, and the macho survivalist Lewis Medlock
(Burt Reynolds), this scene alone would be enough to qualify *Deliverance* as a
film about white, middle-class masculinity in crisis. But the larger crisis the
film explores has little to do with the rape. Indeed, as Linda Ruth Williams
points out, a "collective disavowal" rules both the film and the critical reception
of it, as the rape must be buried along with the male bodies that keep piling up
in its wake.[16] The imperative to disavow knowledge of the rape is emblematic
of the film's larger concern with the perils of emotional, sexual, and "natural"
expression and its concern, as well, with the equally perilous repression of
emotional, sexual, and "natural" impulses. The film, Williams speculates par-
enthetically, "could be seen almost as a treatise on the many forms of repression" (9), and, we might add, their inadequacy in the face of the secrets and the
violence that threaten to erupt at every moment. Damned if they do, and
damned if they don't,[17] the men in Boorman's film are caught between two
competing, but oddly complementary, truths structuring masculinity and male
experience: male power is secured by inexpressivity, even as inexpressivity
damages the male psyche and the male body.

The political realignments of the late sixties form the more or less invisible
backdrop to James Dickey's 1970 novel and, like the liberationist guidebooks
with which the novel shares a context, *Deliverance* is intent upon psychologizing the trauma its protagonists endure, and prescribing a personal, rather than
social, "cure." But the text does not rest in the psychological; it *sexualizes* the
psychological. Thus, the novel moves from the sociopolitical to the psychological to the sexual, mimicking the movement in the liberationist discourses on

male (in)expressivity. The narrative follows pretty closely the men's liberation narrative, offering a diagnosis of blocked masculinity and a prescription for release. Critics of the novel have liberally used the language of repression and expression, blockage and release, to describe the narrative's treatment of male violence and the encounter with the "primitive" elements of human nature. James Griffith notes the major motif of "constipation, choking, and blocking" in the novel, and Michael Glenday points to the novel's representation of Ed as seeking "release from the alienation of his business life" (151) and from the "disabling stresses of city life" (153). While John Boorman's film does not explore so fully the causes of its protagonists' "blockage," it does frame the river trip as an escape from the city and its stresses, and represents the men as potentially "liberated" by the flow of the river. The central metaphor of both novel and film— the wildly flowing river about to be dammed, its power channeled into the civilizing projects of metropolitan Atlanta—invites us to see its protagonists, too, as characterized by the tension between flow and blockage.

But here the similarities end, and we are somewhat surprised to discover that the Hollywood production deflates the myth of masculinity at the heart of the poet's text. Challenging our assumptions about the relative "difficulty" of the literary as opposed to the popular, Boorman's film is, indeed, more "difficult" to swallow than Dickey's novel, and leaves this viewer baffled at Dickey's and his champions' claims that Boorman sacrificed "art" to "create a more commercially palatable product" (Suarez 161).[18] In my view, what makes Dickey's novel more "literary" than Boorman's film is the same thing that makes it less critical and less contemporary. Drawing on an American literary tradition which, in Nina Baym's memorable phrase, is structured around "melodramas of beset manhood," Dickey frames his story of male regeneration as a classic frontier narrative, with certain key features: masculine regeneration through violence, the flight from a feminizing civilization toward a virile wilderness, the centrality of a male bond that occurs outside the domestic sphere, and a belief that these very specifically white and male values are universally true, equally available to all, and unmarked by gender and racial specificity.[19] As we saw in chapters 2 and 3, this type of traditionalism seeks to abstract cultural products from the material conditions of their production, and to erase the historical specificity that shapes particular narratives at particular times. What makes Dickey's novel so much more conservative and, in my view, "palatable" than Boorman's film, is its comforting repetition of certain myths about white masculinity in an era in which such myths were increasingly open to attack. While Dickey's novel is primarily interested in reinventing an old narrative that will enable him to map a new route to men's psychological health, Boorman's film, rather shockingly, offers a darkly pessimistic view of the therapeutic powers of male release and, instead, leaves its protagonists hysterically torn between repression and expression. While the novel details the therapeutic power of the male wound and thus further confirms the healing power of male violence and release, the film offers no true release for its protagonists, only more blockage and a newly urgent need for repression. Bobby never talks about the rape, Drew must die because he cannot come to terms with the decision to suppress evidence of the hillbilly's death, and Lewis's body literally implodes with the force of his unexpressed male energies, a bone hideously protruding from his leg and his entire body attempting to keep a lid on his agony. Ed's face, as played by Jon Voight, seethes with storm after storm of unexpressed emotion, as the violence escalates and the imperative to keep silent becomes more pressing. Where Dickey's novel gives us the canoe trip as a ritual to heal the wounds of a civilized, enervated white masculinity, Boorman's film gives us a group of devastatingly wounded white men.[20]

Both Dickey's novel and his original screenplay tell the story of a man whose natural, violent, and sexual impulses have been blocked by the social and who is "transfigured" by the violent and sexual experience in the wilds. Explicitly evoking a frame of "Before and After," the novel and screenplay locate the experience in the woods in relation to Ed's overall feeling of inertia, ennui, and suppressed anger in the civilized world. Although Dickey does not explicitly identify the agents of Ed's blockage, his emotional flatness is linked to women and the feminizing effects of white-collar work. For Ed, women "represent [the] normalcy" that produces male boredom (29), and women are aligned, as well, with a vaguely defined "society" that inhibits men. Returning to work after the lunch at which Lewis introduces the idea of the canoe trip, Dickey's Ed comments on the suffocating feminization that marks this world of work: "I was halfway up [the street] when I noticed how many women there were around me. Since I had passed the Gulf station on the corner I hadn't seen another man anywhere" (17). Entering the stream of returning secretaries with "barren, gum-chewing faces," Ed acknowledges that "I was of them, sure enough" (17). It is against this brief glance of a feminized social world that the masculinized natural world of the river will unfold; the feminized stream of secretaries flowing toward work provides the context against which the masculinized river can flow toward a recuperation of the male body and male psyche that has been endangered by the requirements of the social.

For Dickey, the route toward remasculinization flows through the body, as the novel attempts to recover a biologistic essence of maleness that has been tamped down, or blocked, by civil society. Ed gets revitalized and remasculinized in the woods, and can come home to his wife's "normalcy" having incorporated the experience of violence into his own body. The wounds he suffers during the trip are key to his remasculinization, as his earlier blockage gives way to an orgy of "release" that conflates the violent with the sexual, and frames his killing of the mountain man (who had earlier threatened to rape him) as a sexual and remasculinizing experience. As Ed sites the approaching sexual predator/partner, Dickey utilizes a sexualized vocabulary that makes of this experience a substitute for the "kind of love" the two men would have "made" (154) had Lewis not interrupted by killing Bobby's rapist: "His eyes were moving over the sand and rock, faster and faster. They were coming. When they began to rise from the ground they triggered my release" (163). In the process of this climax, Ed falls on his own arrow, penetrating his flesh and producing a fresh sense of sexualized pleasure, a "liberation" into the bodily and irrational: "There had never been a freedom like it. The pain itself was freedom and the blood" (166). One of several therapeutic penetrations represented in the novel, this one allows Ed to experience a primal masculinity radically removed from anything as socially constructed as gender and, thus, to evade the "feminization" that might in another context be produced by such wounds, and the "homosexualization" that might be produced by the desire to be penetrated.[21] The novel represents this primal male-on-male violence as a "natural" expression of male sexuality, and in "nature," gender and sexual orientation become irrelevant. That is, according to Dickey's novel, social understandings of gender and sexuality have no place in this primal nature; and, thus, Bobby is not "feminized" by the rape, and Ed does not endanger his manhood or his heterosexual identity by desiring to "make love"—via an arrow if not a penis—with the mountain man. The male body belongs to the natural and not the social.

The novel maps the geography of the male body against the geography of the land, as is evident in the very first scene, where the characters study a map of the area. The narrative begins with an unidentified, but powerful, subject— "it"—a material and mythic subject straining to escape constraints: "It unrolled slowly, forced to show its colors, curling and snapping back whenever one of us turned loose. The whole land was very tense until we put our four steins on its corners and laid the river out to run for us through the mountains 150 miles north. Lewis' hand took a pencil and marked out a small strong X" (7). "It" is the land, the river, the map, and the men, and James Beaton's gloss on this scene further emphasizes the dynamics of blockage and release that the novel will explore. The map/river stands in for the male psyche whose energies will be set free: "The map, reluctantly pinned down by the steins, is certainly a figure for the undisclosed psychological landscape the novel is about to reveal; so is the river itself, apparently blocked and subdued by Medlock's ominous inscription, a figure for the natural strength and imaginative fluency that Gentry must free from the depths of his psyche" (Beaton 295). This "natural strength and imaginative fluency" is constructed as a bodily essence of maleness, one that literally flows through, or is blocked within, the body. The male psyche, thus, is a fully *embodied* one, and it is through the body that Ed finds the "release" that he seeks.

The male body in Dickey's novel is represented as the source of male power, an elemental force that must be recaptured and channeled if middle-class white men are to regain virility. The novel draws heavily on what Gail Bederman has identified as a nineteenth-century narrative invested in "remaking manhood," a narrative that leans on a racialized discourse of "civilization" to reconstruct a white manhood widely understood as enervated and lacking the passion and virility that marks "primitive" masculinity. "Manliness," long thought to be contingent upon control, an iron will, and, most of all, self-restraint, was the basis of civilization, white supremacy, and male power; but as the economy moved toward consumerism, and immigrant, African American, and working-class men became more visible as the embodiment of a powerful, physical masculinity, middle- and upper-class white men began to be anxious about that "manliness." Educators, medical men, and politicians undertook to solve what Bederman refers to as the "neurasthenic paradox" haunting middle-class white men.

> According to Victorian doctrine, only civilized white men had the manly strength to restrain their powerful masculine passions. But what if civilized, manly self-restraint was not a source of power, but merely a symptom of nerve-exhaustion and effeminacy? What if civilized advancement led merely to delicacy and weakness? Then the male body becomes not a strong storage battery, highly charged with tightly leashed masculine sexuality, but a decadent wreck, an undercharged battery with a dangerous scarcity of nerve force.   (88)

This paradox was never "solved" in any final sense, and Bederman suggests that the conflict between manly self-restraint and a masculine expression of primitivism or savagery remains the hallmark of manhood in the Progressive Era. Indeed, as *Deliverance* suggests, this conflict still structures masculinity.[22] The paradox of blockage and release animating men's liberation discourse of the seventies replays the neurasthenic paradox in strikingly similar terms. Calling neurasthenia the late nineteenth-century version of "executive hysteria," Elaine Showalter describes it in terms that echo the diagnoses of emotional constipation in the 1970s, and notes that for "middle-class men the preferred treatment for neurasthenia was travel, adventure, vigorous exercise" (*Hystories* 66).

Dickey's *Deliverance* follows its Victorian progenitors' attempts to negotiate this paradox by invoking Darwinism, natural selection, and a racialized discourse of male power. Like G. Stanley Hall, the Victorian educator who used recapitulation theory to alleviate middle-class white men's anxiety about their distance from the primitive masculine,[23] Dickey sends his "bored and rudderless" (Griffith 47) protagonists on a journey toward the primitive that ends with the incorporation of that primitive into themselves. In the process, the novel also suggests that the genetically flawed mountain men, unlike Ed, remain stuck in an earlier evolutionary phase, overwhelmed by, and not capable of schooling, their primitive impulses. The mountain men teach the city boys that there is a reservoir of primitive masculinity available that can, in Bederman's terms, " 'innoculate' them against the weakness of excessive civilization" (94). But the mountain men use that force incorrectly; in Dickey's mythology, the "civilized" protagonists are alone capable of tapping into that primitive reservoir and using it to increase their power. It's important to stress that it is the "damming" of a masculine, bodily power, that Dickey is celebrating; for the mountain men represent an inadequate solution to the problem of the primitive, a purely bodily expressiveness that threatens civilization and, not incidentally, white masculinity.

Central to Dickey's mythology is a frank appreciation of the male body as a "dammed" vessel of primitive impulses, and it is Lewis's body that commands the most appreciation and awe. Lewis welcomes Ed's objectifying gaze, as the two men share an unspoken contract not unlike that between the film star and the spectator: "Everything he had done for himself for years paid off as he stood there in his tracks, in the water. I could tell by the way he glanced at me; the payoff was in my eyes. I had never seen such a male body in my life" (90). Lewis's survivalist ethos is based on a belief that the body "is the one thing you can't fake" (41); "the machines are going to fail, the political systems are going to fail," and "the whole thing is going to be reduced to the human body" (40). "Life is so fucked-up now," Lewis echoes Ed in saying, "that I wouldn't mind if it came down, right quick, to the bare survival of who was ready to survive" (41). While Ed does question how Lewis's survivalist ideas jibe with his more or less normal, everyday life, the novel does not undermine the essential truth of what Lewis says. In fact, as the arrival of the "primitive" mountain men indicates, Lewis is precisely right about survival coming down to the body.

Ed describes the rape in terms that suggest that the mountain men embody an unschooled primitive conceptualization of the male body that is in marked contrast to the power that Lewis's body (and, ultimately, Ed's, too) represents. He sees in them a "brutality and carelessness of touch," an utter "disregard for another person's body" (98) that makes the rape appear as a simple expression of a primal, unsocialized male power, rather than an assault on Bobby's masculinity: "There was no need to justify or rationalize anything; they were going to do what they wanted to" (100). Where Ed respects the awesome power of Lewis's male body, these men have no respect for, or even awareness of, the body as the site of gendered identity or the source of male power. Like the "savages" who people the pages of Victorian writings on the relationship between manly civilization and masculine primitivism, the mountain men have not evolved into a state where they can *use* their power, channel it and thus increase it; theirs is not, in other words, a *productive* power. As Ronald T. Curran argues in his reading of the conflict between biology and culture in the novel, Dickey draws on images which reinforce the "popular conception of man's evolution" (85) including numerous references to *Tarzan*, "instinct," comparisons of Ed to animals, and an overall narrative about the survival of the fittest.[24] At the end of the novel, "these civilized whites have returned alive from the 'primitive' land of the rednecks" (Curran 85), and their masculinity has been revivified by the effort. As Curran puts it, Ed and Lewis may be city boys at heart, but "they have reserves to tap beneath that limp-wristed veneer of small-town respectability. Good old 'instinct' is there when needed" (88). The gendered meanings of this racialized discourse don't register for Curran, except insofar as he invokes the effeminization of "limp-wristed." The racial and gendered conflicts forming the backdrop to Dickey's novel get displaced onto biology, and with them the wounds to the social position of white men in the post-liberation era.

In Dickey's *Deliverance*, the release of violent and starkly sexualized male energies enables the recuperation of masculinity made necessary by the stresses and enervation of city life. Ed triumphs and, in returning to his "civilized" life, literally incorporates the river and its awesome power: "it ran nowhere but in my head, but there it ran as though immortally. I could feel it—I can feel it—on different places on my body" (234). Ed's revitalization stems not only from the experience of white-water rafting but also from his experience of violence controlled. The now dammed river runs through Ed's veins, making of his body a living testament to the power of a released masculinity, and one made even more powerful for its "damming."[25] Ed's wounds are therapeutic. In an earlier scene, after cutting the arrow out of his side (the aftereffect of the satisfyingly sexual "release" found in killing the mountain man), Ed "luxuriates" in his wound, jumps into the river, and experiences an odd painful/pleasurable "penetration" leading to another release: "the river went into my right ear like an ice pick. I yelled a tremendous, walled-in yell, and then I felt the current thread through me, first through my head from one ear and out the other and then complicatedly through my body, up my rectum and out my mouth and also in the side where I was hurt" (177). The river signifies a primitive masculine force whose damming need not be mourned, since its power now flows in the veins of the civilized man whose self-restraint and ability to withstand pain becomes the mark of a newly reconstructed masculinity.

Boorman's *Deliverance* registers the importance of popular ideas about evolution to this story, but ends up demonstrating the bankruptcy of the myth of masculinity that the novel embraces. The myth of the saving power of a primitive but restrained masculinity, the film suggests, is based on certain premises that are no longer tenable. The film both exaggerates and ironizes Lewis as the figure of that myth. Lewis likens their trip to the "first explorers" discovering virgin territory and, thus, at least implicitly, positions the "rednecks" as the "redskins" of American frontier legend. Indeed, Lewis speaks for what Bederman identifies as Teddy Roosevelt's particular prescription for "reinvigorating" male authority that promised "American men they could achieve virile power if only they took up the white man's burden" (214). Lewis speaks for evolutionary fitness, racial superiority, and male power, as he looks forward to a time when "the machines are gonna fail, the system's gonna fail. And then . . . Survival. Who's going to survive. That's the name of the game." The very visibility of the genetically deformed hillbillies functions to underline Lewis's credo as a version of early twentieth-century solutions to the problem of "race suicide" in the eugenics movement.[26] Although Dickey's novel represents Lewis as far more sympathetic with the "natives" of this strange and foreign land, Boorman's film emphasizes the difference between Lewis's strong, bounded, and powerful body, and the deformed and decadent bodies of the hillbillies.

Yet it is Lewis who suffers the most visible wound; it is his body that comes to signify the failure of the myth of masculinity and the hysteria that follows that failure.[27] Boorman uses Lewis to elaborate on the key contradictions structuring masculinity throughout much of American history: is masculinity secured by manly restraint of primitive impulses, or the expression of those impulses? In Boorman's treatment, the male body becomes, not the source of male power, but the text on which is written the emotional, physical, and social traumas of contemporary masculinity. The film meditates on male inexpressivity, and constructs emotion as a psychophysical force that gets trapped in, and thus endangers the stability of, the male body. The film joins the men's liberationists in representing the dangers of male repression as *bodily* dangers, as both the narrative and the camera construct the male body as a simmering cauldron of warring impulses that, lacking a proper outlet, are doomed to endlessly recirculate, poisoning the male body and the male psyche. But, unlike the male liberationists, Boorman's tale of male blockage eschews the release that would cure masculinity. Ed's failure to release his emotions, and his hesitation in channeling those emotions into the violent revenge the novel touts, is metaphorically figured in his inability to shoot an arrow, his "draw-hysteria."[28] The film constructs an elaborate metaphorical system around the shooting of arrows, and the key sign of Ed's inability to unblock is the scene where he yearns to "Release!" the arrow that will save his life by killing the man who intends to shoot him. Significantly, he falls onto his own arrow and suffers the wound that signifies his inability to release. That inability is linked to the film's concern with repression and the effects of that repression on the male body. The male body becomes both the site of emotion and the means for expression: this is, strictly speaking, a hysterical body, which evinces the somatic symptoms of some emotional, psychic, or even sociopolitical trauma.

Throughout the film, the body "speaks" the psychological and emotional condition of the group, and the wounds the men suffer offer visual evidence of the costs of male repression. Bobby's rape is the occasion for repression, and it sets in motion a representation of the hysterical male body, as the trauma of the rape is written on the bodies of each of the characters. Lewis's body, more than any other, registers the trauma of Bobby's rape, as the imperative to "forget" that trauma causes that previously hard and bounded body to implode, and a horrifyingly phallic projection of bone and tissue becomes visible on its surface. Prior to the rape, Lewis's body is represented as solid, impermeable, unpenetratable, bounded by the wet suit that sheathes the buff Burt Reynolds. The camera dwells lovingly on this body, eroticizing and objectifying it, as his bulging arms signify a physicality always on the verge of the excessive. A human phallus, Reynolds/Medlock is the very figure of the power of a "dammed" masculinity: stony-faced and emotionally inexpressive, Lewis's bottled-up power is quite literally written on his body. As if in reaction to the repression instituted almost immediately after the rape, Lewis's body appears to produce its own phallic wound from the inside, a kind of penetration imposed by his own body to mirror the penetration suffered by Bobby. The phallic nature of this wound—nowhere indicated in Dickey's novel, where the injury is simply described as a break—draws attention to itself, and begs for some kind of interpretation. The graphic nature of Lewis's wound becomes a visual register of the crisis in masculinity figured by the rape. Drew, too, appears to be penetrated (by a bullet), but the film's representation of his corpse as horribly mangled evokes nothing so much as an image of a masculinity strangling itself. But, as I noted earlier, the rape is merely the precipitating event; what truly traumatizes these men is the imperative to repress itself. The hysteria figured in the film, thus, is produced by the conflict between a socially conditioned requirement that men not speak of a "feminizing" trauma and a naturalized, even biological impulse toward the expression of male rage that would align the protagonists with the "primitive" mountain men. That conflict might best be described as the conflict between nature and culture, biology and the social, and it is written on the hystericized bodies of the film's main characters in an exploration of what film theorists have recently suggested is a surprising prevalence of male hysteria (and masochism) in Hollywood film.[29]

Paul Smith, in particular, has argued that male action and adventure films produce the male body as hysterical by following a three-stage narrative whose closure always fails to rein in the anxieties provoked by images of eroticized and/or wounded male bodies. These films, according to Smith, frame the male body in a narrative that moves from objectification/eroticization, through a temporary destruction that "masochizes" the male body, and ends in a regeneration of that body and a reemergence of the phallic masculinity that was damaged by the second, and even the first, stage of the narrative (96–98). Questioning the critical impulse to see male masochism as subversive of traditional constructions of masculinity, Smith notes that such masochism appears almost always as a merely temporary violation of phallic norms, submitted to a narrative pull that inevitably works to rephallicize masculinity in part by erasing or "forgetting" the (vulnerable) male body (102).[30] Yet Smith finds, even with remasculinization at the end of narratives like the *Lethal Weapon* films and many of Clint Eastwood's films, a kind of hysterical residue remains, as the body cannot so easily or completely be exorcised nor its objectification and "masochization" entirely forgotten.

In fact, Smith's use of the concept of hysteria suggests that a never fully successful repression is not only an effect of this type of narrative structure, but is, in fact, its *subject.* These films are *about* the necessary repression of the male body, just as hysteria is an acknowledgment of the impossibility of "forgetting" the trauma of a visualized and masochized male body. The "hysterical moment" Smith isolates marks the inevitable return of the repressed body *and* the difficulty of representing the male body, for "repression in the male subject seems to prohibit the speaking of the male body, to block its symbolization" and leaves us with "the unsymbolizable of male sexed experience" (104). Unsymbolizable, that is, except through hysteria:

> The hysterical moment . . . marks the return of the male body out from under the narrative process that has produced what appears to be its transcendence, but which in fact is its elision and its forgetting. In other words, although there is in these movies a conservatively pleasurable diegetic path which ends up suppressing the masculine somatic, the body nonetheless returns from beneath the weight of the symbolic. What I mean by this hysterical residue, then, is an unresolved or uncontained representation of the body of the male as it exceeds the narrative processes. The meanings proffered by these movies concern the male body as that which has to be repressed.
>
> (103)

The male body has to be repressed, its representation "blocked," even as this repression and this blockage perpetuate the hysteria and the physical and psychic trauma they are meant to manage. Male hysteria, thus, is the perfect vehicle to figure the particular dynamics of wounded white masculinity in the era I'm discussing: like the men's liberationists' somatization of the social and political symptoms of a decentered white masculinity, the hysterical male body registers, in personal and bodily terms, the trauma of the social. Neil Hertz suggests as much when he notes, in an essay on "Male Hysteria Under Political Pressure," "a recurrent turn of mind: the representation of what would seem to be a political threat as if it were a sexual threat" (161).

The language in which the men's liberationists describe the evils of male blockage constructs a hysterical male body, but cannot name it as such. This construction relies on a post-Freudian notion of a closed psychic economy in which repressed material can produce hysterical symptoms; but the men's liberationists seem loath to register the psychosomatic nature of the disease they anatomize. This body, in which dangerously blocked, substantial male energies circulate without proper outlet, draws on the persuasive power of male pain, a pain that must be "real," as opposed to psychosomatic, if men are to claim the moral high ground of victimization. The images of white male bodies in pain guarantees the authenticity of male traumas; as we saw in chapter 3, authentic wounds are posed against "political" wounds. Psychosomatic illness also carries the taint of the womanly, as hysterics are most often represented as theatrical, dissembling malingerers striving for attention. As Elaine Showalter points out, a "century after Freud, many people still reject psychological explanations for symptoms; they believe psychosomatic disorders are illegitimate and search for physical evidence that firmly places cause and cure outside the self" (Hystories 4). For the men's liberationists who represent the male body as traumatized by the restraint of natural impulses, the cause of somatic disturbance is a vaguely apprehended "society" or "civilization" that works to thwart male release. In this sense, male hysteria itself becomes both subject of, and subject to, repression in the discourse of male liberation.[31]

Like the emergence of the wounded male body to signify social or political trauma in the post-liberation era, the representation of a hysterical male body draws on the persuasive power of bodily injury to gesture toward a more social or political disempowerment. Adam Knee's analysis of male hysteria in Eastwood's 1971 Play Misty for Me points to the centrality of hysteria as a response to the threatened "blockage" of male impulses and to the fact that a male silence and repression that functioned in earlier eras and their films to secure male power, "no longer functions effectively in a changed social landscape" (Knee 96). Knee traces the male hysteria evinced in this men's liberation-era film to a historical renegotiation of gender norms and meanings. The protagonist played by Eastwood "is at pains to repress physical impulses of various sorts"—to block what the film explores as dangerously masculine desires and emotion. His performance "suggest[s] a violence seething beneath the surface (and largely stuck there)" (92), while the violently feminist woman who stalks

and kills gives free reign to such impulses. For the Eastwood character, such repression produces hysterical symptoms, primarily a voicelessness which figures
his inability to "release" his pent-up emotions.

In Boorman's *Deliverance*, Ed's facial expressions register the same kind of
emotional trauma and voicelessness as the Clint Eastwood character in *Play
Misty for Me*, and his body bears the wounds of his repression as well. Ed looks
nothing so much as terrified and hysterical, and the film leaves little doubt that
Ed is as traumatized as Bobby. It is while the mountain man dies from Lewis's
arrow that the film gives us the most extended shot of Ed's face registering a
mix of warring emotions. This is not the image of a man transfigured by terror
or power; it is, instead, the image of a man who will remain haunted by trauma
and the repression of that trauma, never able to express the emotions that
might liberate him from that repression.

Importantly, while the rape precipitates the crisis that necessitates the repression that produces hysteria, it is in the process of killing or burying the
mountain men's bodies that Ed gets wounded. Thus, the film literalizes the fact
that the male body is "that which has to be repressed" (Smith 103): the efforts to
literally *bury* the male body, and the impossibility of doing so, preoccupy the
second half of the film. While Dickey's novel might be the story of "a modern
mind in search of a body," as James Beaton puts it (294), Boorman's film is
characterized by a futile attempt to escape the male body, a concern emblema-
tized by the men's frantic efforts to hide the male bodies that keep piling up as
they progress down the river. When Ed wrestles the man he has killed down the
side of the cliff and into the water, the futility of getting rid of these bodies/the
body becomes clear, as Ed and the corpse become entangled underwater. It is
telling that the final image in the film is the return of the repressed, the inadequately buried body emerging from the now placid and still water of the man-
made lake.

Boorman's *Deliverance* is so intent on hystericizing the male body and exploring the dangers of male repression that it breaks out of the action-adventure paradigm Smith analyzes and, thus, might be seen to critique that paradigm. As I've already suggested, Dickey's novel and screenplay much more
closely follow a path toward remasculinization, while Boorman's film seems intent on exploring the "hysterical residue" Smith finds left in the wake of the
three-stage narrative from objectification to masochism to regeneration. The
film does indeed follow the first two stages of this narrative, distributing various forms of objectification and masochization among its four main characters, but perhaps most directly narrativized through Lewis. But whereas the action films that Smith analyzes "forget" the male body, its display and
subsequent wounding,[32] *Deliverance* deprives its characters and its audience of
the transcendence of a remasculinization and triumph over the body. If the

film does nod to what Smith suggests is the father of all such narratives, by having Ed bear vaguely stigmata-like wounds to his chest and arms, no resurrection follows that wounding and no "deliverance" is, in fact, offered. Although there are any number of places where we might identify the dissolution of this narrative, and point to the male trouble caused by the transition from novel/original screenplay to film, one scene will serve nicely. That scene, important to both the screenplay and the film, takes place at the end of the journey, when Ed returns from getting his wounds dressed to find Bobby at the dinner table with the group of locals who are hosting them.

This scene *should,* according to Hollywood convention, mark the start of the regeneration stage of the male action narrative, a healing of the wounds exposed in the earlier stages. Indeed, Dickey's screenplay uses this scene to literally register the "beefing up" of Ed's manhood, as he nourishes himself on a dinner presented as a well-deserved reward for having survived his ordeal. The point of the scene as Dickey writes it is to signify Ed's deep-down bodily *pleasure:* "Food begins to come at him from all sides. Shyly he takes a little of this and a little of that, and then he is eating madly, trying to thank the various people who are passing him things. He begins to wolf things down, in one of the best moments of his life" (Dickey 1972; 132). Even the sheriff, who greets the survivors' story with some skepticism, reads Ed as heroic and ratifies the "best moments of his life" view of the ending. "You done good," the sheriff tells him. "You'uz hurt bad, but if it wudn't for you, you'd all be in the river with your other man" (Dickey 1972; 144).

The film, in contrast, makes this a far edgier scene, not least by the suggestion that these quite ordinary inhabitants of Aintry seem ridiculously removed from the inbred, redneck townspeople Lewis argued would hang the city boys for murder with not so much as a trial. But the tension that really animates the scene comes from the subtly but undeniably changed relationship between Ed and Bobby. Bobby, despite having arguably experienced the worst horrors of all on the river, appears protective of and anxious about a palpably vulnerable and quasi-hysterical Ed. For his part, Ed begins eating tentatively, as if his mouth is sore or his stomach unstable, only to burst into wracking sobs. This outburst is quite brief, and therein lies its pathos. Ed "releases" his pent-up emotions— once again, written on his expressively contorted face—but only for the briefest of spurts. We are left with the image of a man who desperately needs to be purged, but will remain emotionally constipated. In this context, it is worth recalling that Dickey's Ed, journeying toward his release on the wild river, wryly comments on the billboards by the side of the road which register a construction of southern masculinity as, on the one hand, constipated and, on the other, intent upon a too-civilized release: "From such a trip you would think that the South did nothing but dose itself and sing gospel songs; you would think that the bowels of the southerner were forever clamped shut; that he could not open and let natural process flow through him, but needed one purgative after another in order to make it to church" (38).

In the film, Ed experiences nothing so curative as a purge, and the image of a repressed and unhappily civilized masculinity competes with an image of an expressive and dangerously primitive masculinity. In marked contrast to the film, the novel represents Bobby's rape as one of a series of encounters with the primitive, and the male-on-male violence is greeted less with anxiety about Bobby's masculinity and more with a kind of begrudging awe for the power of the uncivilized masculinity modeled by the mountain men. While the novel offers the rape, oddly, as part of the "cure" for what ails a citified and denaturalized masculinity, the film demonizes the mountain men precisely for the kind of release-oriented, "expressive" masculinity that underwrites all the violence the film explores.[33] But the rape is something of a red herring in Boorman's film, the crisis in masculinity it explores residing elsewhere. And, here again, the differences between the novel's and film's representations of the rape are instructive. Whereas Dickey represents the rape as more or less a fact of nature, the expression of a natural instinct that exceeds any political or social interpretation we might be tempted to place on it, Boorman represents the rape as a ritual humiliation, an explicit feminization of Bobby. The famous "squeal like a pig" sequence, most viewers of the movie will be surprised to learn, is entirely absent from the novel and from Dickey's screenplay. Instead, Ed tonelessly notes the stark reality of the act, seeing "no need to justify or rationalize anything; they were going to do what they wanted to" (Dickey 100). No mention is made by Dickey of Bobby being a "sow," and it is actually *Ed* who is referred to as "fat," not Bobby (101). The rape is only important insofar as it "transfigures" Ed, and makes him "beastlike" by "releasing his aggressive urges" (Suarez 167); within the lexicon of the novel's myth of masculinity, such urges are natural, bodily forces that must find an outlet. And, finally, the rape is represented as a *collective*, rather than an individual, act, one set of men gaining temporary ascendancy over another set of men, and all somehow united in the fact of the rape. "We all," Ed notes, "sighed" when the mountain man "drew back, drew out" (100). This is a battle, and one whose purpose is primarily to set the stage for the regeneration and "transfiguration" of Ed. Dickey does not make us wait long for this; the screenplay instructs "Close-up of Ed as he rises, transfigured by terror and by the turn events have taken. He is beastlike with the power of having the gun" (1972; 66). In Dickey's lexicon, being "transfigured by terror" and "beastlike with the power of having a gun" is a *good* thing, a positive turn of events.

In contrast, Boorman uses the rape to figure not only the social trauma suffered by these city boys displaced from nature but also the impossibility of healing that trauma. Given that outcome, it comes as no surprise that, in his new book *Summer of Deliverance: A Memoir of Father and Son*,[34] Dickey's son Christopher confesses to being anxious about Boorman's version of the story, particularly its representation of "homosexual rape." He worries that "the rape scene was becoming what the movie was about. . . . It was all going to be about butt-fucking." But the father/novelist/screenwriter knows that the action is elsewhere, and explains: " 'I had to put the moral weight of murder on the suburbanites.'" Christopher glosses this statement by saying that his father "had to portray the mountain men as such monsters that the suburbanites would decide not only to kill but to try to cover up their crime" (45). But why would the men's being monsters require that their bodies be buried, their crime forgotten, the trauma repressed? So that "every man watching will think, Yeah, bury the son of a bitch" (C. Dickey 45), so that every man watching will agree to collective amnesia, to the repression not only of trauma but of the male body itself.

While I think Christopher Dickey was right when he predicted that the film would best be remembered, with a collective male shudder, for the demasculinization inherent in the "squeal like a pig" scene—a demasculinization that mirrors that threatened by the damming of the river—I want to suggest that the film's residual damage to constructions of masculinity be sought elsewhere. Lewis speaks of the damming of the Cuwalahassee as a "rape," and this "extremist" point of view is reinforced by the images of destruction that Boorman juxtaposes with this dialogue in the opening frames of the film. The explosion that destroys the natural beauty of the landscape is, thus, paralleled to the explosion of primitive male energies evident in the mountain man's rape of Bobby. *Both* the "system" that Lewis excoriates *and* the savagery that Dickey's novel embraces are linked to a masculinity out of control and, thus, Boorman's film offers no safe or positive alternative masculinity. The seeming opposition between the machine-driven forces of civilization and the machine-ignorant forces of primitivism falls apart, leaving the film's four protagonists with no route toward the recuperation found at the end of Dickey's narrative. Since release has been demonized, blockage becomes a mode for managing, although never curing, the trauma experienced by the men in the film. Not at all marked by sentimentality or nostalgia for a time when men were men, the film's tone is more of a sad acknowledgment that the crisis in masculinity it chronicles has become incurable—indeed, the norm of a masculinity that can never find health through violence. All that is left is an image of a hysterical male body, torn between the competing, and mutually unsatisfying, imperatives to repress and express.

FEMINISM AND MASOCHISM: *THE PRINCE OF TIDES* AND
THE PLEASURES OF REPRESSION

Pat Conroy's *The Prince of Tides* begins where Boorman's film ends: with a wounded masculinity and a hysterical male body. Torn between the competing imperatives to block and release what the novel construes as natural and inevitably destructive male energies, Conroy's Tom Wingo is the very image of a vulnerably powerful, powerfully wounded white man, the embodiment of a new masculinity perpetually in crisis. The humid southern landscape and tidewaters of South Carolina function as an appropriate backdrop for this novel about the blockage and flow of tears, emotions, and sexuality. Like *Deliverance*, *The Prince of Tides* uses flowing and blocked water to analogize the power of "dammed" masculinity. Reversing the setup of Dickey's *Deliverance*, in which city boys are sent into the wilds of nature, Conroy places his country boy in the wild city, a city that, importantly, works to "mark" Tom as the embodiment of a retrograde, "primitive" white masculinity. Like Ed Gentry, Tom feels the "indignities" of city life and experiences "a feeling of displacement, profound and enervating." For Tom, though, it's not the "feminizing" effects of city life that endanger his vitality; it is the fact that, in the city, his "hardwon singularity" is endangered. "The city *marks* my soul with a most profane, indelible graffiti" (32), Conroy writes. Tom is marked as we have seen white men marked throughout this study, and *The Prince of Tides*, more than any other text we've attended to, explores the complex causes and effects of that marking. In New York City to help his sister Savannah, famous feminist poet, recover from her latest suicide attempt, Tom agrees to regular therapy sessions with Savannah's psychoanalyst, Susan Lowenstein. The emotionally blocked Tom must be taught to express himself and, *literally*, to let the tears flow. These sessions are meant to flesh out Savannah's story and give Dr. Lowenstein the knowledge she needs to cure her, but it is Tom's story that occupies the center of the narrative and of the therapy. At issue in this therapy is the question of whether it is healthier to repress or express past trauma, and the related question of how white masculinity can survive in a post-liberationist America in which white men have been "marked" as the bearers of power, privilege, and a violent sexuality.

"My wound is geography" (1), begins the novel, and thus is set in motion an emotionally saturated exploration of the personal and social traumas of Tom Wingo, a feminist man who is "damaged" by a family history of violence, and who feels himself displaced in a world in which he, as a southern white man, "embod[ies] everything that is wrong with the twentieth century" (9). As we have seen throughout this study, the social and political disenfranchisement of white masculinity gets displaced onto images of wounded white male bodies. In Conroy's novel, the sociopolitical and bodily are so intertwined as to be virtually indistinguishable. Conroy's representation of Tom is a masterful combination of lost entitlement, wounded masculinity, and liberal responses to the challenges that affect southern white men in the post–civil rights, post–Stonewall, post–women's liberation era: an odd combination of self-flagellating guilt and self-indulgent confessions of inadequacy. Within the first few pages of this very long novel, Conroy frames Tom's story in relation to the decentering of straight white men in the post-sixties era, emphasizing the wounds suffered by living through these historic changes:

> I grew up in South Carolina, a white southern male, well trained and gifted in my hatred of blacks when the civil rights movement caught me outside and undefended along the barricades and proved me to be both wicked and wrong. . . . Then I found myself marching in an all-white, all-male ROTC program in college and spit on by peace demonstrators who were offended by my uniform. . . . I thought I would enter my thirties quietly, a contemplative man, a man whose philosophy was humane and unassailable, when the women's liberation movement bushwhacked me on the avenues and I found myself on the other side of the barricades once again.   (9)

Wounded by the twentieth century's marking of white masculinity—and the repression that marking institutes—Tom claims those wounds as evidence of his goodness and as guarantees that, despite how others mark him, he belongs among the ranks of the dispossessed, the disenfranchised, and the injured.[35] Tom is characterized as a masochist who takes pleasure in displaying his wounds. "Bushwhacked," "spit upon," "undefended," Tom is placed by Conroy in precisely the contexts where his masochism can find full expression—as in the scene where he and brother Luke attend a reading of Savannah's poetry "sponsored by Women United to Stamp Out Penises or one of those other maniacal splinter groups." "Among this terrifying group," Tom trembles, "we feigned a state of penislessness" (36). Like the Ellen Jamesians in *The World According to Garp* (see chapter 3, this volume), these radical feminists read all men as the carriers of a violent and abusive male power; but the difference here is that Conroy's novel suggests that, on the whole, the feminist assessment is right.

Like Updike's *Rabbit Redux,* as we saw in chapter 1, *The Prince of Tides* revels in the representation of disempowered white masculinity. As the novel begins, Tom's been fired from his job as high school football coach; is mourning the institutionalization of his twin sister, the successful but suicidal feminist poet, Savannah; has not yet been able to cry over the tragic and epic death of his broth-

er Luke; is totally dominated by his mother Lila, and outstripped professional-
ly and otherwise by his physician wife Sallie, who is having an affair with a man
who, unlike Tom, can express his feelings. He is traumatized not only by the social realignments of the twentieth century but also by a terrible childhood of
psychological and physical abuse, capped by the rape of himself, Lila, and Savannah by three escaped convicts who are then mauled and decapitated by a
tiger (yes, a *tiger*). The rapes and the carnage following them pale in significance, however, next to Lila's forcing her wounded sons to bury the bodies and
her catatonic daughter to help clean up the blood and gore, and her stern command that no one ever talk about the experience to anyone. The regime of imposed silence does more damage than the actual violence it was meant to mask.
"I don't think the rape affected me as profoundly as my adherence to those laws
of concealment and secrecy my mother had put into effect" (489), Tom later recalls, and the novel thus sets up its central question: is it better to express or repress? This question is complicated by the fact that male expression is intimately tied to violence. Torn between the competing imperatives to repress and
express, the former instituted by maternal injunction, the latter modeled by his
violent father, Tom is crippled, blocked, and closed down.

The novel constructs white masculinity as naturally violent, and male sexuality as naturally explosive, and thus suggests that men *should* be blocked and
masculinity destroyed. Conroy leads in this direction by representing the damage caused by a masculinity defined by the uninhibited expression of impulses.
Tom's father Henry is the figure for this masculinity, as are the men who rape
Tom, his sister Savannah, and his mother Lila in a horrible orgy of a primitive
masculine expressivity. Tom learns to "hate the fact that [he] is male" (118); "I
equated fucking with power," he confesses, "and hated the part of me where that
flawed and dangerous truth dwelt" (342). *The Prince of Tides* does nothing to
dispute that truth, but it does suggest that Tom's awareness of it makes him an
extraordinary man, a man who chivalrously protects the women in his life by repressing his own "natural" maleness and violence. Such repression pushes him,
again and again, into spectacular displays of wounded and humiliated masculinity. The clearest example of this comes when he suppresses an impulse to
hit Sallie after she confesses to an affair and, instead, sinks into a bog of self-
doubt and self-deprecation. This passage is worth quoting in its entirety because
it models so perfectly the logic through which a violent masculinity is naturalized, and man is wounded by the necessary suppression of that nature. The result is a construction of the male body and the male psyche as always on the
verge of explosion and further traumatized by the necessary force of repression.

> I felt an irresistible desire to strike her, felt the ghost of a violent father as-
> sume dominion over the blood, felt his surge into power around the heart;

my fists clenched, and for a moment I fought with all my strength against the man it was my birthright to be. I controlled myself and sent my father into exile again. I loosened my fists. I breathed and cried, "Is it because I'm getting fat, Sallie? Please tell me it's that. Or because I'm losing my hair? Or maybe it's because I've told you I've got a little dick."   (30)

Tom's sense of self seems utterly "feminized" here as elsewhere, and the novel suggests that his sickness stems from a crisis in gender identity: he is torn between a patriarchal and violent manhood and a weak and humiliating one, the former passed on as his paternal birthright, the latter imposed by maternal dominion. The body here is both vessel of rage and object of hatred; it is as if the suppression of his bodily, masculine power produces a desire to diminish the body's power and, in doing so, destroy the body itself. The violent energies that are Tom's "birthright"—given by nature and not culture—get channeled into a self-deprecation that verges on the masochistic.

This masochism is one symptom of Tom's pathology, a sickness that has social, familial, and biological causes.[36] Conroy's representation of masculinity as *inevitably* and *naturally* violent works alongside his representation of Tom as a feminist man to suggest that this blocked but sensitive man is torn against himself, his politics permanently and essentially at odds with his "birthright." Tom's repression of his violent impulses gets "channeled" into a masochistic stance, and his feminism also becomes a symptom of that masochism,[37] a fact brought home with some regularity in his verbal sparring matches with the feminist psychoanalyst Susan Lowenstein. Convinced that Tom is a "classic male," Dr. Lowenstein lectures him about his sister, her poetry, feminism, and masculinity; challenges his "self-pitying male ego," and characterizes him as just another one of her "whiny" male patients who "talk about the agony of being men" (437–38). But while Lowenstein questions the logic of white male victimization—"Oh, I've heard this sad song before . . . about the old agony of command," she complains (437)—the novel sanctions it by piling psychic, emotional, and physical wounds onto Tom's once sturdy but now buckling back. Lowenstein's feminist critique gives way in the face of Tom's pain. Lowenstein is also proven wrong when she gets swept away by Tom's particular brand of charm, and experiences her own sexual and emotional healing with him.

Tom's feminism is part of his problem, not its solution, for "a man who calls himself a feminist is the most ridiculous figure of our silly times" (437). He is the perfect image of the "enlightened male" mocked by Goldberg, the man who "has responded to feminist assertions by donning sack cloth, sprinkling himself with ashes, and flagellating himself" (Goldberg 16). In *The Prince of Tides*, such self-flagellation becomes the source of satisfaction and pleasure for Tom, whose feminist convictions position him as a heroic, if quixotic, individualist fighting against a system of sexual difference whose inevitability makes his quest seem futile and even masochistic. Like Leonard Michaels, Conroy suggests that there are essential differences between men and women, and that, while men can accept a feminist critique of male privilege and even become feminists, change is limited to the exceptional case, the individual man who sees the light but is, by definition, paralyzed when it comes to social action.[38] This tension between the social and the individual plays out in what Fred Pfeil might refer to as a narrative of "therapization," in which the political and social groundings of trauma or "dysfunction" are jettisoned and, with them, the possibility that any genuine social change can affect the "unchangeable way things are" (Pfeil 152).[39] This is an apt description not only of Tom's pathology but also of his feminism. The novel suggests, in fact, that his feminism is *part* of his pathology, less a political stance than an individual quirk. Tom's feminism is a political response to a personal trauma, but the novel ultimately recommends a therapeutic and not political solution.

This is even more true of Barbra Streisand's 1991 film, for which Conroy cowrote the screenplay. Whereas Boorman's *Deliverance* aspires toward a European-influenced, arthouse type cinema that experienced a new popularity in early 1970s Hollywood,[40] and thus could afford to risk some uncomfortable responses in its audience, Streisand's *The Prince of Tides* goes in exactly the opposite direction. In a decade known for producing box-office driven blockbuster films, with proven action-adventure directors and big name (often macho) stars, Streisand's film can be seen as her attempt to play with the big boys. Given that possibility—and the film was, in fact, marketed and reviewed as a "big" film—it might seem odd that Streisand chose this particular story, a story about male rape that would risk alienating a large portion of its potential audience.[41] But it could also be the case that Streisand's film attempts to compete with more visibly "big" movies by cashing in on the new visibility of the white male victim, a figure who was popping up everywhere in the early 1990s.[42] With that figure comes a stunning abdication of decades of radical feminist and antiracist analysis, as the personal overwhelms the political and a backlash against the gains of the women's and civil rights movements becomes undeniable. Into this context comes *The Prince of Tides*, a film that sentimentalizes the white male victim, foregrounding the therapeutic narrative and all but erasing the feminist one. While the novel places Tom's struggles firmly within a historical, if also a familial, narrative, Streisand's film represents Tom as wounded only by the repression of his feelings (prompted, rather simplistically, by the rape), a repression demanded by his mother Lila. Streisand demonizes Lila even more than does Conroy's novel—in part, one suspects, in order to empty out the maternal position so that her Susan Lowenstein can fill that position, too. Mother, therapist, and lover all rolled into one, Streisand's Lowenstein heals the wounded Tom. Savannah is virtually a cipher in the film, and while she is a poet, she is *not* a "feminist" poet. The decentering of Savannah's character and her trauma thus parallels the film's erasure of a feminist discourse. Neither Lowenstein nor Tom are "feminists," either, and this rescripting renders Conroy's parable about the wounding of contemporary white masculinity all but indifferent to gender. In the scenes where Lowenstein and Tom spar over the meanings of masculinity, Streisand shifts the battle onto the far safer ground of parental authority and childish responses to that authority. Where Conroy's Lowenstein accuses Tom of being a "classic male," Streisand's counsels Tom to "stop acting like a petulant child." Similarly, the film displaces Tom's fear of being "marked" as a redneck white southern male onto one scene, in which Lowenstein's obnoxious but gifted husband mocks him at a dinner party. This scene does appear in the novel; but, there, it is part of Conroy's more general critique of "liberal" urban sentiment and its unthinking stereotyping of the South. Importantly, while the film does show Henry Wingo's physical violence, this violence pales in comparison with the film's representation of Lila's psychological violence.[43] In structure, editing, and narrative flow, the film makes it clear that Lila's injunction to repress is far more damaging to Tom than his father's injunction to express. Streisand evacuates the novel's meditation on the dangers of a primitive, inevitably violent masculinity and, in doing so, participates in the general movement from the political to the personal, the social to the individual, that I have been charting throughout this study.

In fact, as Adam Thorburn points out, the film is structured by a relatively straightforward narrative of remasculinization, in which Tom is cured of the wound caused by his "emasculating" rape and the equally unmanning maternal domination. With the help of beautiful Susan Lowenstein, Tom proves his heterosexual and masculine credentials and comes into full possession of his sexual (and phallic) manhood. Oversimplifying Tom's crisis, the film fails to register the depth and complexity of the novel's representation of masculinity as dangerous, and Tom's crisis as the inevitable result of a conflict between the "natural" requirements of a primitive masculinity and the social and personal choices Tom wants to make. The film erases Tom's hysteria, or more precisely, sees his repression as a result of his failure to believe in the healing power of therapy, crying, and the free expression of emotional and sexual energies. Because the film has no interest in a critique of a violent (or even inexpressive) masculinity, no irony attaches to Tom's remasculinization, and the ambivalence so central to Conroy's novel evaporates in Streisand's zeal to deify Lowenstein as Tom's savior.

In contrast, Conroy's solution of Tom's crisis seems deliberately unsatisfying and unconvincing, but not out of place in a novel that seeks to put the lid on its simmering energies by offering clichéd solutions to the problems it raises, and insisting that emotional repression *does* characterize a protagonist whose prose almost literally drips with emotion. Clichés, however, need not be read as the sign of a weak or overly melodramatic (not to say trashy) novel; in fact, at one point in the novel, Conroy suggests that clichés are central to the expression of southern-ness: "We were born to a house of complication, drama, and pain. We were typical southerners. In every southerner, beneath the veneer of cliché lies a much deeper motherlode of cliché. But even cliché is overlaid with enormous power when a child is involved" (109). This statement suggests that the "purple" quality of this narrative, its melodramatic excesses and banal sentimentalities, is significant as a statement of a southern mythos and aesthetics. Thus, we might see the novel verging on self-parody at moments, a reading that might further foreground what I take to be Conroy's simultaneous critique and naturalization of constructions of masculinity.

Two clichés are worth noting here, particularly because they are offered as the foundation of a narrative closure that is full of holes. The first is the idea that Tom overcomes both his father's and his mother's influence and learns to cry—thus releasing all of his repressed emotional energies and enabling a healthy masculinity. In fact, the novel ends in a veritable wash of tears, as Tom and Sallie, Savannah and father Henry, collapse together in a wet heap of reconciliation and emotional expressivity. It is his father's tears that command most of Tom's attention, as the novel ends with the restoration of the once powerful but now wounded patriarch, the archetypal "boys never cry" man; the maternal presence is entirely eliminated as Tom narrates:

> There was my father, the source of all these lives, the source of all these tears, crying now, crying hard and without shame. The tears were water, salt water, and I could see the ocean behind him, could smell it, could taste my own tears, the sea and hurt within me leaking out into the sunlight and my children crying to see me cry. The story of my family was the story of salt water, of boats and shrimp, of tears and storm.   (660)

Tom's return to his family, the release of his emotions, and the cure that comes from telling the family's story to Lowenstein and healing himself by sleeping with her, all appear to have alleviated his blockage, earlier described by the second cliché: "There's only one difficult thing about being a man, Doctor. Only one thing. They don't teach us how to love. It's a secret they keep from us" (438). As is typical of such statements, the "they" is unspecified, and men appear to be the passive recipients of a gender ideology that damages them. But just when Conroy appears to be opting for the therapeutic solution, he backs down and leaves his protagonist wounded and, more importantly, *still* blocked. Tom goes back to Sallie, even though he remains "incapable of responding to love from a woman." Therapy and the emotional release of crying notwith-standing, Tom remains "closed." He knows, and Sallie knows, that he "could never make her feel loved or needed or wanted even though that's what I want-ed to give her more than anything else in the world" (660).

While Conroy's representation of Tom's emotional blockage can be seen as part of a clichéd image of dominant masculinity, something more interesting is going on here. Tom is blocked, closed down, *not* because his violent father has taught him that "boys never cry" (115), and not even only because his mother insists on silence as the price of family loyalty; Tom is blocked because he knows that uninhibited expression will push him to tap into that reservoir of maleness where violence lives. Tom must remain "closed" because violence re-mains the "natural" expression of masculinity. Male blockage is necessary, even as it wounds Tom. Recall the earlier passage in which Tom confesses to an "ir-resistible desire to strike" Sallie, a desire that Conroy attributes to an inevitably violent patrimony, an elemental maleness that circulates through Tom's "blood" with a "surge of power about [his] heart" (30). Heroically battling this primitive impulse, Tom resorts to self-deprecation (he has a "little dick," "is getting fat," "is losing [his] hair" [30]). Which is better, the novel forces us to ask, Tom hitting Sallie? Or Tom opting for self-deprecation over violence? Tom can either beat his wife, or "fight with all [his] strength against the man it was [his] birthright to be" (30). But since this fight is framed as *unnatural,* Tom is positioned as a heroic if wounded man who must constantly buck nature and his masculine inheritance. The best he can do is collapse into a pathetic heap, confessing his inadequacies. Suppression of violence leads to humiliation, and the novel sets itself up to explore the pleasures of that humiliation. The novel is saturated with loss and, despite Tom's return to his family, it ends on a note of pure loss, a lack that signifies the perpetuation of a desire that can never be ful-filled: The novel ends with Tom confessing that "it is the secret life that sustains me now," a life encapsulated by his nightly ritual of whispering "Lowenstein, Lowenstein" (664). No recuperation for Tom, whose masculinity remains de-fined by lack, loss, and vulnerability, the only alternative, Conroy suggests, to the violence expressed by Henry and the mythologized rapist, Callanwolde. The novel, thus, subtly contests the ideology of male release it seems to exem-plify. In the process, it offers an answer to Kaja Silverman's question of what it might mean for "the typical male subject, like his female counterpart," to "learn to live with lack" (65).

In the final analysis, the novel suggests that emotional blockage hurts men but is necessary if men are to participate in a civilized social and familial world. Tom is hurt by the repression imposed on him by Lila, but the novel also sug-gests that the male expression of "natural" impulses is dangerous. In this re-spect, it's interesting to note, again, that Streisand's film rewrites Conroy's narrative by making it a simple story of remasculinization, rather than a more complicated representation of a masculinity perpetually in crisis. Along with downplaying the novel's explicit discourse about masculinity and feminism, the film fails to do justice to the sheer excessiveness of the novel—an excess that is integral to its exploration of the perils of repression *and* expression. For example, Streisand's representation of the rape scene foregrounds Tom's physical violation, Lila's horrifying injunction to silence, and Tom's feelings of inadequacy for his failure to help his mother and sister. Rather than have Luke bring in Caesar (remember the tiger?) to kill the rapists, Streisand has Luke shoot two, Lila stab the other, and Tom lament, "Luke two, Mama one. While I did nothing." While there are certainly many reasons why a filmmaker might not choose to show a tiger biting the head off one rapist, and generally mauling the others, Streisand's rewriting of this scene is symptomatic of the film's more general rescripting of Conroy's representation of Tom's crisis.

The scene in which Caesar kills the rapists is represented in vivid detail in the novel, but I am less interested in that description than I am in how Caesar is framed—specifically, how Conroy creates a kind of primal continuum between the violent Henry Wingo, Caesar, and the men who rape Lila, Savannah, and Tom. The tiger is one of Henry's crazy schemes to make money, and these schemes are presented with a kind of wry affection for the father's financial inadequacies. But the tiger is also a figure for Henry, its crime his crime: Caesar is "fired" from the circus for biting off the head of a cute, childlike seal whose claim to fame is his ability to play "Dixie" on a horn. Caesar, thus, is provoked to violence by the innocent expression of a southern sentimentality, and Henry is provoked to violence by an equally "innocent" expression of a masculine imperative. That Tom later threatens to destroy Lowenstein's husband Herbert Woodruff's prized Stradivarius violin after the pompous snob plays "Dixie" to mock the redneck southern boy suggests that Tom, too, identifies with the tiger. Having Caesar kill the rapists foregrounds the animalistic masculinity performed by them, a masculinity that is only one small step away from that performed by Henry. But the novel's deification of Caesar complicates this picture, and shows clearly that such primitive masculinity is also worthy of awe and respect. Primal, male violence is good, provided that it can be controlled, channeled into the protection of women and children rather than their destruction. That control, when managed properly, makes male health possible. But the problem is that it's nearly impossible to manage properly: the novel thus is about the damming of a natural primitive force, and how such a damming produces a masculinity perpetually in crisis.

Set, appropriately, in the "primitive" tidewater, Conroy's novel is rich in the language of a primal masculinity. A language of survival and fate also permeates the novel, as the narrative's epic quality lends weight to this tale of male wounding and pain. At the very beginning, Tom describes his family in such terms, when he calls his father's family "a passionate but unlucky clan whose decline after the Civil War was quick, certain, and probably inevitable" (3). Yet, if this clan is in inevitable decline—produced, in part, by its violent, self-defeating, and masochistic masculinity—that decline never ends entirely, and Tom lives as the embodiment of a new masculinity, one that pays the price for violence suppressed. In both *The Prince of Tides* and *Deliverance*, male rape plays a part in the representation of a dominant masculinity in crisis, but not because the penetration of a male body by another man results in an emasculation. Rather, rape becomes the emblem of a masculinity split against itself. Connected to a primal maleness, rape appears to be the "natural" expression of masculinity; but this expression turns against men whose lives are lived in the social. Dickey's *Deliverance* is alone in its belief in the absolute separation of the natural and the social, and the novel's movement toward remasculinization makes of it a far simpler, and somehow less contemporary, narrative than either Boorman's *Deliverance* or Conroy's *The Prince of Tides*. The latter two embody the full force of a dominant masculinity in crisis, a crisis that perpetuates itself as a reconstructed norm.

That crisis and its management is fully evident in the popular studies of male sexual problems that, as I've argued, cover a political critique of masculinity and male power with a naturalized discourse on bodies. Like the men's liberationists whose critiques of the "male role" are built on an uneasy relationship to feminism, popular books aimed at reassuring men about their sexuality in post-liberationist America are full of contradictions both over what constitutes masculinity and how nature and society play into that constitution. By focusing on the biological bases of a rhetoric of blockage and release, I have suggested that a politicized construction of sexuality has prompted a return to an evolutionary, and resolutely "apolitical," understanding of male sexuality. Further, because of the changed social and political terrain—due largely to the success of feminism in changing the terms of the discussion of gender and sexuality—these writings on male sexuality construct the male body and masculinity as inevitably torn between the imperatives of blockage and release, repression and expression, indulgence and restraint. The power of an elemental masculinity gets channeled back into the body, as injunctions against the free expression of male impulses and energies create a state of crisis. Since these energies are represented and understood as "natural" and material, failure to find an outlet has consequences for the male body and male psyche. The body that emerges in these discussions is a body whose power is secured *not*, as it turns out, by the expression of those energies, but, instead, by the necessary if damaging suppression of them. Thus, contemporary men are, if only implicitly, represented as hysterical, their simmering bodies carrying the signs of the social and political crises of the era.

This construction of masculinity, which entails the naturalization both of male inexpressivity and male violence, is surprisingly resilient. As I was finishing up this chapter, I happened to read David Denby's review of Paul Schrader's film of Russell Banks's novel *Affliction* in a recent issue of *The New Yorker*. Part of what draws Denby so passionately to this film is its exploration of the pain inflicted by a pathological but, nevertheless, "normal" masculinity passed by fathers to their sons. Denby's response to the film indicates his belief in the "naturalness" of what I want to insist is a socially constructed masculinity, a masculinity characterized by emotional inexpressivity leading to violence: "Wade's 'affliction' is a heritage of lovelessness which manifests itself in rage. . . . [His father] still razzes the love [his sons] try to express for him. No wonder Wade can't find the rhythm in his relationships and is always lunging at people and then apologizing. . . . They are father and son, and Wade is unable to escape the destructive element in the old man's temperament. Murder is in the air, and in this movie violence seems right—not morally but as the *inevitable expression of the rage that fills men when they feel weak or lost*" (95, emphasis added). Male violence is inevitable, produced by the repression of feelings and language; and, moreover, this violence functions as evidence of men's *wounds*.

Representations of a hysterical, masochistic, or wounded white male body testify to the real, material effects of a perceived displacement of white masculinity away from the center, from the normative, from the mainstream. But, as we have seen, such representations also work to recenter white masculinity, to carve out a new place for white men in relation to changing notions of normativity. In post-liberationist American culture, an unmistakable romance with the figure of the victim—coupled with a much longer American romance with the figure of the heroic, sometimes successful, sometimes doomed, rebel—pushes a wide range of writers, filmmakers, and cultural commentators to imagine white men as both victimized by those changes and pumped up to rebel against them. The paradoxical logics I have read in post-liberationist texts evince the complexity of the category, "white men," and thus caution us to break ourselves of the habit of understanding that category as a noncategory, a nonconflicted and self-evident signifier for dominance itself. But the representational and rhetorical strategies through which the wounded white man comes to occupy the position either of true rebel or true victim should give us pause: what happens when others get evacuated from that position? What happens to "liberation" when the social group with the most economic and political power imagines itself in need of liberation? As I have argued throughout this book, white men *have* been marked, and the responses to that marking have included both the predictable and the surprising. Predictably, the perceived disempowerment of white men has produced a backlash against feminism, civil rights, and entitlements programs understood to be at odds with white men's interests. Surprisingly, an undeniable attraction to vulnerability has pushed white masculinity gradually farther away from a fully phallic power. While my intention has not been to dwell on the actual pain suffered by white men who thus feel themselves separated from a fully empowered position, it's clear that the striking prevalence of images of wounded white male bodies attests to the reality of that pain. At the same time, the substitution of the personal for the political has worked to erase and invalidate the pain of others—primarily those others who have been engaged in marking white masculinity. The rhetoric of crisis enables a slippage between the personal and the political, the material and the abstract, and in late 1990s American culture, that rhetoric shows no signs of abating. The wounded white man, forced into visibility by others, is a figure that, paradoxically, testifies to the power of liberationist movements in reshaping American identity and discourse *and* threatens to erode the gains that those movements achieved. It is my hope that *Marked Men* has contributed some insight into how such an erosion can be forestalled.

NOTES

INTRODUCTION: VISIBILITY, CRISIS, AND THE WOUNDED WHITE MALE BODY

1. A word on terminology: while some analysts of the contemporary crisis in masculinity do not specify *white* masculinity, my desire to do so stems from my conviction that the very particular dynamics of embodiment I am isolating here depend on whiteness and masculinity, insofar as the white man is the figure in American culture understood to be normative, his body unmarked. While some of what I say—particularly about male versus female representations of bodily experience—might apply to men of color, my argument is specifically directed at representations of bodies and subjectivities understood as unmarked by either gender or race. In recent books and articles on masculinity in crisis, there often comes a moment when the writer finds himself in a bit of a bind as to the racial category of the masculinity under analysis. This moment usually comes in the course of detailing how "men" either resent the inroads of, or try to appropriate the tactics of, "black men." A representative instance is found in the last chapter of Michael Kimmel's *Manhood in America: A Cultural History*. In the process of detailing why "men" might turn to the men's movement, Kimmel points out that some men "seek to reclaim the proving ground from interlopers—like blacks, gays, and women" (298). The "interlopers" are racially (and sexually) marked, but the seekers are not. While Kimmel explicitly states elsewhere that his book "describes only one version of 'Manhood in America'—albeit the dominant version" (6), his language in the above instance unwittingly works to unmark white masculinity. Scholars who struggle with competing impulses to generalize by gender and specify by race are struggling against deep-seated linguistic conventions that work to reproduce the normativity of whiteness and masculinity. For clarity's sake, I will use the construction "(white) masculinity" to refer to ideas or work that does not specify a racial category but which, in my view, implies one. At different points in

the study, class differences will come into the foreground, as will concerns about homosexuality and heterosexuality. I might have used the terms *dominant* or *hegemonic* or *normative* masculinity instead of "white" masculinity, but I have chosen to foreground whiteness because it refers to a bodily (but, of course, not *only* bodily) register of difference.

2. These two "calls to action" are representative: "It is time to try to speak about masculinity, about what it is and how it works. . . . Despite all that has been written over the past twenty years on femininity and feminism, masculinity has stayed pretty well concealed. This has always been its ruse in order to hold on to its power. Masculinity tries to stay invisible by passing itself off as normal and universal" (Antony Easthope, *What a Man's Gotta Do* 1). And: "Naming 'whiteness' displaces it from the unmarked, unnamed status that is itself an effect of its dominance. Among the effects on white people both of race privilege and of the dominance of whiteness are their seeming normativity, their structured invisibility" (Ruth Frankenberg, *White Women, Race Matters* 6).

Other analysts of masculinity have articulated similar "calls to action" that take off from the idea that making masculinity visible is the first step toward eroding male privilege. See Peter Lehman, *Running Scared*, 4–5; and Calvin Thomas, 15–18. For interrogations of whiteness and visibility, see, also, Walter Benn Michaels; David Roediger, *Towards the Abolition of Whiteness;* Toni Morrison; and George Lipsitz. See also Shelley Fisher Fishkin's survey of recent work on whiteness in American studies: "Interrogating 'Whiteness,' Complicating 'Blackness': Remapping American Culture." The *Minnesota Review* published a special issue entitled "The White Issue," no. 47 (Fall 1996), which contains reviews of most of the new work on whiteness, fiction and poetry, several critical essays, and much interesting speculation on what motivates this new turn toward whiteness.

3. "Hidden from history" is a trope most often used to describe the exclusion of nondominant individuals and groups from the narratives of history. It is important, I think, to make a distinction between two kinds of invisibility: the invisibility of those who inhabit the margins of history (and literature and theory and politics and so on) is not the same thing as the invisibility of those who can be said to inhabit the center of cultural and political power. Whereas the former are invisible in the sense of being underrepresented, the latter are invisible behind a mask of universality.

4. The presumption that whiteness, heterosexuality, and masculinity are unmarked and noncategorical is based on what Ross Chambers terms "in(di)visibility": the assumption that the normative is singular and uniquely individual, while the "other" is both pluralized and homogenized (144–45). There may be lots of different others, but they're all the same in their differences from the unmarked norm. Going one step further, Chambers argues that the existence of

multiple marked categories safeguards not only the singularity of the un-marked but also enables the equation between the unmarked and the individual.

5. For a further interrogation of the category of the visible, see Phelan's chapter, "White Men and Pregnancy: Discovering the Body to Be Rescued," 130–45; Robyn Wiegman, *American Anatomies*, 21–42; and John Fiske, *Power Plays, Power Works*.

6. Versions of this narrative appear in Susan Jeffords, *The Remasculinization of America*, xi–xii, and *Hard Bodies*, 118; Michael Kimmel, *Manhood in America*, 298–99; and James William Gibson, 10–12. Susan Faludi's *Stiffed: The Betrayal of the American Man* offers a journalistic, anecdotal, and somewhat sentimental account of the causes of the current crisis in masculinity. Based in large part on interviews with men from various walks of life (including a large number of economically displaced or "downsized" workers), Faludi mounts a case for an understanding of the current crisis in what she calls "historical" terms. Noting that most explanations for men's current sense of their own disempowerment rely too heavily on trite psychological or simplistic biological models, she aims to analyze the "betrayal of the American man" in relation to large historical shifts—particularly, the shifts from an industrial to a service economy, from a society of usefulness to an "ornamental" society. While *Stiffed* is a valuable contribution to the current literature on masculinity, it suffers from a sentimental and, paradoxically, ahistorical nostalgia for an older masculinity that, in Faludi's view, was stable and secure. The heyday of this masculinity was World War II (Ernie Pyle is the privileged exemplar of it), and Faludi seems oddly unaware of how her desire to reconstruct this older masculinity works against the very historicism she claims to be pursuing. Further, while being scrupulously careful to avoid blaming women and feminists for men's predicaments, Faludi does not quite get beyond the seventies "men's movement" ideas that she herself claims were inadequate. The villain in Faludi's narrative remains a vaguely sketched and non-agential "society" that promises men everything but delivers little. Noting that the "male paradigm of confrontation" proved useful to the women's, civil rights, and gay rights movements in the 1960s and 1970s, Faludi insists that men do not take a liberationist stance because of their very allegiance to the male paradigm: "The male paradigm," she writes, is "particularly unsuited to mounting a challenge to men's predicament. Men have no clearly defined enemy who is oppressing them. How can men be oppressed when the culture has already identified them as the oppressors, and when they see themselves that way?" (604). As I will argue here, men have, in fact, taken up a liberationist rhetoric and have done so not only to reclaim lost entitlements but to join others in the field of the "oppressed."

7. I take the term "Sonyist" from Fred Pfeil's *White Guys*, 106–107, which he

takes from McKenzie Wark, "From Fordism to Sonyism: Perverse Readings of the New World Order," *New Formations* 15 (Winter 1991). Pfeil's book is the best example of an analysis of straight white masculinity within the frame of an economic analysis.

8. See Katherine S. Newman, *Falling from Grace* and *Declining Fortunes;* and Barbara Ehrenreich, *Fear of Falling.* Joel Schumacher's 1993 film *Falling Down* also tropes on this theme.

9. In addition to Haraway, see Michael Warner, Dana Nelson, and Robyn Wiegman (*American Anatomies*), for discussions of how the very concept of American citizenship (and the Western universalist "man") has depended on a disembodiment of whiteness and masculinity.

10. I want to differentiate between these metaphorical wounds and the more literal wounds suffered by groups such as returning Vietnam veterans or prisoners of war. As Susan Jeffords argues, vets were represented as victims, their increasing visibility enabling a substitution of wounded white men for other "casualties" of the Vietnam era (*The Remasculinization of America,* 116–27). While such literal wounds quite clearly served symbolic purposes, as Jeffords documents, those representations are grounded in the historical real in a way that the manufactured traumas I analyze here are not.

11. David Savran, in a 1998 book on white masculinity and masochism in postwar American culture, constructs an argument that is parallel to mine, but with certain key differences. Savran sees masochism—and, more interestingly, reflexive sadomasochism—as a key "masculine fantasmatic" in this era, and one that has historical as well as psychoanalytic explanations. He understands the prevalence of the white male victim as a product of the social and political changes of this era—feminism, civil rights, the loss of the Vietnam War, the rise of a service economy, and the disenfranchisement of the middle class—and argues that white men must adopt some kind of strategy to evade the "feminization" that comes from taking up a victim position. In Savran's analysis, the late 1960s and early 1970s produced a new masculinity whose "softness" would later require strategies of remasculinization. In his reading of a wide range of literary and other texts, Savran uncovers a white male subject split between a traditionally masculine, sadistic, virile self and a traditionally feminine, masochistic, vulnerable self. Masochism, in Savran's reading, ultimately works to reinforce the traditional masculine portion of this self, as the ability to take pain "like a man" works to override the taint of femininity that comes from positioning oneself as wounded, pain-wracked, victimized subject. Most interesting for my purposes is Savran's argument that reflexive sadomasochism produces a "dramatization of the male subject at war with himself . . . turning against himself, by producing himself as the ground on which irreducibly opposing forces collide and do battle." Savran's argument rests on the idea that

"no longer having others on whom to inflict his power and his point with impunity, the male subject began to turn against himself and to prove his mettle by gritting his teeth and taking his punishment like a man" (176). While this is entirely persuasive in some contexts—here Savran reads the *Rambo* films, Sam Shepard's plays, Robert Bly's *Iron John,* and the Joel Schumacher film *Falling Down*—the middlebrow texts that occupy me in this study evidence a slightly different dynamic. Where Savran suggests that white men's sense of their own victimization *causes* the crisis in hegemonic masculinity, I am arguing that the recourse to victimization attempts to *solve* that crisis. Not only did the sixties and seventies produce a new ideal of "soft" masculinity—which, in Savran's reading, later required remasculinization—but these decades also witnessed the *marking* of white masculinity precisely as the embodiment of the sadistic, traditionally masculine force that Savran reads as having lost its dominance. Further, while the texts Savran reads keep in place a binary (and heterosexualized) construction of gender, as he notes, I want to focus attention on a masochism that is less a struggle between masculine and feminine than it is an attempt to reconstruct the masculine—*not* as "tough" enough to take self-inflicted or other punishments, but as attractively vulnerable in a culture that is so taken with the dynamics of victimization. While Savran argues that white men need a strategy to remasculinize themselves in the wake of their feminizing decentering, I will argue that remasculinization is not the best way to characterize the goals of the texts I'm looking at. The masochistic male subjects I consider do not use their ability to withstand pain as a sign of their masculinity; instead, they use the pain itself to reimagine a new conceptualization of masculinity, and one that just might evade the passive-feminine-masochist, active-masculine-sadistic binaries that Savran analyzes. Finally, unlike Savran, I want to avoid understanding these reconstructions as stemming from "backlash." As I will argue throughout this book, while there is certainly ample evidence of white men attempting to recoup the losses of the post-liberation era, I want to change the angle of vision slightly so as to place the renegotiations of masculinity *within*, not *against*, the various struggles characterizing post-liberationist American culture.

12. Evidence of this dynamic abounds, but appears with particular clarity in a recent news report on a "Diversity" pilot project instituted by the Washington State Ferry System. One worker, articulating dismay at the proliferation of identity markers in American culture, worries that white men, the last defense against a "balkanized" conceptualization of American identity, are becoming just another "special interest" group: " 'We used to all be just ferry workers, but now everyone's divided up into little groups: blacks, women, gays, even white males. Can you give me one reason why we need a white man's group? I don't need anyone to defend me' " (Egan 12A). It seems unlikely that "blacks, women,

[and] gays" were ever considered just ferry workers, for the privilege of being just anything (American, for example) has historically been reserved for those whose bodies and subjectivities have remained unmarked. Yet this worker's claim that white men do *not* constitute a "group" in this sense, and his anxiety over the implication that they might, testifies to the shifting nature of identity politics in U.S. culture in the 1990s.

13. George Yudice argues, similarly, that the presumption that whiteness is racially unmarked proves both a "privilege" and a "liability": "The privilege comes from occupying the 'naturalized' position in a social system in which whiteness, like righthandedness, is taken to be the standard. The liability ensues from the lack of an increasingly valued (some might say commodified) 'difference' or 'markedness,' which many whites are lamenting more and more" ("Neither Impugning nor Disavowing Whiteness," 258). Robyn Wiegman argues that it is the rise of visual culture that is at the root of a (symbolic if not real) decentering of white masculinity. She posits that "corporeal abstraction" of white masculinity—its invisibility as a bodily entity—"exists in overt contradiction with a visual culture predicated on the commodification of those very identities minoritized by the discourses and social organization of enlightened modernity" (*American Anatomies* 49).

14. George Lipsitz argues that it is an "overdetermined inadequacy of the language of liberal individualism to describe collective experience" that has made it difficult to articulate a collective experience *not* based on victimization (381). He notes the troubling fact that "young whites" appear to "have no knowledge of the disciplined, systemic, and collective *group* activity that has structured white identities in American history" (382–83). I will return to Lipsitz's points in my next chapter, and suggest that this denial of white and masculine "group" identity is often undermined by a rhetoric of victimization.

15. Judith Butler and Marjorie Garber are two theorists who have done excellent work on the liminal and, in Garber's terms, "category crisis." Recent feminist celebrations of gender and performance, based on a not altogether accurate reading of Butler, have led some critics to see the performative aspects of masculinity as necessarily subversive, even when the performance of masculinity might serve the interests of a white and male ruling class. See, for example, Yvonne Tasker's consideration of the spectacle of masculinity in Hollywood action films of the 1980s. Noting that it is de rigueur these days to talk about men "performing the masculine" in films, Tasker wonders about the "possibility of making a distinction between a parodic performance of masculinity and the oppressive enactment of that performance" (243). See also Lee Edelman's response to Frank Lentricchia's "performance" of heterosexual masculinity in his reading of Wallace Stevens. Self-consciousness does not, in itself, guarantee subversion of dominant representations or, more importantly, any change in

existing power relations. Indeed, as Tania Modleski points out, self-conscious-ness and self-criticism can actually serve an "inoculating" function which al-lows "business to proceed as usual" (6).

16. See also Abigail Solomon-Godeau, who remarks: "Masculinity, however defined is, like capitalism, *always* in crisis. And the real question is how both manage to restructure, refurbish, and resurrect themselves for the next histori-cal turn" (70). While I think that this kind of skepticism, shared by Modleski and others, is warranted, I want to resist the assumption that a remasculiniza-tion necessarily follows in the wake of crisis—if, by remasculinization, we mean the kinds of operations analyzed so convincingly by Susan Jeffords. I'm not contesting Jeffords's readings, but instead am working to complicate the narrative and rhetorical understanding of "crisis" and the multiple ways in which that crisis is articulated, worked out, and managed. See also Andrew Ross's "The Great White Dude," 167–75; and George Yudice's "What's a Straight White Man to Do?" Both of these essays confirm that skepticism over the "re-form" of straight white masculinity is warranted by the overwhelming evidence of the ability of straight white masculinity to make itself over into any politi-cally and culturally marketable image—including that of the "progressive" man. Such skepticism is also the prevailing spirit behind Fred Pfeil's *White Guys*.

17. See, for example, Clyde Griffen and Gail Bederman. Griffen assumes that a "defensive" construction of masculinity necessarily relies on the creation or perpetuation of separate masculine and feminine spheres. Others, including Kimmel and Kevin Mumford, have no problem with the crisis model.

18. See Kaja Silverman, "White Skin, Brown Masks"; Christopher Newfield, "The Politics of Male Suffering"; Paul Smith; and Carole-Anne Tyler.

19. For an analysis of this film, see my " 'What guy will do that?' Recodings of Masculinity in *sex, lies, and videotape.*"

20. See Judith Roof for a somewhat sardonic review of recent work in mas-culinity studies. Focusing on several books that I would call "pro-feminist," Roof wonders just what is at stake when men start calling for the visibility of masculinity: "The struggle for the right kind of visibility continues among men in a battle that seems to shift the stake of identity politics from authenticity and a 'right' to speak to the crucial importance of being seen speaking" (357).

21. Studlar is relying heavily on Theodor Reik's work on masochism, as does Kaja Silverman. Two points that Reik stresses are relevant to my discussion: the idea that masochistic narratives resist closure; and the idea that the masochist requires an audience. David Savran makes the intriguing point that the econo-my of desire that fuels reflexive sadomasochism poses the watcher (who can be incorporated into the masochistic subject or separate from him) as a destabi-lizing third term mediating between a "masculine" sadism and a "feminine"

masochism (182–83). I am not addressing Reik's work directly, since my project is not to add to theoretical reconsiderations of masochism and male subjectivity. Rather, here I am making a different kind of point: the prevalence of masochism, and the similarly "feminine" hysteria, in recent books and articles on masculinity is both cause and symptom of the crisis I'll be delineating throughout this book. The fact that white masculinity becomes visible primarily through its wounding—and white men renegotiate their position by exploring pain—is the point I want to stress.

22. On this question, see Janice Radway, *A Feeling for Books*, and Joan Shelley Rubin. Classic critiques of the middlebrow include Dwight MacDonald's *Partisan Review* essay on "Masscult and Midcult" and Clement Greenberg's essay on "The State of American Writing."

23. See, for example, John Fiske ("Popular Discrimination"), Dick Hebidge, and other key figures of British cultural studies. See Meghan Morris, and Susan Bordo, "Material Girl," for critiques of this approach.

24. While it might come as a surprise to place King in the middlebrow, that is where, in fact, I think he belongs. I will make this argument in some detail in chapter 3.

1. MARKING MEN, EMBODYING AMERICA: JOHN UPDIKE AND THE RECONSTRUCTION OF MIDDLE AMERICAN MASCULINITY

1. Almost all critics of the Rabbit series say, at least in passing, that Updike's hero is "representative" of the "ordinary" American. Most ignore how gender is implicated in the assignation of the "ordinary," and with the exception of Dilvo Ristoff, Jan Clausen, and Joyce Markle, these critics rarely qualify "American" with "white." For readings of the political and/or historical contexts and significance of the Rabbit series, see Jeff Campbell, Raymond Mazurek, and Matthew Wilson. For analysis of Updike's use of popular culture, see Stacey Olster.

2. The fact that white masculinity has remained unmarked is evidenced by the bulk of critical and theoretical work on gender (which means women) and race (which means nonwhite people), as well as critical work on Updike's Rabbit novels. While there have been surprisingly few studies of Updike which admit to being ideological, a few critics have considered the gendered and racial meanings in the novels. Some have done so directly, while others have subsumed questions of gender and race under a more general analysis of politics or ideology. Early studies of gender and race in the novels concerned themselves with determining the sexism, misogyny, and/or racism of the protagonist, the novels, and/or their creator—most of which concluded that Harry (if not Updike) is sexist and racist. Mary Allen's "John Updike's Love of 'Dull Bovine Beauty'" is the classic piece on sexism. For readings of racism in the se-

ries, see Edward M. Jackson, and Mariann Russell. For a preliminary study of masculinity in the series, see Mary Catherine O'Connell.

3. While it is clear that Updike distances himself from the unheroic Rabbit, presenting him as a kind of case study in Middle American anxiety, there is little evidence to suggest that Updike identifies against his protagonist, and with the "others" who force recognition of Rabbit's markedness.

4. As I noted in the introduction, this is a key characteristic of masochistic narrative, and one that has been analyzed by Studlar, Silverman, and Savran.

5. Barbara Ehrenreich notes that in the discourse on Middle America, the working class was simultaneously heralded as figure for the great middle classes ("the silent majority") and vilified as other to those middle classes, as "vulgar" or retrograde. Further, the professional middle-class men writing these accounts were invested in differentiating themselves from the stable and rule-bound traditionalism that they "found" in Middle America. At the same time, the working class is understood as a reservoir of masculinity. Ehrenreich writes: "The boyish physicality of the working class stood for a kind of manliness that white-collar professionals had long since surrendered to the bureaucracy. . . . The economic injustice that made some men 'workers' could be interpreted positively as a collective addiction to hard work and self-discipline," something that middle-class white men worried that they were on the verge of losing (Ehrenreich, *Fear of Falling* 120). See Gail Bederman for an analysis of similar anxieties in relation to masculinity in the last decades of the nineteenth, and first decades of the twentieth, century.

6. The stories by and about the "forgotten" and "silent majority" all assume, but don't explain demographically, their factoring out of black (or Hispanic or Asian) Americans. Lemon, whose *The Troubled American* was a report on a Gallup poll commissioned by *Newsweek,* simply says that the magazine "commissioned The Gallup Organization to interview 2,165 *white* adults comprising a cross-section of *white* America. Included in this total sample were 1,321 *white* Americans whose incomes ranged from $5,000 to $15,000—representatives of a group which, by itself comprises about 55 per cent of the U.S. population" (7–8, emphasis added). While Lemon uses the qualifying "white" to describe his sample, that qualifier quickly disappears, and the "Middle American" becomes raceless again. Despite that racelessness, however, these representative Americans feel discriminated against—by virtue of their whiteness. Middle Americans are both raceless (Middle Americans without qualification) and raced (a beleaguered white majority); more importantly, Middle Americans are not only constructed as white but as victimized *because* they are white.

7. The focus on the racial animosities motivating Middle American resentments enables the disappearance of differences between or among white Amer-

icans *and* works against the creation of alliances across race. What drops out of the analysis of Middle Americans versus the "young, poor, and black" is any recognition of a white ruling class that might be held responsible for the economic and social woes of the working and middle classes. Scammon and Wattenberg, for instance, note that the "confrontation in Chicago" at the 1968 Democratic National Convention "etched the lines of social class as sharply as they have ever been drawn in America"—between "elitists" and "plain people" (62). What or who constitutes these two categories is never specified, but elsewhere in *The Real Majority* the "middle" is defined in such a way as to insure its majority against the poor and the rich. Richard Lemon makes repeated references to Middle America's anger both at the poor (imagined as black welfare "loafers") and the rich (imagined as white tax evaders); but the references to the rich are not backed up by his interviews, in which the overwhelming target of scorn and hostility is black America. John Clarke, in his analysis of the rise of the New Right in the United States since the mid-1960s, suggests that the conservative elite poses Middle Americans against a "liberal elite," thus making itself disappear from view. As Clarke notes, "This is the classic populist interpellation of the contemporary New Right: the construction of a (implicitly majoritarian) popular opinion whose views are embodied in the agenda of the New Right itself against the socially and politically isolated elite liberals" (141).

8. Part of the intense focus on race is due to what Scammon and Wattenberg suggest is the rise of "The Social Issue" to replace traditional economic party allegiances around the middle of the decade. Thus, according to Scammon and Wattenberg, the Democratic Party splinters, and white Americans unite in a protest against the protests of others. Defined primarily as civil rights, "racial problems," "crime and lawlessness," or "integration struggle," the "Social Issue" signifies white anxieties about race. As Donald Warren observes, 1968 was a year extraordinary for marking "the demise of the Rooseveltian coalition of the intelligentsia, the minorities and the working class" (xix). This demise would open the door to the New Right and a new "popular wisdom" in which the "average American" was constructed in line with "anti-collectivist and pro-individualist sentiments" against a "liberal elite" (Clarke 128). This new "popular wisdom" enables the erasure of the conservative white elite, as well as the scapegoating of people of color and others who benefit from the Great Society programs of the 1960s. As Hodgson shrewdly observes, the Nixon conservatives were ready and waiting to "capture" this Middle America, creating an "alliance between the rebellious Middle Americans—whether they came from a fundamentally Protestant tradition in the South or Southwest or were mainly Catholic 'ethnics' in the urban Northeast and Middle West—and a conservative economic elite whose most noticeable characteristic was emphatically not its social conscience" (Hodgson 421).

9. Dilvo Ristoff has argued that Harry Angstrom shares some characteristics with the MARs as Warren describes them; but I would add that he lacks the (albeit conflicted) will to mobilize and protect group interests. In this sense, I think Ristoff is wrong when he says that Harry is the epitome of Warren's MAR. His neighbors, the white militants who burn down the house, are more in line with the MARs because central to the ideology is protest. Harry's protest is so weak as to be negligible. I am extremely grateful to Ristoff, however, for mentioning Warren's study.

10. In addition to Lemon, Warren, and Scammon and Wattenberg, see also Wattenberg, *The Real America.*

11. Perhaps this explains the fact that (mostly white and male) critics were overwhelmingly "troubled" by the novel. White masculinity is in trouble in this novel, and any recuperation of its powers is, ironically, accomplished through its aligning itself with the disempowered. See Donald J. Greiner, 87–88, for a summary of reviews of *Rabbit Redux,* many of which suggest an uneasiness that I would trace to the way in which the novel works to decenter white masculinity. Greiner observes that critics were much more pleased with *Rabbit Is Rich,* a novel that contains little to trouble white masculinity.

12. Updike's representation of Skeeter participates in a construction of blackness that is already old news by 1971. This representation owes to Norman Mailer's "The White Negro," in which blackness is equated with "hipness," and in which blackness serves to fill a lack experienced by whiteness. Eldridge Cleaver expands on this in *Soul on Ice,* of course, and Updike has clearly read both these pieces. The fact that, by 1971, images of blackness—and, more specifically, black masculinity—had become more overtly threatening suggests that *Rabbit Redux* looks nostalgically back to a "safer" time, rather than forward into the age of black power, an age in which whiteness is truly threatened, instead of being energized, by blackness. See also Thomas Schaub, 137–62, for a discussion of Mailer's construction of an "aggressively masculine individual."

13. A number of critics have traced the centrality of space imagery in the novel. See, particularly, David L. Vanderwerken, and Jack DeBellis.

14. Roediger analyzes in great detail the "wages of whiteness," the benefits (social, economic, political) that come with white skin for working people in the United States, but interestingly, seems to exempt "culture" from the arenas in which whiteness shines as the standard and norm (see *The Wages of Whiteness*). I'm not suggesting that Roediger argues that people of color in the United States wield any kind of substantial cultural clout; his argument is, rather, that it is in the cultural sphere that white people have already begun to value nonwhiteness and, more importantly, might agree to allow a pallid white culture to "wither away."

15. In the new Fawcett Columbine trade paperback edition of *Rabbit Redux*

(1996), the following words have been deleted: "He has escaped. Narrowly," the passage ending with the sentence, "His heart is hammering, hard." According to an assistant editor at Alfred A. Knopf, Updike very often revises his work for new editions, and apparently Knopf sees no reason to indicate changes on the copyright page or anywhere else (author's conversation with Ken Schneider, January 28, 1997). This change indicates to me that Updike is retreating from a risky representation of homoeroticism and the appeals of blackness. There are other, racially significant, changes, including a last-minute and entirely unconvincing framing of Skeeter within the discourse of "victimism" and racial disadvantage.

16. The novel also suggests that America must deal with the Soviet challenge as one might deal with a woman who, like Jill, was "liking it, being raped" (246). Each of the four chapters has an epigraph from space, the first and third from the Soviet Soyuz 5 mission (to couple with the American Apollo), the second and fourth from the Apollo mission to the surface of the moon. The first chapter epigraph sets the stage for the maneuverings to follow:

LIEUT. COL. VLADIMIR A. SHATALOV: I am heading straight for the socket.

LIEUT. COL. BORIS V. VOLYNOV, SOYUZ 5 COMMANDER: Easy, not so rough.

COLONEL SHATALOV: It took me quite a while to find you, but now I've got you.
(12)

By the third chapter, entitled "Skeeter," we have this message: " 'We've been raped! We've been raped!'—*background voice aboard soyuz 5*" (183). This gesture reassures that American imperial might will triumph, but leaves in its wake a troubling image of male-on-male sexual violence.

17. The death of Jill, in one sense, proves that Rabbit's racist neighbors are right: it is the white woman who is threatened by the black man. But the novel, I would argue, does not simply reinscribe this classic scenario of white male fear. Jill is destroyed *not* by Skeeter per se, but rather, by the bond between Skeeter and Rabbit, as Rabbit realizes: "Rabbit understands. They are at war. They have taken a hostage" (262). This is what men do in Updike novels, most of which have at least one triangular configuration. Here there is also a joke, courtesy of *The Carol Burnett Show*, which predicts the racial configuration within the triangles: the Lone Ranger, asked to choose between his wife and Tonto, chooses Tonto—and Tonto chooses the wife. See O'Connell, and Mary Allen, for the strongest indictments of Rabbit's guilt in letting Jill die.

18. A more spirited condemnation can be found in Kermit Turner's essay on *Rabbit Redux,* in which he rails against the "permissive society" represented in

(and endorsed by?) Updike's novel. See Ehrenreich, *Fear of Falling*, for a critique of the notion (still dominant) that the sixties were a "permissive" era.

19. Raymond Mazurek notes that Updike's "commentary on postwar America" in the Rabbit novels is organized around what Richard Ohmann has called an "illness narrative" in which social and political ills get represented as personal, individual malaise. Mazurek suggests that this tendency compromises the more or less accurate representation of history within the novels. But I would suggest that the "illness" that the novels detail is much more specific than a general malaise. It is a disease that afflicts white men far more fully than others—and it is no accident that the vast majority of the writers Ohmann reads are white and male.

20. Greiner writes: "Accounts of space flights and race riots all but surround him in the earlier novel. From the newspaper items he sets as a linotypist to the nightly blarings of the televised news, the despair of his life is linked to the disintegration of his country. Public matters invade domestic affairs, and inarticulate Rabbit finds himself forced to discuss such controversies as Vietnam and civil rights about which he knows little but worries much. In *Rabbit Redux* he is ripped from the self and hurled to the world. He does not belong there, and he knows it. . . . How, he wonders, can he react to the spectacular demands of astronauts and blacks when he cannot meet the mundane requirements of family and friends?" (85).

21. *New York Times*, July 16, 1979, A10; quoted in Carroll, 220.

22. See, particularly, Marjorie Garber, Peter Lehman, Sally Robinson ("What guy will do that?"), and Susan Bordo ("Reading the Male Body").

23. Male bodies are mysterious because so seemingly incidental to male experience, unlike female bodies which define female essence, according to Updike. In a bizarre essay on the male body entitled "The Disposable Rocket," Updike is admirably clear on this point: "The male body skims the surface of nature's deep, wherein the blood and pain and mysterious cravings of women perpetuate the species" (519). "To *inhabit* a male body, then," Updike concludes, "is to feel somewhat detached from it. It is not an enemy, but not entirely a friend" (519, emphasis added). As becomes clear in *Rabbit at Rest*, bodily vulnerability is coded as feminine, no matter what the gender of the embodied person. When Rabbit undergoes an angioplasty, this becomes absolutely explicit. In a vividly detailed description that goes on for pages and pages, Updike nicely conveys Harry's simultaneous anxiety over and pleasure in this feminizing penetration. As the doctor is "inside" Rabbit, he wonders "is this what having a baby is like," and goes on to speculate on how women and "queers" feel being "screwed" and "buggered." In a moment of pure panic, Rabbit experiences an utter vulnerability in which his social powers, entitlements, and privi-

leges recede behind the overwhelming sense of feminized risk: "The mechanically precise dark ghost of the catheter is the worm of death within him. Godless technology is fucking the pulsing wet tubes we inherited from the squid, the boneless sea-cunts" (226–27).

24. Despite the license afforded by this "uncivilized" world, it is not Ronnie Harrison whom Rabbit penetrates, but his wife, and Updike thus deftly sidesteps the consequences of the fantasies about the penetration of male bodies that his protagonist has entertained. That Rabbit's fantasy of anal penetration is realized with a woman rather than a man confirms that, despite his flirtation with homosexual ideas and images, Updike is unprepared to send Rabbit on that particular somatic pilgrimage. (Updike settles for Rabbit being "penetrated" by Thelma's urine, a pretty weak performance, given Thelma's "impotence" and the fact that "women cannot *aim*" [394–95].) Thelma, ill with lupus and in love with Harry, gives her beloved the "gift" of anal penetration, and Harry loves it. Not only has Harry taken the next step on his "somatic pilgrimage," but he has, Updike makes clear, faced death by anally penetrating Thelma. Part of this is due to Thelma's terminal illness, but the description of the experience also owes to cultural presumptions about anal eroticism and death—and thus articulates a common equation between *homosexuality* and death, even if it is here displaced. On this question, see Bersani.

25. Credit for this idea goes to Monika Hogan, a student in one of my classes on recodings of masculinity in contemporary American culture several years ago.

26. Indeed, we see very little production going on in this novel; all economic activity occurs in the service sectors, such as hospitals, restaurants, tourist attractions, golf courses, malls, car dealerships, and rehab centers. For example, cars appear at the car lot (we never hear about where they're made and by whom), and the cars themselves are, according to Nelson, not even "real"—they are simply the conduits through which debits and credits are managed. When Harry was growing up, this was an industrial city: now it's part of postindustrial America, and postindustrial America is falling apart. As Harry says at the beginning of the novel: "Everything falling apart, airplanes, bridges, eight years under Reagan of nobody minding the store, making money out of nothing, running up debt, trusting in God" (6). Reagan himself is, for Harry, the perfect emblem of a culture devoted to the unreal: Hearing of Bush's antics, "it makes Harry miss Reagan a bit, at least he was dignified, and had that dream distance; the powerful thing about him as President was that you never knew how much he knew, nothing or everything, he was like God that way, you had to do a lot of it yourself" (244).

27. What is intriguing about the representation of Nelson's habit is the way in which Updike links Nelson's addiction to Lyle's homosexuality, his identity

as a gay man who, in Updike's terms, is "addicted" to a dangerous form of sexuality. It is so typical of Updike that it is Janice who articulates this point of view so baldly and crudely. Claiming that Nelson has been "corrupted by queers," she utters a secular version of the wrath-of-God argument some people have made about AIDS (233). Harry is somewhat sympathetic to Lyle, the gay man who has HIV—primarily because he feels a brotherhood with him since they have both been close to death. But his misinterpretation of Nelson's problem as *sexual*, rather than drug-induced—he keeps asking "just how queer is the kid, anyway?"—makes it clear that Updike is drawing some kind of analogy between drug abuse and gay sexuality. Just as drug abuse signifies inappropriate consumption, sex between men signifies inappropriate sexuality. Updike is certainly not the first writer to link these things; the connection of gay sexuality with addiction has a long history, but a history given added fuel in the age of AIDS. In having the embezzled money fund both Nelson's habit and Lyle's use of experimental drugs to fight AIDS, Updike represents gay sexuality and AIDS as occupying the same illicit space as illegal drug use. This is not the more common link between homosexual activity and intravenous drug use; this one is more metaphorical.

2. PALE MALES, DEAD POETS, AND THE CRISIS IN WHITE MASCULINITY: SCENES FROM THE CULTURE WARS

1. Crichton uses Tom's female attorney to voice this sentiment, and poses that attorney against the feminist journalist who maligns Tom in print. At one point, Connie Walsh, the journalist, accuses Louise Fernandez, the attorney, of being "just another minority woman trying to get ahead with the patriarchy by getting down on their knees" (352).

2. The scene in which Meredith "harasses" Tom is a study in male ambivalence—not only on Tom's part but on Crichton's as well. Wanting to represent Meredith as in control—and thus lay the groundwork for Tom's harassment claim—Crichton clearly has problems representing Tom as anything other than fully phallic. At one moment, he "felt dominated, controlled, and at risk," and at another, he "felt a burst of anger, a kind of male fury that he was pinned down, that she was dominating him, and he wanted to be in control, to take her" (112–13). While this ambivalence might serve as a springboard for an exploration of how men are socialized to respond to their own sexuality, instead it merely becomes unimpeachable evidence of that old construction of male sexuality: the penis has a mind of its own and, thus, male sexuality is automatic and unstoppable. This goes on for another few pages, with Tom alternating between feeling anxious and wanting to "fuck her. Hard" (115). At one point, Meredith coughs—a cough that will come back later to haunt her as the supposedly irrefutable sign that she's faking her own desire and pleasure—and

Tom takes this as a signal to stop. He pulls away, Meredith appears to be angry at being left unsatisfied, and he leaves with her threatening to kill him. But, as it turns out, this is not a case of a tigerish female sexuality seeking expression, and we later learn that Meredith set up the whole thing as a step in a complex plot to forward her corporate career. The harassment, it turns out, is a red herring—no one harassed anyone else, not really, and the novel thus devolves into a more or less hysterical portrait of female treachery and male innocence.

3. I am using "culture wars" in a more specific sense than the phrase sometimes has in public discussions of contemporary American culture. A key term of the conservative insurgency of the late eighties and nineties, "culture war" is often used as a catchphrase to capture a widespread, vaguely apprehended, baggy monster of a cultural condition that is characterized by violent mass culture, single-mother homes, promiscuity, and a general decline of what conservatives term "traditional values." This "culture war" starts in the 1960s, according to conservative orthodoxy, and is picking up speed all the time. In contrast, the "culture wars" I'm talking about were a series of much more specifically pitched battles between conservatives invested in reshaping higher education and liberals resisting that reshaping. The precipitating factors of this culture war are the rise of multiculturalism and the new "politicized" scholarship; the seeming escalation of campus activism; and the rise of "political correctness." However, rather than seeing these as the "cause" of the culture war, I will argue instead that it is in *articulating* this "reality" that the culture wars actually get produced. In other words, I am placing in doubt the idea that events or trends on campuses produced the culture wars, and am suggesting that the books that claim to be responding to a new reality are actually producing that new reality. The crisis is produced discursively.

4. The reigning "authority" on "victimism" is Charles Sykes, who has recently argued that the United States has become a "Nation of Victims." Sykes, yet another conservative thinker to weigh in on the questions of political correctness, academic shenanigans, and the political clout of "racism" as an interpretive category in American culture, argues that we have witnessed, since the early 1960s, the growth of a culture of "victimism" in which personal responsibility and moral choice have given way to an ethos of blame and the projection of individual guilt onto social forces. Citing the rise of therapeutic culture and the general medicalization of "addiction" and personality "disorders," as well as feminism and black activism, Sykes makes a persuasive case for the prevalence of "victimism" in American culture. But this turns out to be a disappointing book, for several reasons: First, although he gives token acknowledgment to how this "victimism" hurts what he terms "authentic victims," Sykes is clearly more interested in the ways in which an all-powerful elite of feminists and black activists have conned the nation into jumping onto the

bandwagon of victimism—that is, of blaming "society" for any individual crimes. Second, despite the promise of the early pages, Sykes gives very little insight into how this revolution in social consciousness has come about and been sustained, the obligatory jabs at the 1960s notwithstanding. And, finally, while he does indeed see that middle-class white men, the class seemingly most immune to victimization, have appropriated the rhetoric and emotional power of "victimism," he fails to see this as a political move. The picture that emerges from Sykes's analysis is of a flat field of social relations, in which white and black are equally prone to "racism," and in which men and women can equally be victims of "sexism." Power is entirely absent from Sykes's worldview, and thus his analysis is ultimately not very helpful. Nevertheless, he has put his finger on one pulse-point of the American body politic, and one that can illuminate, from a different point of view, the issues I am considering here. The symbolic power of the victim has indeed gained cultural currency. But, more to the point, the appropriation of "victimism" by the socially privileged represents an attempt to hold onto a slipping symbolic power which is no longer vested in the white man as "universal."

5. Much has been said about the conservative assault on the humanities. Early commentators who analyzed and critiqued the rhetorical and ideological strategies of the right's attack on the academy (and on political correctness) focused primarily on the targets of those attacks, either proving wrong the characterizations of institutions or even classes described by individual writers such as Dinesh D'Souza; or linking the attacks to a larger conservative war against liberalism, feminism, multiculturalism, and so on. While this counter-critique has been effective in undermining the right's claims to represent the "truth," it has also had the effect of consolidating an essentially defensive position for the left. More recent forays into this minefield have focused on the economic and social conditions encircling the culture wars, pointing out that they are best thought of as symptoms of massive social realignments taking place under the sign of the New Right; or, as a smokescreen behind which the right hides its even more sinister racial and economic agendas. Some leftist critics have taken the culture wars as an opportunity to think seriously about the usefulness of "identity politics" for progressive intellectual and activist movements. But most of the defenses mounted by the left have, even if unwittingly, left intact a stubborn assumption: that gender and race have meaning only for women and people of color, and not for those who are engaged in the crusade to "depoliticize" academia. Rather than focus on how the right's position exhibits predictable ideas about race (that is, people of color) and gender (that is, women), I want instead to focus on how D'Souza and Bloom speak of and for a white masculinity suffering the pains of its fall from a disembodied universality into an embodied specificity. See the following volumes for a wide range

of responses: Patricia Aufderheide, ed.; Jeffrey Williams, ed.; Christopher New-field and Ronald Strickland, eds.; Michael Bérubé and Cary Nelson, eds. For single-authored studies, see Todd Gitlin, *The Twilight of Common Dreams;* John Wilson; and Henry Louis Gates.

6. My decision to treat *Illiberal Education* as a melodramatic narrative, rather than a serious critique, stems in part from the fact that D'Souza's book hardly qualifies as a serious critique. For one thing, his "evidence" is often shaky, the testimony offered by various students questionable. Its influence is traceable to its sensationalist style, and it is at least a little ironic that a book that bemoans the lack of gravity and seriousness in the contemporary academy is itself such shoddy work.

7. Throughout the book, D'Souza presents the administrators of major universities as entirely cowed by the demands of "minority activists" and feminists, and entirely behind diversity initiatives. He speaks, for example, of the "Michigan Mandate"—a plan under which I was hired at the University of Michigan in the early 1990s—as being a fully successful victory in the fight for diversity. Yet the ultimate success of this mandate is by no means clear, nor is it clear that the administration remains committed to it. I raise the specific case of Michigan only in order to suggest that beneath the narratives D'Souza constructs are counter-narratives that might lead *not* to a vision of the success of the revolution on campus, but to a better understanding of the flaws and blindnesses in such plans.

8. D'Souza's basic point—that the university is organized around "victimism"—is never really supported in this book. In fact, no one but D'Souza even uses the language of victims and victimization to describe what's going on on campus. His informants talk quite a lot about race and gender, about new kinds of scholarship, and about affirmative action programs; but the framing of these issues as all about "victims" is D'Souza's own. In this sense, we might say that he raises the specter of victimism in order to then construct a new class of "authentic" victims.

9. Is it a coincidence that the anecdote which follows upon the heels of Thernstrom's story is about a visiting law professor whose students objected to lines from Byron's Don Juan (included in that professor's own textbook) normalizing female consent to rape? (The lines are "A little she strove, and much repented, / And whispering, 'I will ne'er consent'—consented.") D'Souza elevates the wounded white male professor into the position of authentic victim, while quite obviously concurring with the professor's own glib dismissal of the students' points of view. In the chapter on "censorship" at Michigan, D'Souza puts scare quotes around "date rape" in the process of whipping up righteous indignation on behalf of a white male student disciplined for expressing what D'Souza sees as a politically incorrect attitude toward date rape—that is, that

accusations are often false. For a discussion of the cultural right's construction of date rape, which also depends on a claim that rape should not be considered a political offense, see Grant Farred.

10. Rosa Ehrenreich, in "What Campus Radicals?" writes from Harvard and points out the obvious: one, Harvard is still a bastion of conservatism, and, two, D'Souza's account fails to take into account the fact that students tend to see their professors as all-powerful, rather than as easy targets—a fact that could explain why the three students did not go to Thernstrom directly. He was, after all, responsible for their grades. See also Jon Weiner, "What Happened at Harvard," for a second look at Thernstrom's position.

11. Gerald Graff highlights this paradox when he notes that the "West-Is-Besters are doing precisely what they denounce others for: reveling in self-pity, presenting themselves as helpless victims, and using the curriculum to prop up a flagging self-esteem" (49).

12. A footnote, however, instructs us that "this incident was witnessed by the author's research assistant, Wendy Adams, who was enrolled in Bergin's class and took written notes" (259). Now, here is a footnote to put fear (and paranoia) into any university professor: whose rights are being violated here? Where's the tyranny? Does D'Souza assume that a real student—again, who knows if she's real?—is, necessarily, innocent or disinterested?

Alice Jardine, in "Illiberal Reporting," suggests that D'Souza utilizes the tactics of McCarthyism, despite the typical conservative claim that it is the left that practices such tactics. She suggests, rightly I think, that the book "raises questions and images of the covert agent, of the intellectual spy, of infiltration, of a certain provacateurship, of flying false colors, and of adopting a rhetorical style to match" (129). Certainly, the idea that D'Souza has an army of "research assistants"—undoubtedly funded by the Olin Foundation—taking notes in college classrooms around the country would suggest that Jardine is right. At one point, several years ago, there was a rumor going around on my campus (University of Michigan) that conservative foundations were "planting" student "spies" in women's studies courses. While I have no direct knowledge of this, it is clear after reading *Illiberal Education* that D'Souza certainly had a lot of student help in collecting his "evidence."

13. In the chapter on affirmative action at Berkeley, D'Souza clearly identifies with the Asian American students on whose behalf he is so indignant and, in the process, identifies against African Americans who, elsewhere in the book, are the primary examples of "minority activists." Asian American students come off as conservative, hardworking, committed, and smart—the real innocent victims of Berkeley's diversity initiatives. These students contribute, D'Souza says, to Berkeley's "visual diversity. Yet in another sense they stand in sharp contrast to the mood of languorous abandon. Most of them are impec-

cably groomed, conservative in dress, moderate in manner" (32). That "mood of languorous abandon" seems, instead, to characterize black students, one of whom D'Souza describes as "vivacious" in contrast to the Vietnamese student he interviews. "Passionate" about her oppression, this student is used by D'Souza to support his claims that affirmative action actually hurts even those minorities it's meant to help. Delighting in his exposure of the contradictions within this young woman's political positions, D'Souza leads her to a realization of her own victimization, not at the hands of a racist society but through the institutionalization of "diversity" (33–35). Although I don't want to minimize the fact that individual students might, in fact, have good reason to resent such initiatives, it seems significant that D'Souza doesn't take the more obvious, and perhaps incendiary, tack here of arguing that it is primarily white students who are the objects of institutional discrimination. Further, in arguing that Asian American students and Jewish students are most often victimized by Berkeley's policies, D'Souza shamelessly invokes a history of anti-Semitism in American higher education, claiming that affirmative action is entirely of a piece with earlier attempts by Ivy League institutions to limit the number of Jews in attendance.

14. Although it hardly seems necessary to make this point, I want to stress it all the same. Critiques of identity politics often obscure the history that has made identity politics such a potent response to institutionalized inequities. After all, as Jerry Watts pointed out in a response to Todd Gitlin's argument against identity politics, even if an African American doesn't "choose" to speak or practice identity politics, identity politics might choose to speak *him:*

> [W]hen a black person speaks, the way in which American culture works intellectually—and this happens in the left and all kinds of circles—what happens is that you come as the bearer of a parochial view. Your status as a speaker is determined *a priori* by your race position. I can speak about black Americans, but I'm seen as speaking about a parochial entity, when I might actually be making a generic point about American citizens, and who these people are. But the way I'm culturally understood as a *black* speaker makes me inherently parochial. . . . So I can't buy the idea that we're in this ideal speech moment where each group is in some sense just now perversely deciding to become parochial around this question of commonality.

This roundtable discussion is included with Gitlin's essay, "The Rise of 'Identity Politics,' " in Bérubé and Nelson, eds. (323).

15. Bloom does distance himself somewhat from the Great Books program that was so central to the University of Chicago of his undergraduate days. His problem with this program is, significantly, that it's not elitist *enough:* he criti-

cizes it as "amateurish" and argues that it "has a coarse evangelistic tone that is the opposite of good taste; it engenders a spurious intimacy with greatness" (344).

16. James Atlas, in his review, also notes that "for all its dense theoretical discourse, 'The Closing of the American Mind' is an autobiography" (69).

17. Bloom appears to be ambivalent about Nietzsche, as a good number of reviewers noted. On the whole, however, I think he's less critical of Nietzschean philosophy than he is of the Americanization of that philosophy. Claiming that the American left (and, particularly, its academic branch) has based its political program on a misreading of Nietzsche that sees the "death of God" as the sanction for value-relativism, Bloom appears to want to *save* the "real" Nietzsche from this bowdlerization. Such a desire would be entirely consistent with the overall tenor of the book, with its contempt for what Bloom takes to be an indigenous American anti-intellectualism. Americans, Bloom seems to say, do not understand Europe; and it is only at their peril that they attempt to appropriate European models of thought. While most of the negative reviews of *The Closing of the American Mind* saw Bloom as anti-American and anti-democratic, some reviewers also suggested that the book suffers because Bloom ignores a specifically American tradition of political philosophy that is better equipped to offer insight into American society and culture. See, particularly, Thomas G. West.

18. Quite a number of commentators, in trying to come to terms with the odd fact of the book's success, suggested that Americans seem unaccountably fond of books that tell them how inadequate and ignorant they are. See, particularly, Robert Pattison.

19. Spelman suggests that this argument *might* postulate the irrelevance of gender difference since, if all bodies are equally "incidental" or "inessential," then it should not matter if one has a female body or a male body. Indeed this has led some feminist philosophers to read in Plato an argument for gender equality—or, more specifically, gender transcendence. But, as arguments about transcending gender (or race) tend to do, this one, too, ultimately promises transcendence only to those whose bodies and minds are unmarked by the difference that gender makes—the difference, that is, between Man as universal and Woman as particular.

20. Or rather, in the classic conservative argument, Bloom claims that racism and sexism are perpetuated by people of color and women, who fail to see the promise of America's "color-blind" society. See Michael Omi and Howard Winant for an analysis of how this "ethnicity" model of race in America has remained dominant despite overwhelming evidence that it fails to explain racial arrangements, meanings, and animosities in American culture.

21. Things become even more sinister, as Bloom's digressions into sociobiol-

ogy raise the specter of eugenics. In a striking passage, he worries that the white middle class is not reproducing itself because "humorless" feminists have insisted on the rights of women (of all classes and races) to control their own bodies.

> When one looks at the earnest, middle-class proponents of birth control, abortion and easy divorce—with their social concern, their humorless self-confidence and masses of statistics—one cannot help thinking that all this serves them very well. This is not to deny the reality of the problems presented by too many children for the poor, the terrible consequences of rapes and battered wives. However, none of those problems really belongs to the middle classes, who are not reproducing themselves, are rarely raped or battered, but who are the best-rewarded beneficiaries of what they themselves propose. (236)

Bloom can understand why it might be a good idea for the "poor" to have access to birth control and abortion, but middle-class white women are selfishly refusing to do their part for the race. This inflated rhetoric of crisis recalls the hysteria whipped up by turn-of-the-century educators and medical men around the perceived decline of white, Anglo-Saxon "stock" and values: "By having fewer children and by allowing their vigor and potency to decline, middle-class and patrician Americans placed the future of American civilization in doubt. . . . Mainstream Anglo-Saxon Americans were killing themselves, their culture, and the future of their children's society because they had lost the strength, honor, morals and grace of their forebears" (Green 282). See Bérubé and Newfield, eds., for discussions of the relationship between the culture wars and immigration.

22. Part of Bloom's faith in assimilation undoubtedly stems from his experience as a Jew attending university in the 1940s. But, as I've suggested, that assimilationist project depends on whiteness, as is clear when he turns his attention to the specific case of black students. Bloom exonerates the body politic for its failure to "digest" black students, and excoriates these students for being "the only group that has picked up 'ethnicity'—the discovery or creation of the sixties—in an instinctive way" (93).

23. I am taking a bit of a liberty with Bloom's language here: he speaks of today's students as "spiritually detumescent" (230), and I take that to mean that he and his fellows were "spiritually tumescent." He speaks of entering the University of Chicago and being "thrilled" by the "phallic" towers—and by the fact that he could describe them as such.

24. This is not to say that a certain kind of leftist thinking about the importance of race, for example, is responsible for *The Bell Curve;* it is to say that they

share a context, and one that is, perhaps, inescapable in post-sixties American culture. Conservatives do not hesitate to point out such strange couplings; D'Souza, for one, gleefully accuses "minority activists" of essentializing race and thus reproducing Nazism (187). See Russell Jacoby and Naomi Glauberman, eds., for a sampling of academic and journalistic responses to the publication of *The Bell Curve*, many of which suggest that it signals another whip of the backlash against the egalitarian educational policies of the late 1960s and 1970s.

25. If the goal of any politics is to affect the distribution of power, is there more power on the side of difference or on the side of similarity? The dilemma for feminists or multiculturalists might be articulated as follows: while it can be politically efficacious to stress gender and racial difference (else they disappear under the sign of the universal), emphasizing difference can fuel strategies of containment. For the forces of conservative reaction, the dilemma might be articulated quite differently: is it better to emphasize gender and racial sameness, in the interests of curtailing claims that the disenfranchised deserve restitution for past and present ills? Or, is it better to emphasize difference, in order to facilitate the categorization and exclusions which work to safeguard the privileges of the dominant classes, not to mention the racial and gender "purity" of institutional spaces?

26. Lest my claim that Bloom dips into sociobiology appear overblown, compare the two passages below, one drawn from a leading sociobiologist and the other from Bloom's book.

[The female] has much more invested in each of those eggs than [the male] has in his sperm and this asymmetry is particularly apparent in higher vertebrates. Males can usually walk . . . away from the consequences of a copulation. . . . The consequences of a bad decision . . . fall particularly heavily upon females and hence it is not surprising that they tend to be the more discriminating sex.　　　(David Barash, *Sociology and Behavior* [New York: Elsevier, 1977], 147; quoted in Fausto-Sterling, 184)

Man in the state of nature, either in the first one or the one we have now, can walk away from a sexual encounter and never give it a second thought. But a woman may have a child. . . . Sex can be an indifferent thing for men, but it really cannot quite be so for women. This is what might be called the female drama. . . . [W]omen, now liberated and with equal careers, nevertheless find they still desire to have children, but have no basis for claiming that men should share their desire for children or assume a responsibility for them.
　　　(Bloom 114)

27. The evocation of female modesty resonates with what Sarah Blaffer Hrdy notes as the "single most commonly mentioned attribute of females in the lit-

erature on sociobiology": coyness (122). A recent, avowedly "post-feminist" book by Wendy Shalit, *A Return to Modesty*, has a good deal in common with Bloom's version of sexual reality. See Katha Pollitt for a witty review of a raft of books that base their "sociological" arguments on the weak foundations of personal experience and muddy theoretical thinking.

28. Eve Sedgwick rightly notes that Bloom blames the sexual revolutions of the sixties for "dissipating the reservoirs of cathectic energy that are supposed to be held, by repression, in an excitable state of readiness to be invested in cultural projects" (*Epistemology* 56). Sedgwick argues that, given the philosophical context of Bloom's remarks, the gay liberation movement must take most of the blame for the unfortunate expression of what would better be left repressed; but, throughout *The Closing of the American Mind*, feminism commits an even greater sin: it takes sublimation out of the cultural and into the political realm, putting all energies into the project of "overcoming what is variously called male dominance, machismo, phallocracy, patriarchy" (Bloom 101).

29. The various profiles of Bloom that appeared in magazines after the phenomenal success of *The Closing of the American Mind* all paint him as a kind of decadent hedonist. In an article in the "Style" section of the *Washington Post*, for example, Bloom appears thus: "Here in his apartment next to the University of Chicago, he arranges himself along his black leather couch, a pose in which his legs seem to be crossed at least three or four times. There's a gargoyle voluptuousness to him—his double-breasted Parisian suit; his magnificent ears where the light shows through and illuminates veins, the shine of his bald head, teeth that he bares now and then for emphasis, and an elaborate nose leaking smoke like a dozing dragon." And then Bloom speaks (against the "moralists" who crusade against smoking): " 'There was a time when, ahh, people, you know, used to find something *beauuutiful* in smoke, people used to love *faaactories*, the sky full of smoke, it represented energy, prosperity' " (Henry Allen 39). Invoking Bloom's "curlicues of perversity," the writer then goes on to detail Bloom's unorthodox attack on American orthodoxy. But is "perversity" also a code word here, echoing and interpreting that languorous, sensuous, long-legged male pose? Questions about Bloom's sexuality are kept resolutely out of such portraits, but bubble up occasionally in descriptions of him as a "bachelor" who "has never married and has devoted his undivided attention and care to his students" (Zuckert 73). Writing in *Rolling Stone*, William Greider comes closest to "outing" Bloom when he notes that the "old bachelor" "sounds a bit envious" of the sexualized rock culture he derides; "He denounces Mick Jagger with such relish that one may wonder if the professor himself is turned on by Mick's pouty lips and wagging butt" (245). However Bloom chose to express his sexuality, two things are clear: first, that he positions himself far above the reproductive and familial dramas he describes; and,

second, that his model of an ideal educational system relies heavily on an eroticism between men.

30. More than any other film or novel I've taught in my various courses on masculinity, I have found that *Dead Poets Society* is a sacred text for students who were in high school in the late eighties. While I have backed down somewhat from my cynical view of this film in that context (and *still* find a good deal of resistance to any critical stance on this film), here I want to insist that, while it might be true that the film is an "innocent" exploration of the pleasures of poetry and the pains of conformity for some viewers, it is, simultaneously, an incredibly conservative text invested in mourning the passing of a hegemonic masculinity and the elite institutions in which it forms.

31. Quotations are from Lionel Ovesey, *Homosexuality and Pseudohomosexuality* (New York: Science House, 1969), 24–25.

32. On this score, as Modleski wryly points out, the film is entirely dishonest, exhibiting as it does such pronounced nostalgia for a time when "there were no dead women poets" and "live females apparently could not tell the difference between Shakespeare and a schoolboy's poetry" (140).

33. Hammond notes that Neil dies because he fails to make the transition into adulthood; "he is unable to achieve identification with either his repressive father or the liberal (and unswervingly heterosexual) Keating. His sacrifice allows Todd to find his 'voice'; his barbaric yawp is 'Neil.' The forbidden love is given eternal life and remembrance through death" (63). While I think that Hammond is right to stress the romantic representation of loss and death here, I want to extend this analysis away from the personal and individual, and read in this ending a larger social drama.

3. TRAUMAS OF EMBODIMENT: WHITE MALE AUTHORSHIP IN CRISIS

1. As numerous feminist critics and critics of African American literature have suggested, "literary history" has most often meant history of a very limited sphere of literary production. Genres are excluded from the "literary," and such exclusions are more often than not readable in gender, racial, and class terms. While the white male author may have been able to hide behind the mask of a disembodied creativity, women and people of color have always been *marked* as "female authors" and "African American authors," for example. Betsy Erkkila has most recently articulated suspicion over the "death of the author" in American ethnic and women's studies. Noting that "Historically, women, blacks and other minorities in Anglo-European countries have not been burdened with too much individualism, subjectivity, identity, or authorship" (572), she argues for a "comparative study" of American literature, one that acknowledges different histories and narratives within the American. See also Nancy Hartsock, who asks, "Why is it, exactly at the moment when so many of

us who have been silenced begin to demand the right to name ourselves, to act as subjects rather than objects of history, that just then the concept of subject-hood becomes 'problematic'?" (196). I also take up these questions in chapter 2 of my *Engendering the Subject*.

2. On the Romantic Author, see Martha Woodmansee, Christine Battersby, and Woodmansee and Peter Jaszi, eds.

3. Part of the problem with the film's representation of this "primal" mas-culinity is that it draws from two traditions that are themselves connected with homosexuality: Whitman and the Beats. On the Beats and their paranoid rela-tion to, and rebellion against, normative masculinity, see Savran (ch. 1), which I will discuss below.

4. The novel creates a receding horizon of authorship as its protagonist-au-thor writes a series of fictions about a protagonist-author. The novel is an-nounced as "the writings of Peter Tarnopol," a truly beleaguered author whose aesthetic philosophy and desire to live a life of the mind is constantly disrupted by women, forced embodiments, and psychosomatic disintegrations. The first part contains two of Tarnopol's short stories, starring author Nathan Zucker-man, and the second narrates in artfully fragmentary form "My True Story." Roth frames the whole as a therapeutic enterprise, Tarnopol's generally failed attempt to come to terms with his catastrophic marriage, and indeed, with his many relationships to women, and to what Roth refers to as "fifties-feminese." The two "Useful Fictions" include a coming-of-age story called "Salad Days" (which includes Portnoy-like sexual fantasies) and a longer and much more complicated narrative about marriage, sexuality, and victimization, entitled "Courting Disaster (or, Serious in the Fifties)." "My True Story," the collection of texts (letters, transcripts of psychiatric sessions, confessions, and first-per-son narration) that comprises the bulk of the novel, is Tarnopol's attempt to make order out of the chaos of his life, first with wife Maureen, and then with "Susan the Submissive," the upper-class self-effacing woman with whom he lives but refuses to marry.

This is the first, and generally forgotten, appearance of the author-surrogate whom most critics read as a barely disguised figure for Roth. While there are other episodes in the Zuckerman saga that are relevant to my discussion here—particularly *The Anatomy Lesson*, to which I will refer later—what distinguish-es those later treatments from this one are two important things: *My Life as a Man* is the only novel in which another author-figure intervenes between Roth and Zuckerman, enabling Roth to envision writing as kind of therapeutic if masochistic enterprise and, producing, as well, a dizzying array of selves and pathologies that work to create a picture of Tarnopol as thoroughly belea-guered and horribly wounded author-man; and, second, the obsession of this

novel with an emerging feminist discourse and shifts in gendered power relations, makes it more appropriate for my purposes here.

5. The "feminization" of America in the late 1950s and early 1960s was laid at
the feet of two different enemies of true masculinity: institutions that produced sheeplike conformity (including marriage), and a consumer culture that
threatened to level the class-based distinctions between the elite and the masses. Although the causes and effects of this crisis in dominant masculinity differ
in important respects from earlier crises, the mid-nineteenth-century cultural
crisis Ann Douglas dubbed "the feminization of American culture" shares
some of its rhetorical features. As Douglas argues, our modern notions of a
gendered split between high and low culture take root at this time. The writers
on whom the reputation of "serious" American literature rests point to "the
conspirational [sic] interaction between genteel religion, feminine morality,
and polite literature against the interests of genuine masculinity" (355). The
cultural politics of this era, then, instigated a marking of an emerging mass culture as feminine and, thus, produced the specter of a masculinity *and* high culture at risk. Tania Modleski has (rightly, I think) taken Douglas to task for having reinstitutionalized a whole system of gendered binary oppositions linking
the feminine with mass culture and a debased consumerism, and the masculine
with high culture and a pure production. See her "Femininity as Mas(s)quer-
ade," reprinted in *Feminism Without Women*.

6. While almost all critics of the novel join in with Peter in gleefully blaming
Maureen for what ails him both sexually and artistically, Milan Kundera really
revels in Maureen-bashing, pointing, in the process, to all the evils she represents: mass culture, victimism, and the body's dominion over the mind. His
commentary is worth quoting at length: "Maureen, this queen of vulgarity, no
matter how frankly monstrous and repugnant she may appear, never seems like
a caricature or a simplification. . . . She seems true to us [sic] not because she
exists in reality, but rather because we fear her and pay our respects to her po-
tentiality. I know her by heart through my nightmares; from the time I was
eighteen I have feared one day becoming her victim, and all my life I have constantly been defending myself against her dreaded attacks" (162).

7. See Ehrenreich, *The Hearts of Men*, for an analysis of the fortunes of this
norm in the second half of the twentieth century; and Pfeil, for a more recent
analysis of what has replaced protector-provider masculinity at the end of the
century.

8. See Savran; Ehrenreich, *The Hearts of Men*; and Corber, for analyses of the
conflicts within hegemonic masculinity in the 1950s.

9. Christine Battersby echoes this point when she argues that the aesthetic
we have inherited from the Romantics prizes femininity in male "geniuses,"

while deploring it in both women and "ordinary men." See, particularly, her introduction, 1–11.

10. McWhirter argues that James, unlike Wallace Stevens (in Frank Lentricchia's reading), was unable or unwilling to resolve the problem of the feminized artist by internalizing "the sexual other within"—that is, by internalizing the phallic, patriarchal masculine norm against which the artist appears less than adequately masculinized. James, on the other hand, according to McWhirter, was strangely energized by his distance from that norm, opting for a masochism that McWhirter argues enables James to find power in the rejection of his work by the masses.

11. Interestingly, references to James keep coming up in readings of another Zuckerman narrative, *The Anatomy Lesson,* in which the male author suffers not only writer's block but an intensely painful, but somatically mysterious, neck ailment. A number of critics have noted Roth's near-obsession with James in the later Zuckerman stories (collected in *Zuckerman Bound,* and supplemented later by *The Counterlife*). Adeline Tintner argues that in *The Anatomy Lesson,* a novel that explores physical pain as a "metaphor for the burden of the writer's consciousness" (Tintner 59), Roth makes use of, and even rewrites, the autobiographical texts that occupy McWhirter in his essay on James's masochism. For Tintner, "the burden of the lesson in anatomy is Zuckerman's discovery that he cannot disengage himself from his body" (60).

12. Lovelina Singh refers to Tarnopol as one of Roth's "victim-heroes," Roth men who experience a "masochistic attraction" to unsuitable women. While Singh traces this dynamic to the protagonists' misogyny—and notes, as well, that there is something "essentially Jewish" about their ambivalence about eroticism and morality—I'd like to stress something else here: the centrality *not* of the misogyny that produces the victim-hero but, rather, the centrality of the performance of a powerfully wounded masculinity. This performance is, undoubtedly, fueled by the misogyny with which Roth afflicts Tarnopol; but its effects are less to consolidate male power as to reconstruct a normative masculinity.

13. As I suggested at the end of chapter 2, following Ehrenreich, the concept of the "latent" homosexual became increasingly elastic in the 1950s, as it was used to discipline even the tamest of male rebellions. See, *Hearts of Men,* 126–30; and, also, Robert Corber, for an exhaustive discussion of the place of homosexuality in Cold War crises in masculinity.

14. "Courting Disaster (or, Serious in the Fifties)" is modeled after *Lolita* in its subject matter, as well as in the gendering of its aesthetics. Here, Zuckerman marries a woman who has been abused by men her entire life, and has a young daughter who "seduces" him eventually, and with whom he runs off in the end. Like Nabokov's novel, Tarnopol/Roth's story is replete with horror and disgust

at adult female bodies, while attempting to erase the materiality and specificity of the adult male body. Both texts attempt the latter by opting for textuality over referentiality—that is, by, as Nabokov would have it, preferring "art" to "life."

15. The classic Charles Atlas narrative of the puny boy overcoming his "disabilities" to grow into the strong and physically imposing man is evident in *Misery*, as well, where Paul regrets the atrophy of his physique: "He had been a puny kid and so he had tried to take reasonably good care of himself as an adult, but his muscles were now the muscles of an invalid and the puny kid was back and all that time spent doing laps and jogging and working out on the Nautilus machine had only been a dream" (83).

16. As Harry Brod has argued, American Jewish men live a complex relation to hegemonic (white) masculinity, caught between a European Jewish tradition of intellectualism, and an American anti-intellectualism:

> Forced to affirm the value of the life of the mind, which is indeed traditionally valued in Jewish culture, against anti-Semitic attacks on it, many Jewish men have been forced into an overly rigid identification with this ideal to the extent that they perpetrate an overly zealous denial of the complementary life of the body, to their own great loss. The ideal of the intellectual Jewish male is held to so strongly because it emerges *both* from within the intellectual traditions of Jewish culture *and* as a defense mechanism against attacks on Jewish men for not conforming to dominant, more brawny standards of masculinity.   (91)

Brod goes on to argue that an alternative, but still patriarchal, masculinity emerges from a "culture of resistance," in which intellectual power is valued over physical power. It is this patriarchal "alternative" that Roth's novel explores, wherein masculinity is defined through intellect and through distance from the body.

In her essay on Jewish masculinity in Roth, Barbara Gottfried points to the bifurcation of masculinity into the "nice Jewish boy" and the "Jewboy" in Roth's work. She quotes from Roth's *Reading Myself and Others* (New York: Penguin, 1985), the following elaboration on that distinction: "the 'Jewboy' (and all that word signifies to Jew and Gentile alike about aggression, appetite, and marginality) and the 'nice Jewish boy' (and what that epithet implies about repression, respectability, and social acceptance . . . [were] the Cain and Abel of my own respectable middle-class background" (35, 37; quoted in Gottfried, 38). While this bifurcation is evident in *My Life as a Man* on a very limited basis, I don't think that the use of the word "Jewboy" in this context carries with it the meanings that Roth points to here. That is, there's no indication of his army "buddies" seeing Zuckerman as a man of "appetite" or "aggression."

17. See Christopher Newfield's reading of masochistic masculinity in *The Scarlet Letter* ("The Politics of Male Suffering"). Newfield, too, sees this masochism as ultimately functioning in service to hegemonic masculinity even if constructed as its seeming opposite.

18. In a strong feminist critique of the novel, Janice Doane and Devon Hodges have amply documented the novel's antifeminist sentiments, including its disqualification of feminist discourse from cultural value. They note, for example, that what Garp finds distasteful in his mother's huge book is its "mundane prose style and simple-minded organizational scheme" (67). In his comment about the Sears, Roebuck catalogue, Garp indicates that this low cultural form, the sprawling feminist memoir, belongs less with even the lowest of "literary" works, and more with the pragmatic, if vulgar, texts concerned with "reality," consumerism, and so on. Doane and Hodges argue that the novel is intent on establishing a dichotomy between feminist writing—which simply transcribes "experience"—and men's writing—which constitutes "art"—but they don't address the importance of the marketplace in the novel's representation of the high-low dichotomy. What, in part, constitutes the debasement of "art" in the novel is its commercialization, which is, in turn, linked with the perceived feminist-ization of the cultural sphere.

19. Garp is distinguished as a more discerning *reader* in the novel; whereas women—Jenny, Helen, and the trashy Mrs. Ralph—voraciously consume books, Garp spends much of his time reading a small number of "good" books. "Garp's way with a story was to find one he liked and read it again and again; it would spoil him for reading any other story for a long while. When he was at Steering he read Joseph Conrad's 'The Secret Sharer' thirty-four times. He also read D. H. Lawrence's 'The Man Who Loved Islands' twenty-one times; he felt ready to read it again" (111).

20. The linking of feminism with mass culture returns us to the discourses of culture war, and their attempt to liberate the work of art from the grip of these two enemies (and the third, deconstruction). "Postmodernism" might serve as a kind of umbrella description of this triumvirate, and Irving is notorious for positioning himself against the postmodern. Aligning himself with Dickens, Irving rails against the type of metafiction that concerns itself only with language and form, and against the literary critics who conspire to turn the work of art into an intellectualized puzzle with little connection to the intention or creative consciousness of an author—or, even worse, read the work of art as an ideological statement. Irving eschews both the "literary" and the "sociological," and he means these terms to refer to criticism as well as fiction: fiction and criticism err when they go too far into either the abstracted realm of a writerly, language-based formalism, or the "gossipy" realm of the "bleeding heart confessional type of writing" (Priestley 490) and its critical equivalent in

"the destruction of art by sociology and psychoanalysis" (*Garp* 525). What is left once these options are eliminated? Criticism according to Irving, one suspects, will always be a kind of violation; as for fiction, Irving stakes out a fictional terrain where the personal and sentimental are the supreme values, and where the author is capable of expressing his original and unique vision even while transcending the "confessional" or merely autobiographical. In his defense of Kurt Vonnegut against the critics, Irving offers a particularly heated repudiation of the contemporary critical sensibility, which he imagines to be in cahoots with the "new fiction," and against what he calls "the aesthetics of accessibility" ("Kurt Vonnegut and His Critics" 41–42). See Evan Carton for an interesting discussion of how *The World According to Garp* works to foreclose on *any* kind of interpretation.

21. From the beginning, Irving's representation of the elder Garp is saturated with reproductive terms and meanings, expressing a certain amount of anxiety that the masculine can so easily be reduced to a reproductive vehicle. For instance, we're told this about the ball turret and the gunner's place within it: "This ball turret was a metal sphere with a glass porthole; it was set into the fuselage of a B-17 like a distended navel—like a nipple on the bomber's belly . . . There were wooden handles with buttons on the tops to fire the guns; gripping these trigger sticks, the ball turret gunner looked like some dangerous fetus suspended in the bomber's absurdly exposed amniotic sac, intent on protecting its mother" (18). Later, when Garp begins to fail, Jenny imagines him reverting to a fetus, and then to sperm.

22. See Andreas Huyssen's "Mass Culture as Woman" for a discussion of the modernist artist's fear of being "sphinxed" by a feminized mass culture, and of the representation of crowds and the masses as dangerously feminine. I will return to these issues below in my discussion of *Misery*.

23. See Radway, *A Feeling for Books*, for an analysis of the battle over the literary field. Drawing on Michael Warner's arguments about the construction of the public sphere in republican America, Radway demonstrates that what was at stake in the skirmishes over the perceived debasement of the "literary"— through the advent of book clubs, among other things—was the definition of the public sphere as the space for a seemingly disinterested, "free" exchange of ideas among those Americans "unmarked" by gender, racial, class, and ethnic specificity. Clearly, such struggles are ongoing in American culture.

24. The novel also contains a parody of political correctness, in the character of one Mrs. Poole, who writes to Garp to complain about his second novel's cruel mockery of various human problems and foibles. After a volley of letter-writing that gets increasingly nasty, Garp writes: "You should either stop trying to read books, or you should try a lot harder" (237). In another scene, Irving has a "Mrs. Ralph" reject Dostoevsky's *The Eternal Husband* because the women

characters are "*less* than objects" (257), causing Garp to yell, "The woman is an idiot! My mother would love her" (261).

25. In the film, Hill erases Ellen's own articulation of her displeasure by having *Garp* write the critique of the Ellen Jamesians. This erasure further polarizes Garp and the crazy feminists, eliminating Ellen as the complicating mediator between them.

26. King unashamedly claims the label of "brand name author," accepting his place as the "Green Giant of what is called the 'modern horror story.'" In an essay entitled "On Becoming a Brand Name," which heads a collection of criticism of his work, King comments on the opposition between the "serious" and the "popular":

> I have written seriously since I was twelve, and to me that means that I always wrote in order to make money. . . . There is no particular danger in writing what I will call, for want of a better term, "serious fiction." In writing popular, commercial fiction, there is nothing but danger. The commercial writer is easy to bribe, easy to subvert, and he knows it. I have felt this much more strongly in the last two or three years than ever before. But if this is true, it also means that the commercial writer who can tell the truth has achieved a great deal more than any "serious" writing can hope for; he can tell the truth and still keep up with his mortgage payments.   (16)

While not exactly debunking the opposition between the serious and the popular, these comments do show that these categories are constructions motivated by a desire to keep the commercial outside the gates of high culture. What, King seems to ask, could make an author write more "seriously" than paying the bills?

27. In Janice Radway's wonderful analysis of the Book-of-the-Month Club and the construction of middlebrow culture, she pinpoints the 1986–87 book season as a pivotal moment in the renegotiation of the middlebrow. The Club, purchased a number of years earlier by Time, slowly moves closer to the "commercial" in these years in ways that would change middlebrow culture for good. Among concessions to the "common reader"—and in the interests of financing the more "literary" of the Club's offerings—the Club signed a contract with King's publishers to offer his next three books as Main Club Selections. *Misery* was one of those books and, published in the 1986–87 season, represents a significant moment in the reshaping of the middlebrow. One of the things that I find so suggestive about Radway's history of the Book-of-the-Month Club is the idea, not fully explicit, that the kinds of defenses now offered by the Club against its absorption in mass culture are precisely the same attacks articulated *against* the Club in its early years. In other words, where early critics of

the Club's commercialization of literature warned that this would mean the death of the literary as they then knew it, contemporary defenders of the Club warn that further commercialization will spell the death of the literary as *they now know it*. One of Radway's most canny points is that the Club performs a remarkably similar function to academic English departments in constructing and defending the category of the "literary," despite the tendency of elite academics to see their work as antithetical to such "middlebrow" institutions.

28. Quite a number of King's critics have noted that he has a bit of a blind spot when it comes to women characters. Mary Pharr, for instance, notes that there are two types of women in King's fiction: the nurturing, self-sacrificing woman and the monster. Annie is interesting precisely because her monstrosity stems from her perversion of the archetypal mother figure. See also Gail Burns and Melinda Kanner. About his representation of women, often criticized by scholars and the mainstream press, King himself had this to say in 1983: "Yes, unfortunately, I think it is probably the most justifiable of all those [charges] leveled at me . . . when I think I'm free of the charge that most male American authors depict women as either nebbishes or bitch-goddess destroyers, I create someone like Carrie, who starts out as a nebbish victim and becomes a bitch goddess, destroying an entire town in an explosion of hormonal rage. I recognize the problems but can't yet rectify them" (Underwood and Miller, 47). In her introduction to *Men, Women, and Chainsaws: Gender in the Modern Horror Film*, entitled "Carrie and the Boys," Carol Clover suggests that King's relatively new interest in women characters as villains stems from his sense that feminism has made women angry in ways that are useful for a horror maven. Clover proposes that Brian De Palma's 1976 film version of *Carrie*, endorsed by King, makes possible the kinds of gender dislocations through which fifteen-year-old boys can identify with female figures on the screen.

29. Janice Radway has questioned the elitist representation of romance fiction, writers, and readers in her *Reading the Romance*. There is a growing body of work by romance writers and their champions, defending their craft and their readers from two kinds of attacks: attacks by feminists, who have often argued that romances brainwash women into submitting to patriarchy; and attacks by the literary establishment, which tend to construct romances as trashy and trivial, and, even, dangerous to the cultural order. See the essays collected in Pearce and Stacey, eds., *Romance Revisited*, and in Jayne Ann Krentz, ed., *Dangerous Men and Adventurous Women*.

30. See King, "On Becoming a Brand Name," 16.

31. Andrew Schopp, in the most sophisticated feminist reading of the novel I've seen, argues that the epigraph from Nietzsche sets the stage for the novel's construction of a kind of mirror-effect between Paul and Annie, in which Paul's own monstrosity can be discerned underneath the representation of An-

nie's. He also argues that Annie is monstrous primarily because she is not normatively feminine. While I am in sympathy with this reading, I think Annie is monstrous because she forces Paul to live a life of the body, thus making him more like her, *and* making him less the disembodied author living a life of the mind. See also Bernadette Bosky.

32. On "white trash" and its distance from middle-class norms of consumption, see Gael Sweeney's intriguing reading of Elvis Presley; and Kelly Thomas's discussion of the distinction between the "good" poor and "white trash." Although Rob Reiner's 1990 film of King's novel does not explore Annie's consumption in very great depth, it does represent her as a kind of "trashy" consumer by having her listen to Liberace records and put Spam in her meatloaf. But, as I will suggest later in this chapter, these references seem more or less gratuitous jokes at Annie's expense, since they are not moored to an exploration of relationships between gender, class, and cultural value.

33. In the novel, Paul is also addicted to cigarettes, and goes through a period of withdrawal when forced to quit. In the film, his well-known ritual is to smoke just one, celebratory cigarette after finishing a novel, thus signaling his self-control rather than his weakness.

34. *Misery* is proof that the hopeful note on which Huyssen ends his "Mass Culture as Woman" is premature. Invoking the postmodern blurring of the boundaries between elite and mass culture, and the increasing number of women artists who now occupy a position within the "high," Huyssen writes: "it is primarily the visible and public presence of women artists in *high* art, as well as the emergence of new kinds of women performers and producers in mass culture, which make the old gendering device obsolete. The universalizing ascription of femininity to mass culture always depended on the very real exclusion of women from high culture and its institutions. Such exclusions are, hopefully forever, a thing of the past. Thus, the old rhetoric has lost its persuasive power because the realities have changed" (205–206). Not only is this prematurely optimistic, but this final verdict fails to consider that the gendered dichotomy might be functioning within *mass* culture, as well. That is to say, in seeing the gendering of mass culture as originating only within the high, Huyssen fails to register the importance of this gendering in mass culture.

35. There is a certain amount of debate over the gendered breakdown of King's readership. Claire Hanson, for one, states flat out that "horror fiction is, primarily, produced and consumed by men," then goes on to offer a Kristevan reading of why this might be (152). But others have questioned this assumption. See Schopp (42n5), for a survey of these perspectives. While my own very informal survey of the undergraduates to whom I've taught this book supports the claim that women do read King in relatively large numbers, it's clear enough that, compared to the readership for romance novels, the horror audience looks positively masculine.

36. Many of King's novels before *Misery* focus on collective protagonists and less "human" embodiments of the evil force. The one-on-one battle between Annie and Paul is also a departure in its clear (and salient) gendering of good and evil.

37. See Susan Jeffords, *Hard Bodies,* for a thorough consideration of this dynamic.

38. See, particularly, the essays collected in the section of Cohan and Hark's *Screening the Male* entitled "Muscular Masculinities."

4. MASCULINITY AS EMOTIONAL CONSTIPATION: MEN'S LIBERATION AND THE WOUNDS OF PATRIARCHAL POWER

1. Julie Ellison's intriguing analysis of liberal guilt in the 1990s is relevant to my analysis here, although I would say that Warren Farrell's work is motivated by liberal guilt, while Herb Goldberg's emphatically is not. According to Ellison, liberal guilt is always about race, and it is most often represented as an emotion that afflicts men, or, as Ellison puts it, "it names a form of discomfort that matters politically when men suffer from it" (348). Liberal guilt evinces "ongoing crises of masculinity" (348) that have dramatized "anxieties" about liberalism since the Enlightenment. Liberal guilt "designates a position of wishful insufficiency relative to the genuinely radical" (345)—and, I would add, to the genuinely disenfranchised. While Ellison does not go in this direction, her analysis suggests that liberal guilt, an embarrassing position, becomes the sign of a wounded white masculinity. So, while liberal guilt might spring from an uncomfortable recognition of one's privilege in relation to racial others, it ends up signifying a kind of fantasized (and depoliticized) disempowerment in the face of others' "genuine" disenfranchisement. In the men's liberation discourse that is my subject here, guilt is one emotion that must be disavowed because it works to "block" the flow of positive male energies. Rather than seeing this as a sign of the conservative politics of this discourse, as Ellison might, I will suggest that the impulse behind "freeing" men from guilt over their privileges is central to the project of personalizing, psychologizing, and depoliticizing the very concept of "liberation."

2. Or, one might say, modeled on a particular strain of women's liberation. While it is certainly true that a major impetus behind, and effect of, feminism in the 1970s was what Judith Bardwick calls the "new hedonism" that comes with an emphasis on personal growth and the other code words of the human potential movement, the personal and psychological is always moored to the political and social in feminist discourse and activism. Barbara Ehrenreich and Deirdre English have suggested that, in certain key respects, the "Me!" generation was a male phenomenon, leaving women outside the personal revolutions announced by and enacted in popular seventies therapies. See their discussion of the singles culture and popular psychology (297–311). Alice Echols argues

that early radical feminism, too, was eventually overwhelmed by the rise of a cultural feminism that, like other sixties movements, shifted from the political to the personal in the late sixties and early seventies. See, particularly, chapter 2 of *Daring to Be Bad.*

3. The crisis in masculinity mapped by men's liberation discourse is specifically a crisis in heterosexual masculinity, encapsulated by the shifting meanings of the term *straight.* By the early seventies, "straight" had mutated from a general term used by the hip to describe the "establishment" to a more specific term used to describe heterosexuality. This shift in the meanings of a popular term points to an ambivalence about male sexuality and sexual identity in men's liberationist discourse. These books are generally aimed toward the more hip of America's heterosexual, white middle-class men; but those hip credentials are endangered by an increasingly visible gay population not only labeling all heterosexuals as "straight," but necessarily implicating even the most hip among them in perpetuating the status quo. " 'Damn it all,' " one of Warren Farrell's consciousness-raisers cries in the middle of an excited conversation about same-sex desire, "when I hear you guys talk about bisexuality I feel like my heterosexuality is abnormal' " (246). While being "abnormal" is no cause for shame with this group, being unliberated is; and, thus, bisexuality becomes the safest route toward the release of a liberated—but still hetero—sexuality. I will return to these issues in chapter 5.

4. See, particularly, chapter 2 of *Iron John.* Bly distinguishes between bad and good wounds. The former are produced by shame, by being abused or ignored by others, and by "having no soul union at all with other men" (32–33). Through ancient rituals of initiation, however, a man can find a new wound, bestowed upon him by "The Wild Man" as a therapeutic "gift" of self-discovery. On Bly and the mythopoetic men's movement, see Pfeil's wonderful critique of "New Age" culture in chapter 5 of *White Guys,* and the collection of essays edited by Michael Kimmel entitled *The Politics of Manhood.*

5. I refer to Bly's *Iron John,* Andrew Kimbrell's *The Masculine Mystique,* and Warren Farrell's *The Myth of Male Power.*

6. White, middle-class men—so unimpeachably the norm that neither Farrell nor Herb Goldberg have index entries under "race," "black," "white," "class," "working class," "civil rights," or "ethnicity"—are damaged by the very system that supposedly works to their benefit. Economic concerns are strikingly absent from these texts, except insofar as the man in need of liberation is one suffering from the stresses of a professional or managerial position.

7. See Barbara Ehrenreich, *The Hearts of Men,* ch. 9, for an analysis of how the men's liberationists used the language of Human Potential and of feminism to justify the evasion of responsibility and the breadwinner's role. She notes that "male self-interest could now be presented as healthy and uplifting; the

break from the breadwinner role could be seen as a program of liberal middle-class reform" (119).

8. Herb Goldberg lists nineteen "impossible binds" in which men find themselves (again, passive construction), and each of these binds leads to an "Either way he loses" conclusion (96–106). Nowhere in Goldberg's analysis are the hazards of being male offset by the benefits of being male: from the shockingly high rate of male fetal death (179) to the repressed man who suffers for having erupted in violence and beat his son (72), Goldberg portrays even violent men as wounded and endangered. And, while never identifying the *causes* of male repression (except to point to a vague notion of socialization), Goldberg does not shy away from prescribing a cure: what men need is the therapy he offers, a long and slow process. "[T]he male would be well advised to give himself the gift of a thorough and total experience, allowing it the time it requires and that he deserves. After all he has spent a lifetime denying his feelings. Undoing this process requires a full commitment and a constant awareness of how important this is to his survival" (70).

9. Goldberg describes a study that confirms his analysis of the "impact of the masculine ethos on the body": the study found that male victims of lung cancer "have a poor outlet for emotional discharge and that they tend to conceal or bottle up their emotional difficulties" (Goldberg 117). The citation appears to be from a reputable medical journal, unlike the bulk of Goldberg's sources. It is: David M. Kissin, "Personality Characteristics in Males Conducive to Lung Cancer," *British Journal of Medical Psychology* 36 (1963). It is of course possible that certain personality traits prompt men to *smoke* more than others, thus contributing to a high incidence of lung cancer. In general, pseudo-medical ideas about the psychosomatic causes of cancer and, particularly, ulcers, are no longer even dominant in popular culture.

Kate Millett's *Sexual Politics* traces the literary equivalent of this idea in Norman Mailer: "Believing that violence is an innate psychological trait in the male, Mailer insists that repression can only lead to greater dangers. In the strange personal mishmash of hypochondria and pseudo-medicine to which he subscribes, Mailer finds the genesis of cancer in throttled violence" (331). Fasteau cites Millet's comments in his very smart analysis of "Violence: The Primal Test" (144–46). Fasteau's book is more analytic than therapeutic, and contains fascinating chapters on "Vietnam and the Cult of Toughness in Foreign Policy" and "Speculations on Watergate." Still, the book uses images of wounded masculinity to argue for changes in the male role, and makes ample use of the rhetoric of blockage and release to do so. Like Farrell and Goldberg, Fasteau also tends to paint men as the passive recipients of gender ideology, making liberal use of phrases like, "men are forced," "men aren't permitted," and so on.

10. Of course, the spectacle of male tears has become something quite different in post-Clinton American culture, where the public display of emotion has become evidence of a sincerity that often substitutes for real political commitment, backed by real social policy. We are inhabiting a moment that evinces the further development of the trends I am analyzing here, what Fred Pfeil has referred to as the "therapization" of the social (see Pfeil, 150–53). On tears and gendered conceptualizations of emotion, see Pinch, 128–34. On the public display of sentiment in the 1990s, see Ellison, "A Short History of Liberal Guilt."

11. Recent feminist work on men and emotion has begun to challenge the assumption that emotion is "feminized" in historically constant ways. See Pinch; and Ellison, "Cato's Tears."

12. In this light, we might read the conservative academic attack on "political correctness" and its wider public circulation in the mid-eighties and early nineties as a narrative of protest against the blockage of white and male verbal expression (see chapter 2).

13. Jack Sattel in "The Inexpressive Male" (1976), argued that male inexpressivity "empirically emerges as an intentional manipulation of a situation when threats to the male position occur" (469), but he was arguing against a much more vocal chorus of writers like Goldberg and Farrell. Even as late as 1988, the 1970s construction of male inexpressivity remains dominant. In his *The Inexpressive Male* (1988), Jack Balswick undertakes to contest the "sexual politics" explanation of male inexpressivity and does so by arguing that, because men are physically harmed by inexpressivity, it doesn't make sense to see inexpressivity as *good* for men. This argument rests on the flimsiest evidence of physiological damage: "It *can be* physically and psychologically unhealthy for a person to not release and express emotion. Physically, the inability to cry and express emotion *is thought* to be related to the development of various physical symptoms" (3, emphasis added). Balswick, like Goldberg, is invested in claiming a *bodily* harm produced by male inexpressivity.

14. See also Susan Bordo, "Reading the Male Body."

15. "Many men join them," he writes, "because they want to please their women or to learn how not be male oppressors. Consequently there is a subtle group climate of self-hate and guilt induction. The target is oneself and each male is cautious about using words or relating in ways that are 'typically male chauvinist'" (142). Such self-censorship, Goldberg implies, is yet another form of blockage, and he advises his clients and readers to see feminism as an opportunity for male liberation rather than the occasion for guilt.

16. Herb Goldberg also uses a plumbing metaphor to describe the "wise" penis: "The penis is not a piece of plumbing that functions capriciously. It is an expression of the total self. In these days of over-intellectualization it is perhaps the only remaining sensitive and revealing barometer of the male's true sexual feelings" (39). The penis *is* a piece of plumbing, according to Goldberg, but one

that functions *meaningfully*, rather than "capriciously." Paradoxically, a discourse that attempts to contest the construction of male sexuality as entirely focused on the performance of the penis ends up endowing the penis with the "sensitivity" that both women's and men's liberationists would argue more properly belongs in the emotional, rather than bodily, realm. Men's emotions are only "expressed," then, by the physical acts of erection and ejaculation.

17. The novel's simultaneous use and critique of therapeutic narrative recalls what Andrew Gordon analyzes in Barth's *The End of the Road* (1958). According to Gordon, that novel is less interested in critiquing a therapeutic model per se (in this case, Freudian psychoanalysis) than it is in exposing what Gordon calls (echoing Philip Reiff) the "triumph of the therapeutic" (41).

18. See Peck, 135–36, for a discussion of therapy as a mode of individualized adaptation to social changes.

19. The increased visibility of gay men, and of a trumpeted gay sexuality that is more liberated, adds to the sense of crisis afflicting straight white middle-class men. I will return to this question in the next chapter. The only visible gay man in Irving's novel is "alternately assumed to be great lover or a fag, or both" (117). Trumper meets him in the bathroom of an Iowa City bar, weeping in the "crapper stall" accompanied by the sound of a "self-flushing urinal" (115). Trumper decides to help this victim of a gay-bashing, and as he walks him home, finds himself "marked" by the unnamed man in two separate ways: first, he becomes visible as a potentially gay man, and worries about how he would show "fag-maulers" he was "straight." Tellingly, the only badge of "normality" he can come up with is "raping a girl" (117). The discomfort produced by a "contagion" of homosexuality is matched by the discomfort of a heterosexuality whose "normality" can only be proven through violence. Second, he is literally marked by his encounter with the man, for he is covered by the mélange of smells emanating from a man who was beaten in a filthy bathroom with a cheap bottle of toilet water in his pocket. The one smell missing is the smell of sex, and this becomes clear when Biggie assumes the worst upon Trumper's return, and he can only convince her that he hasn't been sleeping around by making her smell his penis.

20. The question of where Michaels stands in relation to his men's club is complicated by a "Prologue" he added for a 1993 version of the novel. This prologue pretends to be written by one of the men in the group, Harold Canterbury, who accuses Michaels of siding with the "enemy," and does so in terms that invoke political correctness and a version of Goldberg's claim that men join such groups in order to please "their women":

Michaels had betrayed us, and also his sex, and he must truly hate men. . . . By making us look bad, Michaels ingratiated himself with the vast audience of women who read novels. I'm not suggesting that they are different from normal people. Today you have to watch every word, since the last reservoir of human freedom, one's mind, is under squinty-eyed scrutiny and ferocious judgment in the high court of the mindless.   (ix)

Canterbury is clearly confused, and Michaels's conceit, taken perhaps from Nabokov's example of the prologue to Lolita, functions to disarm the criticism even as it articulates it. But is that really what's going on here? Why raise the specter of politically correct man-hating in the first place? This is certainly not my reading of the book—although some of my students have vigorously and more or less convincingly argued for it. Instead, my take is that the prologue illuminates the silliness of the political correctness that Goldberg and others see as motivating the formation of men's groups. It comes from feminism, but it also comes from the larger culture of therapy in which Goldberg is firmly situated and, thus, the novel stands as a critique of men's liberation. But this critique has the odd effect, as we will see, of authorizing the male liberationists' construction of masculinity but without the faith in the possibility of changing it.

5. EXPRESSION, REPRESSION, AND MALE HYSTERIA: MARKED MEN AND THE WOUNDS OF A DAMMED MASCULINITY

1. The publication in 1975 of Susan Brownmiller's Against Our Will undoubtedly fueled male efforts to reconstruct masculinity and male sexuality in response to such a thorough feminist critique. Interestingly, Brownmiller begins by invoking the authority of Jane Goodall to establish that rape is not a natural expression of primate sexuality; instead, in a speculative tale about the first rape, Brownmiller suggests that rape has never been about sexuality per se, but always about power. "In the violent landscape inhabited by primitive woman and man, some woman somewhere had a prescient vision of her right to her own physical integrity, and in my mind's eye I can picture her fighting like hell to preserve it." If the first rape "was an unexpected battle founded on the first woman's refusal, the second rape was indubitably planned. . . . [R]ape became not only a male prerogative, but man's basic weapon of force against woman, the principal agency of his will and her fear. His forcible entry into her body, despite her physical protestations and struggle, became the vehicle of his victorious conquest over her being, the ultimate test of his superior strength, the triumph of his manhood" (4–5). As fanciful as this tale might be, it does accomplish Brownmiller's purpose of rewriting the myth of the "primitive" instinct toward sexual domination by suggesting that even in the far distant past, rape expresses a social, not a natural prerogative.

2. Stephen Farber, reviewing the film for the New York Times, was alone in noting its critical edge, as he enjoined his readers to appreciate the film as a

"major work, important for the artistic vision it brings to the urgent question of understanding and redefining masculinity" (300).

3. As John D'Emilio and Estelle Freedman suggest, both women's liberation and gay liberation discourses challenged deeply held assumptions about the "nature" of sexuality and how it functions in society. "In particular," they write, "both movements analyzed the erotic as a vehicle for domination which, in complex ways, kept certain social groups in a subordinate place in society. No longer a natural 'instinct' or a 'drive,' sexuality emerged more clearly than ever as an issue of power and politics" (308).

4. The great debate over the nature of female orgasm (clitoral or vaginal?) worked, at least in part, to increase male anxiety about sexuality on several fronts. Because Masters and Johnson had implied that major female sexual dysfunction was traceable to male ineptitude or ignorance in believing in the consonance of male penetration and female pleasure, male sexuality becomes the enemy. Second, as Alix Shulman notes, feminist discussion about female orgasm worked to *politicize* sexuality, linking male beliefs about women's bodies to deep structures of social inequity: "In the process of exposing the myths and lies [about vaginal orgasm, the clitoris, and female frigidity], women are discovering that it is not they who have individual sex problems; it is society that has one great big political problem" (301).

5. Purvis mixes his metaphors all over the place in this book that has a slightly hysterical tone to it, as if desperately reaching for the most adequate language to heal over the contradictions that arise at most every turn. Here, the contradiction is between a construction of male heterosexuality as a force of *nature*, and a construction of the male body as a *machine*.

6. Like most post–women's liberation sexologists, Purvis undertakes to reassure men that liberated female sexuality need not mean the death of male sexuality. As this quotation suggests, however, the experts often seem to be trying to convince themselves. In general, recent sexologists hold two contradictory views: they directly reassure men that feminism and the rise of female sexual agency will "liberate" men from sole sexual responsibility and the performance ethos, while indirectly suggesting that this new model of sexuality is doomed to failure, since it goes against the "natural," "instinctual," and "biological" dispositions of male sexuality. The tactic of reassuring men, and in contradictory terms, dates back to postwar sexologists who, as Peter Lehman notes, reassure men that penis size doesn't matter, even as they themselves get "caught up in a phallic discourse" (146).

7. In the interests of battling masculine guilt, Goldberg frames male infidelity as just one more form of "expression" that, if blocked, will cause all kinds of problems. He counsels that "the married man who desires other women, therefore, may have to learn to emancipate himself by acting out his sexual desires

more openly and guiltlessly and discussing his needs and feelings honestly with his wife. He needs to come to look at this sexual appetite as a part of his unique make-up and openly own up to being who he is" (42).

8. See, particularly, Susan Bordo's "Reading the Male Body."

9. This is the title of a 1994 book by Eva Margolies, directed at women who want to help men with sexual problems. This book is full of little gems like the following: "The man who has a sexual problem has lost this primitive ability to become aroused by just feeling" (180).

10. See, particularly, "The Allegory of the Black Eunuchs" in *Soul on Ice*, where Cleaver poses the phallic "Supermasculine Menial" against the limp "Omnipotent Administrator." It is striking that none of these books on "male liberation" address black power, nor do the books on male sexuality have much to say about racial differences. In my view, this silence testifies to an uneasy tension between the acknowledgment and disavowal of the normativity of white masculinity.

11. In *The Myth of Male Power,* Farrell "argues" that male homosexuality is forbidden because, one, it offers an escape from the requirement that men support and protect women; and, two, it raises the possibility that sex can be "free." He writes: "Giving permission to homosexuality in Stage I"—pre-WWII "survival" stage—"involved the same problem as giving permission to masturbation: it was permission for sexual pleasure without a price. Think about it. A homosexual experience might mean two hours of sexual pleasure. The consequences?—two hours of sexual pleasure. A heterosexual experience might also mean two hours of sexual pleasure. But the consequences?—eighteen years of responsibility. In brief, *hetero*sexuality was a bad deal!" (86–87).

12. Such a view, as White argues, "brilliantly adapted Freud to the hedonistic consumption-oriented mood of the 1920s" (59). In the 1970s, the legitimation of male heterosexual release enabled men's liberationists to adapt to the sexual revolution, and to manage the psychological guilt produced by feminist critiques of male heterosexuality as dangerous. Just as the Victorian prescription of male continence was promoted by groups invested in safeguarding the "purity" of women by saving them from male lust, so in the 1970s, restraint of male sexual aggression is promoted by a feminist analysis of a male impulse toward sexual conquest.

13. My discussion here is indebted to Gail Bederman's analysis of late nineteenth-century obsessions with the figure of the black rapist. She writes:

Whites' new belief in the "Negro rapist" drew heavily on Victorian ideologies about male sexuality. The middle class believed that men, unlike "naturally good" women, were beset by powerful gusts of sinful sexual desires. This passionate masculine nature was considerd simultaneously the source of men's greatest danger and of men's greatest power. Succumbing to overwhelming emotion or sexual passion would sap a man's force, rendering him weak and degenerate. Therefore middle-class parents taught their sons to build a strong, manly "character" as they would build a muscle, through repetitive exercises of control over impulse. The middle class saw this ability to control powerful masculine passions through strong character and a powerful will as a primary source of men's strength and authority.   (48)

But the energy with which white men are seen "investigating new visions of what 'masculinity' might be, unfettered by civilization" (49) suggests that such visions can work also to reinforce the belief in the powers of uncontrolled male sexual release.

14. Gunning reads Thomas Nelson Page, Sinclair Lewis and, particularly, Thomas Dixon as white men ambivalently invested in the figure of the black rapist, a figure, Gunning argues, that mediated a host of anxieties about white male and female sexuality. As Gunning argues, the white violence evident in lynching parties enabled a kind of collective white male reempowerment at the same time that it uncomfortably suggested that white men, too, were "savage." Ida B. Wells makes use of this paradox in her antilynching campaign that, according to both Gunning and Gail Bederman, worked primarily by making white men appear more violent and savage than the black men they accused of rape. See Gunning (ch. 3), and Bederman (ch. 5).

15. For a not altogether convincing argument about the rejection of violent manhood in 1970s southern rock, see Ted Ownby.

16. Williams's point is nicely illustrated by a phenomenon reported by Jerry Bledsoe in a 1973 Esquire article, in which it becomes clear that audiences were willing and able to "forget" the trauma at the heart of the film. The release of Deliverance spurred a renewed interest in white-water rafting in the South and elsewhere, as mostly young men took to the water to experience firsthand that "adventure" experienced by Boorman's canoers. Bledsoe reports on the number of drownings produced by what law enforcement and rescue workers called the "Deliverance Syndrome," a syndrome marked by the absolute repression of the rape at the movie's center. As one enthusiast, a professor of microbiology at Emory University, described it, " 'it's the last ultimate challenge . . . This is the rites of passage, man. I mean, for some of us old guys it still is, I guess' " (230). Perhaps more remarkably, a young man from the group that prompted the article—in which one man was wounded and another drowned—gets the last word: " 'I mean you live in the city. You go out to these night spots. What can you do? There's no adventure. There's no challenge. What the hell good is life if there is no challenge?' " (233).

17. "Damned If You Do, and Damned If You Don't" is the title of James Griffith's essay on Deliverance, in which he argues that critics who complain that Boorman "missed the point" of Dickey's novel themselves miss the point that

Boorman had his own agenda, his own story to tell. For Griffith, while Dickey focuses on how a previously "bored and rudderless" Ed "draws strength from nature and is restored to creativity and vitality," Boorman creates a different protagonist, one that "may be as easily found in suburban living: one whose unexamined comforts keep him away from any personal doubts" (47). While this reading seems partially right, it also seems too vague and lacks an argument about why, and to what effect, Dickey's story of "creative growth" diverges from Boorman's story of "self-betrayal" (58). In my view, as will become clear, the answer lies in what the two texts see as the future of a masculinity recently come under attack.

18. Critics of the film tend to attribute its failure to adequately translate Dickey's story to the limitations of time and the difficulty of articulating first person narrative in film. See, particularly, Covel, and Suarez. Only Griffith notices that the film offers an entirely different psychological parable than the novel, rather than arguing that no psychological parable is offered at all.

19. This tradition was, of course, monumentalized by Leslie Fiedler's *Love and Death in the American Novel*. For feminist critiques of Fiedler, see Baym, and also Robyn Wiegman (*American Anatomies*, ch. 5).

20. Critics who hail Dickey's novel as everything from a reworking of the masculine myth of regeneration through violence (Ken Butterworth and others) to a meditation on Hobbesian political theory (Charles Redenius) have been almost unanimously hostile toward John Boorman's film. Dickey himself was unhappy with what Boorman did with his screenplay, lamenting that what gets lost in the translation is the "psychological orientation—the *being*—of the characters, their interrelations, their talk with each other, the true dramatic progression" (1972; 156–57). Literary critics excoriate Boorman for "bowdlerizing" Dickey's novel and the film for "perjur[ing] itself by falsifying the story material on which it is based" (Samuels 152; see also Beaton 306). What is "falsified" in the film is, precisely, the myth of masculinity at the heart of the novel. Similarly, what Dickey sees as the film's erasure of the "psychological orientation" of the characters and their stories is, in actuality, a critique of the psychological truths at the center of Dickey's novel. Critical discomfort with the film, I would suggest, has less to do with aesthetics and more to do with the fact that, while the novel follows a narrative trajectory tending toward the recuperation of masculinity, the film goes in exactly the opposite direction. As Stephen Farber noted in his *New York Times* review, the film "has a ruthless logic that will upset audiences looking for another fable of man against the wilderness"; unlike Dickey's novel, Boorman's film "express[es] a sense of total desolation. There is no sentimentality in the film; it is a serious and meaningful challenge to the belief in rites of manhood" (300).

21. Critics of both the novel and film have had much to say about *Deliver-*

ance's flirtation with the signifiers and meanings of homosexual desire between men. On the whole, critical consensus is that the "homosexual" experience of the rape makes real, and horrifying, the unacknowledged homoeroticism circulating among the characters. (See Beaton and Mellen, in particular.) This is perhaps true of the film, but the novel, as I suggest, takes a different tack.

22. See also David Rosen, for a discussion of how "muscular Christianity" negotiated this conflict; and David Leverenz, for an analysis of its persistence into the present.

23. See Bederman (ch. 6) for a fascinating analysis of Hall's life and work.

24. Bederman performs a reading of Burroughs's *Tarzan* (218–32) that foregrounds the ways in which this most popular of pulp fictions draws on the entire lexicon of images and rhetorics linking white supremacy, male power, and "civilization."

25. Dickey's Ed learns to sublimate his primitive, violent, masculine impulses into his art. When he returns to "civilization," he is freed up to explore his more creative, artistic side. No longer purely cynical about his graphic design business, and more in tune with the artist within him, Ed tries his hand at constructing collages, and hires back an artist-type he had formerly fired because of what he at one time thought of as his employee's artistic pretension. Many of the novel's critics have read the ending of the novel in terms of sublimation, although not always in these terms.

26. Social Darwinism and evolutionary theory tend to become popular in eras of critical social change, substituting nature for culture. As Anne Fausto-Sterling points out, sociobiology enjoyed a robust comeback in the mid-1970s, getting an injection of energy from several studies of "rape" in insects and ducks. This moment witnessed a veritable explosion of feminist discourses and activism around rape, much of which implied or even flatly stated that the courts and other social institutions were complicit in perpetuating the acceptance of rape. Fausto-Sterling notes that "the sudden increase in the use of the word in the biological literature, as a response to the furor raised by feminists, was at the very least a non-conscious attempt to establish rape as a widespread *natural* phenomenon and thus deflect and depoliticize a subject of intense and specific importance to women" (162).

27. Farber, who notes that "the film undercuts everything Lewis says" (300), compares *Deliverance* to Sam Peckinpah's 1971 *Straw Dogs*, arguing that the latter film ultimately opts to reinforce the macho myth denoted by the "code of the Old West, implying that in a savage world a baptism of blood is the first step to becoming a man; violence has a purgative effect on the intellectual hero" (300). Farber's use of the term "purgative" is suggestive here, for as I have argued, emotional "constipation" is what the men's liberationists diagnose as the ailment of repressed, civilized masculinity. Marc Feigen Fasteau, in *The*

Male Machine, also pairs these two films, but errs in conflating Dickey's novel with Boorman's film, as I noted at the beginning of this chapter.

28. This is the term Dickey uses in his screenplay to describe the condition of *some* hunters; Ed is explicitly *not* afflicted by this draw hysteria, and the film's representation of his failure to "release" his arrow (on two separate occasions) is entirely at odds with Dickey's narrative and representation of Ed.

29. Along with Paul Smith and Adam Knee (whom I will discuss later), see also Kirby; Fischer; and Creed.

30. Smith holds Kaja Silverman, Gaylyn Studlar, and Leo Bersani among the writers who theorize masochism as subversive. His point is, in part, that all three theorize masochism outside of its narrative contexts and, thus, fail to track the twists and turns (toward subversion or recuperation) such narratives can take. This seems a valid critique, and one that might be extended to ask: why is it when masculinity becomes the object of study, that so many theorists (including Smith himself) look toward hysteria and/or masochism as the site of a nonphallic or alternative masculinity? What lies behind these narratives of wounding? As I suggested in the introduction, an attention to male masochism can be read as a sign that masculinity becomes visible primarily as wounded.

31. See Showalter for a discussion of the fate of male hysteria from Charcot's practice to the present. She suggests that since World War II—when shell shock was understood as a kind of male hysteria—"male hysteria has reverted to its status as oxymoron or insult. Both male and female therapists hesitate to call men hysterical, although they may look, sound, and act like textbook examples" (*Hystories* 76). Interestingly, men haven't qualified as hysterics because they don't exhibit the kinds of emotional excesses noted in female hysterics; but, as I will suggest, hysteria can be evinced by blockage, as well as release.

Herb Goldberg offers a nontechnical conceptualization of the hysterical body when he speaks of "penis wisdom" (37). The penis, for example, "knows" when a man is not attracted to a woman, and so "decides" not to enable penetration. As I suggested above, Goldberg views impotence as simply a sign of "penis wisdom." Claiming that "men invariably try to accommodate female [sexual] needs rather than fulfill their own" (40), he concludes (against an entire clinical history of male impotence) that men would sooner admit to the medical condition of impotence than confess that their partners don't turn them on (36). The invention of Viagra has, already, fueled such biologistic conceptualizations of impotence.

32. Although Smith doesn't make this argument, one might suggest that the masochistic moment is made necessary by the exhibitionism and objectification of the first moment, a kind of punishment necessary to "purge" the masculine of its perhaps too "womanly" exhibitionism.

33. Don Johnson suggests a similar reading of the rape when he argues that

the encounter with the mountain man enables Ed to "rebuild himself, to discover and use the primitive power the mountaineers represent, power that for so long has been smothered by the flab of the soft life" (21). Johnson makes this point in the process of defending the novel and film against charges that they promote negative stereotypes of Appalachian people. Of course, such an argument depends on an unquestioned valorization of the power of the masculine primitive, a valorization, as I've suggested, that the film actively resists. Not surprisingly, Johnson finds it harder to defend the film against these charges than he does the novel.

34. I'm quoting from the *New Yorker*'s excerpt from the book.

35. In the city, Tom is a misunderstood and oppressed minority of one, a victim of the "grouping" that, Conroy argues, gets repeated each generation. This time around, he's the target of "contempt" just because he's a white southern male (195–96). He compares his situation, in which white southern men are the only permitted object of scorn in a multicultural city, to the situation of blacks in the South, a comparison that reveals the individualist orientation behind the social analysis. Indeed, Tom has the experience of being on the front lines of the fight for integration in southern schools, having been forced by sister Savannah into defending the first black student to attend their high school. Tom becomes the victim of integration, and asks, "Where's Earl Fucking Warren now that I need him?" (378). Conroy describes Tom's racism as issuing from his "passionate need to conform rather than from any serious credo or system of belief" (372), and his fight for Benji Washington is just as shallow. Tom later learns that, in sticking up for Benji, he managed to displace himself, for the first time Benji appears on the football field, it's clear to all observers that he is going to outstrip Tom. Racism and antiracism are reduced to negative and positive attitudes and their effects on individual people, and Tom becomes the white southern man whose good intentions make him the "victim" of integration. Robyn Wiegman reads Conroy's *Lords of Discipline* and Frank Roddam's film of it, as part of a post–civil rights project engaged in positioning white men "as both victim of the [changed] social order and its potential hero" (*American Anatomies* 123). See also Susan Jeffords (ch. 5 of *Hard Bodies*), where she reads the film *Mississippi Burning* as part of an effort to "rediscover white male heroism" by positioning white men as the central figures in narratives about civil rights and feminism (118).

36. The Conroy family pathology is, of course, legendary, and very much like the Wingo family in the novel. Much has been made in the popular press of the dysfunctional Conroy family, and how that family has further tormented the son who tells their story. Along with *The Prince of Tides*, *The Great Santini* and *Beach Music* are largely understood to be autobiographical, and Conroy himself has talked publically about how his family tragedies and his own sever-

al personal traumas have found their way into his fiction. See articles and profiles by John Logue; Peter Castro and Meg Grant; John Berendt.

37. Tom's feminism has some features in common with T. S. Garp's humanism/feminism. As we saw in chapter 3, Irving's critique of organized feminism in *The World According to Garp* is that it politicizes gender and, thus, is as guilty of trapping men and women into limited positions as are the ideologies feminism is devoted to overturning.

38. In fact, the novel, like Irving's *The World According to Garp*, tries to depoliticize feminism, as when Tom complains about Lowenstein's claim that Savannah's poetry is mostly for women. This "cheapens" her art, Tom says, and makes it "banal and predictable." Her politics, according to Tom, is what is "commonplace and trivial about her poetry." What is valuable is Savannah's ability to "take the language and make it soar like a bird or sing like some wounded angel" (164). When Lowenstein replies by saying that Tom "could hardly be expected to understand a feminist viewpoint," he launches into one of his "I'm a feminist" speeches. This exchange is typical of the novel's engagement with feminism as a militantly personalized, pathological, and almost unnatural expression of gender crisis.

39. In his inimitable prose, Pfeil writes: "the discursive regime of the therapeutic is hard at work converting the new and old power relations alike to so many private, individual dysfunctions, the exploited and oppressed into so many pathologized deviants and victims; sensitizing us to cultural differences in lifestyle while inviting us to forget politics, opt for personal over collective empowerment or redistribution of power, and suspect the twisted motives of all those who still attempt to change the unchangeable way things are" (152).

40. See Margie Burns, who argues that *Deliverance*, along with *Easy Rider*, were well received in part because they "seemed to represent a new wave of iconoclasm, or at least relative independence, in film production" (45).

41. Most reviews emphasize the "bigness" of the film. See the reviews in *Rolling Stone* ("emotionally overloaded saga"); Richard Schickel's in *Time* ("Wow! Four movies for the price of one. *The Prince of Tides* may be the biggest bargain of these recessionary holidays. Excessive is the word for director Barbra Streisand's movie—and not an entirely pejorative one either"); Leah Rozen's in *People* ("It's big, it's lush, it's even good"); and Jon Young's review of the video in *Video* ("Give Barbra Streisand credit for thinking big").

42. As it turns out, the film did pretty well, grossing $74.8 million in domestic box office receipts, which made it the eighteenth highest-grossing film of 1991—behind another film about the South's violent white men and its victimized women, *Fried Green Tomatoes*, but ahead of a film about the black male as an "endangered species," *Boyz 'N the Hood*. The top-grossing film of the year was *Terminator 2*, followed closely by *Beauty and the Beast, Hook, The Silence of*

the Lambs, and *JFK.* The source for this information is the Web site maintained by Third Millenium Entertainment (www.geocities.com/Hollywood/studio/2561/box90–94.html). *The Prince of Tides* was also nominated for several Academy Awards (no nominations for Streisand), but did not win any. *The Silence of the Lambs* swept the awards, but this year at the Oscars is most often remembered as the year an animated feature film—and one about a male figure torn between a savage, beastly masculinity, and a gentle, controlled one—was nominated as best picture. That film, of course, was *Beauty and the Beast.*

43. Adam Thorburn, in his review/critique of the film, finds its demonization of Lila, coupled with its pathologization of homosexuality, a symptom of its all too traditional masculinist politics. As he points out, Streisand even suggests that Lila is responsible for Tom's "sexual enfeeblement" because she has "sexually overpowered" him as a child (9).

BIBLIOGRAPHY

Abu-Lughod Lila and Catherine A. Lutz. "Introduction: Emotion, Discourse, and the Politics of Everyday Life." In Abu-Lughod and Lutz, eds., *Language and the Politics of Emotion*, 1–23. Cambridge and New York: Cambridge University Press, 1990.

Allen, Henry. "The Right Absolute Allan Bloom." *Washington Post*, June 18, 1987, C1–C3 ("Style" section). Reprinted in Stone, ed., *Essays on "The Closing of the American Mind,"* 39–43.

Allen, Mary. "John Updike's Love of 'Dull Bovine Beauty.'" *The Necessary Blankness: Women in Major American Fiction of the Sixties.* Champaign: University of Illinois Press, 1976.

Amur, G. S. "Philip Roth's *My Life as a Man:* Portrait of the Artist as a Trapped Husband." *Indiana Journal of American Studies* 14.2 (1984): 61–66.

Atlas, James. "Chicago's Grumpy Guru: Best-Selling Author Allan Bloom and the Chicago Intellectuals." *New York Times Magazine,* January 3, 1988, 12–31. Reprinted in Stone, ed., *Essays on "The Closing of the American Mind,"* 68–72.

Aufderheide, Patricia, ed. *Beyond PC: Toward a Politics of Understanding.* Saint Paul, Minn.: Graywolf Press, 1992.

Balswick, Jack. *The Inexpressive Male.* Lexington, Mass., and Toronto: Lexington Books, 1988.

Barber, Benjamin. "The Philosopher Despot: Allan Bloom's Elitist Agenda." *Harper's Magazine* (January 1988): 61–65. Reprinted in Stone, ed., *Essays on "The Closing of the American Mind,"* 81–88.

Bardwick, Judith. *In Transition: How Feminism, Sexual Liberation, and the Search for Self-Fulfillment Have Altered America.* New York: Holt, Rinehart, and Winston, 1979.

Barthes, Roland. "The Death of the Author" (1968). In Stephen Heath, trans. and ed., *Image–Music–Text,* 142–48. New York: Hill and Wang, 1977.

Battersby, Christine. *Gender and Genius: Towards a Feminist Aesthetics.* Bloomington: Indiana University Press, 1989.

Baym, Nina. "Melodramas of Beset Manhood: How Theories of American Fiction Exclude Women Authors." *American Quarterly* 33.2 (Summer 1981): 123–39.

Beaton, James. "Dickey Down the River." In Gerald Peary and Roger Shatzkin, eds., *The Modern American Novel and the Movies,* 293–306. New York: Ungar, 1978.

Bederman, Gail. *Manliness and Civilization: A Cultural History of Gender and Race in the United States, 1880–1917.* Chicago and London: University of Chicago Press, 1995.

Bennett, William. *To Reclaim a Legacy: A Report on the Humanities in Higher Education.* Washington, D.C.: National Endowment for the Humanities, 1984.

Berendt, John. "The Conroy Saga." *Vanity Fair* (July 1995): 108–113, 138–41.

Berger, Maurice, Brian Wallis, and Simon Watson, eds. *Constructing Masculinity.* New York and London: Routledge, 1995.

Berkenkamp, Lauri. "Reading, Writing, and Interpreting: Stephen King's *Misery.*" In Magistrale, ed., *The Dark Descent,* 203–11.

Bersani, Leo. "Is the Rectum a Grave?" In Douglas Crimp, ed., *AIDS: Cultural Analysis, Cultural Activism,* 197–222. Cambridge: MIT Press, 1988.

Bérubé, Michael. "Disuniting America Again." *Journal of the Midwest Modern Language Association* 26.1 (Spring 1993): 31–46.

Bérubé, Michael and Cary Nelson, eds. *Higher Education Under Fire: Politics, Economics, and the Crisis of the Humanities.* New York and London: Routledge, 1995.

Bledsoe, Jerry. "What Will Save Us From Boredom?" *Esquire* 80 (December 1973): 227–33.

Bloom, Allan. *The Closing of the American Mind: How Higher Education Has Failed Democracy and Impoverished the Souls of Today's Students.* New York: Simon and Schuster, 1987.

Bly, Robert. *Iron John: A Book About Men.* Reading, Mass.: Addison-Wesley, 1990.

Bordo, Susan. "'Material Girl': The Effacements of Postmodern Culture." In Lawrence Goldstein, ed., *The Female Body: Figures, Styles, Speculations,* 106–30. Ann Arbor: University of Michigan Press, 1991.

——. "Reading the Male Body." *Michigan Quarterly Review* 32.4 (Fall 1993): 696–737.

Bosky, Bernadette Lynn. "Playing the Heavy: Weight, Appetite, and Embodiment in Three Novels by Stephen King." In Magistrale, ed., *The Dark Descent,* 137–56.

Brod, Harry. "Some Thoughts on Some Histories of Some Masculinities: Jews and Other Others." In Brod and Kaufman, eds., *Theorizing Masculinities*, 82–96.

Brod, Harry and Michael Kaufman, eds. *Theorizing Masculinities*. Thousand Oaks, Calif., London, and New Delhi: Sage, 1994.

Brown, Wendy. *States of Injury: Power and Freedom in Late Modernity*. Princeton: Princeton University Press, 1995.

Brownmiller, Susan. *Against Our Will: Men, Women, and Rape*. New York: Bantam Books, 1975.

Bucher, Glenn, ed. *Straight/White/Male*. Philadelphia: Fortress Press, 1976.

Burns, Gail E. and Melinda Kanter, "Women, Danger, and Death: The Perversion of the Female Principle in Stephen King's Fiction." In Diane Raymond, ed., *Sexual Politics and Popular Culture*, 158–72. Bowling Green, Ohio: Bowling Green State University Popular Press, 1990.

Burns, Margie. "*Easy Rider* and *Deliverance*, or, the Death of the Sixties." *University of Hartford Studies in Literature* 22.2–3 (1990): 44–58.

Butler, Judith. *Gender Trouble: Feminism and the Subversion of Identity*. New York and London: Routledge, 1990.

Butterworth, Ken. "The Savage Mind: James Dickey's *Deliverance*." *Southern Literary Journal* 28.2 (Spring 1996): 69–78.

Campbell, Jeff. "'Middling, Hidden, Troubled America': John Updike's Rabbit Tetralogy." *Journal of the American Studies Association of Texas* 24 (1993): 26–45.

——. "Updike's Honky Apocalypse: Rabbit Redux." *New Mexico Humanities Review* (May 1978): 53–60.

Carroll, Peter N. *It Seemed Like Nothing Happened: The Tragedy and Promise of America in the 1970s*. New York: Holt, Rinehart, and Winston, 1982.

Carton, Evan. "The Politics of Selfhood: Bob Slocum, T. S. Garp, and Auto-American-Biography." *Novel* 20.1 (Fall 1986): 41–61.

Castro, Peter and Meg Grant. "Pat Conroy." *People Weekly*, August 14, 1995, 55–59.

Chambers, Ross. "The Unexamined," *Minnesota Review* 47 (Fall 1996): 141–56.

Clarke, John. *New Times and Old Enemies: Essays on Cultural Studies and America*. London: HarperCollins, 1991.

Clausen, Jan. "Native Fathers." *Kenyon Review* 14.2 (Spring 1992): 44–55.

Cleaver, Eldridge. *Soul on Ice*. New York: Dell, 1968.

Clover, Carol. *Men, Women, and Chainsaws: Gender in the Modern Horror Film*. Princeton: Princeton University Press, 1992.

——. "White Noise." *Sight and Sound* 3.5 (May 1993): 6–9.

Cohan, Steven and Ina Rae Hark, eds. *Screening the Male: Exploring Masculinities in Hollywood Cinema*. New York and London: Routledge, 1993.

Conroy, Pat. *The Prince of Tides* (1986). New York: Bantam Books, 1987.

Corber, Robert J. *Homosexuality in Cold War America: Resistance and the Crisis of Masculinity.* Durham, N.C.: Duke University Press, 1997.

Covel, Robert C. "James Dickey's *Deliverance:* Screenplay as Intertext." *James Dickey Newsletter* 4.2 (1988): 12–19.

Creed, Barbara. "Phallic Panic: Male Hysteria and *Dead Ringers.*" *Screen* 31.2 (Summer 1990): 125–46.

Crichton, Michael. *Disclosure.* New York: Ballantine, 1993.

Curran, Ronald T. "Biology and Culture: Hollywood and the Deliverance of Dickey's Weekend Backwoodsmen." *Southern Quarterly* 18.4 (summer 1980): 81–90.

DeBellis, Jack. "*2001: A Space Odyssey* in *Rabbit Redux.*" *Literature Film Quarterly* 21.3 (1993): 209–17.

D'Emilio, John and Estelle B; Freedman. *Intimate Matters: A History of Sexuality in America.* New York: Harper and Row, 1988.

Dickey, Christopher. "Summer of Deliverance." *The New Yorker,* July 13, 1998, 38–51.

Dickey, James. *Deliverance.* New York: Dell, 1970.

——. *Deliverance* (screenplay, c. 1972). Carbondale: Southern Illinois University Press, 1982.

Doane, Janice and Devon Hodges. *Nostalgia and Sexual Difference: The Resistance to Contemporary Feminism.* New York and London: Methuen, 1987.

Douglas, Ann. *The Feminization of American Culture.* New York: Avon Books, 1977.

D'Souza, Dinesh. *Illiberal Education: The Politics of Race and Sex on Campus.* New York: Free Press, 1991.

Dyer, Richard. "White." *Screen* 29.2 (Fall 1988): 44–55.

Easthope, Antony. *What a Man's Gotta Do: The Masculine Myth in Popular Culture.* Boston: Unwin Hyman, 1986.

Echols, Alice. *Daring to Be Bad: Radical Feminism in America, 1967–1975.* Minneapolis: University of Minnesota Press, 1989.

Edelman, Lee. "Redeeming the Phallus: Wallace Stevens, Frank Lentricchia, and the Politics of Heterosexuality." In Joseph A. Boone and Michael Cadden, eds., *Engendering Men: The Question of Male Feminist Criticism,* 36–52. New York and London: Routledge, 1990.

Egan, Timothy. "Teaching Tolerance in Workplaces: A Seattle Program Illustrates the Limits." *New York Times,* October 8, 1993, 12A.

Ehrenreich, Barbara. *Fear of Falling: The Inner Life of the Middle Class.* New York: Harper Collins, 1989.

——. *The Hearts of Men: American Dreams and the Flight from Commitment.* New York: Anchor Books, 1983.

Ehrenreich, Barbara and Deirdre English. *For Her Own Good: 150 Years of the Experts' Advice to Women.* New York: Anchor Books, 1979.

Ehrenreich, Rosa. "What Campus Radicals?" In Aufderheide, ed., *Beyond PC,* 133–141.

Ellison, Julie. "Cato's Tears." *ELH* 63.3 (Fall 1996): 571–601.

——. "A Short History of Liberal Guilt." *Critical Inquiry* 22.2 (Winter 1996): 344–71.

Erkkila, Betsy. "Ethnicity, Literary Theory, and the Grounds of Resistance." *American Quarterly* 47.4 (December 1995): 563–94.

Faludi, Susan. *Backlash: The Undeclared War Against American Women.* New York: Crown, 1991.

——. *Stiffed: The Betrayal of the American Man.* New York: Morrow, 1999.

Farber, Stephen. "'Deliverance'—How It Delivers." *New York Times* (August 20, 1972): II: 9:7; reprinted in *New York Times Film Review Annual 1972,* 299–300.

Farred, Grant. "Take Back the Mike: Producing a Language for Date Rape." In Newfield and Strickland, eds., *After Political Correctness,* 174–92.

Farrell, Warren. *The Liberated Man: Beyond Masculinity—Freeing Men and Their Relationships with Women.* New York: Random House, 1974.

——. *The Myth of Male Power: Why Men Are the Disposable Sex.* New York: Simon and Schuster, 1993.

Fasteau, Marc Feigen. *The Male Machine.* New York: McGraw-Hill, 1974.

Fausto-Sterling, Anne. *Myths of Gender: Biological Theories About Women and Men.* New York: Basic Books, 1985.

Fiedler, Leslie. *Love and Death in the American Novel* (1960). Rpt., New York: Stein and Day, 1966.

Fischer, Lucy. "Mama's Boy: Filial Hysteria in *White Heat.*" In Cohan and Hark, eds., *Screening the Male,* 70–84.

Fishkin, Shelley Fisher. "Interrogating 'Whiteness,' Complicating 'Blackness': Remapping American Culture." *American Quarterly* 47.3 (September 1995): 428–66.

Fiske, John. "Popular Discrimination." In James Naremore and Patrick Brantlinger, eds., *Modernity and Mass Culture,* 103–116. Bloomington: Indiana University Press, 1991.

——. *Power Plays, Power Works.* London and New York: Verso, 1993.

Foucault, Michel. "What is an Author?" (1969). In Josue V. Harari, ed., *Textual Strategies: Perspectives in Post-Structuralist Criticism,* 141–60. Ithaca: Cornell University Press, 1979.

Frankenberg, Ruth. *White Women, Race Matters: The Social Construction of Whiteness*. Minneapolis: University of Minnesota Press, 1993.

Garber, Marjorie. *Vested Interests: Cross-Dressing and Cultural Anxiety*. New York: Harper Perennial, 1993.

Gates, Henry Louis. *Loose Canons: Notes on the Culture Wars*. New York and Oxford: Oxford University Press, 1992.

Gaver, Charles. "Gay Liberation and Striaght White Males." In Glenn Bucher, ed., *Straight/White/Male*, 51–70.

Gibson, James William. *Warrior Dreams: Violence and Manhood in Post-Vietnam America*. New York: Hill and Wang, 1994.

Gilbert, Sandra and Susan Gubar. *The Madwoman in the Attic: The Woman Writers and the Nineteenth-Century Literary Imagination*. New Haven: Yale University Press, 1979.

Gitlin, Todd. "The Rise of 'Identity Politics': An Examination and a Critique." In Bérubé and Nelson, eds., *Higher Education Under Fire*, 308–25.

——. *The Twilight of Common Dreams: Why America is Wracked by Culture Wars*. New York: Henry Holt, 1995.

Glenday, Michael K. "*Deliverance* and the Aesthetics of Survival." *American Literature* 56.2 (May 1984): 149–61.

Goldberg, Herb. *The Hazards of Being Male: Surviving the Myth of Masculine Privilege*. New York: Nash, 1976.

Gordon, Andrew. "The Triumph of the Therapeutic in *The End of the Road*." *Delta* 21 (October 1985): 31–42.

Gottfried, Barbara. "What *Do* Men Want, Dr. Roth?" In Harry Brod, ed., *A Mensch Among Men: Explorations in Jewish Masculinity*, 37–52. Freedom, Calif.: Crossing Press, 1988.

Gould, Stephen Jay. *The Mismeasure of Man*. New York and London: Norton, 1981.

Graff, Gerald. *Beyond the Culture Wars: How Teaching the Conflicts Can Revitalize American Education*. New York and London: Norton, 1992.

Green, Harvey. *Fit for America: Health, Fitness, Sport, and American Society*. New York: Pantheon, 1986.

Greenberg, Clement. "The State of American Writing." *Partisan Review* 15 (August 1948): 876–83.

Greider, William. "Bloom and Doom." *Rolling Stone*, October 8, 1987, 39–40. Reprinted in Stone, ed., *Essays on "The Closing of the American Mind,"* 244–47.

Greiner, Donald J. *John Updike's Novels*. Athens: Ohio University Press, 1984.

Griffen, Clyde. "Reconstructing Masculinity from the Evangelical Revival to the Waning of Progressivism: A Speculative Synthesis." In Mark Carnes and Clyde Griffen, eds., *Meanings for Manhood: Constructions of Masculinity in*

Victorian America, 183–204. Chicago and London: University of Chicago Press, 1990.

Griffith, James. "Damned If You Do, and Damned If You Don't: James Dickey's *Deliverance.*" *Post Script* 5.3 (Spring-Summer 1986): 47–59.

Gubar, Susan. "'The Blank Page' and the Issues of Female Creativity." *Critical Inquiry* 8.2 (Winter 1981): 243–63.

Gunning, Sandra. *Race, Rape, and Lynching: The Red Record of American Literature, 1890–1912.* New York and Oxford: Oxford University Press, 1996.

Hammond, Mike. "The Historical and the Hysterical: Melodrama, War, and Masculinity in *Dead Poets Society.*" In Pat Kirkham and Janet Thumim, eds., *You, Tarzan: Masculinity, Movies, and Men,* 52–65. New York: St. Martin's, 1993.

Hanson, Claire. "Stephen King: Powers of Horror." In Brian Docherty, ed., *American Horror Fiction: From Brockden Brown to Stephen King,* 135–54. London: MacMillan, 1990.

Hanson, Ellis. "Undead." In Diana Fuss, ed., *Inside/Out: Lesbian Theories, Gay Theories.* New York and London: Routledge, 1991.

Haraway, Donna. *Simians, Cyborgs, and Women: The Reinvention of Nature.* New York and London: Routledge, 1991.

Harris, Marvin. *America Now: The Anthropology of a Changing Culture.* New York: Simon and Schuster, 1981.

Hartsock, Nancy. "Rethinking Modernism: Minority vs. Majority Theories." *Cultural Critique* 7 (Fall 1987): 187–206.

Hebidge, Dick. *Subculture: The Meaning of Style.* New York and London: Routledge, 1993.

Hertz, Neil. "Medusa's Head: Male Hysteria Under Pressure." In *The End of the Line: Essays on Psychoanalysis and the Sublime,* 161–93. New York: Columbia University Press, 1985.

Hirsch, E. D., Jr. *Cultural Literacy: What Every American Needs to Know.* New York: Vintage Books, 1987.

Hochschild, Arlie. *The Managed Heart: Commercialization of Human Feeling.* Berkeley: University of California Press, 1983.

Hodgson, Godfrey. *America in Our Time: From World War II to Nixon, What Happened and Why.* New York: Vintage Books, 1976.

Hrdy, Sarah Blaffer. "Empathy, Polyandry, and the Myth of the Coy Female." In Ruth Bleier, ed., *Feminist Approaches to Science,* 119–46. New York: Pergamon, 1988.

Hughes, Robert. *The Culture of Complaint: The Fraying of America.* New York and Oxford: Oxford University Press, 1993.

Hunter, James Davison. *Culture Wars: The Struggle to Define America.* New York: Basic Books, 1991.

Huyssen, Andreas. "Mass Culture as Woman." In Tania Modleski, ed., *Studies in Entertainment: Critical Approaches to Mass Culture*, 188–207. Bloomington: Indiana University Press, 1986.

Irving, John. "In Defense of Sentimentality." *New York Times Book Review*, November 25, 1979, 3, 98.

——. "The King and the Novel: An Introduction to *Great Expectations*." New York: Bantam Classics, 1986.

——. "Kurt Vonnegut and His Critics." *New Republic* 181 (September 22, 1979): 41–49.

——. *The Water-Method Man* (1972). New York: Ballantine, 1990.

——. *The World According to Garp* (1978). New York: Pocket Books, 1979.

Jacoby, Russell. *Dogmatic Wisdom: How the Culture Wars Divert Education and Distract America*. New York: Doubleday, 1994.

Jacoby, Russell and Naomi Glauberman, eds. *The Bell Curve Debate: History, Documents, Opinions*. New York: Times Books, 1995.

Jackson, Edward M. "Rabbit Is Racist." *College Language Association Journal* 28.4 (1985): 444–51.

Jackson, Jean. "Chronic Pain and the Tension Between the Body as Subject and Object." In Thomas J. Csordas, ed., *Embodiment and Experience: The Existential Ground of Culture and Self*, 201–28. Cambridge: Cambridge University Press, 1994.

Jardine, Alice. "Illiberal Reporting." In Christopher Newfield and Ronald Strickland, eds., *After Political Correctness*, 128–37.

Jeffords, Susan. *Hard Bodies: Hollywood Masculinity in the Reagan Era*. New Brunswick: Rutgers University Press, 1994.

——. *The Remasculinization of America: Gender and the Vietnam War*. Bloomington: Indiana University Press, 1989.

Jeffords, Susan and Lauren Rabinovitz, eds. *Seeing Through the Media: The Persian Gulf War*. New Brunswick: Rutgers University Press, 1994.

Johnson, Don. "Balancing Negative Stereotypes in *Deliverance*. James Dickey Newsletter 2.2 (Spring 1986): 17–27.

Johnson, Haynes. *Sleepwalking Through History: America in the Reagan Years*. New York and London: Norton, 1991.

Kamuf, Peggy. "Replacing Feminist Criticism." *Diacritics* 12 (1982): 42–47.

Kaufman, Michael. "Men, Feminism, and Men's Contradictory Experiences of Power." In Brod and Kaufman, eds., *Theorizing Masculinities*, 142–63.

Kaye, Harvey E. *Male Survival: Masculinity Without Myth*. New York: Grosset and Dunlap, 1974.

Kimball, Roger. *Tenured Radicals: How Politics Has Corrupted Our Higher Education*. New York: Harper and Row, 1990.

Kimbrell, Andrew. *The Masculine Mystique: The Politics of Masculinity.* New York: Ballantine, 1995.

Kimmel, Michael S. "'Born to Run': Nineteenth-Century Fantasies of Masculine Retreat and Re-Creation (*or,* The Historical Rust on Iron John)." In Kimmel, ed., *The Politics of Manhood: Profeminist Men Respond to the Mythopoetic Men's Movement (and the Mythopoetic Leaders Answer),* 115–50. Philadelphia: Temple University Press, 1995.

——. "The Contemporary 'Crisis' of Masculinity in Historical Perspective." In Harry Brod, ed., *The Making of Masculinities: The New Men's Studies,* 121–53. Boston: Unwin Hyman, 1987:

——. *Manhood in America: A Cultural History.* New York: Free Press, 1996.

King, Stephen. *Misery* (1987). New York: Signet, 1988.

——. "On Becoming a Brand Name." In Chuck Miller and Tim Underwood, eds., *Fear Itself: The Horror Fiction of Stephen King,* 15–42. San Francisco: Underwood and Miller, 1982.

Kirby, Lynn. "Male Hysterial and Early Cinema." In Constance Penley and Sharon Willis, eds., *Male Trouble,* 65–85. Minneapolis: University of Minnesota Press, 1993.

Knee, Adam. "The Dialectic of Female Power and Male Hysteria in *Play Misty for Me.*" In Steven Cohan and Ina Rae Hark, eds., *Screening the Male,* 87–102.

Krentz, Jayne Ann, ed. *Dangerous Men and Adventurous Women: Romance Writers on the Appeal of Romance.* Philadelphia: University of Pennsylvania Press, 1992.

Kundera, Milan. "Some Notes on Roth's *My Life as a Man* and *The Professor of Desire.*" In Milbauer and Watson, eds., *Reading Philip Roth,* 160–67.

Laqueur, Thomas. *Making Sex: Body and Gender from the Greeks to Freud.* Cambridge: Harvard University Press, 1990.

Leder, Drew. *The Absent Body.* Chicago and London: University of Chicago Press, 1990.

Lehman, Peter. "*In the Realm of the Senses:* Desire, Power, and the Representation of the Male Body." *Genders* 2 (Summer 1988): 91–110.

——. *Running Scared: Masculinity and the Representation of the Male Body.* Philadelphia: Temple University Press, 1993.

Lemon, Richard. *The Troubled American.* New York: Simon and Schuster, 1969.

Leverenz, David. "The Last Real Man in America: From Natty Bumppo to Batman." *American Literary History* 3.4 (Winter 1991): 753–81. Reprinted in Peter Murphy, ed., *Fictions of Masculinity: Crossing Cultures, Crossing Sexualities,* 21–53. New York: New York University Press, 1994.

Lipsitz, George. "The Possessive Investment in Whiteness: Racialized Social

Democracy and the 'White' Problem in American Studies." *American Quarterly* 47.3 (September 1995): 369–87.

Logue, John. "Fearless Son of 'The Great Santini.'" *Southern Living* (July 1995): 34–35.

Lounsberry, Barbara. "The Terrible Under Toad: Violence as Excessive Imagination in *The World According to Garp.*" *Thalia: Studies in Literary Humor* 5.2 (Fall-Winter 1982–83): 30–35.

Lutz, Catherine A. "Engendered Emotion: Gender, Power, and the Rhetoric of Emotional Control in American Discourse." In Abu-Lughod and Lutz, eds., *Language and the Politics of Emotion,* 69–91. Cambridge and New York: Cambridge University Press, 1990.

MacDonald, Dwight. "Masscult and Midcult II." *Partisan Review* 27 (Fall 1960): 589–631.

Magistrale, Tony. "Art Versus Madness." In Donald E. Morse, Marshall B. Tymn, and Csilla Bertha, eds., *The Celebration of the Fantastic.* Westport, Conn.: Greenwood Press, 1992.

——. *Stephen King: The Second Decade.* New York: Twayne, 1992.

Magistrale, Tony, ed. *The Dark Descent: Essays Defining Stephen King's Horrorscape.* New York: Greenwood Press, 1992.

Mailer, Norman. *Advertisements for Myself.* New York: Berkeley Medallion, 1966.

Margolies, Eva. *Undressing the American Male: Men with Sexual Problems and What Women Can Do to Help Them.* New York: Dutton, 1994.

Markle, Joyce. *Fighters and Lovers: Theme in the Novels of John Updike.* New York: New York University Press, 1973.

Masters, William H. and Virginia E. Johnson. *Human Sexual Inadequacy.* Boston: Little, Brown, 1970.

Mazurek, Raymond A. "'Bringing the Corners Forward': Ideology and Representation in Updike's Rabbit Trilogy." In Adam Sorkin, ed., *Politics and the Muse,* 142–60. Bowling Green, Ohio: Popular Press, 1989.

McCarthy, Cameron. "Contradictions of Existence: Identity and Essentialism." In Bérubé and Nelson, eds., *Higher Education Under Fire,* 326–35.

McKay, Kim. "Double Discourse in John Irving's *The World According to Garp.*" *Twentieth Century Literature* 38.4 (Winter 1992): 457–75.

McWhirter, David. "Restaging the Hurt: Henry James and the Artist as Masochist." *Texas Studies in Literature and Language* 33.4 (Winter 1991): 464–91.

Mellen, Joan. *Big Bad Wolves: Masculinity in the American Film.* New York: Pantheon, 1977.

Michaels, Leonard. *The Men's Club* (1978). Expanded ed. San Francisco: Mercury House, 1993.

Michaels, Walter Benn. "The Souls of White Folk." In Elaine Scarry, ed., *Literature and the Body: Essays on Populations and Persons*, 185–209. Baltimore: Johns Hopkins University Press, 1988.

Michel, Pierre. "Philip Roth's Reductive Lens: From 'On the Air' to *My Life as a Man*." *Revue des langues vivantes* 42 (1976): 501–19.

Milbauer, Asher Z. and Donald G. Watson, eds. *Reading Philip Roth*. New York: St. Martin's, 1988.

Miller, Nancy K. "The Text's Heroine: A Feminist Critic and Her Fictions." *Diacritics* 12 (1982): 48–53.

Millett, Kate. *Sexual Politics*. Garden City, N.Y.: Doubleday, 1970.

Modleski, Tania. *Feminism Without Women: Culture and Criticism in a "Postfeminist" Age*. New York and London: Routledge, 1991.

Monaghan, David. "*The Great American Novel* and *My Life as a Man*: As Assessment of Philip Roth's Achievement." *International Fiction Review* 2 (1975): 113–20.

Morris, Charles. *A Time of Passion: America, 1960–1980*. New York: Harper and Row, 1984.

Morris, Meghan. "The Banality of Cultural Studies." In Patricia Mellencamp, ed., *Logics of Television: Essays in Cultural Criticism*, 14–43. Bloomington: Indiana University Press, 1990.

Morrison, Toni. *Playing in the Dark: Whiteness and the Literary Imagination*. Cambridge: Harvard University Press, 1992.

Mumford, Kevin. "'Lost Manhood' Found: Male Sexual Impotence and Victorian Culture in the United States." *Journal of the History of Sexuality* 3.1 (1992): 33–57.

Nelson, Dana. *National Manhood: Capitalist Citizenship and the Imagined Fraternity of White Men*. Durham, N.C., and London: Duke University Press, 1998.

Newfield, Christopher. "The Politics of Male Suffering: Masochism and Hegemony in the American Renaissance." *differences* 1.3 (Fall 1989): 55–87.

——. "What Was Political Correctness? Race, the Right, and Managerial Democracy in the Humanities." In Williams, ed., *PC Wars*, 109–45.

Newfield, Christopher and Ronald Strickland, eds. *After Political Correctness: The Humanities and Society in the 1990's*. Boulder, San Francisco, and Oxford: Westview, 1995.

Newitz, Annalee and Matthew Wray. "What Is 'White Trash'? Stereotypes and Economic Conditions of Poor Whites in the U.S." *Minnesota Review* 47 (Fall 1996): 57–72.

Newman, Judie. *John Updike*. London: Macmillan, 1988.

Newman, Katherine S. *Declining Fortunes: The Withering of the American Dream*. New York: Basic Books, 1993.

——. *Falling from Grace: The Experience of Downward Mobility in the American Middle Class*. New York: Free Press, 1988.

O'Connell, Mary. *Updike and the Patriarchal Dilemma: Masculinity in the Rabbit Novels*. Carbondale: Southern Illinois University Press, 1996.

Ohmann, Richard. "The Shaping of a Canon: U.S. Fiction, 1960–1975." *Critical Inquiry* 10.1 (Fall 1983): 199–223.

Olster, Stacey. "Rabbit Rerun: Updike's Replay of Popular Culture in *Rabbit at Rest*." *Modern Fiction Studies* 37.1 (Spring 1991): 45–59.

Omi, Michael and Howard Winant. *Racial Formation in the United States: From the 1960s to the 1990s*. 2d ed. New York and London: Routledge, 1994.

Ownby, Ted. "Freedom, Manhood, and White Male Tradition in 1970s Southern Rock Music." In Anne Goodwyn Jones and Susan V. Donaldson, eds., *Haunted Bodies: Gender and Southern Texts*, 369–88. Charlottesville and London: University Press of Virginia, 1997.

Pattison, Robert. "On the Finn Syndrome and the Shakespeare Paradox." *Nation* (May 30, 1987): 710–20. Reprinted in Stone, ed., *Essays on "The Closing of the American Mind*," 7–11.

Pearce, Lynne and Jackie Stacey, eds. *Romance Revisited*. London: Lawrence and Wishart, 1995.

Peck, Janice. "The Mediated Talking Cure: Therapeutic Framing of Autobiography in TV Talk Shows." In Sidonie Smith and Julia Watson, eds., *Getting a Life: Everyday Uses of Autobiography*, 134–55. Minneapolis: University of Minnesota Press, 1996.

Pfeil, Fred. *White Guys: Studies in Postmodern Domination and Difference*. New York and London: Verso, 1995.

Pharr, Mary. "Partners in the *Danse*: Women in Stephen King's Fiction." In Magistrale, ed., *The Dark Descent*, 19–32.

Phelan, Peggy. *Unmarked: The Politics of Performance*. New York and London: Routledge, 1993.

Pinch, Adela. *Strange Fits of Passion: Epistemologies of Emotion, Hume to Austin*. Stanford: Stanford University Press, 1996.

Pollitt, Katha. "The Solipsisters." *New York Times Book Review*, April 18, 1999, 35.

Priestley, Michael. "An Interview with John Irving." *New England Review* (Summer 1979): 489–504.

Prince of Tides, The (movie review). *Rolling Stone*, January 9, 1992, 55.

Purvis, Kenneth. *The Male Sexual Machine: An Owner's Manuel*. New York: St. Martin's, 1992.

Radway, Janice. *A Feeling for Books: The Book-of-the-Month Club, Literary Taste, and Middle-Class Desire*. Chapel Hill and London: University of North Carolina Press, 1997.

———. *Reading the Romance: Women, Patriarchy, and Popular Literature* (1984). 2d ed. Chapel Hill: University of North Carolina Press, 1991.

Redenius, Charles M. "Recreating the Social Contract: James Dickey's *Deliverance.*" *Canadian Review of American Studies* 17.3 (Fall 1986): 285–99.

Reik, Theodor. *Masochism in Sex and Society.* Translated by Margaret H. Beigel and Gertrud M. Kurth. 1941. New York: Grove Press, 1962.

Ristoff, Dilvo I. *Updike's America: The Presence of Contemporary American History in John Updike's Rabbit Trilogy.* New York: Peter Lang, 1988.

Robinson, Sally. *Engendering the Subject: Gender and Self-Representation in Contemporary Women's Fiction.* Albany: State University of New York Press, 1991.

———. " 'What guy will do that?' Recodings of Masculinity in *sex, lies, and videotape.*" *Genders* 21 (Fall 1995): 141–67.

Roediger, David. *Towards the Abolition of Whiteness.* London and New York: Verso, 1994.

———. *The Wages of Whiteness: Race and the Making of the American Working Class.* London and New York: Verso, 1991.

Roof, Judith. "Hypothalamic Criticism: Gay Male Studies and Male Feminist Criticism." *American Literary History* 4.2 (Summer 1992): 355–64.

Rosen, David. "The Volcano and the Cathedral: Muscular Christianity and the Origins of Primal Manliness." In Donald E. Hall, ed., *Muscular Christianity: Embodying the Victorian Age,* 17–44. Cambridge: Cambridge University Press, 1994.

Ross, Andrew. "The Great White Dude." In Berger, Wallis, and Watson, eds., *Constructing Masculinity,* 167–75.

Roth, Philip. *My Life as a Man.* New York: Penguin, 1974.

Rozen, Leah. Review of *The Prince of Tides,* dir. Barbra Streisand. *People Weekly,* December 23, 1991, 18–19.

Rubin, Joan Shelley. *The Making of Middlebrow Culture.* Chapel Hill and London: University of North Carolina Press, 1992.

Russell, Mariann. "White Man's Black Man: Three Views." *College Language Association Journal* 17.1 (Fall 1973): 93–100.

Samuels, Charles Thomas. "How Not to Film a Novel." *American Scholar* 42.1 (Winter 1972–73): 148–54.

Sattel, Jack. "The Inexpressive Male: Tragedy or Sexual Politics?" *Social Problems* 23 (1976): 469–77.

Savran, David. *Taking It Like a Man: White Masculinity, Masochism, and Contemporary American Culture.* Princeton: Princeton University Press, 1998.

Scammon, Richard M. and Ben J. Wattenberg. *The Real Majority.* New York: Coward-McCann, 1970.

Scarry, Elaine. *The Body in Pain: The Making and Unmaking of the World.* New York and Oxford: Oxford University Press, 1985.

Schaub, Thomas. *American Fiction in the Cold War.* Madison: University of Wisconsin Press, 1991.

Schickel, Richard. Review of *The Prince of Tides. Time,* December 30, 1991, 70–71.

Schopp, Andrew. "Writing (with) the Body: Stephen King's *Misery.*" *Literature, Interpretation, Theory* 5.1 (June 1994): 29–43.

Schuman, Samuel. "Taking Stephen King Seriously: Reflections on a Decade of Best-Sellers." In Gary Hoppenstand and Ray B. Browne, eds., *The Gothic World of Stephen King: Landscapes of Nightmare,* 107–14. Bowling Green, Ohio: Bowling Green State University Popular Press, 1987.

Scott, Joan. "The Rhetoric of Crisis in Higher Education." In Bérubé and Nelson, eds., *Higher Education Under Fire,* 293–304.

Sedgwick, Eve Kosofsky. *Between Men: English Literature and Male Homosocial Desire.* New York: Columbia University Press, 1985.

——. *Epistemology of the Closet.* Berkeley: University of California Press, 1990.

Segal, Lynne. *Slow Motion: Changing Masculinities, Changing Men.* New Brunswick: Rutgers University Press, 1990.

Shalit, Wendy. *A Return to Modesty: Discovering the Lost Virtue.* New York: Free Press, 1999.

Shilling, Chris. *The Body and Social Theory.* London: Sage, 1993.

Shohat, Ella. "The Media's War." *Social Text* 28 (1991). Reprinted in Jeffords and Rabinovitz, eds., *Seeing Through the Media,* 147–54.

Shor, Ira. *Culture Wars: School and Society in the Conservative Restoration, 1969–1984.* Boston, London, and Henley: Routledge and Kegan Paul, 1986.

Showalter, Elaine. *The Female Malady: Women, Madness, and English Culture, 1830–1980.* New York: Penguin, 1985.

——. *Hystories: Hysterical Epidemics and Modern Media.* New York: Columbia University Press, 1997.

Shulman, Alix. "Organs and Orgasms." In Vivian Gornick and Barbara K. Moran, eds., *Women in Sexist Society: Studies in Power and Powerlessness,* 292–303. New York: Basic Books, 1971.

Siegel, Carol. *Male Masochism: Modern Revisions of the Story of Love.* Bloomington: Indiana University Press, 1995.

Silverman, Kaja. *Male Subjectivity at the Margins.* New York and London: Routledge, 1992.

——. "White Skin, Brown Masks: The Double Mimesis; or, With Lawrence in Arabia." *differences* 1.3 (Fall 1989): 3–54.

Singh, Lovelina. "The Sexual *Kvetch* of Philip Roth's Protagonists in *Portnoy's*

Complaint, My Life as a Man, and *The Professor of Desire.*" *Panjab University Research Bulletin* 16.1 (April 1985): 17–24.

Smith, Paul. "Action Movie Hysteria; or, Eastwood Bound." *differences* 1.3 (Fall 1989): 88–107.

Solomon-Godeau, Abigail. "Male Trouble." In Berger, Wallis, and Watson, eds., *Constructing Masculinity,* 68–76.

Spelman, Elizabeth V. "Woman as Body: Ancient and Contemporary Views." *Feminist Studies* 8.1 (Spring 1982): 109–31.

Stabile, Carol. "Another Brick in the Wall: (Re)Contextualizing the Crisis." In Bérubé and Nelson, eds., *Higher Education Under Fire,* 108–25.

Steinmann, Anne and David J. Fox. *The Male Dilemma: How to Survive the Sexual Revolution.* New York: Jason Aronson, 1974.

Stone, Robert L., ed. *Essays on "The Closing of the American Mind."* Chicago: Chicago Review Press, 1989.

Studlar, Gaylyn. *In the Realm of Pleasure: Von Sternberg, Dietrich, and the Masochistic Aesthetic.* Urbana and Chicago: University of Illinois Press, 1988.

Suarez, Ernest. "*Deliverance:* Dickey's Original Screenplay." *Southern Quarterly* 33.2–3 (Winter-Spring 1995): 161–69.

Sweeney, Gael. "The King of White Trash Culture: Elvis Presley and the Aesthetics of Excess." In Matt Wray and Annalee Newitz, eds., *White Trash: Race and Class in America,* 249–66. New York and London: Routledge, 1997.

Sykes, Charles J. *A Nation of Victims: The Decay of the American Character.* New York: St. Martin's, 1992.

Tasker, Yvonne. "Dumb Movies for Dumb People: Masculinity, the Body, and the Voice in Contemporary Action Cinema." In Cohan and Hark, eds., *Screening the Male,* 230–44.

Tavris, Carol. *The Mismeasure of Woman.* New York: Simon and Schuster, 1992.

Thomas, Calvin. *Male Matters: Masculinity, Anxiety, and the Male Body on the Line.* Urbana and Chicago: University of Illinois Press, 1996.

Thomas, Kelly Lynn. "Black Sheep: Representations of Poor Whites in American Literature and Culture." Ph.D. diss., University of Michigan, 1998.

Thompson, Becky W. and Sangeeta Tyagi, eds. *Beyond a Dream Deferred: Multicultural Education and the Politics of Excellence.* Minneapolis: University of Minnesota Press, 1993.

Thorburn, Adam. "Dark Secrets in *The Prince of Tides.*" *The Humanist* 52 (May-June 1992): 8–11.

Tintner, Adeline R. "Roth's 'Pain' and James's 'Obscure Hurt.'" *Midstream* 31.3 (March 1985): 58–60.

Turner, Kermit. "Rabbit Brought Nowhere: John Updike's *Rabbit Redux.*" *South Carolina Review* 8.1 (1975): 35–42.

Twitchell, James B. *Carnival Culture: The Trashing of Taste in America*. New York: Columbia University Press, 1992.

Tyler, Carole-Anne. "The Supreme Sacrifice? TV, 'TV,' and the Renee Richards Story." *differences* 1.3 (Fall 1989): 160–86.

Underwood, Tim and Chuck Miller, eds. *Bare Bones: Conversations with Stephen King*. New York: Warner, 1988.

Updike, John. "The Disposable Rocket." *Michigan Quarterly Review* 32.4 (Fall 1993): 517–20.

——. *Odd Jobs: Essays and Criticism*. New York: Knopf, 1991.

——. *Rabbit at Rest*. New York: Knopf, 1990.

——. *Rabbit Is Rich*. New York: Fawcett Crest, 1981.

——. *Rabbit Redux*. New York: Fawcett Crest, 1971.

——. *Self-Consciousness: Memoirs*. New York: Knopf, 1989.

Vanderwerken, David L. "Rabbit 'Re-Docks': Updike's Inner Space Odyssey." *College Literature* 2 (1975): 73–78.

Wallace, Michele. *Invisibility Blues: From Pop to Theory*. London and New York: Verso, 1990.

Warner, Michael. "The Mass Public and the Mass Subject." In Craig Calhoun, ed., *Habermas and the Public Sphere*, 377–401. Cambridge and London: MIT Press, 1992.

Warren, Donald I. *The Radical Center: Middle Americans and the Politics of Alienation*. Notre Dame: University of Notre Dame Press, 1976.

Wattenberg, Ben J. *The Real America: A Surprising Examination of the State of the Union*. Garden City, N.Y.: Doubleday, 1974.

Weiner, Jon. "What Happened at Harvard." In Aufderheide, ed., *Beyond PC*, 97–106.

West, Thomas G. "Allan Bloom and America." *Claremont Review of Books* 6.1 (Spring 1988): 1, 17–20. Reprinted in Stone, ed., *Essays on "The Closing of the American Mind,"* 166–73.

White, Kevin. *The First Sexual Revolution: The Emergence of Male Heterosexuality in Modern America*. New York and London: New York University Press, 1993.

Wiegman, Robyn. *American Anatomies: Theorizing Race and Gender*. Durham, N.C., and London: Duke University Press, 1995.

——. "Missiles and Melodrama (Masculinity and the Televisual War)." In Jeffords and Rabinovitz, eds., *Seeing Through the Media*, 171–87.

Will, George F. "Literary Politics." In Aufderheide, ed., *Beyond PC*, 23–26.

Williams, Jeffrey, ed. *PC Wars: Politics and Theory in the Academy*. New York and London: Routledge, 1995.

Williams, Linda Ruth. "Blood Brothers." *Sight and Sound* 4.9 (September 1994): 16–19.

Wills, Garry. *Reagan's America: Innocents at Home*. Garden City, N.Y.: Doubleday, 1987.

Wilson, John. *The Myth of Political Correctness*. Durham, N.C.: Duke University Press, 1996.

Wilson, Matthew. "The Rabbit Tetralogy: From Solitude to Society to Solitude Again." *Modern Fiction Studies* 37.1 (Spring 1991): 5–24.

Woodmansee, Martha. *The Author, Art, and the Market: Rereading the History of Aesthetics*. New York: Columbia University Press, 1994.

Woodmansee, Martha and Peter Jaszi, eds. *The Construction of Authorship: Textual Appropriations in Law and Literature*. Durham, N.C.: Duke University Press, 1993.

Wymard, Eleanor. " 'A New Version of the Midas Touch': *Daniel Martin* and *The World According to Garp*." *Modern Fiction Studies* 27.2 (Summer 1981): 284–86.

Young, Jon. Review of *The Prince of Tides* (video release). *Video* (August 1992): 40.

Yudice, George. "Neither Impugning nor Disavowing Whiteness Does a Viable Politics Make: The Limits of Identity Politics." In Newfield and Strickland, eds., *After Political Correctness*, 255–85.

——. "What's a Straight White Man to Do?" In Berger, Wallis, and Watson, eds., *Constructing Masculinity*, 267–83.

Zakim, Eric. "The Cut That Binds: Philip Roth and Jewish Marginality." *Qui Parle* 3.2 (Fall 1989): 19–40.

Zilbergeld, Bernie. *The New Male Sexuality: The Truth About Men, Sex, and Pleasure*. New York: Bantam Books, 1992.

Zuckert, Michael P. "Two Cheers (At Least) for Allan Bloom." In Stone, ed., *Essays on "The Closing of the American Mind,"* 73–76.

INDEX